Caste, Society and Politics in India from the
Eighteenth Century to the Modern Age

The phenomenon of caste has probably aroused more controversy
than any other aspect of Indian life and thought. Some scholars see
India's caste system as the defining feature of Indian culture,
although it is dismissed by others as a colonial artefact. Susan
Bayly's cogent and sophisticated analysis explores the emergence of
the ideas, experiences and practices which gave rise to so-called
'caste society' over a period of 300 years, from the pre-colonial
period to the end of the twentieth century. Combining historical
and anthropological approaches, Bayly frames her analysis within
the context of India's dynamic economic and social order. She
thereby interprets caste not as the essence of Indian culture and
civilisation, but rather as a contingent and variable response to the
enormous changes that occurred in the subcontinent's political
landscape both before and after colonial conquest. In subsequent
chapters, she explores the idea of caste in relation to Indian and
Western 'orientalist' thought, and the upheavals associated with
competing understandings of Indian nationalism and the creation of
the modern Indian nation-state. The book's wide-ranging and
rigorous analysis offers one of the most powerful statements yet to
be written on caste in South Asia.

SUSAN BAYLY is a Fellow of Christ's College, Cambridge and
holds a lectureship in history and social anthropology at the
University of Cambridge. Her previous publications include *Saints,
Goddesses and Kings: Muslims and Christians in South Indian
Society, 1700–1900* (1989).

THE NEW CAMBRIDGE HISTORY OF INDIA

General editor GORDON JOHNSON
President of Wolfson College, and Director, Centre of South Asian Studies,
University of Cambridge

Associate editors C. A. BAYLY
Vere Harmsworth Professor of Imperial and Naval History, University of Cambridge,
and Fellow of St Catharine's College

and JOHN F. RICHARDS
Professor of History, Duke University

Although the original *Cambridge History of India*, published between 1922 and 1937, did much to formulate a chronology for Indian history and describe the administrative structures of government in India, it has inevitably been overtaken by the mass of new research over the past sixty years.

Designed to take full account of recent scholarship and changing conceptions of South Asia's historical development, *The New Cambridge History of India* is published as a series of short, self-contained volumes, each dealing with a separate theme and written by one or two authors. Within an overall four-part structure, thirty-one complementary volumes in uniform format will be published. Each will conclude with a substantial bibliographical essay designed to lead non-specialists further into the literature.

The four parts planned are as follows:

I The Mughals and their Contemporaries

II Indian States and the Transition to Colonialism

III The Indian Empire and the Beginnings of Modern Society

IV The Evolution of Contemporary South Asia

A list of individual titles in preparation will be found at the end of the volume.

4/2007

THE NEW CAMBRIDGE HISTORY OF INDIA

IV · 3

*Caste, Society and Politics in India from the
Eighteenth Century to the Modern Age*

SUSAN BAYLY

University of Cambridge

CAMBRIDGE
UNIVERSITY PRESS

PUBLISHED BY THE PRESS SYNDICATE OF THE UNIVERSITY OF CAMBRIDGE
The Pitt Building, Trumpington Street, Cambridge, United Kingdom

CAMBRIDGE UNIVERSITY PRESS
The Edinburgh Building, Cambridge CB2 2RU, UK
40 West 20th Street, New York, NY 10011–4211, USA
10 Stamford Road, Oakleigh, VIC 3166, Australia
Ruide Alarcón 13, 28014, Madrid, Spain
Dock House, The Waterfront, Cape Town 8001, South Africa

www.cambridge.org

First published 1999
Reprinted 2001
First paperback edition 2001

Printed in the United Kingdom at the University Press, Cambridge

Typeset in Garamond 10.5/13pt [CE]

A catalogue record for this book is available from the British Library

Library of Congress cataloguing in publication data
Bayly, Susan.
Caste, society and politics in India from the eighteenth to the modern age / Susan Bayly.
p.   cm. – (The New Cambridge history of India: IV.3)
Includes bibliographical references and index.
ISBN 0 521 26434 0 (hb)
1. Caste – India.   2. Social classes – India.
3. India – History – 18th century.
4. India – History – 19th century.
5. India – History – 20th century.   I. Series.
DS422.C3B38   1999
305.5′122′0954–dc21   98–38434   CIP

ISBN 0 521 26434 0 hardback
ISBN 0 521 79842 6 paperback

CONTENTS

v

PLATES

GENERAL EDITOR'S PREFACE

The New Cambridge History of India covers the period from the beginning of the sixteenth century. In some respects it marks a radical change in the style of Cambridge Histories, but in others the editors feel that they are working firmly within an established academic tradition.

During the summer of 1896, F. W. Maitland and Lord Acton between them evolved the idea for a comprehensive modern history. By the end of the year the Syndics of the University Press had committed themselves to the *Cambridge Modern History*, and Lord Acton had been put in charge of it. It was hoped that publication would begin in 1899 and be completed by 1904, but the first volume in fact came out in 1902 and the last in 1910, with additional volumes of tables and maps in 1911 and 1912.

The *History* was a great success, and it was followed by a whole series of distinctive Cambridge Histories covering English Literature, the Ancient World, India, British Foreign Policy, Economic History, Medieval History, the British Empire, Africa, China and Latin America; and even now other new series are being prepared. Indeed, the various Histories have given the Press notable strength in the publication of general reference books in the arts and social sciences.

What has made the Cambridge Histories so distinctive is that they have never been simply dictionaries or encyclopaedias. The Histories have, in H. A. L. Fisher's words, always been 'written by an army of specialists concentrating the latest results of special study'. Yet as Acton agreed with the Syndics in 1896, they have not been mere compilations of existing material but original works. Undoubtedly many of the Histories are uneven in quality, some have become out of date very rapidly, but their virtue has been that they have consistently done more than simply record an existing state of knowledge: they have tended to focus interest on research and they have provided a massive stimulus to further work. This has made their publication doubly worthwhile and has distinguished them intellectually from other sorts of reference book. The editors of *The New Cambridge History of India* have acknowledged this in their work.

The original *Cambridge History of India* was published between 1922 and 1937. It was planned in six volumes, but of these, volume 2 dealing with the period between the first century AD and the Muslim invasion of India never appeared. Some of the material is still of value, but in many respects it is now out of date. The past fifty years have seen a great deal of new research on India, and a striking feature of recent work has been to cast doubt on the validity of the quite arbitrary chronological and categorical way in which Indian history has been conventionally divided.

The editors decided that it would not be academically desirable to prepare a new *History of India* using the traditional format. The selective nature of research on Indian history over the past half-century would doom such a project from the start and the whole of Indian history could not be covered in an even or comprehensive manner. They concluded that the best scheme would be to have a *History* divided into four overlapping chronological volumes, each containing short books on individual themes or subjects. Although in extent the work will therefore be equivalent to a dozen massive tomes of the traditional sort, in form *The New Cambridge History of India* will appear as a shelf full of separate but complementary parts. Accordingly, the main divisions are between I. *The Mughals and their Contemporaries*, II. *Indian States and the Transition to Colonialism*, III. *The Indian Empire and the Beginnings of Modern Society*, and IV. *The Evolution of Contemporary South Asia*.

Just as the books within these volumes are complementary so too do they intersect with each other, both thematically and chronologically. As the books appear they are intended to give a view of the subject as it now stands and to act as a stimulus to further research. We do not expect the *New Cambridge History of India* to be the last word on the subject but an essential voice in the continuing discussion about it.

ACKNOWLEDGEMENTS

While this book builds on my research and teaching over many years, it is also a work of synthesis and interpretation and therefore owes much to the work of others. Among the many specialists cited in the notes and bibliography I must mention particularly Professors André Béteille, Veena Das, Jonathan Parry, Romila Thapar and Peter van der Veer whose arguments and insights inspired much that I hoped to achieve in this volume. My earliest attempts to understand the life and history of the subcontinent were made under the supervision of the late Professor Eric Stokes; the field of Indian studies still sorely misses his ebullience and intellectual verve.

In both the planning and completion of the book I have been fortunate in receiving much support and stimulation from present and former Cambridge colleagues and students, especially Dr Seema Alavi, Professor Sugata Bose, Professor Caroline Humphrey, Professor Ayesha Jalal, Professor Alan Macfarlane, Dr Rosalind O'Hanlon, Dr Radhika Singha, Professor Ajay Skaria and Maya Warrier. I thank too Professors Dharma Kumar, Ravinder Kumar, John Richards and Peter Robb.

I am deeply indebted to Dr James Laidlaw and Dr Norbert Peabody, each of whom generously spared much time from his own work to read the entire manuscript in draft. From them both I received penetrating comments on both style and content, as well as careful guidance on the intricacies of anthropological debate. I am deeply grateful for their efforts; for the book's remaining shortcomings I alone am responsible.

My attempt to make this an interdisciplinary work was greatly aided by the generosity of the Cambridge University Isaac Newton Trust which funded my appointment to an Affiliated Lectureship held jointly within the Cambridge History Faculty and the Cambridge Department of Social Anthropology. I also thank my College for agreeing to participate in this scheme. I am especially grateful to Professor Marilyn Strathern and to my other colleagues in the Department who have done so much to welcome me into the lively and

x

learned community of Cambridge anthropologists. I am indebted too to distinguished colleagues in the Cambridge History Faculty who have shown an interest in this project.

For much patient help I am grateful to many librarians and archivists in both Britain and India, notably Dr Lionel Carter of the Cambridge Centre of South Asian Studies, and the staff of the Cambridge University Library, the Christ's College Library, the India Office Library and Records, the Library of University College, London, the National Archives of India, the Nehru Museum and Library, and the Connemara Library, Madras. Particular thanks are due to Dr Sudeshna Guha, Dr Robin Boast, Ms T. A. Barringer and Mr Stuart Cary Welch. For permission to reproduce items from their collections I am grateful to the following institutions: Cambridge University Library, the Cambridge University Museum of Archaeology and Anthropology, Harvard University Art Museums, and the Victoria and Albert Museum, London.

Christ's College has provided me with unceasing support over many years. My past and present colleagues in History have been a particular source of intellectual nourishment; Sir John Plumb, Professor David Cannadine, Professor Linda Colley, Professor Lucjan Lewitter, Dr Miles Taylor and Dr Alan Cromartie have been unstinting in both learning and friendship. I must also thank both the Master, Dr Alan Munro, and Dr Nicholas Gay for patiently explaining the terminology of the genetics researcher to an interested but regrettably uninformed non-scientist.

Dr David Reynolds has long enriched and invigorated my academic life. He too read the entire manuscript in muddy typescript and provided a trenchant critique from the perspective of the international historian; this has greatly aided me in sharpening both the structure and arguments.

As always my greatest intellectual debt is to my husband Professor Christopher Bayly. The example of his own scholarship has been an inspiration throughout my career. Without his exhilarating enthusiasm, his willingness to endure impromptu domestic seminars, and his lively companionship on many journeys to India, this book would have been neither conceived nor completed.

Cambridge,   S.B.B.
February 1998

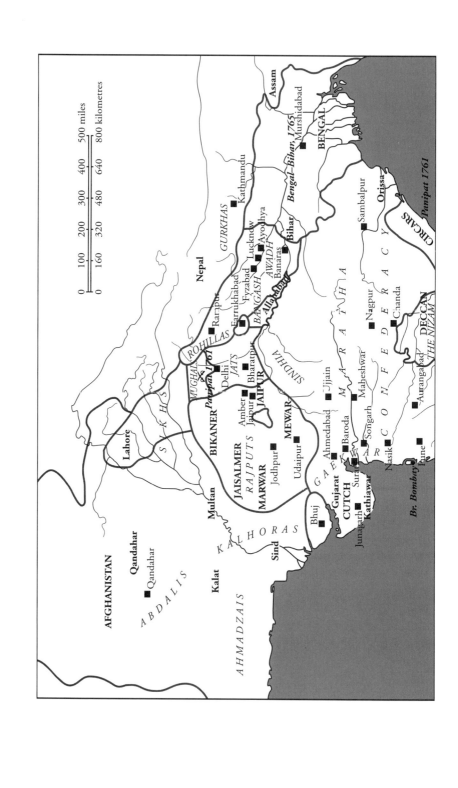

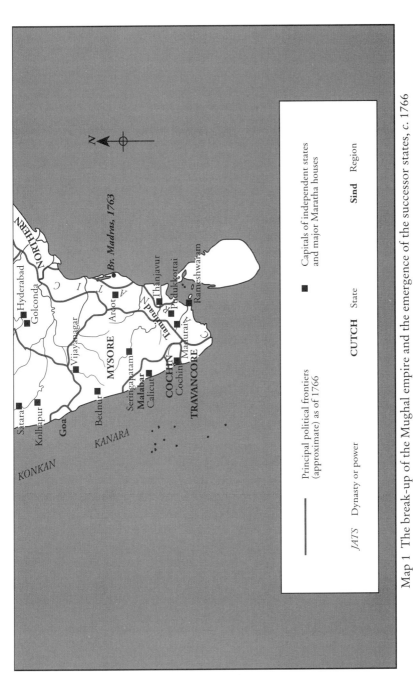

Map 1 The break-up of the Mughal empire and the emergence of the successor states, c. 1766

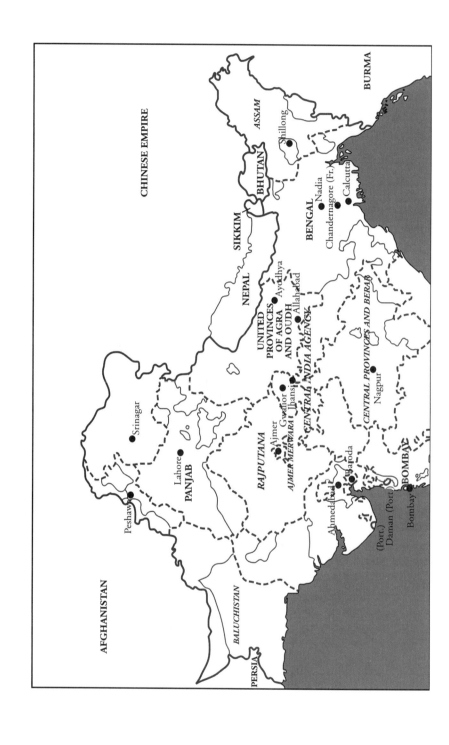

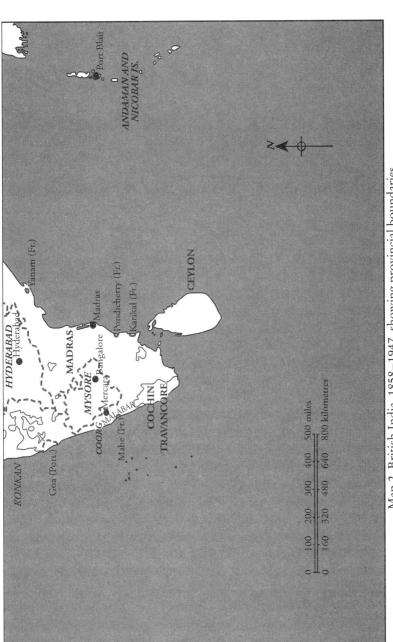

Map 2 British India, 1858–1947, showing provincial boundaries

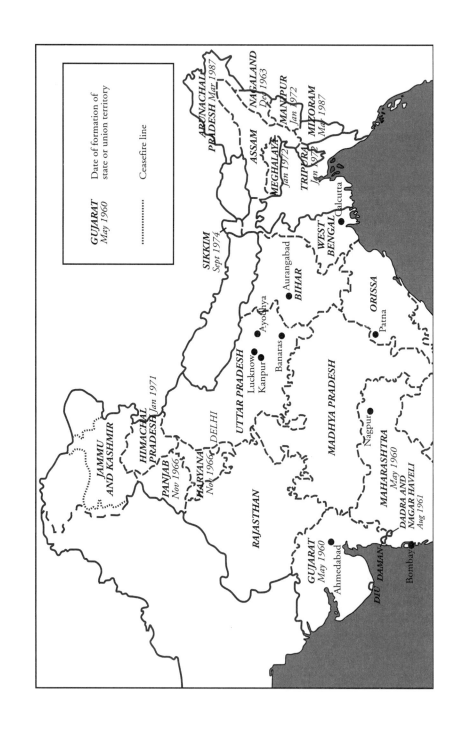

Date of formation of state or union territory

GUJARAT
May 1960

·············· Ceasefire line

SIKKIM
Sept 1974

ARUNACHAL
PRADESH Mar 1987

ASSAM

NAGALAND
Dec 1963

MANIPUR
Jan 1972

MEGHALAYA
Jan 1972

TRIPURA
Jan 1972

MIZORAM
May 1987

WEST
BENGAL Calcutta

Aurangabad

BIHAR

ORISSA

• Patna

JAMMU
AND KASHMIR

HIMACHAL
PRADESH Jan 1971

DELHI

PANJAB
Nov 1966

HARYANA
Nov 1966

UTTAR PRADESH

Ayodhya

Lucknow
Kanpur

Banaras

MADHYA PRADESH

Nagpur

MAHARASHTRA
May 1960

DADRA AND
NAGAR HAVELI
Aug 1961

RAJASTHAN

GUJARAT
May 1960

Ahmedabad

DIU *DAMAN*

Bombay

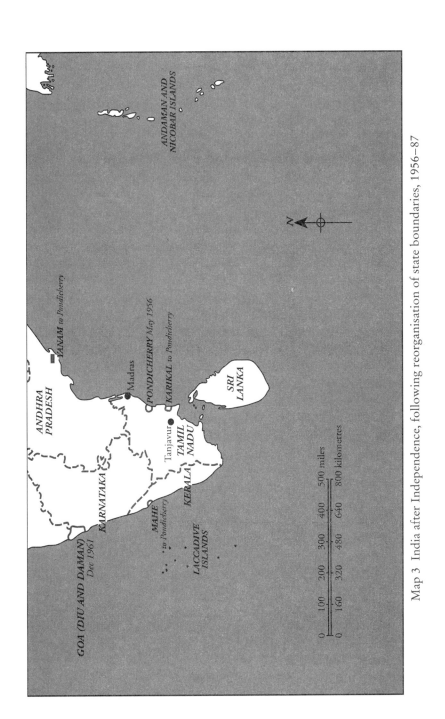

Map 3 India after Independence, following reorganisation of state boundaries, 1956–87

INTRODUCTION

This book is an attempt to account for and interpret the phenomenon of caste in the Indian subcontinent. It deals primarily with the period from the mid-eighteenth century to the present day, though the first two chapters explore the spread of castelike norms and values in the age of the great sixteenth- and seventeenth-century Indian dynasts.

Of all the topics that have fascinated and divided scholars of south Asia, caste is probably the most contentious. Defined by many specialists as a system of elaborately stratified social hierarchy that distinguishes India from all other societies, caste has achieved much the same significance in social, political and academic debate as race in the United States, class in Britain and faction in Italy. It has thus been widely thought of as the paramount fact of life in the subcontinent, and for some, as the very core or essence of south Asian civilisation.

There is of course an enormous body of academic writing on caste. Studies by anthropologists and other social scientists provide a wealth of closely observed ethnographic detail; many propose sophisticated theoretical interpretations. So, given the notorious sensitivity of this terrain, what is the case for an attempt to explore it from an historical perspective?

In recent years historians have broken much new ground in the study of political and economic change in the subcontinent, both before and during the colonial period. But caste, which is best seen as a meeting ground between everyday Indian life and thought and the strategies of rulers and other arbiters of moral and social order, tends to provoke more heated debate than almost anything else in the specialist literature.

It has been common since the days of British rule for both historians and anthropologists to refer to India as a 'caste society', and to treat the values of so-called caste Hindus as an all-pervading presence in Indian life. Since the 1970s, however, there have been commentators, both within India and abroad, who have accused these earlier specialists of massively overstating the importance of caste. Some have gone so far as to question the very existence of an ancient pan-Indian caste system, dismissing the idea of caste society as a fabrication of colonial data-collectors and their office-holding Indian informants. This often perplexes newcomers to the field when they read about the many important Indians, including Mahatma Gandhi and other past and present politicians and social reformers, for whom caste was and is a real force in Indian life, and certainly much more than an orientalist's 'imaginings'.[1]

The subject of caste throws up other difficulties as well. Those unfamiliar with the field often complain that even the best modern historical studies make little effort to explain what they mean by caste, despite the fact that these works so often refer in passing to such mysterious phenomena as *jati* and *varna*, Backward and Forward Castes, Brahmanism and non-Brahmanism, purity and pollution, untouchability and outcasting, caste movements, casteism, 'caste wars', and much more.

Furthermore, in dealing with such major historical events as the 1857 Mutiny-Rebellion and the anti-colonial 'freedom struggle', the literature often identifies groups of Indians by specific regional caste titles, often without making clear whether this kind of group affinity truly overrides individual decision-making in times of crisis. Not surprisingly, many readers wish to understand more fully what is meant when they read that, in 1857, there were areas where 'the Jats' remained loyal, while 'the Rajputs' and 'the Gujars' rebelled; or that in the 1920s, 'the Patidars' of the Gujarat region joined Gandhi in acts of resistance to British rule. They read too of how Gandhi and his powerful opponent B. R. Ambedkar clashed in the 1930s over the issue of how best to 'uplift' India's millions of so-called untouchables.

Those to whom these terms and concepts are unfamiliar will rightly want to know what an endowment of Jat, Patidar, Brahman or 'untouchable' caste identity actually entailed at these times. Further-

---

[1] See Inden 1990. Such works as Dirks 1992a, 1992b, Cohn's 'The census, and objectification' in Cohn 1987, Appadurai 1992 and Breckenridge and van der Veer 1993 improve greatly on studies which treat Western orientalist ideas in isolation, especially in suggesting that colonial rule had the effect of turning such 'constructions' into lived reality. (See also Washbrook 1975.) The present volume shares these historical perspectives but argues that while colonialism deserves much emphasis, so too do the many changes which were underway well before the British conquest. Furthermore, much weight will also be given to factors promoting the assertion of caste values in the years since Indian Independence in 1947.

more, did such affinities change, or did they remain constant and immutable when so much else was changing in India's culture and material environment? Readers of both historical and anthropological works have good reason to ask whether caste is to be seen in any sense as an ancient or primordial essence of Indian life. Should such be the case, how is this to be reconciled with what many historians now say about the fluidity and dynamism of the pre-colonial state systems and economies?

By the same token, non-specialists sometimes find even the most stimulating anthropological discussions of caste hard to reconcile with accounts of nineteenth- and twentieth-century nationalist politics. Those reading these historical treatments of the early nationalist era find once again an emphasis on subtly overlapping affiliations of religious community, class and regional or linguistic affinity. They are therefore taken aback when they then turn to works by those anthropological theorists for whom Indian life and thought are represented in an apparently very different way, featuring fixed and arbitrary schemes or structures of caste identity.

ISSUES AND PREMISES

This study will argue that caste has been for many centuries a real and active part of Indian life, and not just a self-serving orientalist fiction. Yet it will also seek to show that until well into the colonial period, much of the subcontinent was still populated by people for whom the formal distinctions of caste were of only limited importance as a source of corporate and individual lifestyles. This would include much of Bengal, the Punjab and southern India, as well as the far northwest and the central Deccan plain.

Of course long before the age of European expansion, these and other regional societies knew norms and conventions which named, grouped and sometimes ranked people by order and function. There is much debate about the nature of these social forms as they emerged in India's medieval kingdoms, and this study will not attempt a detailed reconstruction of these usages in the distant past.[2] It is clear though that some at least of these diverse and fluid ideas and practices

---

[2] For one such reconstruction see Inden 1990: 213–62 on castes as political assemblages or 'subject-citizenries' within medieval Indian kingdoms.

3

prefigured what we now know as caste; indeed the names of many individual castes as well as other elements of the terminology used in contemporary caste life derive from these earlier regional schemes and groupings. But this certainly does not mean that a single static system of caste has dominated Indian life since ancient times, despite the fact that a reverence for certain generalised caste ideals is extolled in important scriptural writings. Nor did the emergence of the varying castelike observances of the medieval realms translate directly into the very different forms of so-called caste society which anthropologists observe today.

These current manifestations of caste are now far more generalised across the subcontinent than was the case in former times. The book's aim is therefore to show that caste as we now recognise it has been engendered, shaped and perpetuated by comparatively recent political and social developments. The initial premise is that even in parts of the so-called Hindu heartland of Gangetic upper India, the institutions and beliefs which are now often described as the elements of 'traditional' caste were only just taking shape as recently as the early eighteenth century – that is, the period of rapid regional state-building which accompanied the collapse of Mughal rule and the expansion of Western power in the subcontinent.

Furthermore, from the early nineteenth century onwards, British rule significantly expanded and sharpened these norms and conventions, building many manifestations of caste language and ideology into its structures of authoritative government. It was Indians as much as Britons who took the initiative in this process, even though the impact of these moves was all the more compelling because it was supported by the apparatus of an increasingly powerful colonial state, and also by the effects of India's involvement in a Western-dominated global market economy.

Ironically, the practices of representative government, which became more deeply rooted in British-ruled India than in any other part of the non-white colonial world, served further to enhance the importance of caste affinities in the political arena. Both for early participants in electoral politics and to a significant extent in the period since Independence, caste has been an effective tool and resource for the creation of common interests across the boundaries of region, language, faith and economic status.

The argument here is not that Indians have somehow lacked the

4

capacity to develop 'modern' political allegiances. On the contrary, it has often been avowedly 'modern' men and women who have taken the lead here, discovering that by embracing caste principles, or by imposing them on others, one may gain an extraordinarily flexible resource in uncertain times. On the one hand, the assertions of caste have made it possible to build broad allegiances which breach India's many boundaries of region, faith, language and economic status. Yet, at the same time, caste principles have often provided the means of excluding, disempowering or subjugating others. This has proven to be of great advantage in situations where other differentiations – those of class, for example – may be far less effective than an assertion that a group or individual is of alien or inferior caste. This may go far to explain why consciousness of caste differentials has not altogether given way in contemporary India to other markers of social difference – for example, those of class, colour, language or occupation – even though in many situations considerations of caste may overlap or be partially supplanted by any or all of these.

These manifestations of a more consciously castelike social order became increasingly apparent in the turbulent environments of the later Mughal realm, as well as those of the eighteenth-century post-Mughal kingdoms. This explains the book's somewhat arbitrary starting point of 1700. Of course the making or remaking of caste in the forms that we see both in the colonial period and today was a long-term process which cannot be pinned down to specific dates. Even so, the book will attempt to show that the later eighteenth century in particular was a period when India's regional societies underwent profound and complex changes which tended to give more Indians than hitherto a stake in this 'traditional' caste order.

The reasons for this are extremely diverse, and no single book can encompass all the ways in which caste and castelike identities were shaped, debated, attacked and contested even in the relatively recent past. There will, however, be an attempt to identify the most decisive of these changes, and to write about them comprehensibly, avoiding the use of abstruse technical jargon wherever possible. At the same time, the book will seek to build on the best of the existing empirical and theoretical literature. But, like the other New Cambridge Histories, this volume was commissioned as an interpretive synthesis rather than a survey. So what can it achieve that has not already been done by other specialists?

First, it will seek to draw on interdisciplinary perspectives in an attempt to bridge the gaps that often divide historians from social scientists in the treatment of caste. Particular emphasis will be given to the work of anthropologists: this discipline's special skills, and its insights into the values of the small-scale community, can and should be drawn on in the attempt to explore both changes and continuities in the experience of caste. Secondly, the book will attempt to frame its questions along rather different lines from those pursued in other studies. In particular, using both historical and anthropological perspectives, it will ask why caste has so evidently mattered to so many Indians, why it has aroused so much debate both within and outside the subcontinent, and why its norms have been so widely acted on in so many areas of economic, political and religious life, both in recent times and in the more distant past.

The aim here is certainly not to *defend* caste. Nor is it the intention to offer an all-embracing *theory* of caste, or at least not the kind of theory proposed by those social scientists whose goal is to identify a single principle such as purity, power or orientalism with which to explain caste experience, regardless of regional or historical context.

This does not mean that the book will disregard the rich but confusingly diverse theoretical literature, though it will give priority to those approaches which treat caste as a dynamic and multidimensional reality of Indian life, rather than an orientalist fiction or monolithic cultural code. The underlying premise then is that caste is a topic that can and should be explored by those seeking to grasp the complexities of both past and present life in the subcontinent. Indeed, given the vast array of empirical and theoretical studies that have contributed so much in recent years to the disciplines of Indian anthropology, sociology and history, the time is certainly ripe for an attempt at synthesis and interpretation.

What then of value judgements? Generations of well-meaning observers have denounced caste as a source of dehumanising inequalities and enfeebling social divisions. And it is true that in recent times especially, caste has been for many Indians a system of oppression comparable with the racist doctrines of *apartheid*, or the worst abuses of European serfdom. But it is impossible to understand its full effect on Indian life if we see caste only as a scheme of social and material 'disabilities'. On the other hand, nineteenth- and early twentieth-century critiques of caste did have a powerful impact on colonial policy, and on the ways in which Indians themselves have come both to understand and to experience the phenomenon. Many modern south Asians are fiercely disparaging about caste, dismissing it as a legacy of a backward and inegalitarian past. Yet this kind of internal scrutiny was itself a major factor in the shaping of present-day caste society. Its effects are most visible today in a number of far-reaching provisions of India's post-Independence Constitution. Though now widely contested, these empower the state to advance or 'uplift' those of its citizens who are defined as 'backward' or collectively deprived on the grounds of low-caste birth. Ironically, as will be seen in the book's final chapters, the implementation of these provisions has played an important role in perpetuating rather than eliminating the claims of caste for many Indians.

More broadly, this study seeks to show that both before and after the end of British colonial rule, the perceptions and writings of both Indian and foreign observers contributed directly to the shaping of caste as a 'system', both in the distant past and in more recent times. In other words, caste was and is, to a very considerable extent, what people *think* of it, and how they act on these perceptions. Far from being a static reflection of received codes and values, caste has been a dynamic force in Indian life and thought: it has been embodied in what people do and say at any given moment about the conventions and values which they define as those of 'caste society'.

This does not mean that the book will seek to reduce caste to the realm of imagination or 'discourse'.[3] For centuries, south Asians have found ways to make caste or castelike identities serve them in changing and often threatening circumstances. As a means of coping with a diverse and unpredictable social and physical environment, the titles, symbols and lifestyles of caste have proved to be remarkably durable and adaptable. So if caste is neither an orientalist fiction nor a shameful crime to be disguised or ignored in discussing India's history, it must be a fit subject for historical exploration. It is this which the volume will attempt to provide.

---

[3] The term 'discourse' is being employed here in the crude though widely used sense of purely cognitive or unconscious operations without connections to an active social or political domain.

DEFINITIONS AND PRINCIPLES

The English word caste has come to be widely used in south Asia, even by speakers of vernacular languages, though many equivalent terms for human orders or 'communities' exist in the subcontinent's regional languages. (On the origins of the term in English usage, see Chapter 3.) Today, as in past centuries, most Indians who would classify themselves as Hindus (and also many non-Hindus) are likely to be at least broadly familiar with two distinct concepts of corporate affiliation: the jati (birth group) and the varna (order, class or kind).[4]

The term caste is commonly used to refer to both of these. Both may be used of non-Hindus; they sometimes designate distinctions of species or kind amongst gods, animals and even inanimate objects and substances.[5] Nevertheless, both now and in past centuries, the term jati has most often been used for the units of thousands or sometimes millions of people with whom one may identify for such purposes as marriage. There are thousands of titles associated with specific jatis in different parts of the country. A few such titles – most notably Rajput, Chamar and Jat – have come to be quite widely recognised; most will be unfamiliar to people outside a limited geographical area.

In contrast to this profusion of jatis or birth groups, the concept of varna involves a scheme with only four divisions. Thus what would now be called Hindu society is conceived of as being divisible into four very large units which transcend specific regional associations. This scheme is propounded in a variety of widely revered Hindu sacred scriptures (see below, pp. 13–14). It has been most commonly understood as a ranked order of precedence, with the four varnas or idealised human callings appearing in the following order:

- the varna of Brahmans, commonly identified with those fulfilling the callings of priests and spiritual preceptors;
- the varna of Kshatriyas, usually associated with rulers and warriors, but also including seigneurial landed groups;

---

[4] These usages include such regional vernacular terms as *qaum, sampraday, samudi* and *jati*. Like other English terms made familiar through colonial administrative practice, 'community' is still widely employed in both English and the vernaculars. It is often a reference to ethno-religious origin, as when newspapers refer euphemistically to Hindu–Muslim riots as 'clashes of two particular communities'. It is also a term for caste origin, often with an implication that such a 'community' shares an inherited moral mandate to promote common interests by coercive means. (See Chapters 8 and 9 below.)

[5] Sharma 1975; Marriott and Inden 1977.

- the varna of Vaishyas, often identified with commercial livelihoods, though associated with other producers and wealth-creators as well;
- the varna of Shudras or servile toilers.

So-called untouchables (and also the hill and forest populations who are now commonly called 'tribals') occupy an ambivalent place below, outside or parallel to this varna scheme. The titles of these four archetypes or orders, and the hierarchy of ranked callings and moral endowments which characterise them, are defined in ancient religious scriptures which became increasingly well known both before and after the British conquest. It is important to note too, however, that there are many widely revered sacred texts and doctrines which devalue or condemn caste principles. (See Chapter 1, below.)

In the words of the anthropologist R. S. Khare, the concept of jati refers to the experience of caste in the 'concrete and factual' domain of everyday social life, as opposed to the 'ideal and symbolic ... archetypes' which are embodied in the concept of varna.[6] Once caste or castelike norms have come to be widely shared in a given region, a reference to jati can therefore identify people in a very minute and precise way; the designations of varna evoke vast and sweeping generalities. While one would expect to find at least a rough match between the two, there has often been much dispute about the precise order of merit among the various jati populations of a given region. Furthermore, people of different doctrinal traditions and social circumstances have attached differing degrees of importance to these schemes of caste. Indeed all these conceptual principles, and the ways in which people have acted on them, have been far more diverse and flexible than has often been thought, both by academics and by would-be reformers of caste.

For all this fluidity, it is still the case that certain basic ideas subsuming both jati and varna were shared by at least some people in the subcontinent well before the colonial period. The underlying premise here, which is still widely known today, is that those who would nowadays call themselves Hindus are born into fixed social units with specific names or titles. Such a unit is one's caste or 'community'.[7] And, insofar as individuals and kin groups recognise the claims of caste, these embody something broader than the notion

---

[6] Khare 1983: 85.

[7] This is the sense in which the term jati is generally used, though without necessarily overriding its meaning as a reference to broader species-like groupings. (See note 4 above.)

of a common kin or blood tie. Indeed caste is widely described by anthropologists as a notion of attachment which bundles together a given set of kin groups or descent units. Both in the past and for many though not all Indians in more modern times, those born into a given caste would normally expect to find marriage partners within these limits, and to regard those outside as of unlike kind, rank or substance.

Furthermore, both in the past and today, those sharing a common caste identity may subscribe to at least a notional tradition of common descent, as well as a claim of common geographical origin, and a particular occupational ideal. Neither now nor in past centuries would an individual claiming Brahman parentage have been obliged to follow a priestly or preceptoral livelihood. Nor would a man professing princely Rajput descent automatically expect to wield a sword. Yet such claims have often conveyed recognisable messages to other Indians. In particular, those claiming Brahman or Rajput descent would definitely not expect it to be thought that their ancestors were humble labourers or providers of menial service, as would be the case for an individual identified by a low-caste jati designation such as Paraiyan or Chamar. (On the important topic of women's caste status, see below, especially Chapters 1 and 3.) Above all, the concept of caste has come to imply both boundaries and collective or corporate rank. In theory at least, civilised 'caste Hindus' should regard it as wrong and unnatural to share food or other intimate social contacts with those who are radically unlike them in caste terms. In theory too, the central characteristic of 'caste society' has been for many centuries the hierarchical ranking of castes or birth groups. The implication here is that to be of high or low caste is a matter of innate quality or essence. This is what is said in many scriptural codifications of caste ideals; in real life, these principles have often been widely contested and modified. Nevertheless, even people who came to reject caste principles either recently or in the more distant past are at least likely to have been familiar with these notions of corporate moral essences or qualities, meaning that in 'caste society', gradations of rank and precedence are innate, universal and collective. The implication of this would be that all who are born into so-called clean castes will rank as high, pure or auspicious in relation to those of unclean or 'untouchable' birth, regardless of wealth, achievement or other individual circumstances.

THEORIES AND DEBATES

The key problem for Indian social science has been to decide whether caste should actually be seen in these terms, that is, as a coherent system of thought and practice rather than an orientalist fiction or a miscellany of essentialising 'discourses'.[8] This in turn leads to the question of what exactly comes into people's minds when they differentiate between one another in caste terms. How distinctive are these markers of difference? Are they truly unlike those of other stratified social systems, where differences of status would seem to be so much more readily reducible to straightforward material matters, that is, to differentials of economic class, colour, education or religious affinity?

One might not think that caste differentials are so very distinctive, requiring special explanations which treat the difference between high and low castes as being fundamentally unlike the forms of stratification that distinguish the rich from the poor, or the dominant from the weak and subordinated 'subaltern'. After all, people of low-caste origin are often significantly poorer, less well educated, more inclined towards unprestigious forms of 'folk' religion, and even physically darker-skinned than those claiming superior caste rank. None of these, however, is invariably a feature of caste difference. Some other basis of differentiation does seem to come into play, above all in cases where there would appear to be no evident material basis for a claim of caste superiority.

Both in the past and to a significant extent today, the deprived 'untouchable' and the very poor individual of 'clean' caste may appear to be indistinguishable in economic and other material terms. Yet there is still something real and important that divides them, not just in the abstract, but in the bitter realities of everyday experience. Similarly, Brahmans and other 'clean' or high-caste groups and individuals may often be found in deprived material circumstances. Yet such people will not lose the intangible but widely recognised quality that defines them as higher in caste terms than those who may be richer, better educated and even more politically influential than they are, but who will still be seen as their inferiors by the standards of 'traditional' caste ideology. This, however, raises the question of

---

[8] For an influential treatment of this issue see Inden 1990.

11

whether such perceptions have differed at the top and bottom of the scale, either in the distant past or in more recent times. There is much debate on these two related issues, that is, whether 'modernity' has modified or undermined caste values, and whether those deemed to be low-born in caste terms have accepted or contested the jati and varna principles which define them as unclean or otherwise inferior.[9]

Among social scientists, the most compelling modern interpretations of caste are those which have sought to resolve these problems by combining ethnographic fieldwork observations with an analysis of sacred scriptures and other normative texts. The anthropologist Veena Das has been a particularly eloquent and innovative champion of this technique. She has thus rejected the approach of the empirical anthropologists who studied caste in the 1950s and 1960s, notably F. G. Bailey, for whom the learned abstractions of Hindu scripture were an irrelevance to the life and thought of the ordinary 'caste Hindu'.[10]

For Bailey and many of his contemporaries, 'traditional' caste was to be found in India's villages, and the villager's mental universe was one of practical material realities. 'Caste Hindus' worshipped Hindu gods, but the logic of their social relations did not stem from the values of those codes and scriptures which proclaimed the superiority of 'pure' Brahmans over worldly men of wealth and power. These were merely a disguise or *ex post facto* rationalisation for the realities of material advantage and disadvantage. Caste in Bailey's view was therefore not a unique moral or religious system. It was merely a more elaborate form of the social stratifications to be found in many other societies: the true basis of the distinction between those of low and high caste was differential access to political and economic resources.

For Veena Das, as for other important commentators of the past twenty years, texts do connect with this wider world of everyday town and village life, and have done so for many centuries. It is notable too that anthropologists who study 'caste' norms no longer confine themselves to non-literate village environments. T. N. Madan,

[9] Moffatt 1979 argues for 'cultural consensus' between those of low and high caste; see Weber 1958. For opposing views, see Berreman 1967, 1971; Gough 1973; Mencher 1974; Omvedt 1980; Juergensmeyer 1982; and works by historians of the Subaltern Studies school, e.g. Chatterjee 1989. Other important contributions include Freeman 1986; Lorenzen 1987; Randeria 1989; and Deliège 1988, 1989, 1992. And see O'Hanlon 1985. (The distinction between those of low and high caste is now widely seen as being conceived in terms other than or in addition to those of ritual purity and impurity: see note 18 below.)

[10] See Das 1982, also Tambiah 1985; compare Bailey 1957, 1960.

R. S. Khare, André Béteille and Jonathan Parry are among the most highly regarded of those who have taken the study of both 'caste Hindu' and apparently caste-free life and thought to environments of complex urban modernity. This blend of textual and ethnographic approaches has thus opened up a domain of norms and values which would otherwise have remained hidden from view, but which are now widely seen in anthropology as determinants of thought and action both within and beyond the world of caste relations.[11]

India's earliest expressions of caste ideals can be found in the vast body of sacred writings known as the *Vedas*. These texts are thought to have been compiled between 1500 and 1000 BC, though it was in relatively modern times that the *Vedas*, especially the great invocatory sequence known as the *Rg Veda*, were extolled by influential sage-reformers as the defining core of Hindu faith and worship. One of the most famous sections of the *Rg Veda* describes the primordial act of blood sacrifice from which the gods created the four human varnas. The victim in this cosmic creation story is the thousand-eyed Purusa, the first created man. From the dismembered fragments of the sacrificed Purusa came each of the four varnas:

When they divided the Purusa, into how many parts did they arrange him? What was his mouth? What his two arms? What are his thighs [loins] and feet called? The *brahmin* was his mouth, his two arms were made the *rajanya* [*kshatriya*, king and warrior], his two thighs [loins] the *vaisya*, from his feet the *sudra* [servile class] was born.[12]

The sanctity of caste is extolled too in the *Bhagavad Gita*, the great exposition of spiritual teaching which is contained within the ancient *Mahabharata* epic. Without caste, says the *Gita*, there would be corruption of humanity's most precious standards of domestic honour and sexual propriety:

... when lawlessness prevails, ... the women of the family become corrupted, and when women are corrupted confusion of castes arises. And to hell does this

[11] See e.g. Madan 1991, 1992, 1993; Khare 1984; Béteille 1991a, 1991b, 1996; Parry 1980, 1981, 1985, 1994. These are certainly not simplistic portrayals of caste as an all-pervading essence of Indian culture; see also Kolenda 1983, 1986; Fuller 1992. M. N. Srinivas (1965, 1969, 1989) gave the field the important though now much modified concept of Sanskritisation, an historical process of upward group social mobility through the embrace of high or 'Sanskritic' (as opposed to local or popular) forms of Hindu social and religious practice, thus allowing caste society to be seen as mobile and fluid rather than static and inflexible.

[12] *Rg Veda* 2.2.1.1, quoted in Radhakrishnan and Moore 1957: 19; see O'Flaherty 1988: 27–8.

confusion bring the family itself as well as those who have destroyed it ... By the misdeeds of those who destroy a family and create confusion of *varnas* [castes], the immemorial laws of the race and the family are destroyed.[13]

The principles of caste as a universal law of life are further elaborated in the *Manavadharmasastra* or *Manusmrti*, an encyclopaedic treatise in verse on human conduct, morality and sacred obligations. This work is most commonly known as the *Laws* or *Institutes* of the mythical sage or lawgiver Manu; it was probably composed in about the first century AD. Here, as in the *Bhagavad Gita*, the focus is on the concept of *dharma*. This key principle of 'caste Hindu' thought is usually understood as the code of duty, religious law and right human conduct which defines the path to virtue and spiritual fulfilment for all humankind. In the *Institutes* of Manu, the source of this *dharma* is the will of the divine creator who gave each of the four human archetypes or varnas a distinct moral quality, and a calling to follow. God, 'the lustrous one', 'made separate innate activities' for the different orders of humanity.[14] All wellbeing and merit, indeed the preservation of the entire created universe, depend upon this stratified ordering of castes. The term 'dharmic' is often applied to those ways of life which conform to these principles of varna.

How then have modern social scientists sought to relate these ancient scriptural ideals to the everyday life of the 'caste Hindu'? The best-known though most hotly contested attempt to construct a textually informed interpretation of caste has been that of the French sociologist Louis Dumont. Dumont proposed his formulation as nothing less than a synopsis of Hindu civilisation itself, which he saw as being animated by a unique and coherent structure of 'core values'. These he saw as conforming to the structuralist cognitive principles elaborated most influentially in the work of Claude Lévi-Strauss. The view here is that social systems are underpinned by identifiable systems of values and concepts, and that these in turn are organised around universal cognitive and symbolic processes. In both Lévi-Strauss's and Dumont's versions of structuralist analysis, these regu-

---

[13] 'The distress of Arjuna', *Mahabharata* 40–3, quoted in Radhakrishnan and Moore 1957: 105.
[14] O'Flaherty 1991: 12. On the growth of social complexity in ancient India, which is thought to have provided the context for this text's differentiation of ranked human classes, see Thapar 1984 and 1992. On the idea of *dharma* as universalising 'laws of life', see O'Flaherty 1991: lxxvi–lxxvii, also pp. xxxv–xxxvi on *dharma* in the cultural synthesis embodied in the Hindu epics (the *Ramayana* and *Mahabharata*) and the *Laws* of Manu.

larly recurring core patterns or operations of thought take the form of paired binary oppositions.

Famously – and controversially – Dumont specified the opposing conceptual categories of purity and pollution as the first in the sequence of all-important complementary principles which, in his theory, pervade the conscious or unconscious thought processes of all Hindus. These are the archetypal or core principles which Dumont held to be unique to caste, and which he claimed to have observed both in scriptural formulations and in everday life and worship.[15] Thus for Dumont, the facts of life for the Hindu villager are not the straightforward matter of material differences on which Bailey insisted. The difference between those of high and low caste is far from being a disguised reflection of the ability to command material resources. It is instead, says Dumont, the reference points of purity and pollution which provide the important measurements of rank and status for the 'caste Hindu'. 'Preoccupation with the pure and the impure is constant in Hindu life', Dumont declares.[16]

Many anthropologists have found corroborating ethnographic evidence for this. Referring to the Pandit Brahmans whom he studied in their home region of Kashmir, T. N. Madan declares, '[Their] whole way of life is pervaded by a sense of the pure, and consequently, by the fear of impurity.'[17] Other ethnographers too stress the importance attached in everyday speech and action to these complementary concepts of purity and defilement, though many specialists would now insist that the picture is misleadingly simplistic without the addition of further conceptual polarities, most notably those of auspiciousness and inauspiciousness.[18]

---

[15] Both Dumont and his critics draw on such earlier theorists as Emile Senart (1894), Célestin Bouglé (1927), Georges Dumézil (1957) and especially A. M. Hocart (1938) who emphasised the ritualised or sacrificial dimension of the caste system's occupational specialisations. For interpretive overviews, see Deliège 1993 and Kolenda 1983; on Dumont's intellectual pedigree, see Galey 1981 and Appadurai 1992; on Hocart's view of caste as a ritualised redistribution system with principles comparable to that of the royal kingdom, see Dirks 1987.

[16] Dumont 1970: 44. For debate on Dumont's view of caste as a unique feature of Hinduism which has nevertheless influenced or 'contaminated' many non-Hindus (1970: 202–12), see Ahmad 1973; Fuller 1975 and 1996.

[17] Madan 1992: 109.

[18] Such terms as the Hindi *shuddha/ashuddha* for purity/impurity, *sutak* for ritual pollution caused by birth and death, and *shubh/ashubh* for auspiciousness/inauspiciousness are widely used. On the debate about whether 'caste society' embodies power-centred relations of auspiciousness/inauspiciousness which exist independently of those of hierarchy

Thus, many commentators, particularly Veena Das, Richard Burghart and the 'ethnosociologists' inspired by McKim Marriott, have discerned a much wider array of cultural coordinates in 'Hindu thought' than those emphasised by Dumont.[19] Indeed, even Dumont contrasts the Hindu social being, that is, the purity-loving dharmic 'caste Hindu', with another ideal type whom he sees as a second crucial pillar of the Hindu moral order. This is the ascetic renouncer – the so-called holy man or god-person – who for Dumont provides a complementary counterpart to the values of caste society. The ascetic steps outside social norms to follow a path of transcendant spirituality; this may lead to the achievement of ultimate release (*moksha*, liberation) from the bonds of material existence.[20]

Other theorists, most notably J. C. Heesterman, also make much of this seeming tension between the two domains of caste life and other-worldly asceticism. As will be seen in Chapter 4, this is an important consideration for both historians and anthropologists, because both in the past and in more recent times, influential doctrines of anti-Brahmanical and even anti-caste 'uplift' and 'reform' have been constructed around claims that Hinduism's highest spiritual principles exalt 'casteless' renunciation over and above the values of caste.[21]

Furthermore, much like Heesterman, both Veena Das and Burghart are dissatisfied with Dumont's simple binary oppositions, and insist instead on the importance of additional patterns and conceptual categories as reference points, both in scripture and in everyday ethnographic reality. In particular, all three depart from Dumont in emphasising the ideal of kingship and power as an independent variable in Hindu life and thought. Burghart finds three rather than two spiritual

or ritual purity/pollution in Dumont's sense, see Carman and Marglin 1985; Raheja 1989; Madan 1991; Parry 1991 and 1994: 135–8.

[19] See Das 1982; Burghart 1978b, 1983a, 1983b. Ethnosociologists, whose techniques derive from American cognitive anthropology, seek to interpret non-Western cultures using indigenous sociological concepts, rather than those of Western social theorists. See Marriott 1968, 1989; Marriott and Inden 1977; *CIS* Special Issue 23, 1: 1989; Moffatt 1990; Khare 1990; compare Madan 1982.

[20] On the associated doctrine of *karma*, the effects of past actions determining a being's successive rebirths, with *moksha* as the goal of ultimate liberation from incarnate existence, see Keyes and Daniel 1983; Fuller 1992: 245–52. On ascetic renunciation: Weber 1958; van der Veer 1987; Burghart 1983a; Babb 1987.

[21] Heesterman sees no true opposition between the Brahman-centred values of caste society and those of the ascetic who seems to reject the norms of caste life. In classical Hindu scripture Heesterman sees a basis for reconciliation of this 'inner conflict': the Brahman absorbs the ascetic's renunciatory principle and is therefore able to claim to be 'in the world yet not of it' (1985: 43).

ideals extolled as principles of supreme human and cosmic virtue and harmony. These three elements, each of which is a path of virtue and a source of cosmic harmony and righteousness in its own right, are represented as follows: first, the standards of dharmic caste life, as embodied in the priestly functions of Brahmans; second, ascetic renunciation; and third, the exercise of power by righteous kings, and by those who share kingly qualities of initiative, assertion and command.

Yet for Burghart, this apparent diversity still has coherence as a single system of thought and faith, with each of the three ideals interpenetrating and referring back to the others. Kings glory in their capacity to order the world through the exercise of power, yet still shore up their claims to be fonts of righteousness by borrowing from the characteristics of the other two ideals. In the same way, the exemplars of the priestly and ascetic ideals absorb the key qualities that define the other two paths of righteousness.[22]

For Veena Das, Hindu thought involves an even more complex array of patterned mental structures. She identifies a whole series of interconnected conceptual pairings: kings and their 'unkingly' subjects (commoners or Shudras); Brahmans and renouncers; renouncers and unkingly subjects; Brahmans and kings. For each pairing, she then identifies a 'latent' third ideal, arguing for example that the relationship between the Brahman and the king has no meaning without the implied presence of this pairing's shadowy silent or latent principle, that of the renouncer. These webs of interconnecting core concepts, which she describes as a scheme of 'tripartite classifications with one term latent', are for her the basis on which the diversities of Hindu thought can be seen to achieve ultimate coherence.[23]

Marriott's 'ethnosociology' offers yet another highly complex formulation, treating the bonds of caste as a product of mutable, ever-changing 'coded substances', and offering a model of caste society in which status rankings are expressed and experienced as a multidimensional web of ordered ceremonial exchanges and transactions.[24]

---

[22] Burghart's (1978b) sources include seventeenth- and eighteenth-century texts from the Hindu-ruled Himalayan kingdom of Nepal. Compare Malamoud 1981.

[23] Das's (1982) sources include Gujarati caste *puranas* (mythological 'community' histories) dating from about the fifteenth century AD.

[24] For Marriott's view of Hindu culture as 'transactional and transformational', and of the Hindu person as a fluid, unbounded, continually transacting 'dividual' or divisible entity composed of coded substances or essences transferred to others through marriage and other interpersonal contacts, see Marriott 1976 and 1989.

For all the richness and sophistication of these approaches with their insistence on this greater diversity of conceptual reference points and core principles, they have all remained bounded by a surprisingly circumscribed notion of Hinduism. As a result, these formulations do not seem to recognise the extent to which the 'Hindu''s life and thought have been intertwined with the subcontinent's other powerful religious traditions, including those of devotional Islam, as well as Christianity and Sikhism.[25]

Some social scientists have argued that caste norms are based on ideals which are unique to Hinduism, and that 'true' caste is to be found only among those who profess the Hindu faith. Yet this presupposes much firmer boundaries between ethno-religious 'communities' than was often the case in past centuries. Certainly, castelike forms of rank and corporate allegiance have been very prominent in the lives of most people who would nowadays be thought of as non-Hindus. The difficulty here is that so many studies of the supposedly casteless minority faiths have played down those elements of religious and social life which adherents of these faiths have shared with the wider society. Yet if one looks at the millions who subscribe to India's minority faiths – Islam, Sikhism, Christianity, Jainism, and the ostensibly anti-caste neo-Buddhism to be discussed in Chapter 7 – one finds both in the past and today a high level of sensitivity to the nuances of caste, especially in matters of marriage and ritual pollution.

For adherents of the Sikh faith, the distinction between 'peasant' tillers and urban moneyed groups has long been reflected in an awareness of which Sikhs are of 'peasant' Jat caste origin, and which are to be identified by other jati names denoting a background in the literate service occupations. In south India it is common to encounter Christians who take pride in Brahman ancestry, and until recently many north Indian Muslims identified with the caste ideals of the lordly Rajput. Furthermore, as James Laidlaw has shown, most of the powerful north Indian traders who follow the austerely anti-Brahmanical Jain faith are as insistent as their Hindu neighbours on the importance of marrying within named Vaishya merchant jatis, while simultaneously claiming descent from converts of princely Rajput caste.[26] Above all, for the members of virtually all the so-called

---

[25] See S. Bayly 1989 on south Asian religious 'syncretism'; on the historic construction of Hinduism see Thapar 1989 and van der Veer 1988.

[26] Laidlaw (1995: 88–119) shows that while Jains and Hindus regard their faiths as

conversion faiths, the fluid but highly potent phenomenon of the pollution barrier is still a living force in everyday life, with those deemed to be descendants of untouchable caste groups often being denied social ties with others of their ostensibly casteless faiths.[27]

AEQUALIS OR HIERARCHICUS?

With this one important *caveat* then, the view of caste offered in this volume is closest to the multidimensional models of those anthropologists who have emphasised the persistent appeal of renunciatory and kingly ideals, and their interconnections with those of Brahmanical purity. Veena Das and Richard Burghart are among the key influences here. At the same time, there are certain debates which are pursued in the work of other theorists, notably Dumont and his critics, which will be important to the approach being taken here. For Dumont, the presence of the renunciatory element in Hinduism does not alter his central premise, which is that it is fundamental to Hindu thought to rank all beings, all substances and all aspects of worldly social existence by this one overarching criterion of purity and pollution. This for him is an inherently 'religious' principle. It is on this basis, and no other, that the hierarchical rankings of caste derive their meaning. Brahmans therefore stand at the apex of the moral hierarchy which we call caste because they are inherently purer than the people of every other caste.[28]

The great problem which Dumont thereby claims to have solved is how to explain the role of the so-called untouchables whose presence in 'caste Hindu' communities is for him a paramount fact of Hindu life. Dumont saw the presence of these 'unclean' toilers as a fundamental manifestation of Hindu values. In Dumont's theory, the distinguishing characteristic of so-called untouchables is that they and only they must perform the tasks of ritual cleansing and pollution-removal which he sees as indispensable for the existence of Hindus as social beings. These are tasks which keep the 'untouchable' in a permanently unclean state, but which thereby allow those of 'clean'

---

separate and distinct, the same castes exist among both; Hindu–Jain intermarriage is permissible so long as the partners are of matching caste. On Muslims and Rajput lordliness, see Chapter 1, below.

[27] See Chapter 1, note 3.

[28] Important discussions of Dumont and the concept of hierarchy include Kolenda 1976; Appadurai 1986, 1992; Galey 1989.

caste to maintain a state of ritual purity in a world which continually surrounds them with both tangible and intangible sources of defilement and pollution. Thus for Dumont, the distinctiveness of the supreme, pure Brahman is the complementary counterpart to that of the inherently unclean 'untouchable'.

What then are the problems arising from these claims? Many of Dumont's most vehement critics have accused him of disguising or even legitimising the coercive side of caste relations, particularly the concrete realities of disadvantage as experienced by those of low and 'unclean' caste. Among those who have attempted to reassert a material or political economy dimension to caste have been those Marxist commentators who since the 1970s have written sympathetically about caste-based militancy involving so-called 'Dalits' (ex-untouchables). Gail Omvedt in particular has thus rejected older Marxist views of caste as mere 'superstructure' or 'false consciousness' in a world where the true realities of political economy were to be seen as those of class-based oppression. She argues instead that the material effects of colonialism and modern capitalism served to make caste an authentic force in Indian life, and that any truly 'revolutionary' movement in India must take note of the special oppression experienced by those who have been thus coerced and disadvantaged through the workings of this 'redefined caste system'.[29]

Some of those who have argued in these terms have at least hinted at the idea that Dumont's picture of caste may therefore be an accurate if only partial reflection of Indian reality, not in the sense of being a timeless expression of age-old 'traditional' values, but as a product of economic and social change in comparatively modern times. Yet there are still those who have condemned Dumont's entire theory as an exercise in demeaning orientalism, charging him with purveying a false stereotype of Indians as the slaves of an all-powerful 'religious' code, hence dreaming, irrational, otherworldly and devoid of the capacity to take 'modern', secular or individual initiatives. A number of Dumont's critics, notably Mattison Mines, have found evidence of strongly individualist values in Hindu thought.[30] Above all, many see Dumont as recapitulating Western colonial views which supposedly exalted or even fabricated the Brahman-centred perspectives that are central to

---

[29] Mencher 1974, 1978; Berreman 1979; Omvedt 1978, 1982; Gough 1989. See also Meillassoux 1973; Godelier 1986; Shah 1985: 14–15.

[30] Mines 1992.

his analysis, and which are also fundamental for such commentators as Madeleine Biardeau, for whom 'orthodox Brahmanism' is nothing less than the 'permanent heart' of Hinduism.[31]

It true that Dumont's theory treats Indians (or Hindus) as heirs to a system of values which are radically unlike those of the West. For Dumont, the Hindu's hierarchical judgements of human worth are made on a basis of collectively inherited moral qualities, rather than personal endowments or attainments. He maintains that only in modern, secular, rational Western society has there evolved a genuine concept of the individual. For Dumont, no such principle is possible in 'traditional' Hindu thought. The Hindu is a caste being whose social identity derives from collective rather than individual bonds and claims; in Hinduism, he says, only the follower of the renouncer's path can lead a life approximating to that of the Western individual. Thus, in Dumont's famous phrase, Indians belong to a distinct human order or cultural category, that of *homo hierarchicus*. This is a broad category embracing other supposedly 'traditional' non-Western civilisations. Yet for Dumont the Indian variant of this hierarchical being is unique; in their deference to the overriding 'religious' values defined in his theory of caste, Indians (or Hindus) are so different from other peoples that they are almost a distinct species of humankind.[32]

Even Dumont's defenders have generally accepted that there are serious flaws in this sweeping portrayal of the Euro-American as *homo aequalis*, in contrast to the Hindu Indian who is consigned to the category of *homo hierarchicus*. But the key complaint here, as far as the historian is concerned, is the charge that Dumont makes India a land of static 'oriental' spirituality rather than action and agency. More specifically, these critics say that by insisting on Brahman-centred caste values, Dumont and those who share his views make India appear to lack any indigenous values which might have inspired the construction of strong states and the achievement of effective political action, either in the distant past or in resistance to colonial conquest.[33]

A number of commentators have therefore mounted strong objections to Dumont's hierarchical or purity-centred picture of caste values, since this suggests to them a claim that only with colonial rule

---

[31] Biardeau 1992: 15; those criticising Dumont on these grounds include Inden 1990; and see Searle-Chatterjee and Sharma 1994.

[32] Dumont 1970; see Madan *et al.* 1971.

[33] See e.g. Dirks 1987; Raheja 1988a, 1988b; Quigley 1993.

did the subcontinent finally acquire forceful but 'derivative' models of polity and statecraft.[34] It is indeed true that for Dumont, the logic of caste makes those who are collectively pure by birth and essence superior to those who are endowed with mere worldly power. Although kings and other embodiments of the Kshatriya's active, lordly qualities may stand supreme in the material order, Dumont maintains that the Brahman as priest-preceptor derives his status from a source which is beyond and superior to the concerns of the mere material plane.

Dumont's famous phrase for this is the assertion that in caste society power is invariably 'encompassed' by status.[35] Thus he proposes yet another key set of binary conceptual oppositions: following on from his complementary pairings of purity/impurity, Brahman/untouchable and renouncer/man-in-the-world is his insistence on a radical disjunction in Hindu values between priesthood and secular power. In other words, unlike other societies which possess the cognitive capacity to recognise and exalt individual prowess and achievement in the worldly sphere, Dumont argues that in the Hindu social order, the worldly achiever and doer of active this-worldly deeds performs a less exalted task than that of the 'pure' and therefore superior Brahman.

Nicholas Dirks and Gloria Goodwin Raheja in particular charge Dumont with having overlooked much strong ethnographic and textual evidence which would radically reduce the importance of Brahmans and Brahmanical values in Hindu thought and social life. These critics propose a view of caste relations emphasising action, initiative and concepts of power deriving from indigenous cultural concepts and categories, rather than the 'religious' values of purity and hierarchy proposed by Dumont. In this view it is rulers, and those who exercise king-like power through the command of men, land and other material resources, who stand at the apex of India's scheme of moral order and values.[36] Thus in the centuries before colonial rule, Brahmans are to be seen as little more than technicians, performing

---

[34] Chatterjee 1986.

[35] Dumont 1970: 76–9.

[36] Dirks's formulation (1987) which emphasises indigenous notions of royal gifting proposes a view of power which, unlike Bailey's, does not depend on simple economic or material differentiations; Raheja (1988b) insists too on the mechanism of the gift (*dan*) which transfers inauspiciousness and thereby asserts and confirms the power (or 'ritual centrality', rather than hierarchy) of dominant, king-like landed groups.

their specialist rituals as subordinate servants of kings and other men of power.[37] Even in present-day village life, it is the Kshatriya-like qualities of landed elites, rather than Brahman-centred purity values, which are seen by Raheja as structuring the relations between Hindus of differing caste rank.[38]

These attempts to downplay or even dismiss the significance of Brahmans and Brahmanical caste values go against the grain of much that is familiar both from the historical record and in contemporary Indian life. The social scientists who will probably have the most enduring impact on the field are therefore those who have taken Dumont's formulations seriously rather than dismissing them altogether.[39]

At the same time, however, India's enormous complexity and historical dynamism must make any quest for a single model or formula of caste a deeply frustrating experience. Herein may lie the great advantage of exploring these issues historically. The central premise of this volume will be that through historical perspectives, it may be possible to reach a view of caste which captures much of the plurality and multiplicity of Indian life and thought. From an historical vantage point, it may indeed be possible to show that none of the divergent theoretical interpretations outlined above can be refuted absolutely. On the contrary, each of them may actually be correct for some if not all Indians, at least for limited periods, and in at least some areas of the subcontinent, either recently or in the more distant past.

Those arguments which de-emphasise the Brahman and identify the princely warrior as the lodestone of the social order work best for the pre-colonial military states which took shape in comparatively remote frontier regions, well away from the great centres of high Hindu culture and worship. Yet it cannot be convincingly inferred from this that the role of the Brahman was merely a fiction promulgated by ancient law-givers, and then seized upon by British officials and academic orientalists. On the other hand, far from illuminating the life and thought of an unchanging or primordial 'traditional' India, Dumont's theory is probably best understood as a description

[37] Quigley 1993.
[38] Raheja 1988a.
[39] Among the many strengths of these works is that they treat Dumont's category of purity as an element of a dynamic world shaped by the force of the political and the 'religious', rather than an abstract or independent entity. Notably successful examples are Parry 1974 and 1994; and Fuller 1979 and 1988.

capturing some of the rapid and complex changes which were becoming increasingly active in Indian society just before and during the colonial period.

Chapters 1 and 2 therefore explore the changes in political, economic and religious life which helped to spread castelike ways of life in many areas of the subcontinent in the period immediately preceding the colonial conquest. Chapters 3 and 4 deal with thought and 'discourse': Chapter 3 assesses Western colonial perceptions of caste, and Chapter 4 considers the understandings of caste that animated debates among Indians themselves, concentrating particularly on influential social, religious and political commentators of the later nineteenth and early twentieth centuries. Chapter 5 returns the discussion to the domain of everyday life. Its aim is to explore the changing experience of caste in the age of high colonialism. The emphasis here will be on the increasing rigidities of the so-called pollution barrier, by which is meant the formalisation of social barriers separating those of superior caste from the lowest or most unclean and inauspicious caste groups, in circumstances of growing conflict in both town and countryside, in the period before the First World War.

Turning next to the power and resources of the twentieth-century Indian state, Chapters 6 and 7 focus on the electoral arena and the impact of modern political institutions on the experience of caste, first in the late colonial era, and then in the period since Independence. In the two final chapters, an attempt is made to ask in what ways and to what extent contemporary Indians are still affected by the norms of caste. Chapter 8 considers the practical realities of caste in the late twentieth century, asking how far the experience of caste has truly changed or been supplanted by other forms of solidarity and moral obligation in everyday life. Chapter 9 explores the painful and controversial phenomenon of so-called 'caste wars' in present-day India.

It goes without saying that the interpretations offered here will not please all of the field's contending experts. Nevertheless, on the assumption that these are important and compelling matters to explore and comment on, it is to this array of thorny issues that we now turn.

CHAPTER 1

HISTORICAL ORIGINS OF A 'CASTE SOCIETY'

INTRODUCTION: 'HISTORICISING' THE ANTHROPOLOGICAL MODELS

Caste is not and never has been a fixed fact of Indian life. Both caste as varna (the fourfold scheme of idealised moral archetypes) and caste as jati (smaller-scale birth-groups) are best seen as composites of ideals and practices that have been made and remade into varying codes of moral order over hundreds or even thousands of years. The context for this fluidity has been the subcontinent's remarkable diversity in culture and physical environment, and above all the diversity of its states and political systems. Those conventions of rank and corporate essence that are often seen as the defining features of caste have been shaped, critiqued and reconstituted in all sorts of ways, both century by century and region by region. As will be seen in the three final chapters, these processes of invention and reformulation are still taking place today at the local level, and also in the wider context of regional and pan-Indian political and social conflict.

Even in the distant past, recognisably castelike ideologies and practices were followed by some people in most or all of the subcontinent's regional cultures. Yet until relatively recent times, many Indians were still comparatively untouched by the norms of jati and varna as we now understand them. This was true not only of the forest and hill people who are now called 'tribals', but also of much larger groups of powerful plains-dwellers and martial pastoralists. Even under the Raj, caste as a 'system' was far less uniform and all-pervading than many colonial commentators believed. Nevertheless, in the centuries immediately preceding the British conquest, social life in almost all areas of the subcontinent became significantly more castelike than had been the case in earlier times.

But what exactly did it mean to become part of a castelike social order, and what was it that caused these far-reaching changes in thought and behaviour? In the Introduction, it was noted that the social scientists who appear to have the most persuasive models of

25

caste as a conceptual system are those like Veena Das and Richard Burghart who emphasise a multidimensional array of themes, ideals and principles. In these anthropological accounts, which have both challenged and built on Louis Dumont's structuralist formulations, three sets of values – those of priestly hierarchy, kingship and ascetic renunciation – have particular importance in caste society as both opposing and interconnecting reference points for the 'caste Hindu'.[1]

Looked at historically, however, it is possible to see a sequence of relatively recent political and ideological changes which brought these ideals into focus for ever more people in the subcontinent. Between about 1650 and 1850, all three of these core concepts came increasingly to make their mark in Indian life. Yet these developments did not bring all three conceptual principles to bear with equal force at one and the same time. On the contrary, there seem to have been two distinct stages in the making of the elaborately ritualised schemes of social stratification which have come to be thought of as the basis of 'traditional' faith and culture in the subcontinent. (The term ritualisation is being used here to denote an emphasis on forms of differentiation between groups and individuals which appear to demand recognition through distinctive modes of action – rituals – and which derive from some quality of innate or hereditary status, rather than immediate economic or political power.)[2]

What happened in the initial phase of this two-stage sequence was the rise of the royal man of prowess. In this period, both kings and the priests and ascetics with whom men of power were able to associate their rule became a growing focus for the affirmation of a martial and regal form of caste ideal. Across much of India, those who embraced these values sought increasingly to establish firm social boundaries between themselves and the non-elite tillers and arms-bearers to whom their forebears had often been closely affiliated. The other key feature of this period was the reshaping of many apparently casteless

---

[1] Without adhering literally to Das's or Burghart's schemes, the book's attempt to portray caste as both historically shaped and multi-stranded draws on their insights and those of other anthropologists discussed earlier. (On the relationship between dharmic, kingly and ascetic ideals, see below, pp. 49–62, and Chapter 2.)

[2] This is not to overlook the importance of forms of caste which focus on ideals of political power and kingship; indeed king-centred manifestations of caste will be emphasised throughout. Also, in the light of important work on kingship and the royal gift (notably Dirks 1987), it is not being suggested here that politically conceived conceptions of caste were lacking in the element of 'ritualisation'. See Dumont 1970; Humphrey and Laidlaw 1994.

forms of devotional faith (*bhakti*) in a direction which further affirmed these differentiations of rank and 'community'. (See below, pp. 46–9.)

The spread of these lordly or Kshatriya-centred manifestations of caste values is therefore the focus of this chapter. Three important elements of change in the new states and dominions of the post-Mughal period will be discussed here: first, the emerging courtly synthesis between Kshatriya-like kings and Brahmans; second, the diffusion of these values and practices into the world of the upper non-elite 'peasantry'; and third, the continuing power and importance of martial 'predators' and so-called tribal peoples. The significance of these trends, and particularly the importance of individual agency in the forging of more castelike forms of social order, are explored more concretely at the end of the chapter through an account of the rise of the great Maratha-dominated polity of Shivaji Bhonsle (1630–80).

Chapter 2 will then explore the second stage in this sequence, which had its origins before the British conquest but reached its culmination during the period of colonial rule. Here Brahmans, together with scribes, ascetics and merchants who espoused Brahmanical social and spiritual codes, became ever more widely deferred to, even achieving a quasi-independent status in such areas as legal codes and colonial administrative practice. It was in this period that the power of the pollution barrier became for many Indians the defining feature of everyday caste experience.[3]

What will be seen in subsequent chapters is that British rule had the effect of intensifying many of the trends towards ritualisation in social life which were already underway well before the colonial period. Towards the end of British rule, and also in independent India, a process of what one might call de-ritualisation has been apparent. This has meant that Dumont's purity-conscious 'caste Hindu' has come in many cases to look more like a believer in material and political power as the chief measure of value in a dangerous and uncertain world. Yet these trends have never been complete. At no time in the past did all Indians deal with one another on a purely 'ritualistic' basis. By the same token, even in 'modern' environments, contemporary Indians

---

[3] On the important phenomenon of the pollution barrier, that is, the values and practices dividing those of ritually 'clean' and 'unclean' birth, see below, Chapters 2, 5 and 8. (Despite their increasing power, these differentiations retained considerable fluidity and flexibility: see Parry 1970: 84–104 and 1979: 113.)

have not entirely de-ritualised their understanding of social difference. The focus throughout this study will therefore be on the many ways in which the experience of caste has taken root, often being forcibly challenged, and yet still spreading and diversifying in ways which had far-reaching effects across the subcontinent.

CASTE AND THE ORDERING OF PLURALITY

Nothing quite like caste has evolved in other parts of the world. Of course there are schemes of idealised social and moral order outside the subcontinent, especially in east and southeast Asia where Indian gods and social norms are widely known, but these schemes took shape in very different contexts. Japan's *bushido* code defined a hierarchy of warriors (*samurai*), commoners, merchants and 'untouchables' which resembled the fourfold varna scheme but was not associated with a proliferation of smaller *jati*-like birth-groups. In Thailand, ostensibly casteless Buddhist norms have co-existed for centuries with an ideal of kingship derived from India: hereditary Brahman ritualists still serve the Thai royal house, and the deified hero Ram is still the model for Thai rulers (as for the former Khmer kings of Cambodia) in their capacity as protectors of faith and righteousness. Furthermore, both east and southeast Asia have sizable minority populations – pastoralists, swidden cultivators and hunter-gatherers – who have been looked upon by 'civilised' townspeople and sedentary 'peasant' villagers in much the same way that so-called caste Hindus have regarded India's 'tribals'.[4]

Yet in east and southeast Asia, where the expansion of the rice frontier was generally accompanied by the spread of Islam and Buddhism, castelike hierarchies did not emerge from these differentiations between wanderers or 'tribals' on the one hand and sedentary villagers and townsfolk on the other. This should not come as a surprise: in these other Asian lands, diversities of religion, culture and language have been considerably less dramatic than India's. These

[4] For debate on the existence of caste outside India, especially in *apartheid* societies, see Dumont 1970: 243–8; Berreman 1979; Ursula Sharma 'Berreman revisited' in Searle-Chatterjee and Sharma 1994: 72–91; Béteille 1991b: 15–36. (Detailed consideration of the literature on caste in Sri Lanka and Nepal is beyond the scope of this volume.) Potter and Potter (1990) and Bloch (1989) have pointed to the existence of castelike social groupings in China and Madagascar; Bourdieu (1962: 132) refers to the racial divide between whites and Muslims in colonial Algeria as a 'caste system'.

regions' political landscapes were generally much less diverse as well, with ideals of pre-colonial kingship often focused on only one divinely mandated royal house rather than many competing dynasties. Furthermore, in both the distant and more recent past, India's specialist Brahman priesthoods and ascetic preceptoral corporations tended to retain a considerable degree of separation and independence, even from very powerful rulers and their courts. Elsewhere in Asia, most notably in pre-modern Japan and China, both the Buddhist clergy (the monkhood or *sangha*) and its Confucian equivalents were often significantly more closely tied to state power than was the case for their Indian counterparts.

This difference can be attributed in part to the rise of regional Muslim kingdoms in India from the eleventh century onwards. Even where Muslim rulers patronised and interacted with Hindu religious foundations, as they often did, the subcontinent still did not develop a single composite 'national' faith. One further factor in the making of caste was the inheritance of a large body of sacred scripture elevating the Brahman to a status co-equal with or even superior to that of a reigning king, though this is certainly not to say that the *Institutes* of Manu or any other ancient code or text in some way 'created' the phenomenon of caste.[5]

Indeed the emergence of caste cannot be reduced to these factors or any other single causal factor. Yet the fact remains that, in contrast to other areas of Asia, the paramount fact of Indian history has been the subcontinent's remarkable array of contrasting ecologies, languages, religions, modes of production and political systems, as well as its great political fluidity, with persistent oscillations between prosperity and dearth, commercialisation and subsistence, pastoralism and peasant agriculture. One especially striking element of Indian life has been the presence of very large subordinated populations who have been identified as culturally, morally and even biologically distinct from other Indians: these are the people to whom such labels as 'tribals' and 'untouchables' have been applied.

All of these cultural, ethnic and historical diversities are reflected in the profusion of different meanings that Indians have given to the castes or caste-like groupings with which they have come to identify themselves. This was a particularly notable trend of the period

---

[5] On eclectic styles of religious patronage, see Chapter 2, below.

explored in this chapter, this being the time when the great Mughal polity was fragmenting into the fluid regional successor regimes of the late seventeenth and eighteenth centuries.[6] These critical changes in India's pre-colonial political landscape had profound but very disparate social effects. In many respects the subcontinent had become more fully integrated by the later eighteenth century, both physically and culturally. This integration derived from an increase in inter-regional warfare, as well as increasing travel, pilgrimage and commercial exchange, and greater scope for the transfer of writings and social norms from one region to another. Yet the limited standardisation which had occurred under Mughal administration was counter-balanced by equally powerful decentralising trends. These were particularly widespread during the eighteenth century, with its proliferation of competing and decentralised kingdoms and petty chiefdoms.

In these new post-Mughal realms, *parvenu* ruling elites took bold initiatives in the attempt to assert their power and legitimacy, turning to the symbols and language of caste as a prop of their statecraft, and especially to versions of these which emphasised power and benefi-cence. Yet at the same time, most of these rulers had to tolerate the presence of smaller-scale social groupings possessing their own norms and social conventions. These people, who included networks of long-distance traders, armed ascetics and arms-bearing 'tribals', often had only tenuous connections to the ideologies of caste being promulgated in these fluid new dynastic realms.[7]

The great puzzle then is how to relate people's lives in these environments of plurality and dynamism to ideals of jati and varna which apparently reduce human experience to arbitrary stereotypes: high and low, clean and unclean, 'pure' Brahman and 'impure' untouchable. In fact, however, pre-colonial kings and their subjects did not treat caste norms as one-dimensional absolutes, but as reference points to be negotiated, challenged or reshaped to fit changing circumstances. In the period from the Mughal conquest to the early stages of colonial rule, the caste or castelike conventions

---

[6] On the formation of these Muslim-, Sikh- and Hindu-ruled polities (including those of Bengal, Awadh, the Punjab and the Maratha domains), see e.g. Alam 1986; Cole 1988; Grewal 1990; Gordon 1993; C. Bayly 1988; Wink 1986; Peabody 1991; also S. Bayly 1989; Dirks 1992a; Perlin 1985; Kulke 1995; Brittlebank 1997.

[7] These circumstances of volatile politics and rapid but uneven economic growth ultimately came together to create a foothold for British military and commercial expansion across the subcontinent. See note 6, above; also Marshall 1996; Subrahmanyam 1990a.

which had come into being in different regions equipped both the weak and the strong with a means to maximise assets and protect themselves from loss.

This often involved naked coercion: new rulers and other insecure elites frequently invoked jati and varna principles in attempts to assert authority over dependent cultivators and other subordinate groups. But even people whose 'community' was defined as low or inferior in caste terms could see advantage in being known by a recognised title and status which they could associate with sacred norms and mandates, especially when others around them were relating themselves to these same conventions. These strategies of collective classing and ranking proved particularly valuable in circumstances where state power was fluid or insecure, and where large numbers of people had to adjust to the unpredictable in their everyday environments. The experience of caste could even reflect individual achievement, although in theory there should have been no way to force the facts of jati and varna to take account of personal prowess, as for example when a man claimed to be of exalted or 'pure' substance even though his origins were clearly of quite a different order.

So how wide were the diversities, given that caste has often been portrayed as a single homogeneous 'system', rather than a grid of diverse and changeable ideals and practices? In the high period of Mughal power (c. 1580–1700), there certainly were areas where strictly defined orderings of rank and status had come to prevail quite widely, especially among ruling elites, settled cultivators, and specialist mercantile and service groups in zones where intensive cultivation had long been practised. Such norms were common in the densely populated eastern Ganges valley. Similar conventions emphasising conformity to Brahman-derived ideals of refinement and ritual purity had emerged even earlier under the great Hindu dynasties which in the fifteenth and sixteenth centuries were centred on the royal courts and temples of the rice-growing southern river deltas.[8]

Yet even in south India, where Brahman-centred jati and varna codes are often thought of as being especially strict and all-embracing, the great ruler Krishnadeva Raya (1509–29) communicated an ideal of kingship which extolled both Brahman-centred piety and the virtues of lordship and armed prowess:

[8] Stein 1980 and 1989.

The expenditure of money ... [on] buying elephants and horses, ... in maintaining soldiers, in the worship of gods and Brahmans and in one's own enjoyment can never be called an expenditure ... [A king] should protect one and all of his subjects, should put an end to the mixing up of the castes among them ... [and] should always try to increase the merit of the Brahmans ... A king should get the merit of severe fasting and subduing the body only by giving money and not by giving up the enjoyment derivable from the anointments, baths, feasts, smearings, clothes and flowers in the several seasons ... A crowned king should always rule with an eye towards Dharma.[9]

Indeed, much of south India had no uniform 'system' of caste even in the colonial period, and the regional societies which came under Nayaka warrior rule in the sixteenth and seventeenth centuries were far from being textbook illustrations of the fourfold varna scheme. On the contrary, among south India's trading people there was little emphasis on the Vaishya ideal. In addition, many of the superior Tamilnad landowners, who modelled their refined lifestyles on those of superior Brahman land-controllers (*mirasidars*), did not themselves wear the sacred thread of the twice-born, the *suta*. As far as the formal varna scheme was concerned, this meant that they could not claim to be anything but members of the lowest varna, that of the non-elite Shudras.[10]

SEIGNEURIAL RIGHTS AND STATUSES: AN ARCHETYPE OF THE 'HIGH-CASTE'

These former Nayaka-ruled regions then were among the many areas where caste or castelike forms of social organisation were either fluid and open-ended or were based on conventions that were special to one particular regional subculture.[11] Elsewhere, however, there were regions where more standardised understandings of varna had become widespread and where, in particular, armed men of power had come to exalt themselves as heirs to the scriptural Kshatriya ideal. The adoption and spread of the title Rajput among north Indian ruling clans was of critical importance here. In the arid hill country which is now known as Rajasthan, located to the southwest of the Mughals' original strongholds in the Gangetic plain, powerful lords and their arms-bearing retainers had been calling themselves Rajput, a title derived

---

[9] Sarasvati 1926; see Stein 1989: 51–2.
[10] See Rao, Shulman and Subrahmanyam 1992.
[11] See Chapter 3 below.

from the Sanskrit *rajaputra*, 'king's son', as far back as the thirteenth or fourteenth century AD, and possibly much earlier. These people's closest counterparts elsewhere were the users of the south Indian designations Nayar and Nayaka; such titles as Kanyakubja and Maithil had similar connotations in the eastern Gangetic plain. Nevertheless, through a process of assimilation and interaction with the statecraft of the Mughals and their eighteenth-century successors, it was the Rajput version of lordly caste values that became particularly influential across much of the subcontinent.[12]

The Rajasthan region's ideal of Kshatriya-centred caste ideology emerged in its initial form well before the Mughal conquest, through the struggles which transformed the area's most effectively militarised chiefdoms into expansive royal domains. In both the sixteenth and the seventeenth centuries, Mughal armies fought bloody battles in this strategic frontier region, and through a mixture of force and conciliation, its kingdoms were eventually absorbed into the loosely textured Mughal political order. At this time, these armed elites had strong memories of the earlier clan chiefs who had made their mark in turbulent times by adopting known marks of lordship and exalted descent. Whether they were grandees commanding the region's great royal fortresses, or the armed retainers of such lords, such people now had to adapt themselves to the new circumstances of Mughal hegemony. Some clan heads accepted revenue-taking rights and military rank as Mughal clients, while others became 'rebel' opponents of Mughal rule; in either case such lineages had good reasons to identify with the potent though still highly flexible ideal of the lordly royal Rajput.[13]

Thinkers dating back to ancient times have written as if all of India (or non-Muslim India) were a domain of caste, with Brahman-centred caste values being everywhere revered as the core of human order and propriety, *dharma*. But the scholars of the Indo-Islamic courts knew that not all Indians, not even all 'Hindu' Indians, lived their lives by the principles of jati and varna. So to be Rajput or its equivalents elsewhere was more a matter of mediating between the formal world of courts, towns and villages and the big and vigorous populations

---

[12] Tod [1829–32] 1920; Peabody 1991 and 1996; Kolff 1990; Ziegler 1973: 3; Fox 1971; Ziegler 'Some notes on Rajput loyalties during the Mughal period' in Richards 1978.
[13] Richards 1993.

who lived a more open or 'wild' life near the margins of the settled caste Hindu world.

India in the high Mughal period was therefore not yet embraced and integrated by proliferating Brahman-centred pilgrimages and royal rituals, with state power being exercised by and through pan-Indian Brahman service networks. As Chapter 2 will show, these were features of the far more castelike society that was only just beginning to take shape in many regions during the mid- to late eighteenth century. These were uneven processes even in the eighteenth century, with pacific Brahmanical norms often being confined to the lives of major courts and devotional centres, while the ways of prowess still flourished on the turbulent margins. Indeed, even at the centre of many new realms, these nominally opposing ways of life still existed side by side, sometimes in tension, but often interacting and interpenetrating, and with one only gradually coming to predominate over the others.

Yet the varna archetype of the Kshatriya-like man of prowess did become a key reference point for rulers and their subjects under the Mughals and their immediate successors. The chiefs and warriors whom the Mughals came to honour as Rajput lords in the sixteenth and seventeenth centuries may not even have been descendants of Rajasthan's earlier pre-Mughal elites. What mattered instead was that for both the Mughals' client feudatories and those who fought against them, these titles, and the markers of refined faith and social life which accompanied them, spoke in recognisable terms of exalted blood and ancestry.

Surprising as it may seem, Mughal rulers and their deputies actively fostered these assertions of seigneurial caste values. While the empire's power was still expanding, there was obvious advantage to be gained from the establishment of overlordship over an exalted regional military nobility. Indeed for the many Rajasthan chieftains who served in the Mughal armies as leaders of clan levies from their home domains, being Rajput came increasingly to be defined in precisely these terms, that is, as an entitlement to be enrolled in privileged military service within the imperial system. Mughal statecraft therefore consistently acknowledged the distinctiveness claimed by those professing Rajput birth and blood. In 1638 the Mughal dynast Shah Jahan personally placed the red *tilak* mark of investiture on the brow of his Rajput client Jaswant Singh of Marwar, despite the fact that this gesture had strong connotations of Hindu dharmic convention. Even the 'Islamising' emperor Aurangzeb (reg. 1658–1707) included a high proportion of Rajput officers in the upper ranks of the imperial service hierarchy, and exempted them all from payment of *jizya*, the special tax on non-Muslims.[14]

These bonds between Mughals and Rajputs were equally notable in the sphere of dynastic marriage. Despite their allegiance to the ostensibly casteless faith of Islam, the Mughals made much of their marriages to Hindu brides from the households of Rajput grandees. In so doing they created strategic alliances and enhanced their legitimacy as dynasts by conforming to the known moral traditions of south Asian kingship. By these conventions, a true ruler must have many seigneurial co-sharers in his sovereignty. Such a ruler thus proclaims his authority by means of bride-taking and other acts which establish a continual flow of shared honour and allegiance between the sovereign and the lordly lineages who take part in these transactions.[15]

Under Mughal rule, all these usages spread far beyond the royal domains of Rajasthan, particularly across the Gangetic plain and deep into central India. This occurred in part through the continuing out-migration of arms-bearing lineages who called themselves Rajput. It was also a reflection of the willingness of Mughal rulers and officials to recognise titles implying Rajput descent as a marker of such people's assumption of rights to lordship over land. Again there were equivalent usages in the south, most notably in the kingdoms of the Telugu-speaking Nayaka dynasts who claimed to be heirs to the lordships created by the Deccan's Hindu Vijayanagar dynasts of the fourteenth to sixteenth centuries.[16]

Both within and beyond these domains, those who wished to claim ties of blood and privileged clientage with elite lineages became increasingly insistent on their superiority to the unrefined toiling 'peasant' groups. By the later seventeenth century, there were many areas of north and central India where the most fertile lands had become subject to lords based in mud-walled forts who used their bonds of marriage with fellow Rajput, Maithil, Bhumihar or Kanya-kubja patricians to command a flow of resources and deference from

[14] Richards 1993: 179–80.
[15] See Galey 1989; Richards 1978; Dirks 1987; Fox 1971; Stern 1977; Cohn 'Political systems in eighteenth-century India' in Cohn 1987: 483–99.
[16] Stein 1989.

1. The Mughal Prince Parviz in audience with his father, Jahangir. The emperor wears a Rajput-style turban; Mughal court styles were strongly influenced by the conventions and symbols of Rajput lordliness.

non-elite tillers and dependent labourers. By the early nineteenth century, European travel writers regularly observed both fortress-dwelling chiefs and their more prosperous 'peasant' imitators who defined themselves as men of refinement whose forebears had never 'touched the plough'.[17]

In the north, these clusters of petty rural patricians looked to ideals of Kshatriya kingship which had originated within the grander Kshatriya-ruled realms and chiefdoms. Amongst such lineages, the wearing of the sacred thread came to be considered a distinguishing mark of the Rajput seigneur and his regional counterparts, and to be incompatible with the life of the non-elite 'peasant'. And ultimately, as Chapter 2 will show, a high proportion of these men of prowess turned to forms of high courtly culture which exalted the more purity-conscious versions of varna ideology, most notably those which proclaimed the indispensability of Brahmans to human and cosmic order.

Of course these areas still contained large numbers of non-elite tillers. In the Punjab and the western Gangetic plains, convention defined the Rajput's non-elite counterpart as a Jat. Like the many similar titles used elsewhere, this was not so much a caste name as a broad designation for the man of substance in rural terrain. Even well into the nineteenth century, a male Jat was understood to be a man of worth but not a follower of exacting lordly codes. If he tilled land, his holdings were generally organised into common units of ownership (*bhaiachara*, literally brotherhoods), with each co-sharer being a fellow member of the same descent unit (the clan or *gotra*). In theory at least, each of these kin groups was a tightly-knit unit exercising control over the lands and villages of its own self-regulating ancestral territory or *khap*: tradition holds that this control was maintained through the authority of bodies which were known as *sarv-khap* (clan-territory assemblies). To be called Jat has in some regions implied a background of pastoralism, though it has more commonly been a designation of non-servile cultivating people.[18]

---

[17] Pinch 1996: 86.

[18] Pradhan 1966: 94–111 notes Mughal references to these *sarv-khap* assemblies; see also Stokes 1986: 128–42. In the Deccan the most widely used designation for 'peasant' groups was Kanbi. Their closest counterparts were the people referred to as Kammas, Reddis and Lingayats in much of the south, and as Kurmis and Goalas in Hindustan.

During the later Mughal period, the seigneurial rights of the greater landed lineages had come to be widely understood in ritual terms, that is, as a claim of inherited superiority over people who were identified by lower-status caste names. However, the basis of such rights was in the assertion and sharing of lordliness: in the more formally ordered kingdoms and chiefdoms over which the Mughals established their suzerainty, these assertions of rank came to be rooted in the claim that some higher overlord, a king or other man of power, had recognised one's ability to collect and remit revenue, usually land tax, within a particular territory.[19]

As the scale of state power expanded during the later sixteenth century and into the seventeenth, such opportunities became more widely available. In addition to those who could plausibly call themselves Rajput or Nayaka, many of these newer revenue contractors (zamindars) came from families claiming Brahman origins. In such areas as Darbhanga (now in north Bihar), these powerful lineages found advantage in embracing the style and trappings of princely lords (rajas). Darbhanga's Brahman revenue-receivers signalled their seigneurial pretensions by adopting the jati title Maithil; this prestigious honorific had many equivalents elsewhere.[20] Such titles came to be associated with highly formalised jati and varna norms, and in particular with an insistence on the lordly man's duty to protect Brahmans and Brahmanical caste codes.

This kind of caste ideology became much more pervasive during the colonial period. Its most distinctive feature was its insistence on the power of the pollution barrier, that is, an emphasis on the impurity and degradation of so-called untouchables, and for those of 'clean' caste an ideal of strict exclusiveness in relation to marriage, dress and diet.[21] (See below, Chapter 5.) These are the rigorous social codes that have been widely regarded as the core of a single all-pervasive Hindu caste 'system', equipping both the weak and the strong to say in effect: 'Those are my inferiors; they are unclean by birth; by divine mandate their womenfolk are available to me, and they themselves must defer and toil in ways which I do not.' But caste in these forms was not universal even in the Gangetic heartland of Mughal India or in the 'orthodox' Hindu south. Such highly developed manifestations of jati

---

[19] See Tod [1829–32] 1920, I: 127; Westphal-Hellbusch 1974.
[20] Ludden 1985: 166; Brass 1974: 58–9.
[21] For further discussion of this important phenomenon, see Chapter 5, below.

and varna had only a very rough similarity to the looser forms of community which were still prominent long after the decline of central Mughal power.

THE OTHER INDIA: 'MARAUDERS', UPLANDERS AND ARMS-BEARING 'PEASANTS'

Despite the prestige achieved by such people as Rajputs and Nayakas in their home locales, the life of the so-called traditional caste Hindu was still strange to many Indians even in relatively recent times. Long after the rise of the post-Mughal successor states, a large proportion of the subcontinent was still populated by martial uplanders and pastoralists who knew little of Brahmans, purity norms or socially exclusive marriage practices. Yet here, too, the broad status categories employed by military recruiters and other key practitioners of Indo-Islamic statecraft had familiarised many Indians with the idea that, like Rajputs, such non-lordly arms-bearers were also to be identified by specific regional 'community' titles. Indeed the very assertiveness of the seigneurial groups who wished to be known as Rajput had its direct counterpart in the increasing use and recognition of such collective arms-bearers' designations as Gujar, Koli, Kallar, Marava and Rebari.

Yet the forebears of the Tamil-speaking Kallar 'caste' whom Dumont studied in the 1950s would have been hard to recognise as a caste in the modern sense even in the later eighteenth century. Looking at such populations historically, it becomes clear that the turbulent events of state-building and ideological change both before and during the colonial period subjected such arms-bearers as south India's poligars (warrior chiefs), together with their counterparts elsewhere, to a further 200 years of caste-forming influences.[22] Not the least of these was the disappearance of the thick jungle which still covered much of this terrain until the late eighteenth century. Until relatively recent times there were few sedentary 'peasants' either in the poligar country or in such areas as the Koli-dominated territories of Gujarat. The contemporary evidence suggests that hierarchical varna

---

[22] The chiefs known as poligars came to control much of the Tamil and Telugu country in the late seventeenth and eighteenth centuries; most were from the southern arms-bearing populations known as Kallars, Maravas and Vadugas. See Price 1996.

and jati concepts were of little significance among these regions' arms-bearing people until this process of 'peasantisation' was well in train.

Certainly the names by which these martial groups have come to be known often originated as dismissive outsiders' coinages, rather than caste or 'tribal' designations in the modern sense. Yet by the mid-eighteenth century, as Mughal authority fragmented and the rulers of the new regional successor realms fought to consolidate their power, many of the upland, forest and 'tribal' people made dramatic gains. The expanding state systems with which they became involved in this period played a crucial role in pulling the Kallars and their counter-parts elsewhere into the world of jati and varna. This happened gradually at first, and in ways that generally reinforced the arms-bearers' command of ritual and material resources, and then more fully and disadvantageously as the East India Company's forces began to subjugate and 'sedentarise' these groups.

The statecraft of the Mughals and post-Mughal successor regimes certainly did not 'invent' caste. Yet by building on the inheritance of the Rajput domains and other pre-Mughal royal centres, these rulers familiarised a high proportion of their subjects with distinctions between high and low or meritorious and unmeritorious birth. By the early eighteenth century, a whole range of standardised social classifi-cations had become central to the language of officials, scholars and military men. In addition to the titles associated with Rajput status, such broad regional arms-bearers' designations as Kallar and Marava in the south, and Koli, Ahir and Maratha in the west and north, gained prominence both in Indo-Islamic record-keeping and in the usages of such rulers as the south Indian Nayakas.[23]

None of these was a truly castelike usage, signalling corporate affinity within an all-embracing dharmic order. Many were simply the usages of the scribe and the lofty urban moraliser in referring to those whom they regarded as frontiersmen and turbulent rustics, of interest primarily for purposes of record-keeping and intelligence-gathering. So a Mughal chronicler, commenting in 1664 on an abortive uprising involving 'predatory Kolis' from the Ahmedabad region, records: 'The Kolis, who always have the wind of revolt and the passion of rebellion in their heads, made that base person [a 'Balooch' rebel leader] a handle of revolt, and created disorder.' In the Gangetic north, arms-

---

[23] These were successors to south India's medieval Vijayanagar dynasts.

bearing Jat and Rohilla 'plunderer' populations were stereotyped in much the same way in eighteenth-century Persian commentaries.[24]

Crude as it was, this terminology did reflect a rough notion of shared geographical origin, and often a specific liability to revenue payment or military service. Not surprisingly then, these labels, and others which regional officials either coined or took over from their predecessors, were rapidly assimilated into local vernacular languages. This occurred particularly in areas where such terminology reflected moves made by new rulers to differentiate among those of their subjects whose skills could be used in expanding their armies and revenue networks.

Through the operation of these patronage and preferment systems, large numbers of Indians became accustomed to the use of the many corporate titles which the Mughals and their successors had applied to both martial and non-martial client groups. Again, it was the people to whom such titles as Koli and Kallar had been applied who were particularly important here. Although most of the subcontinent's mobile forest- and plains-dwellers were disarmed and coercively 'peasantised' under British rule, during the late seventeenth and eighteenth centuries the waning of Mughal suzerainty brought rich opportunities for these groups. Aspiring dynasts competed for their skills and allegiances, and as they became more deeply involved with the people of towns and sedentary cash-cropping villages, it would have been hard to draw firm boundaries between the martial meat-eaters and the big groupings of rural people who were known to other Indians either by superior lordly designations – Bhumihar, Rajput, Nayaka – or by so-called peasant titles – Jat, Kanbi, Kurmi and Kamma. Until well into the nineteenth century, these groups were all part of the same social continuum as the lordly elites and toiling cultivators who are now thought of as conventional 'caste Hindus'.

Nevertheless, by the standards of those who lived among socially exclusive and varna-conscious 'caste Hindus', the sense of community displayed by Kolis, Kallars and other mobile arms-bearers was decidedly open and fluid. It is particularly notable then that in the new kingdoms and dynamic smaller lordships which came into being across most of India in the eighteenth century, many of the new men of power had precisely this kind of non-elite martial background. A

---

[24] Khan 1965: 227.

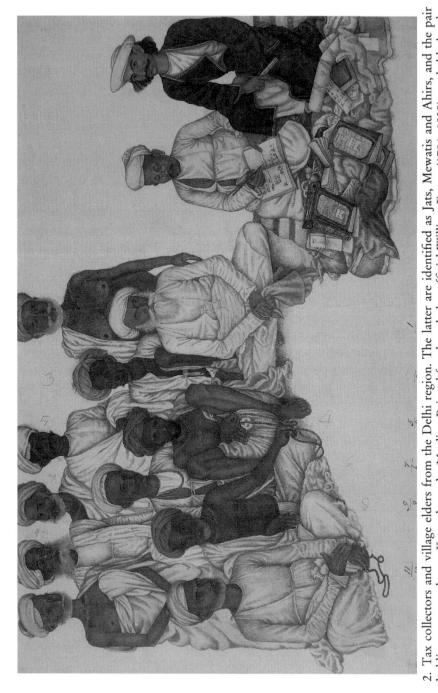

2. Tax collectors and village elders from the Delhi region. The latter are identified as Jats, Mewatis and Ahirs, and the pair holding tax records as a Kavastha and a Muslim. Painted for the scholar-official William Fraser (1784–1835), probably by the

significant number of these chiefs and dynasts were either descendants of humble tillers from the thinly settled lowland plains, or hillmen and pastoralists with an established warrior tradition and a history of uneasy relations with sedentary village-dwellers.

Relatively few of the new lords and revenue magnates were superior 'caste Hindus' in the modern sense. Few wore the sacred thread (*suta*), and most were supported by socially diverse populations of warrior-cultivators who were relative strangers to Brahmanical convention. In the north, many of the individuals and armed lineages who forged these new dominions were identified as Marathas and Jats, and as Kallars and Maravas in the south. Many others called themselves Rajput. But as will be seen below, the armed lineages who expanded the margins of trade and commercial cultivation into remote areas in the Himalayan foothills and along the thinly populated fringes of the Gangetic plainland centres lived very different lives from those of the Mughals' grand patrician clients.

Initially at least, as they competed with their rivals for warrior recruits and other local allies, the rulers and their armed retainers in such dominions as the Jat-ruled Bharatpur kingdom southwest of Delhi, or in the other dry and thinly populated tracts of the poligar country and the western Gangetic plain, had good reasons to stay relaxed about matters of ritual purity. Many were from Muslim minority populations; these rulers particularly found advantage in building open and all-embracing networks of recruitment and affiliation. The non-Muslim soldiers, merchants and revenue contractors who took the new dynasts' patronage also needed to keep their options open: some Brahmanical exclusiveness in diet and marriage-making could signal to both Hindu and Muslim rulers that one's kin were honourable and thus suitable for service within the new realm. Too much, on the other hand, could foreclose options for tactical marriages and alliances with these rulers' other new-found clients.

In these areas where understandings of 'caste' were comparatively loose and flexible, the new rulers did recognise the more formal versions of jati and varna which characterised certain of their subjects and near neighbours. The self-made dynasts thus knew and used the relatively precise and socially exclusive jati and varna titles which were common to the specialist merchants, priests and artisans whose skills were of value to them in the forging of their new domains. At the same time, not even all of these people drew hard and fast boundaries between themselves and the populations of nomadic hill people, pastoralists and forest hunter-gatherers who made up a sizable proportion of the Indian population in this period.

Certainly the eighteenth-century dynasts and lordly groups found it advantageous to interact with unsettled 'marauders' as well as settled villagers and the habitués of the more refined court and shrine centres. This was no longer the case for people who used patrician titles in the later nineteenth century, when the memories of such connections were being widely disowned by 'pure' caste Hindus. Indeed, as Chapter 2 will show, for all the openness and ambiguity of the eighteenth-century warrior rulers in such matters, it was paradoxically the strategic and ideological needs of the dynasts which tilted the balance towards stricter order and rank, both in the making of marriages and in other important areas of caste experience. Even so, it was only in the later colonial period, when a high proportion of the unsettled arms-bearers had been reduced to the status of tied labourers in the service of dominant cultivators, that plains-dwellers came more generally to shun hill and forest people as unclean enemies of the 'caste Hindu'.

Yet in most cases these changes came slowly and unevenly. Even well into the era of the East India Company's political ascendancy, many people who were recognised as Rajputs, or as persons of equivalent honour and refinement in other regions, still had attachments to meat-eating 'tribal' chiefs, recruiting warriors from their kin groups, recognising the power of their gods and forest holy places, and often accepting their daughters in marriage.

It is true that by the mid-eighteenth century, many of the expansive new post-Mughal lordships were encroaching deep into the territories of the supposedly fierce and carnal people who were known by such titles as Bhil, Gond and Santal. Yet these heightened contacts could still be mutually advantageous. As the new dynasts became increasingly dependent on cash revenue and commerce, many hill and forest groups provided a market for commodities from the plains. In many cases too, rulers increased their recruitment of irregular military levies from these turbulent margins, whose populations often still mixed forms of shifting cultivation with armed tribute-taking from adjacent 'peasant' locales. So, far from seeking to disarm or annihilate such people, the Marathas and other post-Mughal dynasts found at least until the later eighteenth century that it made strategic sense to vest the most valuable of these groups with forms of qualified sovereignty (*girasi*), often with a tacit right to raid adjacent populations of sedentary revenue-paying 'peasants'.[25]

In both north and central India, some new dynasts encouraged the itinerant quasi-Brahman bards known as Bhats or Charans to attach themselves to these armed hill lineages whom they called *girasias* (sometimes *girisi rajas*, later anglicised as Gracias or Grasia Rajas).[26] The idea of recruiting Bhats to sing the praises of these so-called *girasiadars* was that these hill chiefs could thereby be exalted in the heraldic style associated with Rajputs, thus becoming more plausibly 'royal', and therefore fit to exercise the kind of parcelled-out lordship that had become the basis of suzerainty both in the Maratha-ruled territories and elsewhere. This seems to have been the means by which many self-made men of prowess equipped themselves with convincing Rajput 'caste' credentials. In the south too there were bardic groups who performed similar functions in the poligar country.

There was always a delicate balance between aggression and harmony in these relationships. Even so, until relatively recent times plains people tended to hold the bearers of 'tribal' titles in mingled fear and reverence. Their hills and forests commanded respect as the domains of blood-taking deities whose powers of *sakti* or activated divine energy empower both kings and gods to contend with the unclean or 'demonic' forces which continually menace the ordered dharmic world. Even well into the nineteenth century many powerful people still understood 'caste' codes to be saying to men of prowess that conformity to Brahmanical norms was not enough, that dynasts and their fellow Kshatriyas had a mandate to associate themselves, however ambivalently, with the gods, peoples and warlike energies of the hills and forest margins.

This idea even entered the great sixteenth-century Mughal text on statecraft, the *Ain-i-akbari*, which records a legend about the founder of one of the great Rajput dynasties being brought up in the wilds by a spear-wielding Bhil. When the young prince succeeds to his throne he is given his *tilak*, his emblem of royal consecration, by being marked on the brow with human blood provided by his Bhil protector. This stands in marked contrast to later versions of this story in which the

---

[25] Skaria 1992; also Tod [1829–32] 1920, I: 190–1; Singh 1988; Unnithan 1994.
[26] Forbes 1813, II: 88–106. On these Bhat 'self-immolators', see Chapter 2, below.

Bhil guardian becomes a mere savage to be subdued and triumphed over, thus proclaiming that the lordly man conforms to models of varna-derived Kshatriya refinement. The blood in the ritual is now that of the Bhil himself, slain by the prince who has won his throne by shedding the blood of the un-dharmic forest 'other'.[27]

DEVOTION AND 'CASTELESSNESS'

Caste terms and principles were certainly not in universal use in the post-Mughal period, but those seeking appropriate terminology could certainly glean much from the available sacred sources – from the Sanskrit *Vedas* and epics, from Manu and the other *dharmasastras*, from the *purana* texts, from Brahmanical rituals, and even from the denunciations of anti-Brahmanical 'reformers'. Furthermore, by the early eighteenth century, more and more Indians could see these schemes of rank and classification being used to advantage all around them.

Yet at this time both the subordinated and the newly advantaged could and did turn to other forms of religion which have been widely described as 'casteless' and anti-Brahmanical. These spiritual traditions derive from the religion of *bhakti* or devotion as expressed by the great *sampradayas* or organised sectarian orders. Initiates of these monk-led orders still bind themselves in loving communion to one of the incarnate forms of the all-India high gods, the most popular of these being Ram the warrior-king, and Krishna the pastoral lover and nurturer. In the centuries preceding the British conquest, these devotional networks spoke to both new and established 'peasants', and also to rulers, traders and artisanal populations, in the anti-Brahmanical language of Caitanya, Kabir and the other historic teachers and mystics.[28]

---

[27] On the Marathas' bloody subjugation of Bhils in Indore, where worship was offered to the eighteenth-century rulers' royal executioner's axe, see Luard 1908, II: 222. Also Unnithan 1994: 109; M. Carstairs 'Bhils of Kotra Bhomat' in Mathur and Agarwal 1974; Deliège 1985; Guha 1996; and the anthropologist Adrian Mayer's account (1985: 215) of a Rajput prince's accession rite in 1918 when a Bhil reportedly performed the hereditary task of applying the installation brow mark with blood from his own gashed thumb.

[28] Among other medieval preceptors in this tradition are Ramanuja, and also the originator of Sikh teaching, Guru Nanak; earlier versions of anti-Brahmanical teaching were disseminated through both Buddhism and Jainism. For historically informed anthropological treatments of the *sampradaya* faiths see Burghart 1978a; van der Veer 1987, 1988; Pinch 1996.

Islam too, which first took root in coastal areas of the west and south through contact with eighth- and ninth-century Arab traders, had a complex history of interaction with the anti-Brahman *sampradaya* faiths. By the sixteenth century, the rise of Muslim-ruled kingdoms in the Deccan and north spread the teachings of Islam to both humble and elite groups in much of the subcontinent, with Muslims comprising as much as one-fifth of the population in some areas. Even after the decline of Mughal power in the early eighteenth century, Muslim *pirs* (adepts of the mystical and devotional traditions known as Sufism) continued to be revered by both Muslims and non-Muslims. These *pirs* or cult saints attracted constituencies which were similar to the followings of Hindu *bhakti* teachers and Sikh gurus, and which shared many of their ideals and spiritual practices. Thus, from these sources too, Indians encountered messages of devotion to a deity who was to be seen as transcendent, but also as dissolving divisions of rank and hierarchy through practices of personalised mystical devotion.

Paradoxically, however, even though both Islam and the popular *bhakti* forms of Hinduism are often described as casteless and egalitarian, few if any adherents of these traditions should be seen as renouncers of caste. On the contrary, in the Punjab, Bengal and the southern poligar country particularly, the many non-elite 'peasants' and pastoralists who became devotees of Muslim *pirs* during the seventeenth and eighteenth centuries seem to have become distinctly more castelike than hitherto through these new-found bonds of discipleship. Of course these ties were not based on Brahmanical purity, but they did foster a sense of Kallar, Rangar or Meo *qaum* or *jati* affinity which was nourished by shared attachment to the *pir* and his power.

Such developments were particularly widespread in areas where the Muslim saint or spiritual preceptor had become a recipient of royal patronage, and an embodiment of lordly powers and virtues, in one of the fast-growing new regional realms and chiefdoms.[29] These trends closely resembled patterns of caste formation which were occurring at this time among hitherto amorphous and open-ended trading and service groups. Such people developed these enhanced jati affinities through attachment to *pir*-like local power divinities (*birs* and *virans*),

[29] S. Bayly 1989.

or to the temples, *maths* and gurus of regional *bhakti* cult deities. Here particularly we see a connection between the movement of merchants and traders into the *bhakti* cults and their growing association with the larger and more settled kingdoms and royal patronage networks of the seventeenth and early eighteenth centuries.[30]

This was also true of the initiated adherents of Sikh teaching in the north, and the followers of the Shiva-Lingayat tradition in the southern Deccan. These adherents of devotional faith had already become castelike 'communities' in their own right well before the era of the post-Mughal successor realms. More generally, however, *bhakti* teaching simply gave to the ordinary so-called caste Hindu an experience of mystical and apparently casteless union with the divine.

Yet even when the *sampradaya* sectarian orders devalued worldly jati and varna hierarchies, their lay adherents did not deny their validity in everyday life. Especially where marriage was concerned, lay initiates who worshipped through a personal guru (preceptor) rather than a Brahman ritualist would still accept that the 'untouchable' Chamar or Paraiyan was radically unlike the devotee of respectable caste origin. Many *bhakti* sects denied initiation to 'unclean' groups; some allowed only those of Brahman birth to become gurus. And at the very least these movements – like north India's Ram-worshipping Ramanandis, and the other *bhakti* networks which played a crucial role in the making of what we now call Hinduism – built on familiarity with jati and varna conventions, even though their devotees were urged to evade or transcend these boundaries in certain circumstances.[31]

Furthermore the activities of these 'conversion' faiths and *sampradaya* networks gave rise to assertive counter-movements like Bengal's early nineteenth-century Dharma Sabha organisations which rallied self-professed preservers of 'orthodox' faith to the defence of Brahmanical authority. Bengal was one of many ethnolinguistic regions where strong caste ideologies existed side by side with ostensibly un-Brahmanical forms of *bhakti* Hinduism, as well as with Sikh, Muslim and even Christian variants of devotional faith. In many cases too, both before and during the colonial period, battles between organised

---

[30] On such networks of affiliation among Hindus see Prakash 1990a: 41–58; Conlon 1977. On *pirs* see S. Bayly 1989; Eaton 1978.
[31] See e.g. Pinch 1996: 27. A similar diversity of messages can be seen in the teachings of Sikhism, and in the many 'indigenised' manifestations of Islam and Christianity which took root in the subcontinent in the centuries before European conquest.

groups of Hindu 'modernisers' and 'traditionalists' helped to heighten awareness of jati and varna concepts for people of varying social backgrounds, both before and during the colonial era.

THE INNER LOGIC OF CASTE

How then did perceptions of caste come to operate in these situations of rapid change over the last two to three centuries? How did the facts of an insecure environment shape the way in which Indians judged and classified both themselves and those of other 'communities'? And how is it that something in the nature of a caste 'system' came to be built out of such disparate principles as a reverence for the pure and the ascetic, and an exaltation of the warlike man of arms?

To return to the tripartite classifications identified at the beginning of this chapter, these questions may best be answered by exploring the uneasy synthesis that has emerged in relatively recent times between three distinct ways of life. These modes of conduct did not precisely match the three superior classifications of the varna scheme, though they came increasingly to serve as idealised reference points for people whose forebears had been comparatively untouched by caste values. These three modes of conduct were:

(1) the way of life of the kingly warrior or man of prowess;
(2) the way of life of the service-provider, meaning both the literate priestly man and the specialist record-keeper; and
(3) the way of life of the settled man of worth, meaning both the productive and virtuous tiller and the man of commerce, both of whom might favour the spiritual model of the ascetic renouncer rather than the Brahman priest.

Taken together, these were the three main areas of opportunity which became available to those with appropriate skills at the time when the declining Mughal state and its south Indian counterparts were giving way to the new seventeenth- and eighteenth-century successor regimes, and thereafter to the growth of European colonial power. None of these pursuits and callings was new to the subcontinent; what was new in this period was the conceptual and practical importance they were acquiring in circumstances of growing social complexity.

As has been seen, many of the new eighteenth-century rulers and their key retainers were members of caste 'communities' only in the sense of having being roughly generalised about by others in these terms, assigned by Brahmanical convention or a ruler's scribes and office-holders to an imprecise category with more or less pejorative overtones: Jat or Kurmi; Kallar or Marava; Rebari, Koli, Ahir or Gujar. From the vantage point of these people who had achieved new power and wealth through arms-bearing, India in the late seventeenth and eighteenth centuries was a world of individual opportunity and prowess, rather than one in which people of power were born into a known place on a ladder of strictly defined ritual precedence.

Yet everyday experience for many Indians was also coming into line with a picture of the civilised environment as one of more intricately delineated relationships between different social and occupational groups. What the rulers and their lordly clients were finding was that these insecurities could best be countered by projecting themselves as heirs to a known heroic tradition, this being the dharmic ideal of the Kshatriya king whose use of force is just, and who protects and orders the world according to strict norms of virtue and propriety.

Such rulers still needed flexibility in the relationships they were forging with other armed people and with the key specialist populations of the wider society. Brahman-centred formalities were therefore not immediately subscribed to by these new dominion-builders. Yet this was a period when lords and dynasts from comparatively humble backgrounds were adopting recognisably castelike ways of dealing with their subjects, drawing on the terms and archetypes of the Kshatriya ideal as a means of structuring their relationships with important retainers, allies and service-providers. So although they did not necessarily emphasise strict norms of purity, these rulers' claims of lordliness came increasingly to rest on a perception of their non-Muslim subjects as subordinated 'caste Hindus' leading a life of dharmic correctness under the supervision of a Kshatriya-like man of prowess. In making these claims, the new rulers already had a known repertoire of terms and concepts to tap into. Many occupationally specialised groups already used identifying titles which were much like modern caste names, and as we have seen, others were fast acquiring a more jati-like affinity through new patterns of migration and devotional attachment.

As will be seen in Chapter 2, a high proportion of these known 'caste Hindu' norms were associated either with named Brahman jati groupings (Nambudiris, Anavils, Chitrapur Saraswats, Kanyakubjas, Chitpavans) or with the specialist pollution-removers who served these varna-conscious groups (Bhangis, Doms, Chamars, Dheds,

Kahars and many others). It was against this background that the ideal of the lordly and righteous Kshatriya acquired its appeal for an increasing number of lords and dynasts in the later seventeenth and eighteenth centuries.

Anthropologists still find that when these titles and archetypes are invoked, Brahmans are widely thought of as people who should minimise their contacts with different classes of being. They should shun adornment and fleshly indulgence, placing an inherited calling to the spiritual above worldly ties and duties, even to the extent of rationing sensual impulses within marriage.[32] This contrasts sharply with the qualities that have come to be associated with those of lordly patrician birth. A lineage claiming Rajput descent is understood to inherit a Kshatriya's mode of conduct, that is, the ideal of the heroic sovereign who sheds blood in a righteous cause and performs feats of prowess through which disharmony and unrighteousness may be dispelled or kept at bay. The king-like being therefore makes contact with dangerous powers and energies and consumes substances that would be incompatible with those prescribed for the Shudra, the Vaishya and the Brahman. Far from limiting his contacts with those of unlike kind, the environment of the man of prowess must be like the good king's realm, highly pluralistic, yet rendered harmonious and productive by his capacity to interact with and order the different classes of gods and humans. This was certainly the picture of the ideal realm conveyed in the dynastic chronicles which were commissioned by many rulers in the new realms and chiefdoms of the eighteenth century.[33]

In theory at least, although one does not need to live a soldier's life in order to be known as Rajput, any more than one has to perform priestly functions to qualify as a Brahman, a male Rajput inherits a mandate to fulfil the Kshatriya ideal: to be an eater of rich foods, a lover of women and a doer of heroic deeds. And since Indians commonly read important messages into what is put on and into the body, there have evolved strong expectations that Rajputs and their regional counterparts should live, eat and dress in styles recalling the virility and worldliness of warriors.

This is certainly the way Rajput rulers had themselves depicted by

---

[32] K. Gough 'Brahman kinship in a Tamil village' in Uberoi 1993: 146–75.
[33] See e.g. Burghart 1978b; Dirks 1982; S. Bayly 1989: 49–55.

the artists and praise-singers (Charans) whom they recruited to their courts. By the eighteenth century these styles were spreading rapidly throughout the subcontinent. Thus, the wearing of certain turbans and jewels, and the cultivation of luxuriant moustaches, came to be widely adopted as marks of lordly identity, both by the lords of Rajasthan and by those who were making similar claims in other regions. These reflect perceptions of sexuality and the body's physical attributes that are found in many other societies, most notably in Islamic west Asia. In the subcontinent, Muslims and Sikhs as well as Hindus commonly regard loosely flowing hair as being charged with sexual energy. A mustachioed man is virile and soldierly, and by the same token a mature woman's hair – indeed her whole body – should be subject to a demanding code of modesty and containment.[34]

This is one of many areas in which the ideal of Rajput dress and conduct has come to overlap with those of the elite south Asian Muslim populations who have preserved a tradition of lordliness and arms-bearing. In both cases, men and women have contrasting obligations. It is expected that the Rajput man – or the man claiming equivalent warrior-like status – should parade his manliness and martial honour, while the sexuality of the Rajput woman should be rigorously controlled. By these standards, to be non-Rajput was to be one of two things: a pure, pacific person who had need of the lordly man's protection to safeguard his women's honour; or someone weak and lowly and therefore fair game, a provider of womenfolk for the patrician's gratification.[35]

Those people in past centuries who wished to classify themselves by these lordly standards had a wide range of rituals, dietary codes and other markers which could be used to signal their distinctiveness in the eyes of others. Above all, however, there was the careful regulation of marriage alliances, so that it has become hard to conceive of caste without the central feature of endogamy – marriage within one's birth-group. Historically, and to a considerable extent today, people who subscribe to the more formalised versions of caste norms will tend to treat the mixing of seed from different human orders as bad, dangerous and uncivilised.[36]

[34] Beck 1976; Das 1976; Das 'Paradigms of body symbolism' in Burghart and Cantlie 1985; Ward 1997; Bennett 1983 esp. p. 259 n. 31; O'Hanlon forthcoming a and b.
[35] Tambiah 1973.
[36] *Ibid.*

Nevertheless, many of these same people have also tended to pay close attention to complex internal gradations of status within a given birth-group, meaning that kin groups will compete to make marriages that are not merely permissible but are also regarded as prestigious. So it is not just that Brahmans marry other Brahmans, or that those wishing to be known as Rajput or Vellala must find suitable matches amongst lineages of acknowledged Rajput and Vellala birth. Most of those whom we now call caste Hindus have come to see the jatis in which they claim membership as networks of hierarchically ranked descent groups. People who subscribe to these views will seek to make marriages not just with fellow Tamilnad Vellalas or Gujarat Patidars, but with the 'best' available sub-class of their own kind or order. In much of India, it has become common for people to try to elevate themselves in relation to others of the same overarching caste group through the policing of blood-lines, often by marrying daughters 'upwards' into higher-status clans or lineages. This practice, which anthropologists call hypergamy, has been widely understood as sustaining and perpetuating ideals of ritualised hierarchy at the core of the Indian moral order. Among the many groups in south India and elsewhere who have not followed this practice of hypergamy, other means have existed to regulate marriage on a similar basis.[37]

On the other hand, until relatively recently many 'clean-caste' people did not insist on the distinction between so-called caste-fellows, who were suitable to ally with, and non-caste-fellows who were beyond the pale of formal marriage ties. In past centuries, many non-elite tillers gloried in a tradition of open-ended matchmaking. Well into the colonial period many of the rural north Indians who called themselves Jats were known for their practice of *karewa*, that is, the taking of wives or concubines from non-Jat 'peasant' or nomadic groups. Far from being seen as low or polluting, this was taken as a sign of manly prowess on the part of those who added to their kin group's stock of womenfolk in this way. It has been only in comparatively recent times that a much more exclusive ideal of marriage modelled on the practices ascribed to the 'purest' and grandest Rajputs and other lordly groups has come to be exalted by former followers of *karewa* or *karewa*-like practices.[38]

---

[37] Important studies of south Asian marriage systems include: Dumont 1966; Pocock 1972; Nicholas 1975; Kolenda 1984. See also Kolenda 1980; Parkin 1990; Uberoi 1993.
[38] See Pradhan 1966: 4, 78; Datta 1997: 101–2.

This marital dimension of caste has been a key concern of twentieth-century anthropology. Under the influence of Dumont, many theorists have seen the marriage bond as the defining principle of the Indian social order, at least for professing Hindus. On this basis, caste becomes radically distinct from the descent-based social systems mapped by ethnographers in other parts of the world. Rather than making bloodlines carry the weight of people's social relationships, 'caste Hindus' have been thought to exalt the webs of alliance created through marriage over ties of blood, descent and affinity. In other words, it is not enough to ask who someone's father was; the key question in 'caste society' is held to be who will take one's kin as brides or grooms.

In times past, even the Indian state seems to have been shaped in these terms: marital alliances with the king and his kin become a critical source of power and status, and kingdoms grew and took shape around elaborate webs of royal marriage ties.[39] Even today, it is still widely reported that caste values define the kin of wife-receivers as conferring honour on the kin of the bride, the wife-givers. It is therefore a sign of true grandeur for a lineage if one's female kin are in demand as brides, and the most exalted matches are those made with the most exclusive descent groups.

If we ask how these trends evolved historically, in other words, who took the lead in embracing and spreading these conventions, we must stress again the role of the arms-bearers and self-made dynasts of the relatively recent past. Even men who achieved power through acts of individual prowess, and then went on to lead the sort of lordly and lavish life deemed appropriate to a Rajput, still felt a need to show the world that they were adherents of a known moral code. This prescribed order in all things, starting with the most fundamental matters of blood and procreation, and emphasising the nullification of those innumerable ritual pollutions which emanate from all forms of active human life.

There have been countless ethnographic studies treating the importance of marriage rules as a universal given of Indian – or Hindu – life, and thus as a defining feature of caste.[40] Both now and in the past, certain kinship structures have been regarded as characteristic of

[39] Stern 1977: 52–78; Dirks 1987; Parry 1979: 11.
[40] See note 36 above.

specific jatis, with anthropologists making much of the different ways in which defenders of caste norms in particular ethnolinguistic regions have defined the classes of kin with whom a given jati or varna should either encourage or ban marriages. Anthropologists say that a 'caste Hindu' is heir to two distinct but related forms of birth group. The first of these is the jati, or status community, which is made up of many separate biological descent units, and is often identified with the defining moral code of one of the four varnas. The second is one's particular line of biological descent, with the added complication that women change these affiliations at the time of marriage.

Membership of these blood-based descent groups is reckoned at three or more different levels: the out-marrying clan, often termed *gotra*; the out-marrying *kul*, a unilineal descent group of more limited depth than the *gotra*; and the hearth unit or family household, with its single male head and joint access to property and food.[41] Almost everywhere, people whose so-called caste lifestyles permit divorce and the remarriage of widows have been seen as distinct from the more refined populations who regard these practices as low and uncivilised. All this can be related to the ideal of marriage as the paramount social act, to be understood not as a private matter, but as a sanctified binding of kin units through the 'gift of a virgin' (*kanyadan*) from one descent group to another. So people from a wide range of different regions and status groups would say that the marriage union has meaning only if the bride is never-married and indisputably chaste. By this same logic, the severing of the all-important marriage bond is a cosmic and social rupture that makes the wife – never the husband – a person of radical and permanent inauspiciousness.[42]

Even today, it is common for widows whose kin claim superior caste origin to lead a penitential life, breaking their bangles, shearing their hair, and abandoning the red cosmetic which a married woman applies to her hair parting to signify auspiciousness and fertility. Historically, the penances undergone by widows sometimes included *sati* (self-immolation by fire), much to the horror of British and Indian social reformers. As far as caste is concerned, this logic decrees that to allow divorce, or to accept widows as brides, must be the hallmark of people who are without the means to police their blood-lines scrupu-

[41] For an introduction to debate on this topic see Davis 1976; Kolenda 1978: 14–22; Parry 1979.
[42] Madan 1993: 291–2; Fruzzetti 1982.

lously, and who cannot afford to 'waste' the labour and child-bearing potential of available women kin in the interests of propriety and seemliness.

Looked at in these terms, caste as it has been lived and conceptualised becomes important in everyday life at the point when kin groups and individuals must look beyond their individual descent group for marriage partners, since the ideology of caste so consistently stigmatises marriages within the same direct blood-line, that is, one's clan or lineage (*gotra, kul,* etc). For people claiming exalted caste status, the making of marriage choices did become particularly complex at some point in the recent or distant past, with the greatest merit accruing to those who have been able to display the most elaborate and restrictive kinship rules.

THE PARADIGMATIC CASE: MARATHA KINGSHIP
AND THE VALUES OF PROWESS

The career of the celebrated Maharashtrian dominion-builder Shivaji Bhonsle (1630–80) provides a telling case-study in keeping with the broad trends outlined above. The story of Shivaji's moves to consolidate his hard-won military and revenue-taking power may therefore be understood as exemplifying the first part of the two-stage process which was referred to at the beginning of this chapter. In other words, what we see in this dynast's life-long manipulation of the Kshatriya ideal supports this chapter's argument about the complex new developments in Indian social and political life which brought the royal man of prowess into prominence as a maker, shaper and reference point in the assertion of more formalised caste ideals.[43] This remarkable self-made dynast made the fluidities of caste work for him in two strikingly different ways. First, Shivaji was notably eclectic in his recruitment practices, offering high office to men of skill and loyalty with little regard to their faith or formal caste background. At the same time, this man of rustic non-*dwija* (i.e. non-twice-born) origin made caste truly matter to large numbers of people both within and beyond his new domain. He did this both by building classifications of jati and varna into his court rituals and statecraft, and most

---

[43] There are certainly ambiguities here; Shivaji has been widely treated as an illustration of the Brahmanisation of kingship rather than the assertion of active martial agency. On Shivaji's rule in the context of the kingly Kshatriya ideal, see Heesterman 1989.

famously, by inventing the means to have himself literally reborn into the status of a lordly thread-wearing Kshatriya.

This celebrated *parvenu* state-builder thus made a conscious decision to use caste as a strategic asset, garbing himself in the trappings of Kshatriya kingship as a means of stabilising his fortunes and those of his client groups. Other 'new men' in both north and south India subsequently emulated his techniques, finding that they too had good reason to manipulate caste symbols as a means of self-advancement.

Clearly caste was not a matter of fixed or inherited essences for Shivaji and his imitators. The Bhonsles are thought to have originated among the large, amorphous populations of non-Muslim Deccani tiller-plainsmen who had come to be known by the names Kanbi and Maratha. These people's religion was focused on *bhakti* devotional themes and gave little prominence to Brahmans. Even long after Shivaji's time, their social norms were loose and socially inclusive rather than formally castelike in the modern sense. Like the term Jat, which was its Gangetic equivalent, Kanbi has been for many centuries a broad designation for virtually all Gujarati- and Marathi-speakers who sustain themselves as ordinary cultivators. In the Maharashtra plateau country, a thinly populated land where agrarian livelihoods were difficult and insecure, the counterpart of Kanbi was Maratha. This term of modest distinction was used by rural people who had improved their lot through soldiering, mostly by taking up military service under the region's fourteenth- and fifteenth-century sultans. Initially, the term Maratha seems to have been no more specific or castelike than 'Dakhni', this being the designation for the Indian-born Muslim soldiery of these same rulers.[44]

By the sixteenth century, the term Maratha was acquiring a more exalted significance, having become an honorific for people like Shivaji's own family of soldiers and petty office-holders who had been rewarded for service under the Deccan's Muslim sultans with special rights and land tenures (*inams* and *watans*).[45] In a relatively short space of time, the hereditary holders of these offices had come to differentiate themselves from the humbler tillers on whom they levied taxes in the name of their Muslim overlords. Few if any of these people wore the sacred thread (*suta*). Neither Kanbi nor Maratha

[44] On the distinction in Gujarat between rustic Kanbis and refined superior 'peasants' (Patidars) see Chapter 5, below.
[45] Gordon 1993: 15.

signified a primordial 'caste' identity, or an ancient tradition of religious and social differentiation which was specifically Hindu in origin. On the contrary, as in the case of the title Rajput, these designations would not have acquired their modern-day significance without a great deal of sustained interaction between Muslim and Hindu dominion-builders in the relatively recent past.

A series of far-reaching changes was therefore set in train through Shivaji's bid for personal dynastic power beyond his original home terrain. In an environment where the Mughals and their great Rajput client lords were the best-known embodiments of kingship, Maratha–Kanbi origins were clearly not the appropriate antecedents for a would-be dynast. By the early 1670s Shivaji had used his formidable armies to create a core domain of directly administered revenue territories within the former realms of the Deccan Muslim sultanates. He also engaged in expansive revenue-taking operations which rapidly eroded the Mughals' sovereignty in their central Indian provinces, and as far south as the Thanjavur (Tanjore) delta of Tamilnad. Yet all these attainments were evanescent and vulnerable. No new man of power was safe from challenge in these uncertain circumstances. Within the loose grid of Mughal overlordship, everyone's environment was full of threatening newcomers; anyone's patrons and allies could be challenged or annihilated without warning.

But this man of modest origins was not content to leave himself as vulnerable as the refractory border chieftains and rebel generals whom the Mughals were still able to outmanoeuvre. In a period when only the grander Rajput rulers were known formally as thread-wearing Kshatriyas, Shivaji embarked on a strategy of unabashed self-promotion. His aim was to identify himself as a sovereign in terms that were intelligible both to his nominal Mughal overlords and to the peoples of the Deccan and central Mughal provinces from whom he was claiming military service and revenue dues.[46]

As has already been seen, Mughal and Rajput conceptions of kingship had been interpenetrating and reinforcing one another since the sixteenth century, both through the marriages which Mughal rulers contracted with Rajput princesses and through the interactions of their court cultures. Shivaji also drew to his court service people who had

---

[46] On the merging and overlapping of Indo-Islamic and Hindu-derived forms of statecraft in the Maratha realms, see Wink 1986.

knowledge of both the Indic Muslim culture of the former Deccan sultanates and the syncretistic Vijayanagar-*nayaka* court traditions of the far south. Not surprisingly then, he turned to a mixed array of Vijayanagar, Mughal and Rajput symbols through which to assert his claims of lordliness. The key symbolic act of his reign came in two distinct stages. The first was Shivaji's recruitment of a Brahman preceptor from one of the devotional *sampradaya* sects, this being a known mark of kingship both in the classical scriptures and in the practices of contemporary Rajput courts. His second move was to gather Brahman priests and literati with the necessary ritual and genealogical skills to declare him a descendant of royal Rajput forebears. In 1674 these specialists invented an investiture rite for their new patron and installed him as *chhatrapati*, meaning lord of the *chhatra*, the ceremonial canopy which signifies both godhead and kingship in Hindu temple tradition.[47]

These acts of statecraft transformed Shivaji the self-made conqueror into Shivaji the living embodiment of exalted thread-wearing Kshatriya kingship. The striking thing about this is that it was done in the teeth of strong resistance from eminent Brahmans in the great sacred centres of north India. These literati made much of the respected Hindu scriptural sources which held that mankind was living in a degenerate cosmic age, the Kaliyug. The hallmark of this dark epoch, they said, was the complete extinction of the Kshatriya varna. Only unworthy Shudras exercised power in this blighted world, which meant that there could be no grounds for investing Shivaji or any other self-made dynast with the thread and ritual devices of a Kshatriya. A similar principle had been pronounced by scriptural experts in south India, where both Kshatriyas and Vaishyas were widely thought to have disappeared at the dawn of the Kaliyug.[48]

Remarkably, however, Shivaji assembled another set of Brahmans who also had links to the holy city of Banaras, and through them with Mewar (Udaipur), the most prestigious of the great Rajput kingdoms. These Brahmans said, in effect, that great men like the Mewar rulers were Kshatriyas because their actions had made them so. This was quite different from a picture of varna as having been reduced to a permanently truncated state, and it was also very far from a represen-

---

[47] O'Hanlon 1985: 20–1; Gordon 1993: 86–90; Wink 1986: 34–49, 57–9, 268–71.
[48] Grant Duff 1921, I: 204–6.

tation of caste as an immutable fact of birth and blood. On the contrary, what was being proposed here was that in present social and political circumstances there was need for the virtues of the Kshatriya. Therefore a man who acted as a Kshatriya by preserving the order of *dharma* (ordered moral conduct) and, above all, by sponsoring the performance of Brahman rituals would indeed deserve to be recognised as a true embodiment of the scriptural Kshatriya varna.

On this basis it was perfectly proper for Shivaji to send to Mewar, as indeed he did, for knowledge of the proper vedic rituals to perform in the domain of a Kshatriya king. It may even be that the assertion of these arguments on behalf of the great new powers of the late Mughal period helped to lay the foundations for the view of caste propounded in a very different form during the late nineteenth century by the radical theorists of the Arya Samaj, to the effect that even Brahmans were made and not born – in other words, that pious people should see the status of the Brahman as being determined by his personal virtue and learning, and not by his birth.

So Shivaji had himself reborn as a Kshatriya through investiture with the sacred thread, and by the anointing of his body with the sweet and transforming essences of Brahmanical rituals, in particular the sacred products of the all-nurturing and sacred cow: milk, curds and *ghee* (clarified butter). His ritualists reinforced the royal status of his new domain by initiating the ceremony of the vedic fire sacrifice at his rite of enthronement. These rites of king-making became a model for many other self-made dynasts in the eighteenth and early nineteenth centuries, as will be seen in Chapter 2.

This remaking of kings as Kshatriyas was much more than a matter of decorative rites and ceremonies. Real acts of statecraft were performed on this basis, and in a way that spread recognition of these more formalised jati and varna ideals to a considerable portion of the rulers' subjects. In classical sastric scripture, the thread-wearing king is by definition a maker and preserver of varna and can create lordly people (Kshatriyas) in his image. Indeed, the scriptures say that he must do so: if he does not issue and confirm jati and varna titles and order his retainers and subjects in the idiom of caste, he is no true embodiment of kingliness.

Rulers really did behave in this way in the turbulent eighteenth and early nineteenth centuries. In theory at least, a king was a perpetual provider of land and revenue-taking grants, like the *deshmukh* statuses and *patil*ships which were supposed to emanate as a ceaseless demonstration of power by the Maratha rulers. With this flow of assets and retainerships went the provision of 'caste' identities to the king's subjects.[49] In both the north and the south, aspiring dynasts and their lordly retainers recruited soldiers and other followers on this basis. Those who became part of these networks therefore had good cause to follow the lead of a patron who was willing to vest them with a jati title or other castelike designation. The forms of caste which were thus embraced identified such people as part of a 'community' in their lord's own image, or in the image of his affiliates and retainers.[50]

This goes far to explain why the tradition of the lordly conqueror and arms-bearer continued to be so widely acknowledged even into the nineteenth century and beyond. The descendants of recently sedentarised 'peasant' and pastoralist arms-bearing groups did become significantly more cohesive over time, but without necessarily embracing the same forms of jati and varna as other so-called caste Hindus. These included such people as the users of the Tamil titles Marava and Kallar. In the former domains of the south Indian Nayaka rulers, East India Company forces contended for much of the eighteenth century with the fortress-based poligar chieftains whose ethnically diverse groups of armed retainers they knew as 'Colleries' (a rendering of Kallar).[51] As with these other groups, Marava and Kallar 'caste' identity were clearly not ancient facts of life in the region. Insofar as these people of the turbulent poligar country really did become castes, their bonds of affinity were shaped in the relatively recent past.

We can see this happening in the seventeenth and early eighteenth centuries, when self-made dynasts like the Pudukkottai poligar chiefs were trying to secure their gains in areas which were cross-cut with dozens of conflicting and overlapping lordships. This gave the more successful of these armed clansmen an incentive to tell the world that they were rulers and the kin of rulers, with a mandate to enforce order and propriety in all things, including the policing of blood-lines by members of the 'royal' house. Even so, the local dynastic chronicles made it clear that the wider world knew Kallars as untamable

[49] Dirks 1987; Fox 1971; Gordon 'Legitimacy and loyalty in some successor states' in Richards 1978.

[50] See, for example, Pinch 1996: 86.

[51] As noted above, this term comes from the Tamil name Kallar, which had the same connotations as the western Indian usage Koli, implying a background of upland pastoralism and an allegedly 'thievish' or predatory way of life.

despoilers of order and decency, and that Kallarness was hard to reconcile with Brahman-centred 'caste' values.

For these groups, becoming castelike was primarily a matter of being drawn into cults with only the most ambivalent connections to the formal pantheon of puranic Hinduism. Long after the demise of the Marava- and Kallar-ruled poligar realms, Kallar and Marava identity was still being preserved as traditions of martial prowess emphasising the cults of club-wielding hero tutelaries. As was seen above, many of these were not even nominally Hindu, but included Muslim *pirs* (saints) and deified warriors like the Kallars' cult hero 'Khan Sahib'. This was Muhammad Yusuf Khan (d. 1764), a self-made Muslim dominion-builder who had made the fortunes of many Kallar war-bands in his bid to build an independent dynastic realm within the former Mughal *subah* of Arcot.[52]

North India too contains many former arms-bearing groups who acquired new bonds of affinity and castelike cohesion in the relatively recent past in much the same way, that is, without attaching great significance to Brahmans, and without conforming to standards of purity which disparaged the shedding of blood and the worship of warlike deities. These include many users of the titles Jat, Ahir, Koli and Kanbi who underwent what has come to be called caste formation in comparatively modern times. This occurred through service to self-made chiefs and rulers as recently as the seventeenth and eighteenth centuries, and through allegiance to cult traditions which celebrated the virtues of warriors and heroic dynasts.

None of these new dynasts would have survived without recruiting warriors from pastoral frontier areas and treating with armed hillmen and forest people from areas which had previously been beyond the margins of conventional Indian statecraft. At the same time, no-one's gains were safe from their expansive rivals. So whether they were rulers or retainers, the newly advantaged arms-bearers had strong incentives to secure such gains as they had made by identifying themselves with the ideals of lordliness that had become so widely deferred to in the new realms. These patricians who exalted the values of virility and lordliness were crucial in the making of what we now call caste. Their origins were often humble; their claims of dynastic legitimacy required them to tell the world that they were worthy to

[52] S. Bayly 1989; compare Dirks 1987.

wield power. So even if they themselves were not visibly castelike in the sense of following strict marriage rules and other 'pure' domestic practices, it was increasingly important for them to name and rank important classes of their subjects and dependants in a castelike fashion: it was this that made them recognisable as Kshatriyas, makers of order in a civilised or dharmic realm.

Yet the claims of prowess on its own were not sufficient to meet the needs of insecure dynasts in these increasingly complex realms. In the age of the later eighteenth-century warrior-dynasts an uneasy balance came to be struck between the claims of Kshatriya-like warrior-rulers and the very different ideals and values of the Brahman, the trader and the pacific scribal specialist. These classes of people came to play an increasingly critical role as contributors to 'traditional' caste ideologies, and it is on them that the spotlight falls in Chapter 2.

CHAPTER 2

THE 'BRAHMAN RAJ': KINGS AND SERVICE PEOPLE
c. 1700–1830

INTRODUCTION

The great paradox about the warrior dynasts who were the focus of the preceding chapter is that their world of predominantly martial and kingly values came to be so rapidly transformed by the spread of a significantly different set of caste ideals. These principles, which have much in common with the Brahman-centred values identified in Louis Dumont's account of 'traditional' caste ideology, belong to the second part of the two-stage process described in Chapter 1. It is this second stage – which brought ideals of Brahmanical rank and purity to the fore in Indian life, without ever fully supplanting the ideals of the lordly man of prowess – to which the discussion will now turn. Once again there will be an emphasis on Marathas, Rajputs and other builders of great kingdoms and chiefdoms. But, unlike the Maharashtrian dynast Shivaji Bhonsle, who proclaimed himself part of a pan-Indian network of arms-bearing Rajput lordliness, the grandees to be discussed in this chapter are those for whom supra-local Brahman, writer and merchant connections became the focus of their identity as dharmic 'caste Hindus'.[1]

The key change to be explored here is that within only a few generations, the post-Mughal rulers' dominions had become widely known and praised for the size and wealth of their resident Brahman populations, and for the 'pure' forms of worship and social refinement which had been embraced by many of their subjects. This was true even of some domains where the rulers were Muslim. As far as the Hindu-ruled kingdoms were concerned, by the mid-eighteenth century, networks of Brahman service specialists had actually taken over dynastic power in a number of important post-Mughal realms, most notably in the Maratha domains. These rulers and their Brahman

---

[1] On interactions between these caste ideals and those relating to values of ascetic renunciation, see below, pp. 74–6; also Chapter 1, note 1.

clients then took the lead in projecting norms of purity-consciousness onto an all-India plane. They achieved this through the sponsorship of great Brahman-centred royal rituals, and the support of pan-Indian holy places and devotional traditions. Elsewhere too, many dominion-builders were becoming far more dependent on the services of non-martial scribes, ritualists and trader-bankers who were either Brahmans themselves, or followed conventions which are now thought of as Brahmanical.

These developments had far-reaching effects on the experience of caste. With at least qualified support from rulers, Brahman priests – together with scribes, ascetics and merchants who followed Brahmanical social codes – generated around themselves a distinctively caste-like society throughout the subcontinent. Their norms differed significantly from the model of caste life which was still widely favoured by the men of prowess. In many ways, however, the two tended to move in the same direction, that is, towards an order of hierarchy emphasising purity and ritualised status differentials.

Far then from reflecting continuities from an ancient Hindu past, the caste-centred India that we see presented anthropologically in the work of Dumont and other social scientists was largely a creation of this period, though many of its features were further consolidated under British rule. This, however, raises the question of why Brahmans became so much more conspicuous and powerful in these turbulent eighteenth-century environments. And, furthermore, why was it in this period that the Brahman's and merchant's ideal of a 'pure' dharmic way of life became so influential in the world of the so-called caste Hindu? It is these questions that this chapter will address.

THE EXALTATION OF ROUTINE AND SERVICE

To an even greater extent than in the era of Mughal rule, the great men of eighteenth-century India were those who had expertise in commerce, priestcraft and the scribal arts. These all-important groups of service gentry, trader-bankers and priestly ascetics are the non-martial service-providers referred to in the threefold list of callings described above in Chapter 1 (p. 49). Though they were known and acknowledged before the decline of Mughal power, these ways of life gained dramatically in prestige and prominence with the advance of the new eighteenth-century successor realms, and the rise of the European trading companies. Even where they did not actually supplant the rulers who had recruited them, it was these men of the pen, lamp and ledger who helped to define and popularise the ideas and ranking schemes of a more formal 'caste Hindu' way of life.

The driving force here was the transformation of the Maratha warbands, Sikh *misls* (martial confederations) and all the other small-scale martial formations of the early post-Mughal dominion-builders into fully developed realms and kingdoms. These rulers had a growing need for specialists with access to supra-local resources and information. Even in the Sikh-ruled Punjab kingdom, where a surprisingly large number of Brahmans gained preferment under the reign of the great war-leader Ranjit Singh (1780–1839), prowess on its own was clearly not enough. As they struggled to consolidate their increasingly complex armies, tax-farming networks and commercial systems, the new dynasts of the Punjab, the far south, the Deccan, Hindustan and even Nepal found an ever-growing need for men of piety and learning to maximise their revenue, to maintain their records and intelligence networks, and to grace their courts and sacred foundations with the civilities expected of an established royal dominion.

Furthermore, as Europeans began to penetrate regional trading and revenue networks, they too attracted such people as their clients, informants and commercial partners. In these circumstances, men who could claim Brahman or honourable mercantile origin were often especially advantaged, and their power and visibility had a great impact on scribal and commercial families who could claim neither Brahman nor Vaishya origin. Even successful 'peasants' were attracted by the norms and standards that were being defined by these promoters of formalised caste ideals. And although these people's rustic imitators often met resistance when they claimed new honours and titles for themselves, significant numbers of cultivators like the tiller-Kanbis of Gujarat began to join with the bankers and traders of their home locales in Brahman-style 'purification' of their marriage and domestic practices.[2]

Here again the expansion of the Maratha realms set standards which affected everyday life and thought far beyond these rulers' home terrain. Within these realms, a great multitude of Brahman families rose to prominence through ties of service to their courts and

---

[2] Breman 1985.

rulers.[3] Of these great Brahman lineages, the most powerful of all were the Bhats of Danda Rajpuri. By the 1740s the heartland of Shivaji Bhonsle's former domain was being ruled in all but name by this Marathi-speaking Brahman family. This was the lineage of urban service specialists who had made the office of the Maratha king's chief minister their own hereditary preserve, adopting the title Peshwa for this paramount role of service to the Maratha polity. The achievement of the Peshwa-ship by this line of Deccani Brahmans created unparalleled opportunities both within and beyond the Deccan for families and individuals who could also claim Brahman antecedents. Among the most successful of these were *lokika* (non-priestly) Brahmans whom the Peshwas recognised as fellow users of their own particular jati title, Chitpavan. At the same time they also offered preferment to other local and immigrant Brahmans with commercial, priestly and service backgrounds.[4]

The Peshwas' immediate forebears were modestly placed regional revenue-takers, *deshmukhs;* their ancestors were the lowlier kind of literate Brahman traders, cultivators and non-celibate domestic ritualists from the Konkan coast, rather than scholar-ascetics with preceptoral ties to the great Gangetic or southern sacred centres. Within Maharashtra, Brahmans with this kind of occupational adaptability remained a tightly knit minority. They were generally looked down upon by the larger populations of Marathi-speaking Brahman lineages who called themselves Deshasthas, and who claimed superiority over Chitpavans and other service-seeking Brahman incomers on the grounds that they the Deshasthas were the Maratha country's primordial priestly elite.

Yet in spite of (or perhaps because of) these modest antecedents, the Chitpavan Peshwas were typical of the literate and moneyed specialists who rose to prominence in partnership with new rulers with a hunger for the credentials of kingship, and also for practical expertise and service. In both north and south India, such rulers were happy to vest these hitherto rather marginal people with rights and honours which were equally beneficial on both sides.[5] In so doing, they contributed

---

[3] One such family, the Devs of Cincvad, claimed hereditary affiliation to an historic preceptor-devotee of the god Ganesh; their ritual and fiscal services to Maratha rulers were rewarded with land and revenue rights (*inam*s). See Preston 1989; Perlin 1978.

[4] Gordon 1993; Conlon 1977; Johnson 1973; Perlin 1978; Wink 1986: 67–85; Divekar 1982.

[5] Johnson 1973: 55–9; Conlon 1977; Gordon 1993.

very powerfully to the shaping of more formally Brahmanical caste conventions in the wider society. This may seem surprising: many rulers, including the new Maratha power-brokers, remained highly eclectic and wide-ranging in matters of religion, directing benefactions to the shrines of regional *bhakti* gods and power divinities, and encouraging their soldiery to exalt the powers of Muslim mystics (Sufis) and cult saints (*pirs*). Such strategies were followed by other 'Hinduising' dynasties including south India's seventeenth- and eight-eenth-century Nayaka and poligar rulers. Similarly, great shrine and monastic enclaves – such as Tirupati and Sringeri – received support from important Muslim rulers, including the Hyderabad Nisams and Tipu Sultan of Mysore.

Nevertheless, by the later eighteenth century, both the Chitpavan Peshwas and the great lines of Maratha warrior-rulers, who built dominions in central and western India from the 1760s onwards, had made their mark all over India as patrons of supra-local Brahmanical worship and learning. One of the key figures here was Ahilyabhai Holkar, the widowed daughter-in-law of the Indore realm's great ruler Malhar Rao Holkar. Ahilyabhai was one of several women who confounded the usual conventions debarring women from kingship, succeeding to power in the Holkar dominions in 1767. Her strategy of pious largesse, which was directed towards such fast-growing pan-Indian devotional centres as Gaya, Banaras and Rameshwaram in Tamilnad, was dictated particularly by her anomalous status. Not only was Ahilyabhai a woman claiming sovereignty; she was a Kshatriya's widow who had not performed *sati* (self-immolation). Nevertheless her expiatory benefactions were acceptable at the *choultries* (pilgrims' hospices) and *pathshalas* (centres of Sanskrit teaching and textual recitation) which were becoming a major feature of these and other important pilgrimage towns.[6]

Although most of those receiving benefactions from royal patrons like Ahilyabhai were of Brahman birth, the scholarly and puranic devotional texts which they produced were extremely diverse. At the same time, however, much of what the *pathshala* scholars taught emphasised the unique qualifications of Brahmans to enact the rituals through which worshippers could achieve privileged access to the divine hero Ram, or to the other personified gods of the *bhakti*

---

[6] Gordon 1993: 160–2; Luard 1908: 17–20, 302; Prior 1990; Panikkar 1995: 48–50.

devotional pantheons. Anthropologists have found much complexity and ambivalence in these conceptual categories. This is particularly so in those cases where Brahman scholars writing for eighteenth- and early nineteenth-century rulers appear to devalue Brahmanical purity-consciousness, favouring instead ostensibly casteless ideals of trans-cendent other-wordliness and asceticism. Yet there does seem to be a unifying theme here, at least in those cases where the specialists who wrote for such patrons as the Maharajas of Banaras, and the 'Hin-duising' Gurkha rulers who achieved supremacy in Nepal in the 1790s, drew on those aspects of older sastric teaching which extol the Brahman as an authoritative figure in civilised society.[7]

This unifying message is that the 'pure' Brahman's austere way of life makes him a 'this-worldly' representative of the supreme ideal, that of the transcendent and the renunciatory, 'in the world but not of it'.[8] Thus, whether he acts as ritualist, as celibate preceptor-*guru*, or as *lokika* servant of the king, his presence is auspicious and desirable, indeed a defining condition of '*brahman raj*', a realm of worth and legitimacy. Hence, without wholly overriding the openness and comparative castelessness which had characterised their predecessors' political strategies, many eighteenth-century rulers took steps to Brahmanise their office-holding networks, in some cases recruiting only men of Brahman birth to occupy important posts and offices.[9] Other men of power did much to associate their rule with acts of conspicuous piety at Banaras and the other great Gangetic holy places at which both Brahman ritualists and monk-ascetics had come to congregate in ever-growing numbers.[10] The great lords of the Sikh kingdom became prominent patrons at Hardwar, and the Maratha

---

[7] Burghart 1978b. Ironically, nineteenth-century British military commanders saw their Gurkha recruits as relatively casteless. This points to a distinction between the juridical interpretations of caste, which were structured by Indian rulers like the Gurkhas, and the more pervasive everyday working of caste norms as they developed in the wider society, especially under British rule.

[8] Heesterman 1985: 43; see also Das 1982: 18–56; Parry 1994: 122–3; Laidlaw 1995; Burghart 1978b; van der Veer 1987.

[9] As in the Travancore and Maratha realms. This trend can also be seen in material culture, as in eighteenth-century Kotah where royal paintings gave increasing prominence to Brahman courtiers, even in hunting scenes which had formerly portrayed rulers as embodi-ments of the martial Kshatriya ideal. (I am indebted to Dr Norbert Peabody for this point.) Sato's study of eighteenth-century Kotah (1997) uses annual village revenue records which give precise figures for the numbers of specialist untouchable pollution-removers in each locality.

[10] van der Veer 1988; Parry 1994: 40–2.

grandees' state pilgrimages and benefactions directed massive flows of wealth into the hands of the priestly and preceptoral Brahmans who served them both at home and in the distant all-India sites. This made it easier for their many *lokika* service Brahmans to secure their fortunes by forging links of clientship with the family scribes (*pandas*) and other ritualists who served the pilgrims at these prestigious sacred centres. It also helped to reinforce the claim that served them all so well, this being that the greatness of the Maratha realm was derived in large part from the greatness and piety of its associated Brahman client groups.

A crucial asset then for many scribal and commercial people was their growing ability to build all-India connections. In so doing they were able to exploit the fact that a claim to be Brahman, Kayastha or a Vaishya-type merchant had come by the early eighteenth century to be comprehensible in virtually every realm where the men of prowess ruled, that is from Travancore and the southern poligar chiefdoms to the Maratha, Jat, Rajput and even Muslim Rohilla domains of the north. This was not the case for 'peasant' groups: the sharing of Jat, Vellala or Kanbi origin evoked no such recognition outside the 'peasant''s home terrain. But like the long-distance merchant groups who were also benefiting in this period from the rapid growth of trade and commercialised revenue, the scribal and priestly people gained very greatly from the growth of competitive political systems, and from the hunger of rulers and their rivals and deputies for the right kind of skilled experts.

According to the conventions which had come to prevail in most Indian regions, it took a Brahman to vest a man of power with the thread (*suta*), titles and rituals of kingliness; as was seen in Chapter 1, this transformation was achieved by the Maratha ruler Shivaji in the 1670s. By the eighteenth century virtually every realm contained aspiring Kshatriyas who had amassed new wealth from the proceeds of war and tribute-taking, and from participation in expanding regional commodity markets. Typical of these people who had cash to spend on thread-investitures and other caste-making rituals were the members of martial clans known as Cheros whom the British knew in the later nineteenth century as holders of insecure little lordships in impoverished areas of north Bihar.[11] These Koli-like people probably

[11] Forbes 1894: 25.

owed to their expansive eighteenth-century forebears their practice of being invested with the sacred thread of the *dwija* (twice-born) varna orders at the hand of a ritual specialist – in this case a line of comparatively low-status non-celibate holy men (Gharbashi gosains) from the 'syncretistic' Kabirpanthi sectarian order. In addition, they recruited local Brahman ritualists known as Sakaldwipis and Kanya-kubjas to perform household rituals for them.[12]

These Chero arms-bearers had many counterparts in both north and south India, that is, former 'casteless' uplanders and martial pastoralists who in the period preceding the British conquest had garbed themselves in the trappings of formalised jati and varna by taking initiation from one of the more open and assimilative lines of sectarian holy men. At the same time, many of these groups also began making moves to show the world that they were worthy to feast assemblages of Brahmans, and that they had Brahman scribes and ritualists to serve them and take their *dakshina* (benefactions in coin and kind).[13]

In the case of literate groups who could not claim Brahman origin, in particular the many Deccani and north Indian service families who called themselves Kayasthas or Prabhus, it became common in the post-Mughal successor states to signal claims of shared blood and 'caste affinity' through the adoption of certain other highly regarded social markers, especially restrictive marriage practices. Here, too, this firming up of caste boundaries involved a shift away from forms of community which had been relatively loose and open in previous centuries. Many of these people of the service occupations, whose descendants sought to stabilise their 'caste' status by seeking service in the colonial revenue bureaucracies, were incomers of humble origin who had only recently moved into the scribal specialisms. What they wanted now was to claim some degree of kinship with people like the Kayastha grandees who were already established at Hyderabad, Banaras and the other great courts. Similarly, there were many commercial people with aspirations to service beyond their home locales who found that they could improve their chances of preferment if they could say of a rival that his forebears were less 'pure' than their own. Such considerations had become important both to kings and to

---

[12] Forbes 1894.
[13] Cf. Pinch 1996: 36–8.

their status-conscious courtiers and creditors. All these were now increasingly inclined to listen to the merchant who told them that his conformity to exclusive caste ideals made him truly fit to serve a lordly patron, and to interact with other royal service-providers.[14]

Furthermore, even before the British conquest, there were men of modest birth, mostly Bengalis in the north and literate Tamils and Telugus in the south, who had advanced themselves by becoming commercial agents (*dubashes*) to the East India Company. In the later eighteenth century many Bengali *dubashes* moved up country from the colonial port cities, settling in the great centres like Prayag (Allahabad) where commerce and devotional pilgrimage were profitably intermingled. As they did so, they too began to involve themselves with Brahman ritualists, investing above all in the rites of *shraddha* (funerary purification), and in other observances connected with the conventions of *samskara*, this being the term for the sequence of life-cycle rituals (at birth, investiture with the sacred thread, marriage, and finally death), which mark successive stages in the life of the conformist twice-born 'caste Hindu'. Similar specialists in the south took up new forms of ritualised devotion at the expanding sacred sites of the Tamil and Telugu country, particularly the great pilgrimage complex at Tirupati.[15]

Finally, many of the same incentives to adopt a more 'castelike' life applied to the big groups of artisans and trading people who were also patronised by the expansive new dynasts of the eighteenth century. Here too, nothing was easy or straightforward. Although people with specialised skills and assets to protect tended in any case to be more cohesive and castelike than other Indians, these affinities were generally reinforced as regional economies became more commercialised, giving traders and craft specialists greater opportunities to expand into distant regions. In unfamiliar environments or under the rule of a newcomer dynasty, a man and his kin could try to use the bonds of jati and varna to prove that they were of honourable stock, and hence of appropriate credit-worthiness to deal with others who were themselves engaged in the process of classing and being classed in these terms. Here, too, these claims were often violently resisted both by the regional rulers and by fellow traders or artisans who stood to lose out

[14] See e.g. Leonard 1978.
[15] Parry 1994; also Madan 1982.

in a scramble for enhanced rights and statuses. The so-called honours disputes that so baffled the British in south India in the late eighteenth and early nineteenth centuries were among the more dramatic expressions of these tensions.[16]

MONKS, PRIESTS AND GURUS

Yet reinforcing and intersecting with all these developments was the key trend that has already been identified for this period – namely, the amassing of great wealth and prestige by lineages who could claim Brahman origin. It may seem paradoxical that the rise of the warlike man of prowess so rapidly came to intersect with the exaltation of his apparent opposite, the 'pure' vegetarian 'caste Hindu'. Nevertheless, it is the case that the advance of the arms-bearer and shedder of blood brought with it in the eighteenth and early nineteenth centuries the exaltation of the Brahman, the supposedly 'pure', non-life-taking embodiment of ordered piety. By the middle of the eighteenth century, this could be seen in such areas as the Deccan, in the domains of the Peshwas and newer Maratha potentates like the Holkars, and also further south where the smaller Maratha-ruled realms of Kolhapur and Thanjavur (Tanjore) had come into being.

In this period there were three main areas of advancement in which Brahmans and Brahman-centred values came increasingly to predominate: in the field of finance, in statecraft and war, and in the ritual arena. First, as was seen above, in the Peshwa's domains almost all the creditors and revenue managers were bankers and financiers of Brahman origin who intermarried with the Peshwa's line. These people formed the core of a lavish urban lifestyle that turned Pune (Poona) and the other towns which they patronised into centres of sophisticated high consumption and pious philanthropy.[17]

Secondly, in the Maratha realms as elsewhere, Brahmans were not necessarily admired or deferred to by the rulers and other powerful groups who patronised them. But, like the quasi-Brahman Bhat/ Charan praise-singers described in Chapter 1, these scribal Brahmans had acquired highly saleable forms of expertise. By the mid-eighteenth century their skills had become indispensable to the forms of statecraft

---

[16] Brimnes 1996.
[17] Desai 1980.

which had emerged in the subcontinent's proliferating post-Mughal realms and chiefdoms. Literate people who could claim Brahman origin were obviously well placed to exploit these new opportunities: all over India there were enclaves of Brahmans whose families had specialised for many centuries in sacred learning or temple ritual. In addition, many people with such backgrounds already had a family tradition of secular record-keeping under the Mughals and their predecessors.[18]

Military operations, too, became more elaborate and professional-ised in this period, and the new rulers often placed Brahman officers in command of their armies.[19] Surprising though this may seem, such a career did not entail the loss of Brahman status. Unlike the sort of bloodshed that defiled the perpetrator – the killing of a cow, for example – paid soldiering was widely conceived of as an act of spirituality. In theory at least, a hired man-of-arms was bound to his commander and his calling by a tie of sanctified service (*seva*). This consecrated him to a selfless ideal which corresponded to the attach-ment of the devotee, the self-denying *bhakta*, to his guru and tutelary deity. A man who shed blood on these terms was the antithesis of the wild or 'impure' predator – the Bhil, Kallar or Koli.[20] In many cases an elite war-leader of this kind could even be a meat-eater, a consumer of alcohol and a worshipper of fierce blood-spilling deities without being disparaged as a person of 'impure' birth, like a lowly Chamar or Dom. (By the end of the nineteenth century, many Indians had a much more critical attitude to these un-'Sanskritic' ways of life: see below, Chapters 4 and 5.)

These were not merely metaphors or pious idealisations. Indeed, in this respect the second and third of this series of Brahman-centred specialisms often overlapped. In the age of the eighteenth-century warrior-dynasts, monkhood, soldiering and finance actually merged and intertwined in many areas, most notably in Bengal and the Gangetic north (upper India). In these regions' successor realms, much of the new wealth that had been amassed by providers of military and commercial expertise was in the hands of armed monastic corporations headed by Brahman renouncers (*mahants* or abbots). The largest of these assemblages of naked ascetic warriors were the renouncer *sadhus*

[18] Gordon 1993: 18.
[19] *Ibid.*: 145, 185.
[20] Kolff 1990.

74

of the Ramanandi order (*sampradaya*). The Ramanandis' glorification of the divine royal warrior Ram played a crucial role in disseminating ideals of assertiveness and pious mission that are now widely taken for granted in India as being those of the 'community'-minded 'modern' Hindu. Several of the other great north Indian organisations of Brahman-led Vishnu- and Shiva-worshipping ascetics (*bairagis* and *gosains* or *sanyasis*) had also transformed themselves into bodies of trained fighters selling their services to both Hindu and Muslim dynasts, and investing the proceeds in the burgeoning commercial markets of upper India.[21]

The Brahmans who led these corporations were far from being the only beneficiaries of these new political, economic and ideological developments. Indeed some of the Brahman-led monastic orders, especially the Ramanandis, were so open to non-elite adherents that people of almost any background could tap into their networks of 'spiritual capital'. This was a means of translating personal prowess and achievement into claims of inherited worth and 'caste' status. Nevertheless the power and prestige of these orders gave new prominence to the special kind of preceptor-Brahman who was revered as a being uniquely equipped to act as *mahant* or head of a great renouncer order.[22]

It was also the case that, in all the contending successor regimes, the newly established groups of so-called revenue Brahmans who were described above became increasingly important, not just in their own right, but as benefactors of other Brahmans. Wherever they went, either in search of preferment or simply on pilgrimage, such people attracted yet more Brahmans to the courts and shrine or market towns which they frequented as priests, preceptors and service-providers.

These Brahmans who Brahmanised others, including people of comparatively lowly or uncertain status, played a crucial role in spreading and stabilising the values of 'traditional' caste in this period. In both north and south India this task was regularly performed by the *sampradaya* devotional sects. One such case in the Deccan was that of the mixed array of Konkani scribal and commercial specialists who came to be known as members of a single Brahman jati, the Chitrapur Saraswats. Well into the eighteenth century, this group was

---

[21] Pinch 1996; C. Bayly 1983: 29, 143; Forbes 1813, II: 8.
[22] Buchanan [Hamilton] 1925: 38–9; 1930: 43.

still in the process of developing a sense of castelike cohesion; this was achieved primarily through bonds of preceptoral affiliation to a line of Brahman renouncer-ascetics with a network of hospices and touring gurus based along the Kanara coast.[23]

In other realms, too, most notably those ruled by north India's Rajput houses, the *sampradaya* corporations of ascetic Brahmans became especially active in the eighteenth and early nineteenth centuries. These sects gained prominence in many domains – not just as traders and soldiers but as providers of preceptorship, inducting kings and their subjects into forms of *bhakti* devotion which were definitely not 'casteless' or 'anti-caste'. Instead, particularly in the case of the celibate Brahman gurus (Goswamis) of the Vallabhacarya tradition, their doctrines exalted norms of pious munificence and caste-conscious 'householder' life which appealed strongly to both kings and successful commercial groups.[24]

KINGSHIP AND CONSPICUOUS PIETY

So the non-celibate Brahman priest, the Brahman ascetic and the secular 'service Brahman' could and did interlink and ally with one another. When they did so, the effect was to create a more formally 'castelike' social order among many though not all Indians. In many eighteenth-century realms, record-keeping was not just a preserve of Brahmans but had actually become a means of building caste considerations into the functions of government. In the *peshwa daftar* records, that is, the Maratha rulers' registers of state transactions and revenue obligations, the Peshwas documented acts of adjudication through which they as Brahman guardians of the realm proclaimed themselves arbiters of other people's jati and varna status. In other words, these documents testified to the fact that by ordering their subjects according to caste rank and title, by incorporating them as members of named jati and varna groups, and by endorsing their use of particular caste titles and 'honours', they were fulfilling the ancient ideal of sovereignty as set down in the *arthashastra* texts.[25]

---

[23] Conlon 1977.

[24] As noted by early British travellers including Buchanan [Hamilton] 1925: 39, 108, 143; and Buchanan [Hamilton] 1930: 44. See also Peabody 1991.

[25] As illustrated in the *Ajnapatra*, a treatise on statecraft compiled in 1716 by one of Shivaji's former ministers: see Puntambekar 1929: 88; also Desai 1980.

Elsewhere too, new rulers used this Brahmanical caste logic to demonstrate that their realms were real and legitimate, with a cohesion that transcended the necessarily fragile alliances and revenue networks that they or their predecessors had assembled. In many cases, this involved proclaiming for their domains the status of a sacred entity – a dharmic domain or *dharmabhumi*. This Sanskrit term was translated by British writers as 'land of charity', meaning a kingdom defined by its obligations of pious largesse to Brahmans and holy places, and to the deity from whom the righteous king derived his powers.[26]

Inevitably it was Brahmans who enacted the rituals which forged this all-important compact with the dominion's tutelary god. Usually such a deity was a personification of the kingly Vishnu or Ram. In the southwest, this was Lord Ram with the Axe, Shri Parashurama, a god whose *purana* myth identifies him as a superhuman Brahman who avenges his father's death by killing every living royal and warrior Kshatriya, and then repopulating with Brahmans a new dharmic land of his own creation. The Parashurama tradition is thus a particularly graphic embodiment of the second stage in the schematic formulation set out in Chapter 1, this being a movement from mainly warrior-centred forms of 'caste society' to those in which Brahmanical norms had begun to hold sway. South India's leading post-Mughal 'successor' states included Nayaka- and Maratha-ruled Tanjore (Thanjavur), and the expansive eighteenth-century west-coast domains of Travancore and Cochin, in both of which Parashurama was the royal tutelary. Travancore in particular faced growing pressure from the European trading powers; both Travancore and Tanjore had to contend with competition from expansive rivals and their own internal client groups. All had dynasts who treated caste symbolism as a valuable strategic asset; as in several of the poligar realms, rulers from these kingdoms asserted their claims of dynastic legitimacy by undergoing a spectacular Brahman-run ceremony of rebirth. This was the *hiranyagarbha*, through which the ruler was literally born again as a thread-wearing Kshatriya from within the womb of a specially constructed life-size golden cow.[27]

In Travancore this same eighteenth-century kingdom-builder Mar-

---

[26] Mateer 1871: 1, 17–18; S.Bayly 1989: 66–9.
[27] See Dirks 1987: 37–8. Commercial specialist groups often played a prominent role in this rite, with poligar rulers receiving gold for the model cow from the hands of Komati trader-bankers.

tanda Varma (reg. 1729–58) further confirmed his royal status by feeding and lodging thousands of Brahmans in specially endowed royal hospices (*chatrams*), and pledging eternal largesse to their descendants.[28] Yet caste in its 'traditional' or Brahman-centred manifestations had not become an all-powerful fact of life by the end of the eighteenth century. Even the supposed inviolability of the Brahman's body could be set aside when a ruler's power and authority were at stake. Brahmans were executed for opposing the rule of Shivaji's successor Sambhaji (reg. 1680–9); and while few such executions occurred under the eighteenth-century Peshwas, Brahmans were regularly fined and imprisoned in their domains.[29]

Furthermore, even in kingdoms that became renowned for their patronage of Brahmans and Brahmanical piety, and where both the defilement of Hindu temples and sexual contact between Brahmans and members of lower castes were often severely punished, both rulers and their subjects still drew on the power of blood-spilling divinities and cult heroes, and participated in forms of worship which were decidedly un-'Brahmanical'.[30] So there is little reason to assume, as some orientalists have done, that because rulers looked to Brahmans for so many of these services, caste was for some deep-seated cultural or environmental reason a stronger or more stable institution than the Indian state.

On the contrary, the men of prowess who gained power through commercialising and militarising strategies in the seventeenth and eighteenth centuries pursued forms of statecraft which were real and effective in the everyday world. And when they turned to caste symbolism to enhance the moral and spiritual legitimacy of their realms, they were still engaging in techniques of practical and effective statecraft. None of these was a gesture which enfeebled kings or made the Brahman the sole point of reference in a world of 'traditional' caste organisation. On the contrary, even as their statecraft became more centred on Brahmanical institutions and values, the regional dynasts continued to preside over a decidedly open-ended landscape of peoples and castes. These classifications and schemes of precedence were not thought of at the time as being rigid or immutable. In the seventeenth century, the Maratha ruler Shivaji had made himself kingly by proclaiming himself a Rajput; in the eighteenth century

---

[28] Mateer 1871: 168, 170, 181–2.
[29] Guha 1995: 104–5.
[30] On punishments for intercaste sexual contact see Guha 1995.

some men of Rajput descent turned this ploy on its head, claiming to be Marathas as a path to power and privilege under the rule of the Deccani dynasts.[31]

In both the small and the powerful kingdoms, it suited the ruler's purpose to proclaim rights of endorsement and arbitration over highly diverse subject populations. Neither rulers nor their subjects appeared to expect all within their realms to lead a fully castelike way of life, or to conform to the same jati and varna conventions. On the contrary, the more plural the polity, the wider the range of symbolic and practical assets available to a resourceful dynast trying to survive in dangerous times. So the pursuits, gods and livelihoods that most Brahmans would consider disordered and impure actually became more valuable to the thread-wearing Kshatriya dynasts in the age of the post-Mughal successor states. Such a ruler might appear to favour conventions of order and pious civility, but reality in uncertain times demanded a complex interplay between order and disorder, the 'wild' and the settled, the Brahmanised, the partially Brahmanised and the distinctly un-Brahmanised.[32]

This was borne out in the experience of the great Maratha powers among many others. At Nagpur, for example, Raghuji Bhonsle, one of the half-dozen or so war-leaders who founded independent Maratha principalities in the mid-eighteenth century, established his new domain in lands which had previously been dominated by chiefs of the armed forest- and hill-people known as Gonds. Raghuji Bhonsle and his successors set about the task of asserting dynastic Maratha lordship in their own right – not by 'Brahmanising' themselves and their subjects, but by absorbing and building on their Gond subjects' distinctly un-castelike traditions of martial chiefdom.[33] Well into the nineteenth century, Gonds and Gond symbols were preserved at the heart of the new Nagpur realm's rituals and dynastic lore. This was still the case long after the Bhonsles had begun to conform to more conventional principles of 'Hindu' kingliness, for example by re-cruiting and patronising literate scribal people who entered their service and then received honours and privileges as a 'caste' with the title Chandraseniya Kayastha Prabhu.[34]

[31] Peabody 1996.
[32] Dirks 1987: 245.
[33] Gordon 1993: 124; Wink 1986: 108–10.
[34] Gordon 1993; Bates 1984: 57–8.

THE EAST INDIA COMPANY AND THE WORTHY 'CASTE HINDU'

What then became of this shifting mélange of norms and values with the rise and expansion of European power? It has already been noted that India's seventeenth- and eighteenth-century dynasts built their power through a drive for cash revenue. The techniques used by these rulers to spread and tax commercial cash-crop production prefigured the strategies of Britain's nineteenth-century colonial revenue machine. These moves put severe pressure on people who lacked the credentials of the martial elites and the skills of the specialist service-providers. So, even before the colonial period, the tiller was becoming an ever-more important person in Indian society. Yet he was also, as will be explained below, a vulnerable person who had good reason to become more castelike in the face of an uncertain market and an ever-more intrusive and volatile political order.

Until the 1820s there were few areas outside Bengal, Bihar and the territories around Madras where the British can be described as a true colonial power. Indeed only in the former 'successor state' of Bengal had Britons fully supplanted the looser types of sovereignty which had been in place before the Company took over the *nawabi*'s land revenues in 1765. However, even before the British had achieved political and military ascendancy in other parts of the subcontinent, their operations had made a significant difference to many Indians' experiences of caste. This is not to say that the European presence created India's caste norms, any more than it was the Mughals or the post-Mughal succcessor states which imposed an alien regime of jati and varna on a hitherto casteless society. Nor is it the case that jati and varna are merely 'imaginings' in the minds of Western thinkers and data-collectors.[35]

What is clear, though, is that by the end of the eighteenth century the Company's penetration of the subcontinent had accelerated many of the social changes which were already underway within the regional successor states. This can be seen in at least three areas of interaction with the indigenous society. First, through their eighteenth- and early nineteenth-century subsidiary alliance treaties, the British were able to make heavy revenue demands on many of the regional economies, and

[35] Inden 1990.

secured at least partial monopolies in key zones of trade and artisanal production. In these rapidly changing commercial milieux it therefore made sense for many traders and commodity producers to try to protect their skills and credit networks by strengthening their bonds of 'community'. In many cases the first step in the creation of tighter and more castelike affinities among trading and banking groups was the patronage both of local rulers and of the East India Company authorities. In Bengal for example, this affected the people of mixed origin from whom the British recruited their commercial intermediaries. We have already seen that these *dubash* families had become keen practitioners of caste-centred life-cycle rituals (*samskara*) in the early stages of Company expansion. By the time the British were consolidating their power in the Gangetic hinterland, these groups found themselves fighting hard to maintain their slender gains. This gave them strong incentives to build tighter 'community' or jati connections, while also distancing themselves from traditions and values which resembled those of the province's struggling landed gentry groups.[36]

Many other traders had discovered that there were valuable gains to be made by taking titles and offices from the colonial authorities; and this too had the effect of consolidating castelike ties and allegiances. From as early as the seventeenth century, Company officials in Bombay and the other commercial port cities had been following a pattern that had initially been set by the Nayakas, the Deccan sultans and other regional dynasts, and was then imitated by the Portuguese and other European powers. This involved the vesting of key individuals (*mahajans*, literally big men) from the urban trading populations with official status as chiefs or 'headmen' of their 'communities'. Propping up the authority of a so-called caste headman (*talaivan*) proved a comparatively cheap means of keeping order in towns which were continually being unsettled by booms, slumps and waves of unpredictable in- and out-migration.[37]

None of this meant that Indians were unable to conceive of themselves as individuals with interests and identities which were distinct from those of a jati or other corporate community.[38] But by

---

[36] Mukherjee 'Caste, class and politics in Calcutta, 1815–38', in Mukherjee and Leach 1970: 33–78.

[37] Brimnes 1996; S. Bayly 1989: 326–8, 333–78; for Bombay, compare Pearson 1975.

[38] See Mines 1992.

drawing together around the focus of 'kingly' headmen and caste notables, and by distinguishing themselves as pious benefactors and exemplars of superior virtue and respectability, the subcontinent's specialised trading people were in a much better position to amass capital and recruit labourers, and to transact business with people who would otherwise have questioned their worth, honour and creditworthiness. Thus, as they acquired the trappings of well-defined status communities, such regional specialist groups as the sea-going Madras Paravas and Komati trader-bankers were able to signal to local rulers, as well as potential partners and creditors, that they were possessors of shared resources. These included collectively managed capital and other material assets. Equally valuable to the 'community' was its stock of shared occupational expertise and information, and its other intangible assets, particularly the values and moral standards to which its members subscribed by acknowledging the regulatory power of their caste notables.[39]

The second area of interaction involved the Company's policies of intensive military recruitment. These greatly affected the experience of caste in many areas, since they encouraged such people as Kallars in the southern poligar country and armed 'peasants' from the west and Gangetic north to consolidate their claims of shared status and community.[40] And thirdly, the Company was now beginning to reduce many hitherto independent realms to the status of dependent client kingdoms. These moves had particularly important social implications. Once shorn of their military resources, the regional dynasts and their clients were inclined to turn more consistently to the recruitment of Brahman ascetics and ritualists, and to the sponsorship of Brahmanical dynastic rituals, in the hope of preserving some measure of authority in their dealings with both the British and their own subjects.[41]

So it was, at least in part through the tensions and uncertainties which accompanied the expansion of British military and economic power, that the last of the three ways of life outlined in the previous chapter came into prominence over large areas of the subcontinent.

[39] Rudner 1994; S. Bayly 1989: 321–78.
[40] Alavi 1995: 26–94; S. Bayly 1989: 196–9.
[41] This process has been seen by some as a neutering or 'feminisation' of India's political culture. On the emergence of 'traditional' forms of Hinduism in the former Hindu-ruled realms, see Freitag 1989a: 19–81; Dirks 1987; O'Hanlon 1993: 251; Price 1996; Prior 1990: 100–40.

This set of values was defined as the exaltation of the settled man of worth, meaning both the virtuous tiller and the man of commerce. Once this ideal had begun to be widely embraced, something much more like the 'traditional' life of the so-called caste Hindu came into being for more of India's people than ever before.

For the many people who were facing the insecurities of rural life at this time, the new ideals and symbols of community to which they were turning were visibly unlike those of the arms-bearing man of prowess. Those who were hardest hit, either by the Company or by the regional dynasts in their drives for revenue and agrarian productivity, were especially receptive to the teachings of the devotional orders (*sampradayas*) which exalted qualities of industry, sobriety and thrift over kingly prowess.

This kind of message was spread in Gujarat through the new synthesis of devotional Vaishnavite faith taught by adherents of the Swami Narayan *sampradaya*, and by networks of other ascetic renouncers in Bengal, upper India and some parts of the south. All these teachings said in effect that there existed a divine mandate exhorting humankind to live in an ordered world of town and village. The frugal, sedentary and pious tillers, traders and artisans who lived such a life were therefore not weaklings and bumpkins. They and not the men of prowess who coerced and commanded them were the true moral mainstream of a 'Hindu' social order. And if they were embodiments of worth, merit and godliness, caste for the adherents of these faiths became a matter of policing the boundaries of their 'community', insisting on purity and restriction in marriage, food exchange and other social contacts. Not to do so would leave them too vulnerable to being classed as humble menials rather than worthy and industrious 'peasants' and commodity producers.

For people who were new to revenue payment and cash-crop production, the chief models for this kind of caste ideal were merchants and traders from the towns. In Gujarat, urban commercial people were among the greatest winners in the expansion of the region's buoyant agrarian commodity market. They were also among the most conspicuous early adherents of the Vishnu-worshipping Swami Narayan faith. But this sectarian tradition also attracted large numbers of newly sedentarised pastoralist, 'tribal' and 'peasant' devotees. These peoples' adherence to the new faith went hand in hand with their transformation from loosely organised arms-bearers using titles like Koli, into sober 'caste Hindus' who now identified themselves as Kanbis and Patidars, these being titles denoting the way of life of the worthy, virtuous cultivator. They had many counterparts elsewhere, most notably in the Gangetic plain where users of titles like Ahir, Jat and Goala turned increasingly towards the cow-cherishing rustic piety associated with the cult of Krishna. With its visions of milkmaids and sylvan raptures, and its celebration of divine bounty in the form of sweet milky essences, this form of Vishnu worship offered an inviting path to 'caste Hindu' life for many people of martial pastoralist background.[42]

The British found much to applaud in the spread of these pacific 'caste Hindu' teachings. From the 1770s to the 1830s the East India Company was uneasily adjusting to its new functions as a great Indian polity. With severely limited manpower and resources, its three presidency governments were having to try to quell their numerous rivals, and to manage what had become by 1800 one of the largest standing armies in the world, consisting almost entirely of volatile status-conscious Indian recruits.[43] What Company officials feared particularly were the large groups of forest-dwellers and other arms-bearing people whom they knew by such titles as Bhils, Gonds, Kolis and 'Cotties', that is, Kathis, or people of Kathiawar. They also tended to disparage other arms-bearers whom the Mughals and their successors had found both useful and problematic, especially the notables who had been vested with titles like *girasia* or *girisi raja*, meaning someone from Koli or other arms-bearing lineages with the authority of a 'kingly' self-made Rajput lord. Well into the eighteenth and early nineteenth centuries, such people were still being vested with revenue-taking and military powers in the difficult upland and forest borderlands of north and central India.[44]

During the early decades of the East India Company's rule, British officials came increasingly to worry about the pastoral uplands and other marcher zones on the fringes of their insecure power bases. In James Forbes's influential *Oriental Memoirs*, published in 1813, western India's sparsely settled Broach region is described as 'a wild

---

[42] From the later nineteenth century the title Yadav was widely adopted in preference to Goala. In the Bhojpur region (western Bihar/eastern UP) the cult of the royal warrior Ram was a comparable focus for cultivators using the caste title Kurmi. See Pinch 1996: 84–89; compare Maddock 1993.

[43] Alavi 1995.

[44] Skaria 1992: 51–67; compare Bates 1984: 18–19. See above, Chapter 1.

3. A stereotyped colonial image of Bhil 'tribals'.

tract infested by tribes of wild men, and most audacious robbers, under the names of Gracias, Bheels, Coolies [Kolis], Cotties, and other plunderers ... '[45] As will be seen in Chapter 3, such orientalist writings also made much of the comparatively non-castelike people who dominated such areas, echoing earlier Mughal and Maratha reportage in portraying their inhabitants as dangerous 'freebooters' and enemies of orderly settled villagers and town-dwellers. So it is not surprising that Company officials expressed growing approval of the Swami Narayans and other devotional movements whose teachings were thought to disparage wildness and 'freebootery', and thus to promote acceptance of the Company's rule.

---

[45] Forbes, 1813, II: 105.

THE 'BRAHMAN RAJ' AND THE EAST INDIA
COMPANY: INDIAN 'ESSENCE' OR
HINDU SEDITION?

In the early Company period, however, the British were not consistently hostile to those who appeared 'wild' and casteless in their eyes. Nor were they eager to promote every teaching or institution that encouraged the adoption of 'caste Hindu' lifestyles. In fact, although the colonial state is often said to have 'Brahmanised' or 'traditionalised' Indian society through its techniques of data-collection and law-making, few Britons really thought that a rigidly Brahmanical India would be easy for them to tax and regulate.[46]

Certainly in the early Company period, however much they disparaged wildness and 'freebootery', British officials regularly expressed deep suspicion of 'orthodox' or Brahman-centred piety. The Company's greatest strategic problems at this time occurred in areas where it was in competition with the Maratha Peshwas, and with other powers which had become accustomed to using Brahmanical manifestations of jati and varna to assert their sovereignty. In the 1790s the most important of these conflicts focused on the great regional and pan-Indian pilgrimage centres. As was seen above, important urban locales in both the north and the south expanded very rapidly from the late seventeenth century as new dynasts dramatised their claims of lordship through acts of patronage at the major centres of commerce and pilgrimage. Banaras was particularly important to the schemes of open-ended sovereignty which had served so well in the building of the Mughal and post-Mughal realms, but which were now coming into collision with the Company's wish to exercise power without ambiguities of shared and overlapping authority.[47]

Jonathan Duncan, the East India Company's Resident at Banaras from 1787 to 1795, expressed particular concern about the Peshwas' and other Maratha rulers' long-distance contacts with the city's Brahmans and Brahman institutions. Duncan complained that the Maratha dynasts were behaving in Banaras as if the British were not sovereign there, and treating the Banaras region 'as a sort of Hindoo republic, where all the nations of India consider themselves as at home'.[48] It was

---

[46] On the rise of Company power see Marshall 1987; C. Bayly 1988.
[47] Duncan in Oldham 1876, pt II: 184, 186; Skaria 1992: 51.
[48] Duncan's letters 1792 and 1794, in Oldham 1876, pt II: 190, 191.

against this background that Duncan entered into a far-reaching controversy about whether the Company's new law-codes for Banaras should take account of the special sanctity of a Brahman's body, and above all whether Brahmans should be exempted from execution if convicted of murder.[49]

This debate was closely linked to the battle over whether to treat as capital crimes acts of so-called *traga* (suicide, self-mutilation or proxy killing) involving Bhat/Charan 'self-immolators'. These were the praise-singers described in Chapter 1 who supposedly made a commercial industry out of their tradition of Brahman-like bodily sanctity, hiring themselves out as guarantors of contracts, or as enforcers of debt repayment and providers of security to travelling merchants.[50]

In both cases – in the debates about *traga* as well as those concerning capital punishment for Brahmans – the point was not so much to raise abstract questions about justice and penal policy, but to work out how best to secure the Company's interests in regions which had only just been subjected to an insecure form of British client-ship.[51] So this was a debate about whether Indians would be 'loyal' if ruled under English-style laws which ignored the sanctity of Brahmans, or whether they would treat a casteless law-code as the mark of an impious and illegitimate regime. There were similar battles in this period in other temple towns, most notably in south India, where Company officers became equally exercised about how best to deal with the region's persistent 'caste honours' disputes. These they read as being inherently dangerous to the Company's authority because here too, Britons and their local officials were being forced to decide whether it was safe to depart from the practice of former rulers who had confirmed their lordly status by acting as intermediaries in such conflicts.[52]

---

[49] Singha 1998; Oldham 1876, pt II: 188–9.

[50] See above, Chapter 1: 45. If brigands threatened their clients' goods, or if a signatory reneged on a contract, Bhat guarantors were supposedly pledged to kill or maim themselves, or to substitute an aged kinswoman as the victim; such a woman exalted her kin as if she were a *sati*, a self-immolating widow.

[51] Oldham 1876, pt II: 103–4, 188–9; and see Rabitoy 1974.

[52] Among many accounts of these conflicts is a report on a 'left-hand/right-hand' dispute in *Board of Revenue Proceedings* vol. 161, 14 July 1796 no. 22: 7028–62, Tamil Nadu Archives, Madras. Compare Brimnes 1996; for comparable debates in western India see O'Hanlon 1993: 256 and 1994. For further explanation of the left-hand/right-hand ideology, see p. 108 below.

SPONSORED 'HINDUISM' IN THE CLIENT KINGDOMS

Over the next thirty years, the East India Company found it increasingly difficult to deal with rulers who were able to invoke jati and varna ties as a means of gaining allies and clients in regions where British power was insecure. These anxieties came to be expressed most consistently as fear of the 'conspiratorial Brahman'.[53] In 1818 the Company deposed the last of the Brahman Peshwas. But this did not lead to the immediate annexation of the Maratha domains. Here, as in Rajasthan and much of southern and central India, the Company decided that the best way to secure its fragile hegemony was to exercise power through what was, in effect, a screen of stage-managed Indian kingship. So, interspersed among the growing number of territories which had been placed under direct Company rule, the British declared themselves guardians of a whole series of sponsored realms whose thrones were occupied by 'restored' dependent dynasts.

Most of these domains had been stripped of their armies. Some were placed under the nominal rule of Muslims, though this left many commercial and service groups with a strong incentive to participate in the expansion of castelike lifestyles. But it was above all from the dozens of client realms proclaiming pious Hindu credentials that Indians received far-reaching messages about the meaning of jati and varna in the new world of European hegemony. The East India Company's decision to unseat so-called Brahman rule in the former Maratha realms of the Deccan was the crucial landmark here. Faced with apparent danger from the Maratha-ruled realms, the British chose to use caste logic to explain and justify their overthrow of the Peshwa's rule.

The Peshwas, said James Grant Duff and the Company's other influential Deccan strategists and chroniclers, were not and never had been rightful rulers; they were Brahmans, whose proper sphere in life was that of priest and scribe. So it could only have been through guile and subversion that their line had achieved power at the expense of the descendants of Shivaji Bhonsle.[54] According to Grant Duff, the Company's Resident at the former Maratha capital of Satara from

[53] Singha 1998.
[54] Grant Duff 1921 (I): 531.

1818 to 1823, it had been through the machinations of corrupt and self-seeking Brahmans that this virile and worthy line of kings had been usurped. Once in power, Duff argued, the Peshwas and their other Brahman allies had behaved with the same deviousness and treachery in their dealings with the British. Therefore, under the Company's guardianship, peace and order would prevail in a land rescued on behalf of its legitimate rulers from a lawless 'Brahman tyranny'.[55]

It was on this basis that both the Company's officers and their Indian clients set about articulating the logic of caste as it came to be understood by later generations of orientalists, that is, as a scheme of absolutes which marked out rigidly separate spheres of operation for the 'priestly' Brahman and the thread-wearing warrior dynast. This was not mere orientalist 'discourse'. In the Deccan and elsewhere, it was this view of jati and varna that the Company used to justify the installation, as one of their new client rulers in the Deccan, of the nominal heir to the original line of Maratha *chhatrapati* rulers, Pratab Singh Bhonsle (1818–39), ruling from Shivaji's former court centre at Satara instead of the Peshwas' seat at Pune.

Separate Maratha-ruled kingdoms, including those of Indore, Gwalior, Tanjore and several lesser princedoms, were also confirmed as realms of reconstituted royal authority. Mysore was 'restored' to the rule of the Hindu Wodeyar dynasty which had been overthrown in the 1780s by the greatest of south India's dominion-building dynasties, that of Haidar Ali and his son Tipu Sultan. Several of the south Indian poligars, including the Kallar sovereign of Pudukkottai, were also placed on reconstituted thrones; so too were the Travancore and Cochin dynasts, the Bhumihar rulers of Banaras, the Jat rajas of Bharatpur, and the dynastic lords of the various Rajput polities.

These views about Brahmans were also formed in conflicts between Company officials and other powerful elites in areas like Banaras, where Duncan had blamed the 'lawlessness and daring of Brahman cultivators' for the Company's difficulties in stabilising its military and revenue-taking power.[56] By definition, declared Grant Duff and his contemporaries, India's 'manly, thrifty and hardworking husbandmen' had fared badly where they had been subjected to 'Brahman

---

[55] *Ibid.*: 535.
[56] Oldham 1876, pt II: 186; C. Bayly 1983: 48.

government'.[57] Many of these officials' Indian informants were eager to confirm this kind of thinking with representations of their own about the 'lawless', turbulent or conspiratorial Brahman. At issue in many of these cases was actually the question of who out of many plausible claimants would be vested with proprietorship in an area of disputed revenue and landholding rights. But the language in which this was communicated to the British, and then amalgamated into their revenue settlement reports and other important documentation, was that of caste, or more specifically the danger emanating from Brahmans as a 'tribe' or conspiratorial network of affiliation. Again, this was perceived as a political danger.[58] In other words, from their dealings with contending landholders and revenue-takers, Company officers formed the view that it was reasonable and politic for their client dynasts to aggrandise themselves through acts of harmless pious largesse to priests, shrines and ascetics. At the same time, Brahmans as a class must be restrained from wielding civil and military power.

The effort to sustain and manage the new sponsored 'Hindu' realms generated a vast literature in both English and the vernaculars. These works familiarised both the colonial authorities and a later generation of self-professed Hindu 'modernisers' with norms that had hitherto been a matter of much more abstract or technical learned lore. The ideas dealt with in these increasingly public debates emphasised impersonal and universal values of 'Hindu' piety. These fed directly into later nineteenth-century notions of universal Hinduism and Hindu nationhood, as expressed by a wide range of polemicists and organised movements, ranging from such 'modernising' revivalist organisations as the Arya Samaj, to the Dharma Sabhas and other would-be guardians of more formally Brahmanical Hindu norms. More specifically, one can see the genesis of 'modern' Hindu ideals of binding moral affinity and pious citizenship in these earlier eighteenth- and nineteenth-century attempts to define and glorify the obligations of the pious thread-wearing Kshatriya king. Equally influential here were the closely related writings, and also new devotional practices, which either exalted or contested the power of Brahman ritualists and

---

[57] See O'Hanlon 1985: 24–32; Malcolm 1832 [1972], I: 67–8; Grant Duff 1921, I: 531; Forbes 1813, I: 200–1.
[58] Duncan in Oldham 1876, pt II: 102–3.

ascetics to confirm the self-consciously 'Hindu' ruler's claims of universal virtue and dominion.[59]

These were uneasy manifestations of Hindu kingship. They focused a glaring public spotlight on rulers who claimed to personify universal kingly power, while subsisting, disarmed, on the sufferance of alien Christian cow-killers. With no scope for conquest and territorial expansion, these realms, and the landed client groups who patterned their lifestyles on the same lavish kingly model, sought to establish themselves as exemplars of conspicuous piety. This involved the extension of pilgrimage, the building of temples, the feeding and protection of Brahmans, the founding or reinstitution of Sanskrit teaching foundations (*pathshalas*), the adoption of judicial forms based on sastric law, and many other techniques which shaped both the terrain and the ritual styles of a new, universalising pan-Indian 'Hinduism'. These developments also gave rise to fierce internal power struggles between networks of ritualists, revenue-takers and other service people who came increasingly to employ the language of caste and corporate honour as a means of securing a share of these uncertain royal resources. Thus, through the ambivalent mixture of constraint and sponsorship emanating from the colonial state and its clients, more people who called themselves Hindus were behaving in ways which were coming to define ideals of self-consciously Hindu dharmic identity.[60]

Furthermore, there were so many contradictions in the way that these Hindu realms actually came to operate during the nineteenth century that there was particularly fertile ground here for the assertion of all kinds of pious appeals for an assault on spiritual impropriety and so-called corruption, and thus for regeneration of 'Hindu' moral order. This can be readily seen from the wide range of universalising or 'theistic' teachings which were such a conspicuous feature of the urban 'public' arena during the later colonial period. In the eyes of the mainly young, male, English-speaking city-dwellers who were now beginning to debate the principles of moral and social 'reform' in the subcontinent, both Hinduism and caste were matters for agonising self-scrutiny, both personally and collectively. And the urgency of this was all the more pressing because of the fact that behaving as a 'Hindu' and

[59] See especially O'Hanlon 1993: 256 and 1994; also O'Hanlon 1985: ch. 1; Dirks 1987.
[60] Thapar 1992; van der Veer 1988.

4. This albumen print of high-caste youths wearing the sacred thread (*suta*) is labelled 'Vedic students', presumably from one of the many Sanskrit schools endowed by nineteenth-century 'dharmic' benefactors.

conforming to caste norms were both such new, uncertain and bitterly contested phenomena for so many people in the subcontinent.

All this flux and uncertainty in the political order generated a massive flow of petitions and appeals to the British authorities. From all over India came documents purporting to show which established or aspiring rulers and revenue-takers had legitimate claims to be vested with power under the Company's sponsorship. Every self-professed heir or rival claimant to these domains had scribes, office-holders and other would-be representatives all vying for the right to be recognised as sources of information and specialist expertise in their patrons' dealings with the British and their regional agents. Out of these battles for thrones, offices and revenue-taking rights came the enormous wealth of ethnographic information which was compiled in the form of dynastic histories and court chronicles by 'orientalist' scholar-officials.[61]

A high proportion of these documents were not 'traditional'

---

[61] See Dirks 1989.

records but materials specially assembled so as to make a convincing case for particular would-be dynasts or revenue-takers. Frequently it was in these people's interest, or that of the scribal and commercial people who were writing on their behalf, to subscribe to certain stereotypes about the bad, tyrannical powers which had supposedly preceded the Company's rule. British officials like Duncan were well known to view Brahmans as a class of dangerous and conspiratorial troublemakers. This was not a product of some fixed set of preconceptions about caste, since caste was not something about which the colonial authorities had straightforward views, either in this period or in the later nineteenth century (see below, Chapter 3). It was, instead, a consequence of political conflicts and, in particular, the Company's collision with the Peshwa's realm.

Thus through their dealings with client kings, and their nervous encounters with both 'secular' and priestly specialist Brahmans, the colonial officials of the early nineteenth century began to have a subtle but far-reaching impact on people's experience of caste. The framing of codes of so-called Hindu and Muslim civil law for use in the Company's directly administered territories was especially important here. Even though other colonial theorists did not necessarily conceive of jati and varna as the subcontinent's paramount institutions, these massive legal surveys of the 1820s did exalt 'caste' (though also the ambiguously defined concept of 'sect') as a crucial unit of Indian life, treating jatis in effect as law-making constituencies with the power to generate norms governing marriage, divorce, inheritance and adoption.[62]

Among the most influential of these surveys was Arthur Steele's *The Law and Custom of Hindoo Castes*, first published in 1826. This was intended as a definitive manual of 'caste law' in the Deccan, and it made much of the expertise claimed by the many Pune-based court Brahmans who were now attaching themselves to Bombay's new Government Hindu College.[63] Other works of this kind never saw the light of day: the thousands of entries in H. Borradaile's massive survey of 300 'castes' and 'sects' in Gujarat languished unread and untrans-

---

[62] Steele 1868: vi–viii, and *passim*. Compare Borradaile 1884–7; Nelson 1881. The aim of these exercises was to provide the courts with legal manuals superseding the more abstract works of earlier orientalists like Jones and Colebroke, and to impose consistency on the miscellany of 'traditional' texts cited by 'pandits' and other indigenous experts.

[63] Steele 1868: iv.

lated in the Bombay High Court archives until portions of the work were published in the 1880s by the jurist and antiquarian Sir Mungaldass Nothoobhoy.[64] Even so, the very fact that the Company's regional officials made so much of their power to summon and interrogate great assemblages of 'Shastrees, heads of castes, and other persons likely to be acquainted either with the law, the custom of castes, or the public opinion regarding the authority attached to each' conveyed important messages to the wider society.[65] The signals sent out in this way were often contradictory and ambiguous, but they did tell the wider world that the 'caste Hindu' was a real person to the colonial state, and that given propitious economic and political circumstances, valuable gains could be made by the man who was able to conform to superior jati and varna norms.

CONCLUSION: CASTE NORMS IN THE EARLY NINETEENTH CENTURY

Even well into the 1820s, India was not a homogeneous 'caste society' in the sense in which this phrase is employed today. It does seem, though, that jati and varna titles were in more widespread use at this time than they had been in past centuries. Most rulers and their favoured client groups had learned that they could derive real advantage in uncertain times by classifying both themselves and others in more formally castelike terms. Indeed, by the end of the eighteenth century, the far-reaching changes that had reshaped so much of the subcontinent's economic and cultural life had made India a markedly turbulent place, but one in which more people than ever before were trading, travelling and making war, and hence exchanging knowledge and information with one another, often in fiercely contentious circumstances. This forging of new links between town and countryside, consumers and producers, worshippers and ritualists, readers and literati, threw many different kinds of Indians into contact with one another, thereby raising fraught questions about where to draw social and moral boundaries, and familiarising substantial numbers of people who were new to them with at least some of the norms and principles of jati and varna.

[64] Borradaile 1884–7.
[65] Steele 1868: iii.

In this period then, we can certainly see some signs of the very different India that was to emerge by the end of the nineteenth century. As early as the 1820s, Brahmans and those who admired the norms of a 'pure' and pacific Brahman-centred way of life had become extremely prominent in many parts of India. This had occurred initially through preferment and economic success under indigenous realms like that of the Peshwas. It was then sustained through the apparently contradictory experiences of being first disparaged, then tamed and exalted, under the British-sponsored Hindu kingdoms, and in the legal codes that were created for Company-ruled territories in the early nineteenth century. Those who were most deeply affected by these changes were also much involved in reporting and commenting on these developments to the colonial authorities, thus bringing matters which had previously been confined to narrower specialist circles into a new kind of public domain.

The expansion of commerce and cash-cropping also gave important advantages to many trading and non-elite 'peasant' groups. These were the people who sometimes favoured conventional Brahman-centred piety but who were also often attracted to sectarian faiths like those of the Swami Narayans. In either case, such people were beginning to be active at this time in the forging of what we would now call caste Hindu lifestyles. And here too we can see the expansion of conventions which were implicitly hostile to the values and skills of the lordly men of prowess, and even more inimical to the way of life of the forest and pastoral groups with whom the arms-bearing proprietary groups were often closely associated.

However, in the 1820s no decisive shift had yet occurred in that uneasy synthesis between the three modes of existence described in Chapter 1. None of these had yet come to be substantially devalued in relation to the others. On the contrary, in this period 'caste' norms were still being actively forged around all three archetypes – the man of prowess, the service-provider, and the settled man of worth. Furthermore, many Indians were still highly uncastelike in their social and moral norms. Few would have subscribed to the widely shared conventional wisdom of subsequent generations, this being that a plough-touching Patidar or commercially successful Kalwar distiller was more worthy than a lordly but 'unenterprising' Rajput or Marava clansman.

So caste in the 1820s did not mean what it had come to signify to many though not all Indians by the early twentieth century. Even though the new Hindu- and Muslim-ruled client kingdoms were beginning to be demilitarised and deprived of their power to vest power in 'gracias' and other armed feudatories, India's great military labour market was still in operation in this period. There was still much demand from the Company's armies for irregular forces recruited from the armed forest and pastoral groups whose way of life was still far from that of the Brahmanical 'caste Hindu'.[66] Men of prowess still held sway in important areas of the subcontinent, and what was happening at this time was only the beginning of the long and disruptive process of demilitarisation which had so much to do with the reshaping of caste in the later colonial period.

Thus, as of the 1820s, we see no more than the first signs of the pressures which were eventually to undermine the power and prestige of the lordly proprietors and other arms-bearing groups. As will be seen in Chapter 5, these dislocations were partly a result of the colonial state's increasing revenue demand. They were also due to moves by the Company's law-courts to be literal-minded about the collection of so-called book debt, that is, the sums shown as owing in the ledgers of *saukars* and *banias* (money-lenders and traders); such people's demands would have been less favourably treated at the courts of earlier rulers.

In this period, however, the boundaries between 'pure' and 'impure', clean and unclean, 'caste' and 'tribe', even Hindu and Muslim were still much less clearly defined in everyday life than was later to be the case. Even in the thinking of colonial officials and their informants, much would change during the nineteenth century in 'orientalist' conceptions of caste. So, before going on to explore the shaping of caste in relation to economic and political change in the later nineteenth and twentieth centuries, it is to these varied and complex intellectual debates that the discussion now turns.

[66] Alavi 1995; Kolff 1990.

CHAPTER 3

WESTERN 'ORIENTALISTS' AND THE COLONIAL PERCEPTION OF CASTE

INTRODUCTION

This chapter examines the understandings of caste propounded by Western orientalists from the late seventeenth to the early twentieth century. It is important to explore these because so-called Western 'constructions' of caste had a considerable effect on Indian life, especially where such views were shaped by contributions from Indians themselves. Some at least of these ideas became embodied in the practices of government both during and after colonial rule, as well as being embraced, disputed and reflected on by Indian politicians, literati and social reformers.

Often, though not invariably, so-called orientalists saw Hindus as the prisoners of an inflexibly hierarchical and Brahman-centred value system. Their insistence on this point played a significant part in the making of a more caste-conscious social order. Yet this could happen only in the context of broader political and social changes which were in progress well before the onset of colonial rule, as was seen in the preceding chapters. Furthermore, the continuing movement towards the castelike ways of life to be described in the book's final chapters could not have occurred in so many areas without the active participation of Indians.

So while much of the subcontinent did become more pervasively caste-conscious under British rule, this is not to say that caste was in any simplistic sense a creation of colonial scholar-officials, or a misperception on the part of fantasising Western commentators. Nor is it to say that the 'modernisation' of India would somehow have taken a casteless or caste-denying form under a different kind of political order. It would therefore be wrong either to concentrate exclusively on 'orientalism' in exploring the meaning of caste under colonialism, or to deal with it from a strictly material or political perspective. Thus, before looking in Chapter 5 at the social and economic changes which helped to spread the norms of caste in the nineteenth and early twentieth centuries, Chapters 3 and 4 will attempt to create a more nuanced intellectual history of both British and Indian conceptions of caste. The British side of this story is the focus of this chapter, with Indian theories and debates being explored in Chapter 4.

THE LIMITED POWER OF CASTE REPORTAGE

As of the 1820s, British officials were deeply embroiled in the complex social and ideological changes which had initially exalted the warrior's caste codes, and had then given increasing prominence to those of the 'dharmic' Brahman and merchant. As a trading firm which had only just transformed itself into a fragile military despotism, the English East India Company was struggling to consolidate its new territorial possessions and to identify 'collaborators' in locales where even experienced officials were hard pressed to distinguish friend from foe. In these volatile circumstances, the acquisition of detailed social knowledge had become essential to the Company's operations. As in other parts of the Empire, both Britons and those whom they were trying to rule found advantage in feeding the still insecure colonial state with such data as could be used to tax and police its subjects.[1]

For some modern historians, this quest for information was a 'hegemonic' exercise enabling Britons to divide and enfeeble the peoples of the subcontinent by subjecting them to a demeaning and destructive process of 'essentialisation'. Caste was certainly much referred to in the reportage which shaped both scholarship and official policy in the nineteenth century, that is, in the publications of jurists, missionaries, revenue surveyors, military recruiters and innumerable other observers of Indian life. Indeed, the increasingly powerful and intrusive colonial regime that came into being after the 1857 Mutiny-Rebellion found more and more reasons to count and classify the subcontinent's peoples, and to call on Indians to report themselves as members of specific social, economic and occupational categories, each supposedly possessing its own 'essences' and qualities. Particular importance has been attached to the operations of the all-India

---

[1] See C. Bayly 1988 and 1996.

decennial Census, which was launched in 1871; in its voluminous reports and statistical tables, Indians were counted, ranked and classified by caste, 'tribe' and ethnoreligious 'community'.[2] By the early twentieth century, the massive bureaucratic machinery of the Raj had generated an enormous output of further documentation in which jati and varna were used as basic units of identification.

Two key themes have been identified in this vast array of regional ethnographic surveys, population censuses and other official and quasi-official writing. The first of these is an insistence on the supposedly ineradicable sense of community dividing Hindus from Muslims and other non-Hindus; the second is a view of Indians (apart from so-called tribals and followers of minority faiths) as slaves to rigid, Brahman-centred caste values. This is what Ronald Inden has called the 'imagined India' of false and dehumanising orientalist stereotypes. Historians of the so-called subaltern school have seen these misperceptions and wilful distortions as having passed unchallenged from self-serving colonial reportage into the pronouncements of India's post-Independence ruling class.[3]

Yet the writings of nineteenth-century travellers, missionaries and scholar-officials were far too diverse and contradictory to be portrayed in such one-dimensional terms, regardless of period, and without allowing for important variations in approach and interpretation. The colonial state was certainly hungry for statistical and ethnographic data. And, like the many Christian missionaries who engaged in orientalist reportage, colonial officers regularly used phrasing which offends the modern ear:

'... the Hindoo is mild and timid, rather disposed to melancholy, and effeminate pleasures'.

'The life of the Rajput in British districts is not calculated to develop the manly virtues ... they have lost the taste for manly exercises which harden the muscles and develop the physique.'

'The Arora is the trader "par excellence" [of southwestern Punjab] ... [They] are of inferior physique ... "a cowardly secretive, acquisitive race ... possessed of few manly qualities ..."'

'All Bowries [also known to colonial ethnographers as Badhiks or Bhudduks, a

---

[2] Barrier 1981; Cohn 'The census and objectification' in Cohn 1987; Dirks 1989.
[3] Chatterjee 1986; and see Inden 1990; Prakash 1990; Pant 1987. For a penetrating critique of these approaches see O'Hanlon and Washbrook 1992.

"vagrant" or "gyspy" caste] have been from ages past and are still by profession inveterate and irreclaimable robbers.'[4]

Such pronouncements have been seen as evidence of an orientalist 'project' to deny the existence of civil society in India. By representing the subcontinent as a domain of slavish allegiances, orientalists purportedly fed officialdom with the idea that it was 'scientific' to treat Indians as unvirile, irrational and socially atomised, thus unfit to govern themselves.[5] Yet these writings contained ambiguities and contradictions. The more sophisticated conveyed real uncertainty about whether ties of caste and ethnoreligious community were indeed paramount for all Indians. Among those who did emphasise its power, some at least saw caste as relatively modern in origin rather than an eternal essence of Indian culture. There was even debate about whether caste was indeed corrupting and destabilising, or an essentially benign and moral system which could be used for desirable ends.

So how did the most influential Western commentators perceive the ideologies of caste, and how much significance did they attach to their manifestations in Indian life? There are two points to bear in mind here. First, the importance which these analysts ascribed to caste cannot be explored in isolation, or in an exclusively Indian or colonial framework. On the contrary, their writings about caste need to be considered against the background of wider intellectual debates involving attempts by Western thinkers to address the pressing social and political questions of their time. And secondly, within India itself, the analysis of caste must be related to debates about other aspects of south Asian polity and social order, some of which, notably race and religion, came to acquire equal or greater prominence in so-called orientalist discourse.

It is true that, from the early nineteenth century, scholar-officials were turning increasingly to literate Brahmans and to the Brahmanised scribal and commercial populations who were coming into prominence across India. These groups were particularly sought after as learned informants and as providers of the sastric texts which the

---

[4] Ward 1817–20, III: 185; Crooke 1907: 91–2; Barstow 1985 [1928]: 69; Gunthorpe 1882: 2.

[5] The term orientalism is most widely associated with the work of Edward Said, who identified a wide range of past and contemporary Western thinkers with attitudes justifying or echoing colonial intellectual practices, especially those representing non-white peoples as irrational, violent, childlike, morally undeveloped, 'effeminated' and dangerously inclined towards extreme forms of belief and behaviour. For the Indian context, see Inden 1990.

Company's officers were coming to treat as authoritative sources on 'native' law and custom. Some of these were the same superior literate specialists described in Chapters 1 and 2. Such people's concern to retain the preferment they had achieved under previous regimes gave many of them an incentive to tell the colonial state that India was a land of age-old Brahmanical values, and that its inhabitants could be most effectively controlled by feeding their supposed reverence for hierarchical jati and varna principles.[6]

In some cases it clearly suited both the British authorities and their informants to disseminate a picture of Indian life which disregarded its instances of comparative openness and intellectual dynamism, and emphasised instead those conventions of caste and 'community' which made it appear static and rigidly Brahman-centred. David Washbrook has proposed this for the early colonial south, arguing that in the early nineteenth century Tamilnad's newly vulnerable landed elites found advantage in playing up claims of superior varna and jati origins in their dealings with the colonial judiciary. Both colonial judges and revenue officials had apparently come to see the use of prestigious Brahman and Vellala caste titles as evidence of authentically lordly origins, even though they were also aware that families of comparatively humble birth had acquired rights and property under the region's recently conquered warrior dynasts.[7]

These Madras officials did not see such instances of social mobility as signs of healthy Western-style individualism. On the contrary, they were worried about stability in what they saw as a dangerously volatile region, and believed that the country should be governed in alliance with its 'natural aristocracy'. Thus these superior Tamil landowners quickly found that British judges were more likely to abrogate their privileged revenue rights if these were represented as having been acquired in the recent past by known historic acts of purchase or endowment. It appears then that they learned to tell the courts that they should be allowed to keep their holdings simply because they were Brahmans or ancient Vellala lords of the land. In other words, these were Indians who probably had a perfectly clear idea about where their landholding rights had come from. Yet, in flat contradiction of the colonial state's pronouncements about the superiority of

---

[6] R. Frykenberg 'Company Circari' in Fox 1977: 117–64.
[7] Washbrook 1993.

its individualistic legal and political principles, they learned at this time that it paid to behave like ahistorical 'orientals' who believed in age-old corporate statuses and divinely mandated tradition, rather than individualistic principles of achievement and personal gain.[8]

For other regions too, it has been argued that India came to look like a traditional caste society because the British perceived and made it so. Put in these stark terms, this idea of caste as a colonial 'invention' is unpersuasive. The Tamil *mirasidar* landlords referred to above would certainly have wished the wider world to see them as Vellalas or Brahmans whatever the Madras judges did or thought; British colonial perceptions merely added a further dimension to these concerns. Elsewhere too, jati and varna norms had certainly become increasingly pervasive in earlier centuries even if they were not universally subscribed to at the time of the colonial conquest. Further-more, this view oversimplifies 'colonial' thinking, particularly re-garding Brahmans. Even in the later nineteenth century, when the colonial state's strategies of information-gathering became more spe-cialised and elaborate, supposedly reflecting standards of exactitude unknown to non-Europeans, British writers were not interested in caste to the exclusion of other features of Indian life. Most were uncertain about how to obtain and interpret the knowledge they sought, and did not see their findings as proof that the whole of India subscribed to a single ideology of hierarchical caste values.

Many nineteenth-century orientalists saw both priestly and secular Brahmans as an important but also pernicious force in the society, and were far from credulous about the reliability of the *pandits* and other literate specialists who informed them. And, far from defining all of Hindu India as a Brahman-revering caste society, Western writers regularly noted the prominence of anti-Brahmanical monk-renouncers in the areas they observed, as well as the conspicuousness of distinctly un-Brahmanised peoples and ways of life in many regions. Further-more, many officials commented on the conflicting views expressed by their various would-be informants, recognising particularly that Hindu and Muslim notables were often bitterly at odds in their attempts to represent regional ethnographic facts and 'traditions' to their new colonial patrons.

In reality then, British rule generated a remarkable quantity of

---

[8] Washbrook 1993.

statistical and analytical documentation in which references to caste featured very prominently, but did not create an all-powerful 'colonial' consensus about this or any other aspect of the society. Anyone moving from revenue records to judicial codes, local censuses and the descriptive writings of soldiers, missionaries and other quasi-official observers could meet the same people being represented and 'essentialised' in all sorts of guises, depending on what the commentators in a given region understood by such terms as caste, tribe, race, sect, nationality, religious community and occupation, or by the multitude of vernacular terms that were used as their rough equivalents.

This diversity remained in evidence even after mid-century when the comparatively uncoordinated efforts of earlier regional data-gatherers began to be supplanted by the launching of a whole host of mammoth all-India data surveys. These include the first series of Indian district *Gazetteers* (1869), the decennial all-India Census (from 1871), the provincial statistical reports (e.g. the twenty-volume *Statistical Account of Bengal*, 1875–7), the encyclopaedic *Tribes and Castes* surveys (from 1891), and all the other exercises in centralised enumeration and reportage which became the hallmarks of the Victorian Raj. For all their flaws and 'orientalist' bias, these works are worth taking seriously, not least because so many Indians found it useful to adapt their terms and concepts for their own purposes. This was particularly so from the later nineteenth century, when complex changes in the so-called public culture of the Raj led many politically active men to try to extend their regional prestige and influence by founding the 'modernising' voluntary organisations which came to be known as caste associations and caste reform movements.[9]

THE DIVERSITY OF ORIENTALISM AND THE COMPLEXITY OF THE 'OTHER'

The pronouncement of sweeping generalities about other people's 'essences' was not an invention of white men, or of the colonial state. For many centuries before the British conquest, Indians had been meeting outsiders who saw them as alien and exotic. In the eleventh century AD, the Arab traveller al-Biruni described Indian society in language which in some senses prefigured the writings of the

---

[9] On caste associations, see Chapters 4 and 6, below.

'essentialising' Victorian race theorists. Stressing India's 'exclusive attitudes' and 'laws of purity', al-Biruni declared, 'The Hindus believe that there is no country but theirs, no nation like theirs, no kings like theirs, no religion like theirs, no science like theirs. They are haughty, foolishly vain, self-conceited and stolid.'[10]

In later centuries Muslim writers still knew India as a land of varnas and jatis: 'Binavali is the son of Hiraman, a Kayastha. The Kayasthas are a tribe of the fourth cast [sic] which Brahman has created ...'[11] Mughal commentators, too, made much of the moral and physical essences which supposedly distinguished different Indian populations, disparaging the 'wild', black, dangerous Bhils and 'predatory' Kolis, and expressing qualified approval for others, as in the *Ain-i-akbari*'s account of the Gujarat pastoralists whom the Mughals knew as Ahirs: 'Cunning but hospitable, they will eat the food of the people of every caste, and are a handsome race.'[12] It was the Mughals who developed the technique of grading Indians by skin colour so that officials could record standardised descriptions of criminals, rebels and other trouble-makers. This system, which classifies people as being of fair, 'wheaten' (medium) or dark complexion, passed straight into colonial police practice; it was retained even after the adoption of finger-printing, and remained in use well into the post-Independence period.[13]

Thus the British were certainly not India's first data-hungry rulers. Much that was done in the nineteenth century to classify and aggregate Indians for official purposes was in line with the practices of earlier statecraft. In the sixteenth century, the Telugu-speaking migrant warriors who called themselves Nayakas were able to impose heightened forms of centralised tribute-taking on the realms they founded in the southern Tamil country. As commercial networks expanded in these areas, the Nayakas found that relatively tight jati affinities were developing among the more specialised occupational groups. This kind of cohesion was probably already in existence in certain parts of both north and south India among many urban artisans, fishermen,

---

[10] Quoted in K. N. Chaudhuri 'From the barbarian and the civilised to the dialectics of colour', p. 28, in Robb 1993: 22–48.

[11] Moshan Fani 1973: 233. This seventeenth-century Persian treatise on Indian religions gives prominence to *yogi* renouncer-ascetics.

[12] Khan (1965) *Mirat-i-Ahmadi*: 797; Abu'l Fazl (1891) *Ain-i-Akbari* II: 248; see also Zimmermann's treatment of indigenous racial and environmental theories (1987).

[13] See Chapter 8 below on contemporary use of this terminology in newspaper matrimonial advertisements.

ritualists and specialised pollution-removers such as barbers and washermen. The Nayakas were therefore among the many expansive rulers who treated such groups as collective entities for the purposes of revenue collection.[14] The earliest British revenue surveys and population censuses used techniques and categories which were borrowed directly from these rulers and their successors, as in the case of the *dehazada* surveys which were village-by-village compilations of the size, assets and revenue liabilities of a given region's ethnic and occupational communities.[15]

These changes in economic and political power gave rise to the phenomenon of so-called caste headmanship, or at least gave greater definition to the guild-like forms of organisation and leadership which had apparently been common among traders and artisans in earlier centuries. Among merchants and other specialised populations in these warrior-ruled realms, certain individuals or lineages either had or were acquiring an exalted status as arbiters of craft or commercial standards, and seem to have been distinguished in ritual terms as well. These were the people whom the sixteenth- and seventeenth-century Nayaka lords were inclined to honour as chief notables or *talaivans*, vesting them with the authority of so-called caste headmanship in their home locales, and making them liable for the collection of cash revenue dues from the members of their particular community.[16] Their equivalents in north India were the notables known as *chaudhuris* who were given similar duties and honours under the Mughals and their successors. The East India Company ran its coastal enclaves in collaboration with these people.[17] Generations later there were still ethnographers and census enumerators who took the view that castes in general, or at least many non-agrarian castes, were self-regulating corporations which deferred to the authority of caste headmen and councils or *panchayats* of caste 'elders'.[18]

Why and how did Europeans start to use the term caste? The word's origins are usually said to be Iberian. In the sixteenth century the term *casta* (apparently derived from the Latin *castus*, chaste) was used in Portuguese and Spanish to mean species or breed in both

[14] Ludden 1985: 73.
[15] *Ibid.*: 225 n. 17; S. Bayly 1989: 81 n. 16.
[16] Ludden 1985.
[17] Pearson 1975.
[18] For example, Thurston 1909, II: 348, 367; and Cohn 'The census and objectification' in Cohn 1987: 234.

botany and animal husbandry; it seems though to correspond to the English word cast or caste which had the same meaning and apparently predates the British connection with India.[19] *Casta* came to be used in the Iberian New World colonies to refer to Amerindian clans and lineages. Since its botanical and zoological uses involved the concept of pure or true strains and breeds, in the Americas it also came to be applied by bloodline-conscious Iberian settlers to people of mixed white and non-white descent. In India *casta* was used by early European travellers as an ambiguous term for community, blood-line or birth-group. It appears in sixteenth-century Portuguese sources both as a term for religious denomination, that is the difference between 'Moor' (Muslim) and Hindu (or 'Gentoo'), as well as what we would now understand as jati and varna.[20]

By the mid-seventeenth century, Dutch and English writing on India had adopted these usages from the Portuguese, employing them with equal ambiguity and in conjunction with other imprecise terms including race, class, nation, sect and tribe. In the maritime trading ports, early travellers and officials met forms of social organisation which were apparently much influenced by Brahmanical conventions. This probably reflects the fact that the artisans and mobile commercial people with whom the East India Companies were involved in this period were finding ritual and practical advantage in embracing these 'traditional' caste forms. Describing life in the commercial port of Surat in 1689, the English traveller Ovington reports: 'Among the Bannians [*banias*: commercial caste groups] are reckoned 24 casts [*sic*], or Sects, who both refrain from an indiscriminate mixture in Marriages, and from eating together in common.'[21]

This account is couched in virtually the same language that was in use 200 years later in 'essentialising' colonial pronouncements about the 'effete' and 'unmanly' qualities of India's so-called 'non-martial races'.[22] Ovington insists too that people in a caste society are politically unfree, that caste is both a 'despotic' and an emasculating institution and a tool of 'tyrants'. Thus the 'innocent and obsequious' *banias* have a 'Horror of Blood', says Ovington; they are subjects of a 'Despotick Government [which] breaks their Spirits ... '; this com-

---

[19] Pitt-Rivers 1971; see also Dumont 1970: 21.
[20] Subrahmanyam 1990a: 328
[21] Ovington 1929 [1696]: 168
[22] See Nandy 1983.

bines with the torrid climate to 'weaken and effeminate their constitutions …' His account also stresses the conventions of strict ritual avoidance which he claims to have observed among the Surat *bania* groups, particularly their employment of pollution-removers ('Halalchors'), 'separated from all the rest of the Casts, as a thing Unclean'.[23]

Ovington's remarks obviously prefigure many of the so-called essentialising themes of later 'orientalist' scholarship. Yet they were produced almost a century before Britain's move from trade to dominion in Asia, and in an intellectual and political milieu with little or no resemblance to the England of high Victorian muscular Christianity and imperial cults of manliness. He and the other early Company chroniclers who commented on the supposed 'unmanliness' and political slavishness of Indians were far from being representatives of a 'hegemonic' colonial power, and it is therefore important to place these views and judgements in their contemporary intellectual context. In Ovington's day, English social commentators saw 'despotism' as a European evil. In the Protestant political theory of the time, it was the Church of Rome and the absolutist monarchies of Europe which imposed tyrannical despotism on freeborn Christians, deforming their characters and making them 'womanish' and slavelike. In the travel writing of this period, current debates about polity, despotism and the English constitution were regularly transposed to the Indian setting. This certainly provided later memorialists with ideas that were applied to the circumstances of full-scale empire, but in their own time they cannot be seen as tools being fashioned for explicitly colonial purposes.[24]

By the early eighteenth century, the European commercial enclaves were places where local conditions of trade and social organisation gave foreign commentators very diverse experiences of caste. In the south, representatives of the European trading companies were struck by what they understood to be a deep and contentious division between castes of the so-called left-hand and right-hand (*idangai* and *valangai*). European traders and officials found themselves being drawn into violent conflicts between bodies of artisans, traders and affiliated labouring people who had come to group themselves into these paired multi-jati alliances. These confrontations took the form of

[23] Ovington 1929 [1696]: 163–4, 223.
[24] Compare Bernier 1914; see Peabody 1996 on Tod's Rajput study as an intended contribution to debate on European feudalism; also Kuper 1988.

battles over deceptively trivial matters of ceremonial rank or temple 'honours'. In Madras and other European trading centres, representatives of the European companies reported at length on these conflicts, often compiling extensive listings of the rights and 'honours' which their adjudicators had conferred on particular groups of their contending 'right'- or 'left'-hand clients and litigants.[25]

This left–right ideology was apparently unknown outside the Telugu and Tamil country, and it had virtually disappeared as a focus for so-called honours disputes by the mid-nineteenth century. It seems to have originated in the fluid commercial milieux of the sixteenth- and seventeenth-century Nayaka domains, as a response to changing opportunities for both the local specialist groups who dominated the left-hand groupings, and the long-distance migrant traders who called themselves 'people of the right hand'. European trading operations undoubtedly contributed to the flow of assets which the contending parties were fighting over, and which they were able to translate back and forth into gains and losses in the ritual sphere. But while the involvement of British and other Western adjudicators clearly made a significant difference to some of these disputes, Europeans can hardly be said to have invented any of this, or to have used their law-codes and ethnographies to try to perpetuate it as a 'divide and rule' tactic of the Raj.

CASTE AND THE INDIVIDUAL IN COMPANY-ERA REPORTAGE, 1790–1860

The late eighteenth century saw the production of the first Indian gazetteers in English, these being digests of reportage on topography, economic life and the physical environment, together with accounts of certain regions' political and social landscape.[26] These volumes were partly modelled on the great encyclopaedic Mughal surveys, especially the *Ain-i-akbari*. At the same time they were part of the ever-growing British and European drive to subject all known phenomena of the human and natural world to the gaze of the fact-seeking explorer, naturalist and investigative scientist. The growth of empire was closely

---

[25] For example, Madras Board of Revenue Proceedings vol. 838, 11 November 1819, no. 60–2, pp. 9937–51. See Beck 1972; Appadurai 1974; Mines 1984; Subrahmanyam 1990a: 329; Brimnes 1996.

[26] K. Jones 'Religious identity and the British census' in Barrier 1981: 77; Scholberg 1970.

linked to these activities, though again it would be wrong to reduce all aspects of this period's pre-Rebellion map-making, specimen-collecting and ethnographic writing to an assertion of colonial relationships.

The compilers of the early anglophone gazetteers certainly did not see all Indians as being equally 'Brahmanised' or castelike in the modern sense. Most used the terms caste, tribe, sect and nation interchangeably; such usages often signalled no more than that the groups being described possessed some bond of affinity in the writer's eyes, often of a dangerously conspiratorial or 'criminal' nature, and frequently underpinned by ritualistic or occult attachments. Some of these 'tribes' or 'sects' were clearly thought of by early Western commentators as being part of a ranked 'Brahmanical' order of castes. Others definitely were not, and there is often very little emphasis on rules of food avoidance or other aspects of ritualised purity and pollution concepts in these discussions of caste. It is often unclear in these accounts whether the ties that are held to unite such armed 'predator' peoples as 'Kolis' and 'Bhuddicks' are to be understood as permanent, inherited identities such as we would now associate with jati and varna. Many of the warlike groups which particularly concern these authors were apparently regarded as Pindari-like 'gangs' formed by voluntary self-recruitment, though these were clearly thought to be capable of becoming permanent hereditary attachments over time.[27]

Thus, what these early orientalists saw as caste implied a dangerous capacity for strong and dynamic people from India's 'lawless' regions to form menacing 'combinations' and conspiratorial alliances with one another at will. This is not a picture of passive or 'effeminated' slaves of Brahmanical tradition, even though Brahmanical principles are sometimes thought of as reinforcing such ties and statuses. In Kathiawar, says Walter Hamilton, author of the *East-India Gazetteer* (first published 1815), the 'Catties' (Kallar-like upland arms-bearers from Kathiawar) and 'many other tribes calling themselves Hindoos' have only 'very slender' claims to be considered 'within the Brahmi-nical pale'; their tenets 'with respect to purity and impurity [are] by no means rigid ... '.[28]

This was the era of the Company's confrontation with the many

<hr />

[27] Hamilton 1828, I: 140; Forbes 1813, II: 105.
[28] Hamilton 1828, I: 598.

hinterland realms and peoples whose unsettled ways and complex layered schemes of political authority were seen by its officials as a danger and challenge to the new regime's shaky sovereignty. Not surprisingly then, the key theme of this period's ethnographic writing was order and polity. The picture of 'caste' that emerges in these sources is very different from the accounts of seventeenth-century commercial enclaves like Surat, and makes much more of individual will and conspiratorial 'intrigue' than it does of established orders of rank and precedence.

As was seen in Chapter 2, when the power and status of Brahmans were discussed in the early stages of the Company's political expansion, there was a strong emphasis on the lessons to be learned from the allegedly oppressive, unnatural and corrupting experience of 'Brahman government' in the Maratha country.[29] Evangelical Protestant missionaries took up this theme of Brahman tyranny as a means of attacking Sir William Jones and the other eighteenth- and early nineteenth-century scholar-officials who had ascribed 'purity' and 'sublimity' to ancient Hinduism. The influential four-volume polemic by the Rev. William Ward (publ. 1817–20) characterised Hindu faith as a 'fabric of superstitions' concocted by Brahmans, 'the most complete system of absolute oppression that perhaps ever existed'.[30]

Christian polemics like Ward's were clearly a major if unacknowledged source for later academic theorists, including those modern anthropologists who came to regard the Brahman as arbiter and moral centre of the Hindu social order. Ward actually anticipates Dumont's position on the radical subordination or encompassment of kingly power by Brahmanical authority: the 'Hindoo system', he says, is 'wholly the work of bramhuns [sic]' who had 'placed themselves above kings in honour, and laid the whole nation prostrate at their feet'.[31] This vision of immoral Brahman despotism clearly drew on popular English Protestant mythology of a priest-ridden, tyrannised papist Europe awaiting liberation by the triumph of the Reformation spirit. Beneficent British rule, said Ward, had already been inducing some 'degraded' lower-caste Hindus to throw off their 'bramhinical fetters' [sic].[32] Thus, like the debunkers of Maratha 'Brahman government',

[29] Malcolm 1832 [1972], I: 67–8; Preston 1989: 176.
[30] Ward 1817–20, III: 69
[31] Ibid.: 65.
[32] Ibid.

110

the arguments of Ward and his fellow early evangelicals focused on so-called Brahmanism as a corruption of free will: 'Like all other attempts to cramp the human intellect, and forcibly to restrain men within bounds which nature scorns to keep, this system [varna] ... has operated like the Chinese national shoe, it has rendered the whole nation cripples.'[33]

Non-missionary ethnographers in this period echoed some of these themes when they told their readers about armed raiders, predators and lawless 'tribes' whose ways had become inherently 'thievish' and 'refractory' in the Brahman-ruled domains of the Marathas. In this respect, Walter Hamilton's *Gazetteer* of 1828 is a far cry from the ostensibly confident overviews of a settled and safely domesticated India that emerge from the *Imperial Gazetteers* and other works of late nineteenth- and twentieth-century official scholarship. His approach is 'scientific' and often negative in tone, but unlike the missionaries, Hamilton's work does not characterise caste Hindus in general as submissive, slavish or 'effeminated'.

Wherever Hamilton goes he finds what he calls castes and sects whose nature he sees as having been collectively depraved by a combination of corrupting political and environmental forces. In the Agra region, he reports that the area's 'peculiar political relations' had engendered a 'backward' state of agriculture, and that the territory was inhabited by 'tribes long noted for their habits of rapine, such as the Mewatties and Buddicks ...'.[34] The feudatories of the Gaekwar's domains are 'predatory and piratical states'; the swamps, jungles and mountains south of the former Maratha dynastic capital at Baroda had been, until recent times, the haunt of 'many tribes of professed thieves, who preyed on each other and on the civilized districts ...'.[35] In Kathiawar, armed 'gracia' tribute-takers were still enlisting 'banditti of every caste and country'.[36] This, he said, was an area abounding in 'thieves' and 'criminals' from the plains. These people were able to assimilate themselves more or less at will into existing 'predator' populations of 'Grassias, Catties, Coolies, Bheels, and Mewassies'.[37] All these are a danger to order and good government, he says, but

---

[33] *Ibid.* By publishing Hindu texts, evangelicals hoped to end the Brahmans' supposed monopoly of religious knowledge. See Young 1981: 34–5.
[34] Hamilton 1828, I: 18.
[35] *Ibid.*: 603.
[36] *Ibid.*
[37] *Ibid.*: 604.

'[of] all the plunderers who formerly infested, and still, but in less degree, infest Gujerat, the most bloody and untameable are the Coolies [Kolis] ...'.[38]

Bengal too, according to Hamilton, was a land where 'dacoits and gang robbers' were still 'prominent'. In Hamilton's view, such propensities were to be ascribed 'to a general absence of the moral principle which applies to the Mahomedans as well as to the Hindoos ...'.[39] But unlike the evangelical Christians whose views became more widespread by mid-century, Hamilton did not portray either Hinduism or Islam as inherently immoral or corrupting. He does not call for mass conversion to Christianity, merely for 'exemplary punishments' and good laws. 'The great mass of Bengalese are certainly not constitutionally brutal or inexorable ...', he says.[40] Indeed, Hamilton insists, 'The genuine natives of this province never were a martial race, or disposed to a military life, for which, indeed, their want of personal strength and constitution almost incapacitates them ...'[41]

It is striking then that in this era when the three Presidency armies had become the basis of the Company's new political ascendancy, the distinction between so-called martial and non-martial races was already being made in colonial writing, some fifty years before the concept was built into the formal recruitment policies of the Indian Army.[42] Yet the context here is not so much assertive 'hegemony' as anxiety about the Company's uneven conquests and fragile political power. These arguments obviously reflected the practical and strategic concerns of British soldiers and revenue officials. At the same time, they do not indicate that Hamilton and his contemporaries saw India as a unique society where the prevalence of inflexible caste ideas made Indians radically unlike the peoples of the West. On the contrary, his arguments, like those of this period's other influential orientalists, had as their intellectual source the writings of those thinkers, best exemplified by the social theorists of the eighteenth-century Scottish Enlightenment, who were concerned to define the conditions under which the

[38] *Ibid.*
[39] *Ibid.*: 197.
[40] *Ibid.*
[41] *Ibid.*: 205. Compare Browne's characterisation (1788: 64) of Bengalis as a non-'martial' people.
[42] The writings and remarkable ethnographic paintings of James and William Fraser also played a major role in the formation of nineteenth-century martial race theories, particularly with respect to the Gurkhas. See Archer and Falk 1989; also Omissi 1994; Fox 1985; Peers 1991.

human character could attain the highest state of civilised virtue. This was equated with the formation of an ordered and beneficent polity in which rights and liberties were preserved, commerce, property and inheritance secured, and despotic power held at bay.

One of the great themes of these Scottish Enlightenment commentators was the importance of physical environment in the shaping of 'civilised' political institutions. Hamilton and his contemporaries were strongly influenced by this intellectual tradition, as can be seen in their reports on the dangers they perceived in zones of undomesticated Indian hill and jungle terrain, and on the moral and physical contrasts between the people they thought of as freedom-loving martial uplanders and feeble or non-'martial' lowlanders.

By the mid-nineteenth century, these preoccupations with polity and environmental typologies were being subsumed into debates about the moral and political meanings of race (see below, pp. 126–38). But for all its relevance to the Company's strategic problems, and its obvious prefiguring of later orientalist themes, this remained a very incoherent body of so-called colonial knowledge. The understanding of caste that prevailed in the earlier nineteenth century was far from being the core of anyone's ideas about how to govern or tax the peoples of the subcontinent. Few if any of the early orientalists were concerned to instruct British officials in the running or indeed the fabrication of a colonial 'caste society'. On the contrary, the principal concerns of these writings were largely outside the world of empire, with the same interest in the mapping of human essences being displayed in an enormous range of early and mid-nineteenth-century works which had little or nothing to do with the governance of colonial subjects.

In particular, the European travel writings of such radical political commentators as Richard Cobden (1804–65) are full of references to the evils of misgovernment, and the thievish races, martial tribes and lawless *banditti* who thrive in lax or tyrannical realms. But the so-called races and tribes being anatomised in these accounts are to be found in eastern and southern Europe and the Ottoman lands; few if any connections are made with the strategies of extra-European colonialism.[43] Even in the case of data-collection within the Asian empire itself, until well into the nineteenth century what Europeans

---

[43] Taylor 1994: 185.

thought they understood about India was a product of piecemeal and very disparate forms of knowledge-gathering. The far-reaching linguistic discoveries of William Jones and his contemporaries actually emphasised cultural and historic kinship between the cultures of Europe and south Asia, rather than the superiority of whites over all non-white peoples. In his essays for *Asiatick Researches* and other learned 'orientalist' journals, Jones astounded the learned world with his revelation that India's Sanskrit-derived languages were of the same Aryan or Indo-European root stock as those of Europe.[44]

Jones treated the vedic texts which he studied and translated as an historic record of the coming of Brahmanical religion to India. His writings about this material gave rise to the powerful and far-reaching myth of an ancient invasion of the subcontinent by 'tribes' of the so-called Aryan race.[45] Jones saw these primordial Aryans as heroes of a great adventure of migration and conquest 'at the earliest dawn of history', bringing with them from their west Asian homeland the teachings of a divine law-giver, Manu. It was the teachings of this 'pure' and 'primeval' religion which introduced the fourfold varna scheme into India, Jones wrote. The mythical Manu was India's primordial legislator; it was he who had 'divided the people into four orders ... to which he assigned names unquestionably the same in their origin as those applied to the four primary classes of the Hindus ...'.[46] Linguistic kinship thus proved the historic 'racial' kinship of those who came to be identified with this legacy of shared Aryan or Indo-European migration, religion and political culture, both in Europe and in Asia.[47]

James Forbes, author of *Oriental Memoirs* (1813), built on Jones's claim that a linguistically defined race or nation of Aryans from west Asia had implanted in India the divinely sanctioned principles of the varna scheme. Forbes proposed further subdivisions into eighty-four 'classes or castes', each separated by rigid laws of endogamy, and each therefore differing from the other in 'features, dress and appearance,

---

[44] Jones 1807a, 1807b.
[45] Jones 1807b. See S. Bayly 1995; and Trautmann 1997, especially Chapter 2. Trautmann's valuable study appeared after the completion of this volume; while our approaches and conclusions are very different, it is gratifying to note that we both see ideas of race as having played a major role in India's intellectual history.
[46] Jones 1807a: 59.
[47] See S. Bayly 1995.

as much as if they were of different nations'.[48] Like other early orientalists, Forbes was an environmental determinist who believed that there were profound moral and intellectual differences between those 'castes' or 'tribes' who inhabited bracing temperate climates and those who resided in the subcontinent's hot and 'debilitating' tropical zones. He regarded the inhabitants of rugged Rajasthan as the ultimate specimens of environmentally shaped nobility, 'a noble race of Hindoos, divided into distinct tribes'.[49] The Rajputs' homeland evokes a comparison with Switzerland, that favoured milieu of the European Romantics: 'Like that once free and happy country [Switzerland]', Rajasthan 'may be considered, more than any other oriental region, the nurse of liberty and independence.'[50]

Forbes shared his contemporaries' widely held distrust of those 'castes' which he regarded as being of inherently 'gypsy-like', 'degenerate' and 'thievish' character.[51] In this form, Forbes too sees the Indian propensity to form 'conspiratorial' corporate units as a potential danger to legitimate order and civilisation. It is significant here that, like many later orientalists, Forbes treats ascetic corporations (sectarian *sanyasi* orders or bodies of 'fakirs') as castes, as in his reference to 'fakeers, or yogees, of the Senassee [sanyasi] tribe'. He also saw the Bengal region as a morally enfeebling environment, portraying its inhabitants as a perniciously Brahmanised people imbued with 'deeply rooted prejudices and attachments to *caste*' (his italics).[52]

For many other Western writers in this period, Malabar, lowland Bengal and other 'torrid' locales were regions where significant numbers of people did display a strict and 'unhealthy' concern with concepts of ritualised rank and purity. Yet, for all this insistence on the reality and perniciousness of certain forms or manifestations of 'caste', these publications did not stereotype all Indians as slavish Brahman-lovers to whom reason, individualism and the claims of higher moral allegiances were unknown. In the 1820s and 1830s, at a

---

[48] Forbes 1813, I: 60–1

[49] *Ibid.*, II: 258.

[50] *Ibid.*: 46. On the more widely known treatment of the Rajputs in the work of Tod, author of *Annals and Antiquities of Rajasthan*, see Peabody 1996.

[51] In Oldham 1876: 186, compare Jonathan Duncan's comments on 'Buddhiks' and 'gypsy-like' gangs of 'Dosadhs' (called 'a robber tribe of low caste Hindoos' by Oldham, p. 184). And see Richardson 1801.

[52] Forbes 1813, I: 68; *ibid.*, II: 8, 24.

time when the Company's frail regime was facing declining profits and widespread military challenges on its frontiers, the readers of these same orientalist journals could follow the debates about law, crime and punishment that were engaging judicial and revenue officers in both India and Ceylon. These included many contributions which were said to be by 'native judges' and other educated Asians. They arose from exercises like the surveys of 'native opinion' undertaken in 1806 and 1808 in Ceylon and south India to determine whether a system of trial by multi-caste jury should be adopted in the Company's law-courts.[53]

Far from reaching predictably 'orientalist' conclusions on this topic, these jurists did not argue that the 'native' mind was too caste-bound to embrace the individualist and egalitarian principles which they saw as inherent in the British jury system. Indeed, as far as criminal law was concerned, they argued that in this respect Asians were no different from Europeans. Regardless of faith or environment, it was 'elevating' to the 'moral and political character' to possess the right to be a juror, and to be tried by a jury of one's own 'countrymen'. An important essay published in 1836 in the *Journal of the Royal Asiatic Society* gave prominence to the views of an influential 'native' judicial officer who argued that the members of all 'respectable' castes were indeed capable of exercising individual judgement in legal cases.[54] This capacity for rational and individualistic thought was said to be found even among Shudras ('peasants' of so-called 'clean' caste), whose faculties had supposedly become 'enlightened' since the days of the ancient Brahmanical texts. There is the implication, however, that 'aboriginals' and untouchables were too 'unenlightened' for the mental and moral demands of jury service. What was being expressed here was thus an early formulation of the idea that it was natural for Indians to be ordered by jati and varna, and that this was compatible with good order so long as these caste affinities did not become 'deformed' or excessively Brahman-centred.

Even in the treatment of colonial India's most celebrated display of 'orientalism' – the supposed discovery and suppression of the Thug or

[53] Raz 1836: 244.

[54] The author (Raz 1836) was particularly dismissive of the view that Hindus were so devoted to immutable caste principles as to see only Brahmans as suitable to be made judges and jurors. (Of course, at this time the 'egalitarian' British system excluded both women and the poor from jury service.)

thuggee cult – the learned publications reach surprising conclusions in regard to caste.[55] In the 1830s the great theme in these highly coloured accounts of fanatical goddess-worshipping stranglers who supposedly waylaid travellers and murdered them for profit was that of polity deformed. The writers who claimed expertise on this topic insisted that no such horrors could have flourished in apparently safe and tranquil territories if the Company had not inherited the inadequacies of 'weak native governments' whose corrupt notables had long been in league with the Thugs, protecting the strangler 'gangs' from the laws of the Company and its client states, and sharing the spoils of their 'depredations'.[56]

It is notable that for at least twenty years before the mass trials and 'reformist' legislation of the 1830s, the learned journals had carried reports of occult conspiracies, dangerous criminal 'vagrants' and secret sects of 'hereditary murderers and plunderers' in a variety of Indian regions.[57] What was new in the late 1820s and 1830s was that the famous William Sleeman and his fellow Thug-finders were believed when they assimilated reports of what were probably many different forms of organised and unorganised violence into their vision of a single pan-Indian network of religiously informed 'atrocities'. These accounts certainly made much of the contrast between the rational white man and the fiendishly depraved 'oriental'. In this regard, they therefore prefigure the self-congratulation of those later scholar-officials who had so much to say in the wake of the Mutiny-Rebellion about the ever-present dangers that could threaten British interests in India, and about the role of the eternally vigilant intelligence-gatherer as a civiliser and guardian of empire.

But those colonial officers who believed in the reality of an organised pan-Indian Thug network were often highly ambivalent about its implications with regard to the meaning and importance of caste. As was noted above, a number of early British commentators were inclined to see India as a domain of menacing secret organisa-

---

[55] The colonial 'discovery' of *thuggee* has now come to be regarded as a high point in the development of demeaning 'orientalist' stereotypes in India. See Freitag 1985; Singha 1998: 168–228.

[56] Reynolds 1836: 200, 213. Hamilton's account (1828) contains themes associated with the more famous writings of Sleeman, including the claim that hereditary communities of robbers 'sanctified' their 'execrable deeds' by making offerings to the goddess Kali (Hamilton 1828, I: 605). Compare Tone 1799; and see Singha 1998: 168–228.

[57] Sherwood 1820: 251; also Richardson 1801; and Shakespear 1820 (from an account originally produced in 1816).

tions. These writers used the word caste (as well as such terms as sect, race and tribe) for almost any kind of network or association to which Indians gave their loyalty, often with the implication that these were potentially sinister and conspiratorial bonds of allegiance. Some officials were therefore inclined to define the Thugs as a fixed social or ethnic unit, that is, as the equivalent of an hereditary caste. This is consistent with the adoption of measures which allowed supposed Thugs to be convicted of criminality solely on the testimony of a so-called approver (a confessed Thug), who deposed that an accused person had either been initiated as a strangler or was the offspring of a Thug. In other words, this was a principle of guilt by virtue of blood, descent or association, rather than proven individual acts of criminality.[58]

By the end of the nineteenth century, this principle of guilt by collective genetic or social inheritance was extended very widely under the enactments of colonial India's notorious Criminal Tribes and Castes Acts (1871, 1911).[59] Yet even these draconian provisions were mediated by the idea that some people's shared criminal 'essences' could be expunged through so-called reclamation or rehabilitation. Here, as in other areas of so-called orientalist knowledge, British thinkers and policy-makers were simply inconsistent. Their thinking was particularly unclear about whether being a Thug, or indeed a member of any other caste, 'tribe' or ethnolinguistic unit, was to be understood as a function of inherent essences, or as involving at least some element of individual will and choice. Certainly in other areas of colonial law, Indians came to be treated as individuals to whom British-style rules of evidence and definitions of personal guilt and innocence did indeed apply, regardless of whatever caste or racial 'essence' they might be deemed to possess.

So Indians who subscribed to caste values were not defined by all orientalists as uncivilised, and 'caste society' was definitely not viewed by every British commentator as a domain of irrationality and disorder. Indeed in many accounts of the 'uncovering' of *thuggee*, what most alarms the commentators is the elaborate and ordered way in which the so-called strangler gangs were said to have operated. The really fearful part of this was the implication that Thugs somehow

---

[58] Singha 1998: 210.
[59] On the idea of an ineradicable 'blood taint' of inherited criminality, see Smith 1894. Also Nigam 1990; Radhakrishnan 1992; Yang 1985; Arnold 1986: 221, 227.

inverted the caste rules and proprieties that were beginning to be held up by Europeans as the hallmarks of virtue and normality in India. Thus, Lt Reynolds, one of a number of Company officers who claimed to have penetrated Thug bands in disguise, reported to the *Journal of the Royal Asiatic Society* that the Thugs who 'infested' the state of Hyderabad were generally of superior birth or arms-bearing background, with Brahmans, Rajputs, Sodhis, Ahirs and Kolis all mixing together and even recruiting well-born Muslims into this unholy 'free-masonry'.[60] One of their strategies of concealment, he claimed, was the use of aliases – Hindus using Muslim names and vice versa, and members of one caste using the titles of another.[61]

The implication here is that much of the horror of *thuggee* was this alleged perversion of the norms and markers of a proper, civilised order of caste communities. And in these revelations about peace and order unmasked as criminality, and faith perverted into fanaticism, one can certainly see emerging an identifiably 'orientalist' yearning for a safer and more stable India. This was a vision of a new and secure colonial milieu in which Indians behaved predictably and lawfully, according to the known proprieties set down in the white man's ever-growing catalogues of 'orientalist' knowledge.

CASTE AND THE LATER VICTORIAN DATA-COLLECTORS

By the end of the nineteenth century, the colonial authorities were in a very different position from those of their predecessors who had involved themselves in the collection of social and statistical data. From mid-century, the wider intellectual climate affecting the colonial data-collectors underwent important changes, most notably through the worldwide elevation of ethnology – the now-discredited science of race – to the status of an authoritative discipline attracting both Western and Asian adherents from almost every branch of the physical and human sciences.[62]

Within India itself, the shock of the 1857 Mutiny-Rebellion drove

---

[60] Reynolds 1836: 211.
[61] *Ibid.*: 203.
[62] See S. Bayly 1995; and see below, pp. 126–38. Race science has had a powerful and enduring intellectual impact in both China and Japan as well as India, Sri Lanka and other Asian societies.

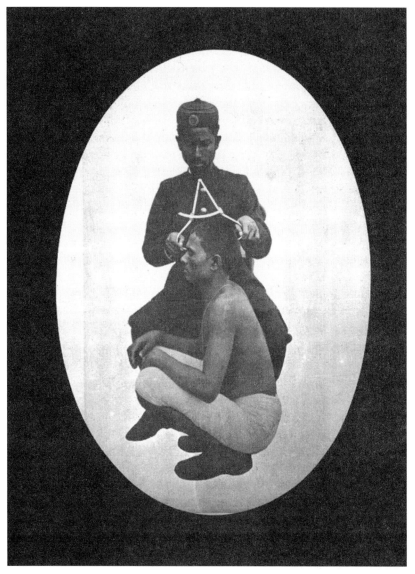

5. A uniformed Indian demonstrates techniques of anthropometric skull measurement. From a set of six lantern slides, probably used for university lectures on evolutionist race science.

both military and civil officials to expand and formalise their networks of control and surveillance, and to pursue the quest for social knowledge in ways which differed significantly from the practices of the Company era. Metropolitan developments and pressures were important here too. The abolition of the East India Company in 1858, and the creation of the many new government departments which ran the post-Mutiny Raj, brought closer Parliamentary scrutiny of Indian affairs, and with it a continuing demand for rigour and detail in the reporting of matters with a bearing on both security and finance.

The taste for ethnographic inquiry was also stimulated by new trends in the world of the intellect. In the colonies, as at home, formal schools of social and scientific thought were taking shape in the academic institutions; these were influential in the education of both Europeans and the growing numbers of Indians and other Asians who were being absorbed into the Empire's increasingly vigorous urban intelligentsias. Whether trained in law, medicine or administration, and even within the military and the missionary organisations, a Victorian professional's career prospects could be significantly advanced if he could claim that his knowledge was 'scientific' and in line with contemporary intellectual and technical trends. Thus, far from being remote from the intellectual ferment which was giving rise to the great debates of Victorian social and scientific theory, in the later nineteenth century there were both British officials and educated Indians for whom the expansion of education and publishing, and the growth and professionalisation of the human sciences, created the essential context for their involvement in 'orientalist' knowledge-seeking.[63]

Much was said about caste in this era of debate and administrative reconstruction, and many officials attached new importance to the old idea of so-called Brahmanical caste 'prejudices' as a force which was stronger and potentially more dangerous among some Indian peoples than others. The 1857 Rebellion had begun with an uprising of the Bengal Army's native infantrymen; the army's many critics now felt vindicated for the fears they had been expressing since the 1840s about the policy of making the Bengal regiments a preserve of lordly landed men. Most of these were Hindus who had been encouraged to lead a

---

[63] On the links between race science in the metropolis and the overseas empires, see Pinney 1988 and 1990b; compare Bell *et al.*, 1995.

life of Brahman-centred piety: this was seen in retrospect to have fostered conspiracy and 'sedition' in the ranks.[64] In the 1860s and 1870s there were attempts to find new and safer recruiting grounds, most notably in the Punjab and Nepal, which had long been perceived in colonial reportage as domains of comparatively 'casteless' martial uplanders. In other areas too, most notably in Rajasthan, there was a push to identify 'manly races' to recruit in place of the discredited Hindustan plainsmen who had dominated the pre-1857 Bengal Army. These concerns generated elaborate attempts to define which peoples, classes or 'races' possessed appropriate martial qualities, with an insistence on minimising the recruitment of 'Brahmanised' Indians, and an attempt to make the new regiments of supposedly casteless Sikhs, Gurkhas and other incomers conscious of shared heritage and identity.[65]

This period also brought the first timid moves to vest small groups of Indians with a limited measure of representative political power as members of the provincial legislative councils. And with the creation of India's first direct income tax, officials hoped to reduce the pressure on those 'peasant' groups who had supported the 1857 Rebellion.[66] These were all developments which pushed officials to record and publish more social data than ever before, and to subject a far wider range of Indians to formal techniques of classification and enumeration. As was noted above, the all-India Census was the key instrument here. In their different and often contradictory ways, the compilers of the decennial censuses treated the phenomena they knew as caste as fundamental to the lives of many if not all Indians, compiling data on the supposed differentials of rank and status between caste groups in ways which stimulated fierce debate among both Britons and Indians.[67]

There was also much 'essentialising' reportage in the monumental

---

[64] Jacob 1857; Hodgson 1857; Alavi 1995. And see below, Chapter 5.
[65] Omissi 1994; and see Chapter 2 note 7 above; also McMunn 1932.
[66] C. Bayly 1988: 195.
[67] The *Report* on the 1853 *Census of the North-Western Provinces* (Calcutta 1854) did not include figures on caste but recommended that future census operations should do so (p. 426). The NWP's 1881 Census placed 121 'tribes' and 'castes' into such general categories as 'casteless tribes', and 'landed', 'trading', 'military' and 'priestly' castes. Under H. H. Risley's direction, the 1901 all-India Census aroused fierce local controversies through its attempt to rank all named castes, and to assign them to a specific varna category; by 1911 Indians were said to believe that the purpose of the Census was not to count people but to determine their caste rank. Padmanabha 1981: 6–7; see also Conlon 1981.

119-volume series of Imperial Gazetteers which was produced under the direction of one of India's most influential scholar-officials, W. W. Hunter (1840–1900). Many other forms of statistical and analytical material emanated from government operations in arenas ranging from state-funded education to the administration of forests, fisheries, hospitals, jails and public works. These and other domains of state power were rapidly creating centralised bureaucracies at provincial and all-India level, and were recruiting ever larger numbers of literate Indians to collect and tabulate their data. Ever larger numbers of people were therefore familiarised with the terminology and conventions of these 'orientalist' enterprises.[68]

This period's profound though uneven economic changes were equally important in the making of these denser and more probing forms of orientalism. The take-off of commercial agriculture, the expansion of the roads, railways and steam-powered shipping networks, and the large-scale movement of labour into new areas of cash-crop production, all generated demands for data and official categorisation, with much discussion of which kinds of people were mentally and physiologically suitable for the Ceylon tea estates, the rubber plantations of Malaya, and the other overseas migration zones. As increasing numbers of Indians were brought into the cash nexus, there was a growing range of situations in which would-be wage workers, military recruits and many other seekers of new economic opportunities found it either necessary or desirable to present themselves to some outside authority or agency for purposes of formal classification. As Chapter 5 will show, it was often people of very low standing in conventional caste terms who made significant gains in these circumstances, even though this process of categorisation helped to strengthen and perpetuate their identification as 'untouchables'.

There were also problems of control in the expanding commercial and industrial towns, encouraging the police and other officials to devise mass surveillance techniques which emphasised corporate 'essentialisms'. In the countryside, colonial officials charged with the imposition or 'settlement' of standard rates of land revenue moved to abolish the revenue differentials which had formerly benefited such

---

[68] Penal establishments, notably the Andaman Islands, were bases for some of India's leading ethnological data-collectors. Among these were E. H. Man and M. V. Portman, whose photographic studies of women clamped into anthropometric skull-measuring calipers are among the most disturbing of all colonial 'orientalist' images. (See Plate 5.)

people as arms-bearers and the descendants of Brahman specialists recruited by pre-colonial rulers. This process generated much talk of tillers who were 'skilful' and productive by nature – the sturdy 'Jat', the 'manly' Kanbi 'race', the thrifty 'Shanar' – as opposed to declining parasitical 'Rajputs', 'thievish' Kallars, or Marava arms-bearers and 'feckless' hill and forest-dwelling 'aboriginals'.[69] These stereotypes both echoed and enhanced the differentiations which many Indians were now making along the lines described in the previous chapter, that is between the upright man of Brahman or merchant *ahimsa* values and the various aggressive, parasitical or 'uncivilised' peoples from whom they were now seeking to distinguish themselves.

None of these developments was wholly new, as was shown above in the discussion of early colonial legal debates.[70] But this typing of people by caste or caste-like statuses was made considerably more comprehensive during the later nineteenth century. Until the launching of the decennial all-India Census, it had never before officially been said that all Indians, rural and urban, elite and lowly, could or should be included in a single master exercise of tabulation which would identify every adult individual by both 'religion' and caste or so-called tribal 'community', as well as by occupation, age and sex.

Indeed the counting of women was one of the great novelties of this process: not until 1872 were women included as 'members' of individual castes by the compilers of local population statistics.[71] It may seem self-evident today that a woman born of a certain jati or 'sub-caste' should be regarded as a permanent 'member' of that caste or birth-group. This is, in fact, an issue on which modern anthropologists have been divided, particularly among those north Indians who are held to practise hypergamous 'upward' marriage. For these groups it is a man's caste identity that has generally been seen as comparatively fixed and stable, while that of an 'up' marrying bride may be seen as undergoing readjustment to match that of her new marital kin. Some of the more perceptive colonial commentators were also familiar with

---

[69] See, for example, Oldham 1876: 92; also Nesfield 1885: 15. Much material of this kind is also to be found in district-level Settlement Reports and provincial Revenue Administration Reports: see, for example, sources cited in Stokes 1978.

[70] On early 'tribal' studies see Pinney 1990b: 278. Pinney 1990a notes that the advent of photography brought a variety of surveys cataloguing Indians by 'community' and racial 'type', notably the Political and Secret Department's 1868–75 *People of India* project containing illustrated profiles of over 400 'races' and 'tribes'.

[71] This was first done in the 1872 Census of the North-Western Provinces: see *Census of British India 1881*, I: 53 (Plowden *Report*).

hypergamous marriage strategies, and were far from simplistic in their account of how this affected regional caste 'systems'.[72] Indeed this is one of the many instances of 'colonial' knowledge being richer and more nuanced than is sometimes thought. It is certainly not a case of fabricated ethnographic findings being somehow imposed on Indians in ways that then made them change their values or everyday actions.

At the same time, growing numbers of Indians acquired an interest in orientalist writings and statistical exercises, particularly the classified caste tables in the provincial Census reports. It certainly was an innovation for these publications to rank, standardise and cross-reference their caste listings on principles derived from Western zoology and botanical classification. These exercises purported to aggregate and rank supposedly comparable castes from different regions under a variety of general occupational headings with the aim of establishing who was superior to whom in any part of India by virtue of their supposed purity, occupational origins and collective moral worth.[73]

These were the bureaucratic operations which made it appear that colonial ethnographers regarded caste as a giant ladder of precedence defined by the logic of the four-varna scheme, with every jati a fixed unit possessing a known place and status which could be measured against that of any other caste group. Actually, not all scholar-officials identified Indians in terms of botanical or zoological specimens, and some at least strongly criticised these exercises. Many data-collectors were well aware that these tabulations were little more than a caricature of the complex and multi-faceted reality of caste.[74]

Yet Indians did have reason to take these listings seriously, most notably when they found the authorities using them for such purposes as deciding which communities were 'manly' enough to provide recruits for the colonial army.[75] Indeed the experience of caste is and

---

[72] Ibbetson 1916: 21–2; Oldham 1870, I: 43.

[73] The 1891 Census used such headings as Agricultural and Pastoral, Artisans and Village Menials, Professionals, and even Vagrants. This was the first Census to attempt an all-India index and classification scheme, with rankings based on local evidence of 'social precedence'. See *Census of India 1891*, Baines *Report*: 188.

[74] For example, the Punjab officials quoted by Ibbetson (1916: 32–5).

[75] *Census of India 1901*, I: 539 (Risley *Report*). Official ethnographers classed a variety of 'martial' groups on the basis of their 'community''s alleged actions during the 1857 Mutiny-Rebellion: see, for example, Ternan 1869: 15 on the Gujars ('a turbulent race ... [who] availed themselves of the disturbances of 1857 to resume their old predatory habits'). Also Omissi 1994: 30.

probably always has been shaped by what was done when rulers and their agents spoke with authority on matters of collective rank and 'essences'. By the end of the century, a growing array of official materials including military recruitment manuals, gazetteers and Census reports featured listings assigning people of particular title and background to a certain order or status ('ruling' or 'military' caste, for example, as opposed to 'scavengers' and 'lower village menials'), with either honourable or ignominious qualities being imputed to each group.

It is no wonder that many Indians took these matters seriously, becoming skilled in manipulating the Census lists, and taking pains to communicate their views and claims about these processes both to other Indians and to the colonial authorities. Indeed, by the later nineteenth century there were some Indians with appropriate scribal and statistical skills who launched their own caste enumeration projects, in some cases adapting colonial Census methods in order to supplement older forms of almanac data produced to popularise regional guru networks and holy places.[76] And as far as the official British Census was concerned, the debates and protests that ensued from the compiling of these listings involved both Indians and British scholar-officials. These exchanges undeniably gave new shape and emphasis to what we would now see as the everyday reality of caste.

CASTE AND THE RACE THEORISTS

From the mid-nineteenth century onwards, British ideas about caste cannot be fully understood without acknowledging the growing force of ethnological race science in the interpretation of social data, not just in India, but in both the West and the wider colonial world. By the end of the century, the emerging academic field of anthropology had become a crucial reference point in the writings of scholar-officials in India. Many were keen followers of the debates which engaged contributors to the new discipline's metropolitan publications, especially those like the *Journal of Anthropology*, the *Transactions of the Ethnological Society of London* and *The Anthropological Review* which were dominated by ethnologists.

---

[76] See Conlon 1977: 132; and see Chapter 9, below, on more recent twentieth-century caste directories.

At the same time, those claiming expertise on south Asian life and thought were active in the shaping of the new discipline's debates and modes of inquiry; by the end of the century, a number of major Indian cities contained flourishing anthropological societies. Both Indian and British writers contributed to these societies' journals. Indeed one of the earliest expressions by an Indian scholar of a nationalist political version of Aryan race theory appeared in 1863 in the *Transactions of the Ethnological Society of London*. This essay was by Gannender Mohun Tagore, professor of both Hindu law and Bengali language at University College, London (1861–5). In the essay, the author cites evidence from Strabo, Herodotus and the *Institutes* of Manu on the origins of 'Brahmanical polity' in ancient India (which he calls 'Aryavarta'), and contrasts the 'wild independence' of India's 'aboriginal tribes' with the 'superior genius' of the 'Aryan race', and the leading role which its builders of advanced political order had played in the 'progressive development' of all humanity.[77]

From these interactions between metropolitan and Indian concerns and institutions emerged two important but very different accounts of caste. Those, like Hunter, as well as the key figures of H. H. Risley (1851–1911) and his protégé Edgar Thurston, who were disciples of the French race theorist Topinard and his European followers, subsumed discussions of caste into theories of biologically determined race essences, and thereby played a critical role in the intellectual history of India and the Empire at large. Their great rivals were the material or occupational theorists led by the ethnographer and folklorist William Crooke (1848–1923), author of one of the most widely read provincial *Castes and Tribes* surveys, and such other influential scholar-officials as Denzil Ibbetson and E. A. H. Blunt. (See below, pp. 138–43.)

To start with the first of these two schools of thought – the racial understanding of caste – the teachings of the nineteenth-century race theorists are rightly abhorred today. Nevertheless, their ideas can still be discerned in the doctrines of many late twentieth-century ultra-nationalist movements both in the West and in the extra-European

---

[77] Tagore 1863. The term 'Aryavarta' was popularised by Hindu nationalists, and also by the Conservative peer Lord Ronaldshay (Governor of Bengal at the time of the 1919 Amritsar massacre). Ronaldshay's ethnological polemic *The Heart of Aryavarta* (1925) sounded dire warnings about the supposedly dangerous nature of India's nationalist political 'awakening'.

world, including those of south Asia's Hindu and Muslim ethnic supremacists.[78]

As has already been seen, references to race – and particularly the idea of ancient migrations by members of a primordial Aryan (or sometimes 'Hindu') 'race' or 'nation' of fair-skinned, vigorous freedom-lovers – featured in the writings of Sir William Jones and his contemporaries. But these eighteenth- and early nineteenth-century orientalists did not conceive of race in the physiological and evolutionary terms which were embraced by later ethnological theorists. With the rise of the new 'scientific' anthropology both within and beyond the Empire, older conventions and typologies were picked up and reshaped in a spirit of deep anxiety about matters which were certainly relevant to empire, but which were not confined to the exercise of power in any one colonial milieu. On the contrary, the evolutionary principles which had been widely embraced in Western countries from the mid-nineteenth century were rooted in a vision of all humanity as contestants in a ceaseless racial struggle. Ethnologists saw these conflicts as subject to merciless and impersonal scientific laws. Some observers of empire interpreted these laws to mean that Britain's global power might one day be superseded by the rise of 'fresher' and more 'vigorous' peoples or nations, meaning the Germans or the Japanese, or even Britain's so-called Aryan 'cousins' in India.[79]

From the mid-century, many of the most influential compilations of Indian ethnographic data were shaped by these ethnological perspectives.[80] This was a form of 'orientalism' which did not treat caste as the defining feature of history and social organisation for all Indians. On the contrary, followers of ethnology portrayed India as a composite social landscape in which only certain peoples had evolved historically in ways which left them 'shackled' by a hierarchical ideology of caste. Paradoxically these 'Brahmanised' Indians were identified by ethnologists as those who possessed superior 'Aryan' blood, meaning that

[78] See Béteille 1991b: 36–56. On race theory in China, see Dikotter 1992; on the Aryan myth and scientific race theory, see Stocking 1968, Poliakov 1974, Stepan 1982, Trautmann 1997 and Leopold 1974; for the use of 'Aryan' as an ethnolinguistic category in modern Indology, see Deshpande and Hook 1979. The assimilation of European racial theories by Indians, including nineteenth- and early twentieth-century Indian nationalists, is discussed in Chapter 4.

[79] Morris 1881; and see Knox 1863; Crawfurd 1863; Hunt 1863; also Metcalf 1995: 80–92.

[80] See *Census of India 1891*, Baines *Report*, ch. 5: 121–30.

they were supposedly descended from the same racial 'stock' as the white European, whose key ethnological endowment was the capacity to achieve 'nationhood'.[81]

Much was made of this idea that, in ethnological terms, so-called Aryan Indians were true though 'debased' kin of their British conquerors, with a common racial heritage of 'virility' and warlike energy.[82] Those who subscribed to these perspectives generally held that the development of caste ideologies had taken the 'Asiatic' branch of the 'Aryan family' into an evolutionary cul-de-sac. Yet according to many commentators, this was potentially reversible. As of the late nineteenth and early twentieth centuries, 'Aryan' caste Hindus were widely said by both Indian and British race theorists to be 'awaking' in evolutionary terms. For many, the proof of this was the formation of such organisations as the Indian National Congress and the Hindu 'revivalist' Arya Samaj, both of which were held to show that Indians were acquiring a sense of 'national' purpose which might ultimately supersede their supposedly divisive jati and varna affinities.[83]

When ethnologists studied caste, then, most of them were doing so as a subsidiary exercise in this supposedly higher and grander task of uncovering the evolutionary heritage of all humanity. Furthermore, even when they contributed to such 'orientalist' exercises as the Census and the Imperial Gazetteers, the race theorists did not necessarily see the entire Indian (or Hindu) population as part of an all-pervading 'caste system' which made all Indians radically inferior to their white colonial rulers.

It is true that Risley, who was the Empire's leading proponent of ethnology from the 1890s until his death in 1911, saw caste as a real factor in Indian life, an 'elemental force like gravitation or molecular attraction' that in his view gave order to the society and saved it from chaos.[84] Risley also anticipated the fieldwork methodologies and even some of the analytical insights of late twentieth-century anthropologists. Indeed there is a surprisingly modern ring to some of his observations. This can best be seen in his advocacy of detailed local kinship studies, on the basis of which he claimed to have found certain 'tribal' populations undergoing what in the 1960s came to be called

---

[81] For a comparable treatment of this theme, see Tagore 1863.
[82] S. Bayly 1995; compare Trautmann 1997: 172–8.
[83] See, for example, Ronaldshay 1925 and Ranade 1900: 278–9, 321.
[84] Risley 1908: 278; see Dirks 1992b: 69.

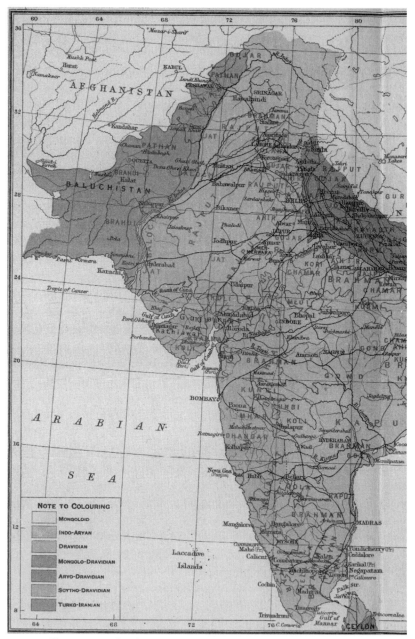

6. Map illustrating ethnologists' race and caste classifications. Based on a map
the *Atlas* volume of *The*

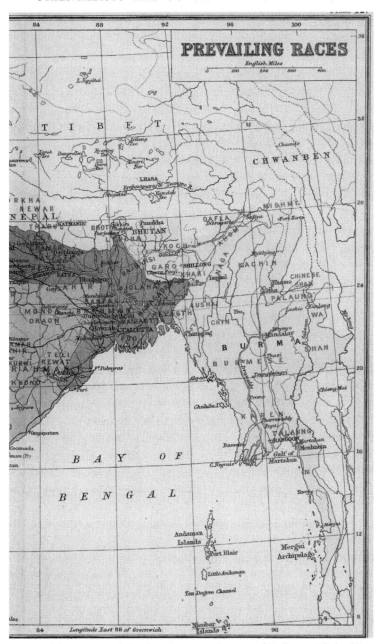

prepared by H. H. Risley for the 1901 Census of India: published in 1931 in *Imperial Gazetteer of India*.

'Sanskritisation', that is, the taking on of the attributes of a conventional ranked Hindu jati.[85]

Risley is best known for his scheme of hierarchical classification which divided Indians into seven racial 'types', with dark-skinned 'Dravidians' defined as the most 'primitive', and fair 'Indo-Aryans' the most ethnologically 'advanced'. His most widely quoted remark is his claim to have discovered an unfailing 'law' of caste, this being that 'the social status of . . . a particular group varies in inverse ratio to the mean relative width of their noses'.[86] As Census Commissioner for the 1901 Census of India and honorary director of the Ethnological Survey of the Indian Empire, Risley's chief priority was the placing of Indian ethnological research on what he called a 'proper' official footing. He conceived of grand schemes for the mapping and measurement of every racial 'type' and 'specimen' in the subcontinent, and shared with other ethnologists the fear that Britain was being outdone by Germany in the official sponsorship of race science.[87]

This was a worrying prospect since ethnology taught that the display of 'masterful' intellect was a mark of collective racial vigour, and thus a sign of a nation's capacity to dominate and civilise its supposed racial inferiors. Only the 'higher races' were fit for 'places of power' on the world stage.[88] Ethnological publications had been speculating since the 1860s about the comparative racial strengths of the British and their 'Teutonic' rivals. Risley argued that it would be proof that Britain was losing its lead as a dynamic and racially purposeful power if Britons failed to exploit India's unique potential as a field for ethnological research.[89]

Thus, to the more romantic and visionary followers of this discipline, the purpose of ethnological inquiry was far more than a matter

---

[85] Risley 1886: 76; also *Census of India 1901*, I, Risley *Report*: 508–9.

[86] *Census of India 1901*, I, Risley *Report*: 498, 500. The ethnologists' favoured technique of anthropometry classified human 'types' on the basis of physical characteristics derived from zoological taxonomies, particularly skull shape (long-headed/'dolicho-cephalic' or short-headed/'brachy-cephalic'). Some specialists also tested skin and eye colour; many advocated classifications based on measurements of nasal width and facial structures. On ethnological principles employed in the 1901 Census, see *ibid.*: 489–557; also Barkan 1992; Bates 1995; Banton and Harwood 1975.

[87] Risley 1894; compare Pike 1865–6: 185.

[88] John Beames, preface in Elliot 1869, I: viii–ix; Hunt 1863–4: 27–9.

[89] Pike 1865–6: 185; Washbrook 1993; Risley 1894. Compare Pinney 1988, 1990b; Crooke 1907: vi. For an illustration of ethnologists' 'orientalism' as applied to matters other than British imperial strategy, see the Hungarian traveller and race theorist Arminius Vambery (1865–6) on the 'idle' and 'fanatic' *dervish* (Muslim mystic).

of solving the colonial state's administrative and strategic problems. All peoples, said the advocates of race science, whether they were writing about Asians, Africans or Europeans, were predisposed to weakness or strength, subjugation or dominance, slavishness or freedom-loving individualism, on the basis of racial factors which could be most accurately mapped in physiological rather than linguistic or environmental terms. Race was perceived as a universal human endowment, and all humankind was subject to its forces of blood and inheritance.[90]

'Civilisation', however, was equated by ethnologists with a bent towards the creation of libertarian political institutions. Those who had achieved this 'civilised' state were thus to be seen as members of ethnologically 'advanced' races. In some cases, however, it was India's 'pre-Aryan aboriginals' and other supposedly 'free' and 'casteless' peoples who were thought to be 'virile' and dynamic in ethnological terms. Commentators with these views often drew racial conclusions from contemporary history, particularly from key moments of colonial crisis including the 1857 Mutiny-Rebellion and the 1855–7 insurrection of the 'tribal' Santal people of Bengal. Surprising though it may seem, these events told some ethnologists that the potential for true 'nationhood' could be discerned in the actions of these Indians, especially such 'pre-Aryan' people as the Santals and so-called Bediya 'gypsies' of Bengal. Both Indian and British ethnologists took this view. Yet another Bengali contributor to a London race science journal, Babu Rajendralala Mitra, says of the Bediya: 'attachment to their nationality is extreme ...; no Bediya has ever been known to denounce his race'.[91]

According to a number of writers, however, ethnological dynamism and receptiveness to 'civilising' influences were most notable in those cases where hill and forest 'aboriginals' had begun to embrace Christianity.[92] Thus religion too was widely regarded as an expression of racial endowments, with the faith of the modern 'enlightened'

---

[90] See the discussion of the treatment of caste, race, tribe and nationality in the *Census of India 1921*, Marten *Report*: 221, where the difference between 'a Parsi and a Maratha, a Pathan and a Telugu, a Bengali and a Burman, [and] a Latin and a Teuton' is held in each case to be a distinction of race.

[91] Walter Elliot 1868–9: 106–7, 114; Mitra 1867–9: 128. See also Campbell 1868–9, and Campbell n.d.

[92] Elliot 1868–9: 128; for a Christian evangelical's view of 'tribals' and their supposed resistance to 'Brahmanism', see Wilson 1843.

Christian being characterised as the apex of human moral evolution, and subjection to Brahmanical 'priestcraft' a sign of comparative evolutionary backwardness.[93] Above all, there were held to be eternal deep-seated antipathies between those who were supposedly higher on this scale of evolutionary attainment and those of inferior or 'debased' and 'degenerate' blood.[94] The ethnologist's tracing of racial interactions presumed a landscape of danger, competition and animosity, with all human history as a manifestation of these unforgiving ethnological principles. As understood by race theorists, the laws of human evolution allowed of no security for those who had made evolutionary 'advances', including those peoples who had established themselves as rulers and civilisers. Even those endowed with superior ethnological qualities were eternally vulnerable; the global 'struggle for mastery' allowed of no permanent winners or survivors, and degeneration or even annihilation were inescapable for even the fittest and most vigorous of racial groups.[95]

This vision of eternal evolutionary race war is explicitly endorsed in the writings of W. W. Hunter, one of the earliest exponents of the new anthropological methodologies within the Indian Civil Service.[96] Hunter's extravagantly written *Annals of Rural Bengal*, published in 1868, portrays the Bengal region as a living ethnological battleground. Its social order, he proclaimed, was shaped by a history of titanic warfare between ancient Sanskrit-speaking 'Aryans' and the rude 'aboriginal races' who had been overrun in the 'primitive time' by the bearers of superior 'Aryan civilisation'.[97]

Far from serving as a static display of conventional 'caste' relationships, Bengal's human 'specimens' provide Hunter with a picture of grim, degenerative racial catastrophe. 'Our earliest glimpses of the human family in India disclose two tribes of widely different origin, struggling for the mastery.'[98] According to Hunter, the incoming Aryans 'came of a conquering stock' and were imbued with 'that high

[93] Wake 1870.

[94] Knox 1863.

[95] Pick 1989; S. Bayly 1995.

[96] Hunter attained renown with the publication of *Annals of Rural Bengal*, written when he was Collector of the remote Bhirbhum district. He became India's first Director General of Statistics (1871) and chief editor of the first Imperial Gazetteers of India.

[97] Hunter 1897: 90, 3. Though unacknowledged by Hunter, G. M. Tagore's *TESL* essay of 1863 contains some strikingly similar formulations. See Morrison 1984.

[98] Hunter 1897: 89–90.

sense of nationality which burns in the hearts of a people who believe themselves the depositary of a divine revelation'.[99] In Bengal, however, the once-noble Aryan conquerors gradually lost out, becoming degenerate and contaminating their 'enlightened' faith with 'degrading superstitions' absorbed from what Hunter calls, revoltingly, the 'squat, black [aboriginal] races'.[100]

On this basis, Hunter, like many of his contemporaries, insisted that the Indian order of castes had been misperceived as an ancient and immutable system based on Hindu *religious* principles, and dividing the entire Indian population into the all-encompassing varnas of classic Indological theory.[101] Caste for Hunter was quite different: a 'cruel' but diverse and regionally specific creation of relatively recent *race* history. It appeared in India in two distinct forms. First, says Hunter, caste in its 'true' sense was a creation of Aryan settlers in Gangetic upper India, where in comparatively recent times the original 'fresh' and virile Aryan 'fighting tribes' had gradually subsided into degeneracy, becoming a society of 'mild-eyed philosophers' strolling aimlessly in their mango groves, creating pointlessly elaborate rituals, and wrangling over empty points of sectarian doctrine. This, for Hunter, was the counter-evolutionary development that produced caste in its 'true' Aryan form, that is, as a 'national code', 'disfiguring' the strengths of unified Aryan 'nationhood' and 'ruining' the 'Sanskrit people'.[102]

Secondly, and in sharp contrast to his idea of caste in this Upper Indian or 'Aryan' form, Hunter gives an account of caste in Bengal. This he sees as a region where what Europeans thought of as caste was actually a 'deformed' institution, one which was fundamentally different from the social norms created by hegemonic 'Aryans' in Hindustan. In Bengal, he wrote, what was called caste was actually a manifestation of race war, that is, a product of the opposition of 'high' and 'low' races, the 'conquerors and the conquered'. Far from representing a purely 'social' distinction between different ranks of the same superior 'Aryan', caste in Bengal was for Hunter an embodiment

---

[99] *Ibid.*: 90.

[100] *Ibid.*: 98. These views about the supposedly corrupting consequences of inter-racial contact were shared by ethnological generalisers like Robert Knox, who discerned the 'mysterious unextinguishable dislike of race to race' as the central principle of humankind's evolutionary history (Knox 1863: 248) and regarded it as a key task of the ethnologist to warn against racial 'hybridisation'.

[101] Hunter 1897: 96–7.

[102] *Ibid.*: 101, 97, 93–5.

of differentiation and irreconcilable revulsion between radically unlike races.[103] As a result, the emergence of what Hunter saw as an extreme ideology of stratification and ritual ranking between caste groups was to be explained in evolutionary racial terms. Vegetarianism and the other rules of a Bengali high 'caste' lifestyle reflected the 'higher' race's deep-seated abhorrence for the 'black-skinned, human-sacrificing, flesh-eating forest tribes'.[104]

Of course there is no intention here to give any credence to this repellent material. Yet it is important to see that for Hunter, Risley and their fellow race theorists, the point of such analysis was that *all* societies had an ethnological story to tell. In this story Indians were not all characterised in the same evolutionary terms. Race theorists did not refer to Indians and Europeans as members of two distinct or homogeneous races, and neither the 'Aryan' nor the non-'Aryan' Indian was dismissed by all race theorists as the evolutionary 'inferior' of all so-called Aryan whites.

Nor, even more importantly, was this ethnological story one in which caste occurs as the paramount institution of Indian life. Like Hunter, Darwin's champion, T. H. Huxley, writing in 1869, conceived of a racially diverse India in which the two predominant groupings were, yet again, strong, pale Aryans and small, dark, defeated Dravidians, the dispossessed ancestors of modern India's 'primitive' southern 'hill tribes'. Emphasising yet again the ethnologist's motif of universal race confrontation, these groups' supposed conflicts, migrations and inter-breeding had purportedly marked out the subcontinent into contentious historic battle zones of separate culture, language and racial 'type'.[105]

Huxley's contemporary, Walter Elliot, wrote in similar terms, subdividing the peoples of south India into no less than six distinct racial categories. In his view the bearers of a particular 'caste' title were never marked off from other groups by the physiological marks and endowments on which ethnologists relied to classify what they thought of as higher and lower 'types' and 'races'. 'Parias', he says, were sometimes 'fair and tall' with 'good' features; other members of

---

[103] *Ibid.*: 111.
[104] *Ibid.*: 131–4.
[105] Huxley 1868–9: 93, who held that some Dravidians 'mixed' with their Aryan conquerors, others being 'extirpated' or surviving in among the Deccan hills '... [remaining] like the Celts of Brittany and Wales, a fragmentary and dispossessed primitive population'. See also *Census of India 1901*, I, Risley *Report*: 508–9.

the same 'nation' were 'black and squat', with 'the lowest and most debased cast of countenance'.[106]

It should be noted then that Victorian race theorists generally subscribed to this view that Brahman-centred caste ideologies were absent or unimportant in the lives of significant numbers of Indians. Caste, as they saw it, was an evolutionary weapon adopted in the distant past by certain Indians, primarily the descendants of light-skinned superior Aryans who devised conventions of exclusion and ritual distance in a struggle to maintain the purity of their 'blood' and race in circumstances demanding extraordinary measures of ethno-logical boundary-making. All this was consistent with the strongly eugenicist overtones of ethnology, which taught that degeneration and racial decline were the inevitable consequence of 'miscegenation' between peoples of advanced and inferior racial 'stock'.

Elliot therefore assigns to a single racial category the Kurumba hill people of Malabar and other so-called 'simple' hunting and pastoral groups whom he sees as close racial kin of the Bengal Santals. For Elliot, these peoples' chief ethnological trait was that they were 'free and unfettered by caste', sharing a common descent from a single 'highly civilised' population with a marked ethnological taste for 'freedom'. Like Hunter, Elliot made much of these and other 'pre-Aryan' peoples, who were supposedly endowed with 'noble' and 'independent' racial traits and whom he saw as having been oppressed over many centuries by so-called Brahman tyranny.[107] Such views were widely reaffirmed after 1900 as offering 'scientific' justification for the claims of those who called themselves representatives of both 'non-Brahmanism' and the interests of so-called primordial or 'tribal' (Adi Dharm and Adi Dravida) peoples.

In contrast to other south Indians, whom he assigns to four separate categories of unfree, servile, predatory and 'civilised' people, Elliot asserts that the Kurumba were formerly 'independent princes' of Malabar; in the Carnatic the same people formed a 'federal commu-nity' of '24 states or castles'.[108] The sad modern plight of these once-strong warrior-pastoralists is for Elliot a demonstration of that key principle of the racial theorists, this being the notion of the decay or

---

[106] Elliot 1868–9: 103, 122.
[107] *Ibid.*: 104, 109, 128.
[108] *Ibid.*: 95, 108. James Wise (1883: 257) says much the same about the Dravidian 'tribe' from whom Bengal's 'Chandala' untouchables supposedly descended.

degeneration of races, a result of various phenomena including racial 'miscegenation' and the superseding of free, 'democratic' government by 'despotism'.[109]

This vision of free tribal republicanism is strikingly reminiscent of Henry Maine's discussion of primordial Indian 'village republics'. Elliot therefore applies to 'Dravidian' south India a form of evolutionary political analysis that was already being spelled out in the works of theorists who were concerned, not just with India, but with all societies in which particular legal and constitutional forms were regarded as markers of free 'citizenries' and 'republican' liberties, both in the past and among living 'primitives'.[110]

Other scholar-officials also distinguished between 'new' and 'old' Aryans', the 'old' being those whose institutions were 'less democratic' than those of later racial colonisers who supposedly shaped the societies of both north and south India. In the Punjab, especially, the first Aryan migrants were supposedly succeeded by waves of 'advancing Jats'. These 'robust and warlike' people were members of a 'fresher race' whose institutions were hailed for their superior ethnological qualities. 'In their institutions they are extremely democratic; every village is a perfect little republic.'[111]

THE MATERIAL OR OCCUPATIONAL INTERPRETATION OF CASTE

To turn now to the second of the two schools of thought mentioned above, this picture of 'fresh', vigorous and 'democratic' Jats had a strong impact on Denzil Ibbetson's portrayal of caste in the Punjab. Ibbetson too perceived Brahmans and Brahmanical standards of rank and hierarchy as a marginal feature of this regional society. On much else, however, materialists such as Ibbetson, Crooke, Blunt, John Nesfield and William Logan differed profoundly from those like Risley who saw race as the paramount factor in the analysis of caste.[112]

---

[109] Elliot 1868–9: 108–9; Knox 1863; Pick 1989.

[110] On Maine's attempts to identify common evolutionary patterns in the history of early Germanic and Hindu polities see Kuper 1991 and Macfarlane 1991.

[111] Campbell 1868–9: 137–8; see also Campbell n.d.: 82–3.

[112] Logan 1887; for Nesfield (1885) a caste's rank depended on whether its traditional occupation belonged to an 'advanced' or 'backward' stage of culture (p. 88); the Kalwar (distiller) was thus of higher rank than the Teli (oil-presser) because there was 'more skill and less dirt in the practice of his art' (p. 23). Compare Hodson 1937: 57–61.

Ibbetson's work, in particular, prefigures some of the most sophisticated insights of modern caste theorists, particularly in its insistence on diversity and historicity in the making of caste. Far from generalising about the whole of India as a uniform 'caste society', Ibbetson saw the Punjab as a highly distinctive environment in which the aspiring theorist of caste had to explain the distinctively non-'castelike' features of much of its rural population. He saw caste ideologies as having come to be manifested in highly varied ways in different regional settings, insisting on the dynamic and fluid nature of caste, and giving much emphasis to material and political factors in the shaping of these different versions of jati and varna.[113]

Although at some points Ibbetson's discussion echoes the standard orientalist clichés about lascivious Brahmans and 'degraded' Hindu 'ritualism', he moves onto another plane entirely in his account of the landowners, cultivators and pastoralists who constituted as much as half of the Punjab's population in the later nineteenth century. These people he describes as open and flexible in their deployment of such 'caste' names as Rajput, Jat, Meo, Gujar and Thakur; they are emphatically not passive, tyrannised victims of received 'Brahmanical' orthodoxies. To him, such titles as Jat and Rajput signalled distinctions of political power which were fluid and variable, and not closed units of hierarchical 'caste' identity. Human agency is preeminent at every stage in Ibbetson's analysis. Thus 'caste' as a Brahman's vision of the world, a vision emphasising rank, purity and what he calls 'artificial' criteria of lifestyle including vegetarianism and prohibitions on widow-marriage, is a known reference point to which these rural 'yeomen' may or may not defer, depending in part on the strength of the anti-Brahmanical Sikh and Muslim faiths in their home locales.[114]

For Ibbetson, then, both the Punjab and the northwest frontier regions were open societies where the difference between the 'Jat' and the 'Rajput' was not a matter of blood or fixed ethnological fact, nor a response to universal Brahman scriptural mandates inherited from the ancient past. In his view, such differentiations were a fluid representation of status as claimed by men of power. Furthermore, 'tribe' and not 'caste' was for Ibbetson the universal fact of rural life in the Punjab; Nesfield says much the same in his account of caste in the

---

[113] S. Bayly 1995: 204–13.
[114] Ibbetson 1916: 5–6, 11.

North Western Provinces.[115] In Ibbetson's work, the word tribe refers to affiliations such as Chauhan, Sial and Punwar, by which, he says, kin-based groups from within his rural 'yeoman' populations define themselves as superior holders of localised agrarian territories.

Ibbetson's emphasis is thus on these factual and visible realities of power and land control as opposed to the open and variable measurements of status which he regards as being embodied in the use of such 'caste' titles as Jat or Rajput. As far as Rajputs are concerned, the title Rajput was not a measurement of superior 'Aryan' blood as it was for the ethnologists; it was instead a reference to the indigenous 'occupational' facts of kingliness and power, and the bonds of affiliation and patronage through which a lord acknowledged the services of his retainers. There was nothing fixed or immutable about these identities: 'In former times, before caste distinctions had become crystallised, any tribe or family whose ancestor ... rose to royal rank became in time Rajput.' And in his own time, the process of shifting and realigning of 'caste' rank was 'going on daily around us'.[116]

With hindsight, it seems likely that the ideas of the ethnologists about human actions as expressions of immutable scientific laws and race essences would have sounded more persuasive to officials with experience of Bengal and the far south, rather than other provinces. This would be consistent with the more paternalist administrative traditions that had emerged in the Punjab and some parts of the Gangetic northwest. In particular, those involved in administering the Punjab canal colonies and comparable schemes of interventionist economic 'uplift' elsewhere would have had reason to be dubious about theories which appeared to deny agency and individual initiative to at least some Indians, especially to the 'sturdy peasants' and 'virile tribesmen' who were expected to make good, 'manly' soldiers, and to be receptive and energetic in their response to 'improving' administrative influence. At the same time, much of what Ibbetson says about caste in the Punjab suggests not idealistic fantasising, but a high degree of accuracy in his observations of Punjab society. Despite his use of dated 'colonial' language, and his inevitable dependence on observations made through the operations of colonial revenue settlement

---

[115] Nesfield 1885: 105–6.
[116] Ibbetson 1916: 7.

work, in his writing we really do see the beginnings of modern, regionally based Indian anthropology.

Furthermore, it is not surprising that these interpreters of caste have had a more enduring influence than their ethnological rivals. Ibbetson and his fellow believers in the occupational and material basis of caste were after all in tune with yet another key strand in the thinking of Western social theorists. This was the attempt in both liberal and emerging Marxist analysis to formulate economic understandings of the past – and also of the contemporary world – with growing importance attributed to modes of property-holding, as well as an interest in the interactions of labour and capital.[117]

Between Ibbetson and Risley, then, there certainly was no homogenising colonial 'consensus' on the subject of caste. In the writings of Ibbetson, and also in Crooke and Blunt, there is no message of doom and degeneration in regard to the familiar old theme of environmentally propitious regions – the Punjab hills, the arid open terrain of Rajasthan – where Rajputs, Jats and Pathans supposedly displayed the 'hardy', 'chivalrous' and individualist qualities of a 'tribal' social and political order. The influence of James Tod, the most influential early historian of the Rajput 'race', is particularly marked here, together with that of other early nineteenth-century commentators whose key point of reference was the theme of constitutional liberties, and the mapping of societies which were supposedly comparable to those from which the freedom-loving Briton had evolved.[118]

It was on this basis that Tod and his admirers had made much of the free-speaking, un-Brahmanised and egalitarian 'tribal' arms-bearers whom they believed to have flourished in zones of temperate terrain and climate. The influence of this environmental logic is apparent in the work of Crooke, Blunt and a number of other writers. In their works, when 'hardy' populations of this type can be identified, they

[117] Studies of European feudal law and land rights by the Victorian medievalists F. W. Maitland and P. G. Vinogradoff were a crucial influence here: see Diamond 1991. Marx himself regarded India as a cellular and fragmented society. Thus while he emphasised material rather than religious or ideological factors, he adhered to fairly conventional orientalist views in representing the colonial conquest and resulting Westernisation as the only social revolution that had ever taken place in the subcontinent.

[118] Peabody 1996; compare Blunt 1969: 24–5; also Balfour 1873 on the Rajputs, a 'brave people' 'of Aryan origin', 'delighting in war and bloodshed' (Balfour 1873, IV: R/p. 31). Nesfield however (1885: 17–18) rejects the idea of the Rajputs as descendants of 'Aryans'; he shares with Ibbetson a view of caste distinctions (as between Jats and Rajputs) as resulting from historic gains and losses of land and political power by both groups and individuals. See S. Bayly 1995: 208–11.

are not to be lumped in with weaker and 'unmanly' lowland peoples for whom caste constituted a very different and much more debilitating bond of social and moral adhesion, and who were therefore corruptible and submissive in the face of priestcraft and despotism. 'The Bengali and his cousin from Assam may be ... identified by their lanky stature ... and want of robustness. With them ... the intellectual have grown at the expense of the physical qualities, ... and they would in troubled times fall easy victims to the stronger races from the upper plains and hills.' For the great majority of plains-dwellers, '[a] powerful priesthood and the bondage of caste repress originality of thought and freedom of action'.[119]

The point, however, is that not all Indians were thought to be like this. 'In ... [Rajputana] the Rajputs have maintained their tribal system and freedom unimpaired [even after the expansion of Mughal, Maratha and British power] ... In a Rajput State the chief is the head of the clan by whom the country was settled. He is not a despot, but exercises a jurisdiction more or less limited over an aristocracy, the members of which are his kinsmen and connections ... This is not exactly feudalism, but something resembling it. It is the only really free constitution within the Empire ...'[120] 'Most ... observers of Rajputs and Jats ... consider them to be of the same stock ... The Jats are a most interesting people ... [Their] character seems to be largely the result of environment – they have grown grave and impassive like the great white oxen which they prize so dearly ... [The Jat] is a fine, manly fellow, and has special interest for us because his tribe supplies some of our best Sikh sepoys.'[121]

'[Rajputs are] ... liable to sudden outbreaks of passion ... [and a] tendency to panic on the battlefield, [with an] inability, as a result of their tribal system, to form a permanent combination against a public enemy ... These defects they share with most orientals, but, on the whole, they compare favourably with other races in the Indian Empire. There is much in their character and institutions which reminds us of the Gauls as pictured by Mommsen [in his *History of Rome* 1866] ...'[122]

[119] Crooke 1907: 9, 15. On the career and anti-establishment views of this maverick scholar-official, see the obituary by H. A. Rose in the journal *Folklore* 1923 (34): 382–5.
[120] Crooke 1907: 90–1.
[121] *Ibid.*: 93
[122] Crooke's introduction to Tod 1920, I: xxxviii.

It is clear then that even at their most arrogantly 'essentialising', these writers were discerning elements in India's social order which they found both admirable and alarming. Furthermore, their responses to this did not involve a stereotype of all Indians, or even all 'caste Hindus', as timid or unmanly.

For Ibbetson too, 'caste' differentials were therefore based on distinctions of occupation, individual achievement and political resources, rather than concepts of higher or lower 'types' and 'races'. His Indians are individuals, achievers of land, power and distinction by virtue of personal attainment and historically dynamic interactions, not passive recipients of race essences or binding cultural codes. And above all, he insisted that the standing of different groups in a particular locality was governed by political considerations, that is, the distinction between those who ruled and those who were politically 'subject'.[123]

It is notable that some of the most sophisticated official anthropology of the early twentieth century was therefore moving in the same direction in its analysis of Indian society as the 'progressive wing' of the Indian National Congress. This can further be seen in the similarity between the views of Sir Malcolm Darling (1880–1964), author of *The Punjab Peasant in Prosperity and Debt* (1925), and the leading Congress Socialists, including Jawaharlal Nehru. It is this emerging public debate about caste within the Indian intelligentsias which is the subject of the next chapter.

[123] Ibbetson 1916: 5. For an attempt to rehabilitate the racial understanding of caste see the Ethnographical reports in the *Census of India 1931* (I, sections A and B); while rejecting Risley's crude differentiation between descendants of 'pure' Aryan invaders and 'aboriginal' Dravidians, J. H. Hutton and his collaborator B. S. Guha of the Indian Zoological Survey tried to use this Census to reaffirm the value of race science, using elaborate anthropometric techniques to create what they saw as a definitive analysis of India's 'racial constitution'.

CHAPTER 4

CASTE AND THE MODERN NATION: INCUBUS OR ESSENCE?

INTRODUCTION

The orientalist writings described in Chapter 3 might be dismissed by some as pseudo-scientific 'imaginings' without relevance to the reality of the colonial experience. But we have already seen that the scholar-officials and their informants were not mere fantasists. However disagreeable to a modern reader, their pronouncements about caste and the other key colonial categories of race, blood and nationality became closely bound up with the operations of the state, together with other important arenas of Indian life. Furthermore, these writings helped to shape the ideologies of faith and nationhood that came to the fore in the final half-century of colonial rule.

Yet this was far from being a one-sided process. On the contrary, the Indians who joined and led these important cultural and political movements were impelled by complex intellectual initiatives of their own. This was apparent both in their appropriation and reformulation of contemporary racial theories and in their treatment of caste as a phenomenon to be critiqued or defended by India's aspiring nation-builders and religious purifiers. This indigenous side of the colonial experience must now be addressed. The debates which engaged Indian moralists and social reformers mirrored and in some cases anticipated the speculations of British scholar-officials. These Indian thinkers were decidedly not mere recipients of Western ideas. This chapter therefore explores the views aired in the subcontinent's emerging public arena, looking briefly at the early nineteenth century, but concentrating primarily on the period from the 1870s to the early 1930s. It will ask why so many Indian polemicists identified caste as a topic of vital concern for the modern nation, and will seek to identify the conceptual roots of these debates, as well as their intellectual and ideological consequences.

INDIAN VIEWS OF CASTE IN THE EARLY
COLONIAL PERIOD

Many of the key themes of late nineteenth- and early twentieth-century debates about caste were prefigured in the writings of Indian thinkers of a much earlier generation. The issue of whether caste was to be regarded as a virtuous or a destructive element of Indian life was raised at least indirectly in works produced in both Sanskrit and the vernacular languages by a wide array of early nineteenth-century literati. Many of these were *pandits*, that is, learned men with a background in the classical Hindu sciences and Sanskrit teaching traditions which had been promoted in both north and south India through the patronage of the Mughals and their eighteenth-century successors; most *pandits* were of Brahman origin. By the early decades of the nineteenth century, increasing numbers of these *pandits* were coming into contact with the polemical writings of evangelical Christian missionaries. In Calcutta, Banaras and other important court and pilgrimage towns, the Indian literati had also become familiar with Western orientalist scholar-officials, many of whom were respectful towards India's intellectual heritage, but fiercely outspoken in their denunciations of the so-called religious and social 'tyranny' exercised by both priestly and secular Brahmans.[1]

Some of these *pandits* applied the techniques of classical Sanskritic learned debate to a consideration of both evangelical and orientalist polemics. Thus, in response to a debate staged in 1804 at the East India Company's Fort William College in Calcutta, an English-educated scholar of Tamil origin cited the authority of classical sastric texts (Sanskrit writings propounding the ideology of *dharma*, correct conduct in caste society) to support arguments refuting a British writer's portrayal of the 'tyrannical' Brahman. This Tamil commentator also denounced the British for violating proper norms of good governance. The basis of his complaint was that Company officials did not pay sufficient heed to their Indian subordinates' caste origins in deciding on promotions, thus disregarding what he regarded as a reliable guide to merit and aptitude.[2]

This writer's views are close to notions of rebirth and *karma* (the

---

[1] C. Bayly 1996.
[2] *Ibid.*: 213.

consequences of past actions which bear fruit in subsequent existences), as expressed by teachers of the *Veda*-centred philosophical system known as Vedanta. For many centuries, proponents of these classical teachings had insisted on knowledge of the Vedas as a prerequisite to salvation (*moksha*, liberation from the cycle of rebirth into the physical world). In this tradition, those of non-twice-born birth (Shudras, untouchables and non-Hindu aliens or *mlecchas*) are automatically debarred from access to this 'salvic' knowledge. Lowly or non-twice-born birth is to be understood as an indication of unmeritorious conduct in past lives, hence a sign that such persons lack the appropriate aptitude (*adhikara*) for those ways of life for which people of superior varna are inherently qualified.[3] This notion of varna as a reflection of inherent karmic attainment and worth was subjected to much critical scrutiny and debate by Indian thinkers from the later nineteenth century onwards, as will be seen below in the discussion both of Vivekananda and other Hindu 'modernists' and 'revivalists', and of the many commentators who wrote in defence of 'traditional' dharmic or Brahmanical faith.[4]

Elsewhere too, Indian literati used similar learned techniques to counter the critical accounts of caste and Brahmanical authority which they encountered in Western orientalist writings. Of particular interest here is the work of Subaji Bapu, an astral expert (*jyotish*) who was based in Sehore in the princely state of Bhopal during the 1820s and 1830s.[5] This learned Maharashtrian was the protégé of Lancelot Wilkinson, one of several early orientalists who attempted to enlist 'native' intellectuals into educational schemes based on a goal of synthesis between Western and 'Oriental' learning.[6] Subaji antagonised more conservative *pandits* for praising the scientific and technological achievements of the West.[7] Nevertheless, in response to British writings attacking caste as a moral evil, Subaji composed treatises considering these anti-caste critiques against the background of his classical Sanskrit learning.

In these works, written in about 1839, Subaji presents divinity

[3] Young 1981: 162–3; Flood 1996: 232–49.

[4] For anthropological treatments of *karma* theory, see Kolenda 1964; Keyes and Daniel 1983.

[5] The identification of Subaji Bapu was made by the Sanskritist Richard Young: see Young 1981: 80–92; C. Bayly 1996: 260.

[6] C. Bayly 1996: 257–75.

[7] Young 1981: 82–6.

(*bhagwan*) as having created different physical environments for the world's different peoples, with a different system of faith and social order appropriate to each. Regarding India, Subaji's picture of the essence of Hinduism is consistent with Louis Dumont's. For Subaji, like Dumont, the system of spiritual teaching which is unique to India is one in which Brahmans and Brahmanical varna principles are the defining essence of faith and values.[8] Thus, according to Subaji, the presence of Brahmans and the active performance of Brahman ritual form the basis of Hindu faith and Hindu social order. Unlike the distant northerly regions of the globe where nights are long and temperatures too cold for proper daily ablutions, India, he says, is endowed with favourable environmental conditions which make it possible for Brahmans to exist. As a result, only in India can humans live the life of purity that those of superior varna may achieve through controlled diet, ritual cleansings, and other forms of dharmic correctness, thus equipping Brahmans to perform rituals and to act as gurus (preceptors) on behalf of the wider society.[9]

Such beneficent conditions are absent elsewhere, according to Subaji. In his view, this means that *mlecchas* (non-Aryans or non-Hindus) are to be seen as mono-caste; here he differed from those Hindu authorities who regarded non-Hindus as casteless and thus excluded from the ideals and benefits of the *varnasramadharma* world order (the code of correct living patterns appropriate to one's caste and life-stage).[10] For Subaji, the people of *mleccha* societies are all uniformly Shudras; a benevolent Creator had endowed such peoples with forms of faith and scripture through which they might in due course achieve salvation, but without the great boon of expert gurus and Brahman priests to chart a more direct path to enlightenment and ultimate release. It was on this basis that Subaji, like other early nineteenth-century *pandits*, used his knowledge of the Sanskrit learned sciences to refute claims emanating from both Christian missionaries and Western orientalists about the superiority of their faith and social values, which they represented as being rooted in traditions of casteless universalism.[11]

In addition to these learned defences of so-called 'Brahmanism', the

---

[8] *Ibid.*: 92.
[9] *Ibid.*
[10] *Ibid.*: 90–2.
[11] *Ibid.*: 91, 146.

arguments of later Indian 'modernists' who attacked aspects of varna and jati were also anticipated at this time in the works of important English-educated commentators whose writings have been much discussed in accounts of the emergence of so-called neo-Hinduism or Hindu 'revivalist' faith. The most prominent of these thinkers were Bengali intellectuals, most notably the celebrated Calcutta Brahman *litérateur* Raja Ram Mohun Roy (1772–1833) whose techniques of argumentation often, in fact, resembled those of more 'traditional' *pandit*-polemicists, especially in his insistence on analytical exploration of sastric texts and other Sanskrit writings.

Roy's prime targets were the forms of polytheistic Hindu worship which he saw as degenerate corruptions of the supposedly high classical Hinduism of earlier centuries. He was a particularly fierce critic of the *puranas*, that is, the traditions and mythological texts which glorify the personified gods of theistic Hinduism; these in his view were a major source of what he saw as the debased state of contemporary Hindu life. But in attacking this puranic heritage, Roy inevitably challenged the legitimacy of caste. The adherents of the important spiritual reform movement which he founded in 1828, the Brahmo Samaj (Society of the Supreme Being), saw themselves as advocates of a new, universal and casteless religion. Ironically, however, the Brahmo Samaj ultimately became itself an exclusive and largely endogamous (socially separate) community within Hinduism.[12]

CASTE DEBATES AND THE PUBLIC ARENA

From the later nineteenth century, all these ideas were given new impetus by their collision with two new forces in Indian life. The first of these was the encounter with notions of individual rights and nationhood which derived primarily from the writings of Western social theorists of the period. The second was the increasing self-confidence of the large and growing Indian intelligentsias which had been expanding rapidly since the 1850s.

The emergence of sisable and assertive intelligentsias was one of the great features of Asia's colonial societies. This was particularly true of India where, by the mid-nineteenth century, this broad category

[12] Jones 1989: 29–42, 164–7.

included perhaps half a million Indians of modest landholding, trade and service backgrounds who had acquired the necessary contacts and qualifications to make the leap into one of the 'modern' livelihoods. The most successful built careers in law, medicine, publishing, or the ever-expanding government service bureaucracies. Those of lesser attainments manned the shops and offices of the colonial cities. Even these humble clerks and storekeepers read the same periodicals and joined many of the same cultural and political organisations as the lawyers, teachers and middle-ranking civil servants who comprised the more advantaged upper layer of this educated minority.

Well before the First World War, such educated Indians routinely joined princes, landlords and other 'traditional' notables in the life of what can legitimately be described as an indigenous public arena. For members of the Bengal *bhadralok* and their counterparts elsewhere, the founding and support of colleges, libraries, debating societies and other 'modern' voluntary associations had become a permanent feature of colonial civic life. So too was involvement in Indian-run philanthropic bodies professing aims which ranged from the dissemination of so-called practical and scientific knowledge, to the 'rescue' of widows and prostitutes, the protection of cows and the dissemination of sacred texts.[13]

The activities of so-called caste associations and movements of pious renewal like the Arya Samaj provided yet more links between the anglophone city-dwellers and the much wider array of traders and other people of substance whom the British referred to as 'native gentlemen'. All these forms of collective action were nourished by the growth of a vigorous native press which drew even the non-literate into debates about forms of allegiance which were coming increasingly to be defined as those of community, race and nation.[14] And like their counterparts elsewhere in Asia, these members of the 'respectable' classes took a central role in framing the histories, law-codes and political creeds which told the wider world how to perceive the inherited moral essences of their homeland.

This is why it is important to explore the ideas of the many Indians who made their mark in controversies about the spiritual and political meanings of caste. When anglophone commentators expressed their

---

[13] S. Bayly 1999.
[14] Haynes 1991; C. Bayly 1996. On caste associations see below, p. 160; and Chapter 6.

views about faith, caste and nationhood as intersecting concerns of the modern 'public man', other people listened, especially when these pronouncements appeared in the columns of leading nationalist news-papers, or were uttered on important platforms like those of the big regional and pan-Indian social 'uplift' organisations. And, with the expansion of educational and economic opportunities, increasing numbers of Indians found themselves in a position to act on what they heard and read about these matters, much as in the more distant past, when the leading of a 'caste Hindu' life reflected both the impact of everyday practical experience and the encounter with 'essentialising' judgements made by rulers and savants. Furthermore, many echoes of these late nineteenth- and early twentieth-century debates are still apparent today in the ambivalent way in which educated Indians often speak and write about caste, and in the language of the populist political and social movements which will be discussed in the last three chapters of this volume.

Beginning in the late nineteenth century, controversies about whether caste was a degenerate social evil or an embodiment of progressive spirituality and nationhood were pursued both in the liberal anglophone journals, especially the *Indian Social Reformer*,[15] and in pronouncements by defenders of 'orthodox' Hindu tradition. Those who involved themselves in these debates included such major sage-polemicists as Swami Dayananda Saraswati, founder of the Arya Samaj, literally 'Aryan Society' (1875), and Swami Vivekananda, founder of the Ramakrishna Mission Movement (1897). Many other important social and political activists took part as well, most notably M. G. Ranade and other leaders of India's most influential pre-First World War 'reformist' voluntary association, the National Social Conference (see below, pp. 155–8).

The key contributors to these debates did not accept the existence of hierarchical jati and varna affinities as neutral facts of Indian ethnography. In their eyes, the values and solidarities to which they attached the English term 'caste' raised issues requiring 'public men' (and sometimes women) to take a stand in the rapidly proliferating printed media. These controversies were strongly influenced by the theories of race and nationality that were discussed in Chapter 3. Those who debated these issues saw themselves as promoters of a

---

[15] This influential journal was founded in 1890 (Heimsath 1964: 200).

boldly modern initiative which sprang from authentically Indian roots, and which they described as emanating from the vigour and race genius of the Hindu 'nation'. What they wrote was therefore an explicit challenge to those orientalists who saw caste as an immoral and atomising institution which had prevented Indians from acquiring the bond of a universal ethical code, thus debarring them from the achievement of nationhood.

A wide range of topics was taken up in these indigenous critiques of caste. These included the claims of Brahmans to possess unique sacred knowledge; the age of marriage and other intimate matters of corporate honour and sexual propriety; and the origin and moral meaning of untouchability. And in putting all these controversial matters before an impersonal audience of the 'enlightened', those who debated these issues were united in portraying their Indian homeland as a realm in which universal standards of reason and morality did indeed apply.

This vision of a united India endowed with a progressive public conscience was widely held by those who claimed to speak to and for the nation. Here there were obvious borrowings from European ethnological theory: many commentators took pains to show that India had reached the requisite evolutionary level to be considered a true nation, that is, a living entity possessing the capacity to identify its own strengths, and to remedy its own 'disabilities' and unhealthy 'sectional distinctions'.[16] Furthermore, by subjecting caste to this searching public scrutiny, these advocates of uplift and national renewal saw themselves as helping to create a new set of standards by which the 'modern' Hindu could expect to judge the conduct of those who shared the subcontinent's so-called 'national faith'.

There are two main issues to be be explored in this chapter. The first is the making of a modern 'Hindu' nation as an enterprise that bore directly on what these polemicists told their readers about caste. The second is the very striking consensus that was forged from these debates. Whatever position they reached as either 'traditionalists', 'liberal' reformists or a hybrid of the two, there was very considerable common ground among those who commented on these matters. Virtually all of these thinkers exalted ideals of purity, hierarchy and moral community as being both truly virtuous and truly Indian. As a result, the new, free and spiritually regenerated India which they

---

[16] *ISR* 7 Apr. 1912: 379.

visualised was, in almost every case, an India in which the forms and values of so-called traditional caste were to remain prominent and active, even if in a modified 'modern' form. This was true even in the case of the many public moralists who campaigned for 'modern' causes including education and other freedoms for women, as well as the 'uplift' of untouchables.

RACE, CASTE AND THE NATION

As was seen in Chapter 3, many Western race theorists were both impressed and alarmed by the growth and assertiveness of such organisations as the Hindu 'reformist' Arya Samaj. Indeed, by the late nineteenth century, large numbers of Britain's Asian subjects had come to speak and write about faith in ways which reflected the campaigns of a whole host of so-called religious revivalist organisations. It was largely through their influence that the terms Hinduism, Islam, Buddhism and Sikhism had all come to be used in indigenous speech and writing as racial, territorial and ethnic categories with fiercely polemical overtones. Their connotations were not neutral or passively descriptive; they referred to something that was much more far-reaching than 'religion' in the narrow sense in which old-style historians of religion once defined their subject.

For many Indian nationalists, then, there were pressing reasons to employ the terms Hindu and Hinduism to designate the qualities of history, blood and intangible essence or 'race genius' which were perceived as binding true Indians to their sacred motherland. Shared faith and spirituality were not the only component of this 'Hindu' identity, but they were certainly important. All over India, proponents of Hindu nationhood were seeking to codify those texts and bodies of pious obligation which could be regarded as an appropriate core of faith for the modern Hindu. Many who embraced such goals were well versed in the writings of those Western race theorists who saw India's Muslim and Christian conquerors as 'peoples of the Book' whose unity of faith had given them the will to subdue the divided and 'backward' Hindu.[17]

By the 1930s, this idea that true religion required binding codes and

---

[17] See Sen 1993: 31–2 on the legal theorist Henry Maine's view of the Brahmo Samaj, which for him was not a religion because it was not based on a formal scriptural code.

texts had acquired an even more assertive edge among many 'modernising' Hindu nationalists. According to Shiv Kishan Kaul, a leading proponent of so-called Aryan Hindu regeneration, the Hindu nation had been for too long stagnant and divided. To restore Hindu greatness, every Hindu must be supplied with what he called the fundamentals or 'essentials' of his faith. Once consolidated as a body of 'essential and fundamental truths', this modern rendering of the 'Aryan heritage' would enlighten the 'mass mind'. This enterprise was to be seen as rational, systematic and 'in harmony with the spirit of modern science'.[18] With a 'united and uniform faith', Hindus would acquire the power to rally, expand and conquer; this, he believed, was the lesson of faith allied to modernity to be learned from the examples of Soviet Russia, Fascist Italy and Nazi Germany. In 'the current history of the world', said Kaul, the force of faith had proved itself in these societies to be an ideal instrument in the making of progressive modern nationality:

Some of the most rational modern countries have perforce infused faith where reason was supreme so as to accelerate the reconstruction of society. Thus we see Bolshevism, Fascism and Nazism in their fullest force.[19]

This distinctly chilling view of Hinduism as a faith of science, power and 'modernity' had long-standing roots in both Western and indigenous theories of nationality and race. Like many of his contemporaries, Kaul was clearly familiar with European writings which portrayed the future of humankind as a Darwinian 'struggle for mastery' between greater and lesser races and nations, with the weak marked for extinction by their qualities of moral, physical and cultural backwardness. This had led him, like many other theorists of Indian racial supremacy, to try to meet this challenge by proclaiming the greatness and vitality of Hinduism. This in turn meant that India's Hindu heritage had to be represented as something more than an array of sacred texts and cult beliefs.[20]

Kaul's apparent sympathy for authoritarian models of the nation-state clearly set him apart from such important thinkers as the Bengali poet Rabindranath Tagore (1861–1941) and the militant nationalist turned holy man Sri Aurobindo (born Aurobindo Ghose,

---

[18] Kaul 1937: 56, 78, 82, 91, 130.
[19] *Ibid.*: 95.
[20] See Chapter 3, above; also Poliakov 1974; Leopold 1974; Thapar 1992; Stocking 1968.

1872–1950). Both Tagore and Aurobindo were concerned that the Indian state in the making should not be overcentralised, and would give due weight to the free interplay of local 'communities'.[21] Yet while these two thinkers were very unclear about where authority would reside within this web of 'community' allegiances, they did imply that caste institutions could be made to function as a benign underpinning of the future communitarian society. At the same time, however, there were considerable difficulties for all those who were seeking to write persuasively about Hinduism as a civilisation with its own eternal and binding essences of race and culture. What exactly was a Hindu? the theorists kept asking; what was the hallmark of this unique Hindu heritage that Indians were being asked to exalt and nurture?

From many of India's most influential thinkers the reply was that the Hindu was a person for whom the divinely mandated institution of caste was the central fact of social and spiritual life. For better or worse, the phenomenon of caste came to be regarded both by many Indian 'modernisers' and by European theorists as a defining feature of Hindu ethnicity, morality and even biology. As a result, those who debated the so-called modernisation of Hinduism from the late nineteenth century onwards, framed their vision of the Hindu heritage around these emotionally charged concepts of nation, caste and race.

NATIONALISTS AND 'ANTI-CASTE' THEORY

When India's aspiring nation-builders discussed their goals, they generally appealed to an impersonal 'public' audience which was supposed to be bound by common ties of race, culture and spirituality. Furthermore, among these thinkers there was wide agreement about the importance of probing and critiquing the phenomenon of caste. Yet those involved in this process were deeply divided about whether caste was good or bad for the modern Hindu, and whether its solidarities could be reshaped as a bond of unifying national imperatives. By the end of the nineteenth century three basic views of caste had emerged among Indian participants in these debates:

1. *The incubus view*: 'caste' in all its forms as a divisive and pernicious force, and a negation of nationhood;

---

[21] Bose 1997: 72–3.

2. *The 'golden chain' view*: 'caste' as varna – to be seen as an ideology of spiritual orders and moral affinities, and a potential basis for national regeneration;

3. *The idealised corporation view*: 'caste' as jati – to be seen as a concrete ethnographic fact of Indian life, a source of historic national strengths and organised self-improvement or 'uplift'.

Those who endorsed the first of these positions included a wide range of Indian commentators who identified themselves as reformists, a label which was extensively employed on public platforms and in the English-language press in the years before the First World War. The use of this term proclaimed the existence of a community or confraternity of the enlightened, working in harmony towards improvement and 'uplift' in the life of the nation. In this category were the adherents of the National Social Conference, an enterprise founded in 1887 by the Bombay High Court Judge M. G. Ranade (1842–1901) and the Madras civil servant R. Raghunatha Rao (1831–1912) with the aim of persuading Indians to 'modernise' their values and behaviour. Its adherents included jurists, academics and other eminent members of the anglophone intelligentsia. What was said on its platforms helped to define an ideal of enlightened social improvement which is still made much of in Indian public life today.[22]

One of the chief aims subscribed to by adherents of the Conference was to campaign against the 'evils' of caste. As will be seen below, particularly in the discussion of Justice Ranade's writings, this did not mean that all Conference adherents regarded *every* aspect of caste as an 'evil'. Nevertheless, Conference supporters were expected to endorse so-called uplift for untouchables, as well as the education of women, the banning of child marriages and the abolition of penitential seclusion for widows. These were all aims which raised painful questions about how the life of a reformist 'caste Hindu' could be made to reflect progressive social and national values. Furthermore, these were goals which assumed that the Indian nation was in effect a Hindu nation, or at least that matters which were of spiritual and moral concern to people who classed themselves as Hindus were the chief concern of the modern nation-builder.

---

[22] Heimsath 1964; on Ranade, a founder-member of the Indian National Congress, see Johnson 1973: 94 and Wolpert 1989: 37–46, 107–9; on Raghunatha Rao, a high-ranking official in the Madras Presidency administration and co-founder of the *Hindu* newspaper, see Rao 1908, Jones 1989: 177. Though a generous benefactor of Hindu pious foundations, Raghunatha Rao claimed sastric textual authority for his condemnation of the un-'Vedic' and un-'Aryan' practice of pre-pubescent marriage.

The National Social Conference had many vocal Indian opponents, among them the radical Maharashtrian B. G. Tilak (1856–1920). Tilak and other 'Extremist' members of the Indian National Congress led militant public agitations for *purna swaraj* or immediate home rule, but were deeply conservative in social and spiritual matters, viewing the reformist challenge to so-called caste evils as an attack on the national faith, and an affront to divinely mandated standards of decency and bodily purity. Indeed, until the First World War, that is, in the years before Gandhi pushed the Indian National Congress into taking a stance on such matters as the age of consent and the treatment of untouchables, it was spokesmen for the National Social Conference who aired topics which nationalist leaders held to be too divisive for discussion on Congress platforms. As a result, until well into the twentieth century it was left to the 'reformists' of the Social Conference to try to define what they called a national social philosophy for India at a time when nationhood was widely regarded, both in India and elsewhere, as an expression of collective moral, spiritual and racial essences.[23]

Many of the most outspoken Conference caste 'reformists' were steeped in the theories of contemporary Western ethnologists and eugenicists. Such leading Social Conference adherents as T. V. Vaswani therefore justified their stance against the so-called evils of caste on the basis of appeals to Aryan 'race genius'. This bond of race was extolled as the one force which could override 'sectional division' and lead the disparate peoples of the subcontinent to nationhood. In a speech to the first Sind Social Conference in 1909, Vaswani quoted both Carlyle and the Vedas as his inspiration as a nation-builder. He told his audience that, like all other advanced societies, India was heir to a unique essence or spiritual principle, and that the social reformist was the chief guardian and embodiment of this racial and cultural heritage. 'I have faith in the divine destiny of the Aryan race; I believe that every social reformer must be in tune with the genius of his nation.'[24]

Caste, Vaswani said, was an evil that was entirely alien to 'the true genius of our Race':

The social reformer seeks not to eliminate but to evolve the Idea immanent in the

[23] See McLane 1977; also Oman 1907: 99–100.
[24] *ISR* 18 Apr. 1909: 390.

history – the thought and culture and life and age-long aspirations – of the Hindu race ... We plead for reform which proceeds along lines of our national evolution and yet seeks to adapt our social life to the requirements of modern times.[25]

Many of Vaswani's reformist contemporaries, including Rao Bahadur M. Audinarayana Iyer and the Madras jurist C. Sankaran Nair (1857–1934), also called for the rooting out of what they called 'self-inflicted disabilities' from contemporary Hindu life. They too identified caste as a form of divisive prejudice which denied all the values of modern nationhood. In the interest of 'higher national efficiency', those sharing in the ideals of the National Social Conference were exhorted to fight the many 'prejudices and caste rules' which had hitherto shackled Hindus to practices which they deemed backward and pernicious, especially child marriage, and the imposition of harsh austerities on widows.[26]

The resolutions agreed on by the 1909 National Social Conference therefore summed up the most widely shared reformist position, which was that caste was a 'national' problem for the freedom-loving people of India to solve through their own will and initiative, and that its evil practices were to be attacked primarily in the domain of faith and morality. These goals were commonly expressed in a language which contained many echoes of Western eugenics and evolutionism.

Caste, said the essayists who commented on these resolutions, was an alien and slavish institution which had been created in relatively recent times under pernicious ethnological and historical circumstances. Caste values were the badge of a 'degraded' and unfree people, and a source of 'irksome and painful customs' which had rigidified a once free and open social order, 'trenching on the liberty of anterior times', and 'shackling' Indians within a 'prison house' of superstition and social oppression.[27] According to the polemicist G. K. Devadhar, over the centuries the institution of caste had sapped the 'natural vitality of the race ...' with the result that 'individual liberty' had been curtailed, 'individual consciousness' weakened and the 'national consciousness' disastrously enfeebled. 'A nation whose individuals are moral weaklings, social slaves and intellectual dwarfs [*sic*] [can] never

[25] *ISR* 18 Apr. 1909: 390. On the assimilation of Aryan race theories by other Indian nationalists, see Chowdhury-Sengupta 1995; and Jaffrelot 1995 and 1996.
[26] *ISR* 3 Jan 1909: 206; *ISR* 1 Nov 1908: 103; see Heimsath 1964; McLane 1977; Singh 1968; Natarajan 1959.
[27] *ISR* 3 Jan 1909: 206–9; *ISR* 15 Dec 1912: 184.

... make a strong and powerful nation intellectually, morally and spiritually.'[28]

These arguments raised the deeply problematic question of who it was that had imposed the 'fetters' of caste on the free and ethnologically vigorous Indians of the distant past. There were already troubling assertions about this by would-be leaders of the so-called non-Brahman castes or races. The most extreme versions of these views were disseminated after the First World War by such militant populists as E. V. Ramaswamy Naicker (1879–1973), founder in 1925 of south India's vehemently anti-'Aryan' Self Respect Movement (see Chapter 6, below). Even before the First World War, however, there were commentators whose arguments foreshadowed the key premise of the later non-Brahman ideologues, which was that there was not and never had been a single united Indian nation. On the contrary, the claim of so-called non-Brahmanism was that India's history had been dominated by a deep and permanent split between 'Aryan' tyrants and those who had allegedly been enslaved by this supposed race of foreign oppressors in ancient times, with the villains being the Brahman law-givers who had been cited as architects of the varna scheme in Western orientalist writing since the time of Sir William Jones. This view was emphatically refuted in the 'reformist' writings of such nationalists as Vaswani and Ranade. Caste, in their view, was to be seen as an affliction of the whole nation, and while there was widespread acceptance that caste had 'hindered popular progress and the growth of popular freedom', this weakness was not permanent; it was only a matter of time before India regained the capacity to develop strong and cohesive political institutions.[29]

This is what made 'caste reform' such a crucial matter to so many theorists of Indian nationhood. For those who regarded themselves as 'modernisers' and 'reformists', caste was backward and pernicious, a shameful obstacle to the moral and political regeneration of the nation, hence an inheritance of 'evil customs' requiring earnest soul-searching and the reformation of personal behaviour by all 'forward-looking' 'men of principle'.[30]

These appeals were not conceived as an unthinking echo of

[28] *ISR* 15 Dec 1912: 184.
[29] Ketkar 1909–11, I: 78–9, n. 3; on non-Brahmanism see Washbrook 1990; Barnett 1976; Irschick 1994: 202–3.
[30] *ISR* 3 Jan 1909: 206–7.

European writings on caste and nationhood, although they shared many of the same premises. But as we have seen, when nationalist thinkers like the early Social Conference leaders discussed caste, they tended to see the issues involved as being inseparably linked to an ideal of nationality which perceived Hinduism as an expression of national 'race genius', and not as a bond of sectarian or scriptural 'religion'. Thus Justice Ranade expressed his vision of India's march to nationhood as a form of racial predestination: 'I profess implicit faith in two articles of my creed. This country of ours is the true land of promise. This race of ours is the chosen race.'[31]

For other theorists too, caste was amenable to scientific analysis. Some portrayed it as a kind of biological infestation spreading from its Hindu hosts to the point that 'even Muslims' had succumbed to its 'contagion'.[32] Justice C. Sankaran Nair was one of the many 'practical social reformers' who expressed such views. This 'reformist''s calls for 'abolition of the existing caste system, emancipation of the depressed classes and ... [support for] every [other] healthy social movement' of the day were quoted approvingly in the *Indian Social Reformer* and other 'modernising' organs.

At the same time, the most striking feature of these campaigns is how much common ground the so-called reformists found with their socially conservative opponents. Virtually all of these thinkers exalted puritanical ideals of bodily containment and spiritual purity, whether they were for or against the key 'progressive' causes such as female education and widow remarriage. In the early 1900s, men like Justice C. Sankaran Nair, who were apparently making a revolutionary call for Indians to become egalitarian and casteless, were actually addressing their audiences in a language that managed simultaneously to invoke 'modern' eugenics and ethnology on the one hand, and the key principles of Brahamanical varna theory on the other. These reformists therefore invoked both science and Hindu piety in the attempt to claim that theirs was the true understanding of moral conduct for the race and nation. Far from being the highest and purest of values, they said, what was wrong with conventional Brahmanical codes was that they were not pure and moral enough. Indeed they were an obstacle to

---

[31] Quoted in Masselos 1974: 82.
[32] *ISR* 20 Sept 1908: 25, 28. This essay quotes H. H. Risley and endorses anthropometric measurement as a source of 'proof' about the supposed racial differences between Hindus and Muslims.

the purity enshrined in Brahmanical ideals: they told men that it was virtuous to take infant brides, thus inculcating lust; where they also banned the remarriage of widows, these codes were equally to be deplored for placing further sexual temptations in the path of the householder, thus inviting indecency and 'social impurity'.

These themes had all appeared many times before in past centuries in the teachings of the *bhakti* saint-hymnodists and other exemplars of anti-Brahmanical spiritual ideals. What was new in this period was that these ideas were being reformulated in the light of colonial science and administrative practice, and on platforms which were available to a new kind of anglophone intelligentsia. But it was still with an eye to a pious Hindu's understanding of purity and decency that the Conference's 'reformist' adherents urged the 'desirability of a gradual relaxation in the rigid rules of caste', and this aim was linked to other goals which were held to be essential to the regeneration of national life.[33]

CASTE CONFERENCES AND PROPONENTS OF CASTE UPLIFT: NEW EXPRESSIONS OF 'MODERNITY' IN INDIAN PUBLIC LIFE

All these were matters which had been fixed on by other avowedly reformist bodies over the preceding twenty to thirty years, most notably by the hundreds of so-called caste conferences and caste associations which had their heyday from the 1880s to the 1930s. These regional organisations claimed to speak as moral exemplars for certain named jati and varna groups; in most cases they involved people of scribal, trade and middle-status cultivating backgrounds. Some of these, like the north Indian Kayastha population, which generated a particularly vocal and combative series of rival caste associations, were of clean or superior status in Brahmanical terms; others, like the celebrated Tamilnad Shanar/Nadars, were regarded as very low in dharmic terms. It was this that gave small groups of educated and newly prosperous men good reason to claim that they spoke for communities which had been wrongly stigmatised as unclean and 'backward'.[34]

---

[33] *ISR* 3 Jan 1909: 212–13; 7 Apr 1912: 379–80; 14 Apr 1912: 390.
[34] Carroll 1978; Conlon 1977; Washbrook 1975; Hardgrave 1969.

The formation of these often shortlived and evanescent caste organisations was partly an expression of the 'modern' man's search for ways to show his vigour and respectability to the wider world. They were also a response to the all-India Census, and to the other worrying state operations which told Indians that their membership of a specific jati or varna was to be made a matter of public record, and that these findings might then be used in such important matters as military recruitment and the creation of electoral constituencies. The caste associations' ideas about how their 'communities' could achieve a creditable reputation in the wider world were therefore drawn from an uneasy synthesis of dharmic and European conventions, with an emphasis on norms of 'pure' behaviour which would have been acceptable both to a teetotal Brahman and to an apostle of strait-laced Victorian Christian proprieties.[35] These themes were echoed by the National Social Conference, whose delegates were from much the same background as the more 'reform'-minded of the caste associations' leaders. They too found it natural and 'modern' to express themselves as pro-temperance, and keenly sympathetic to 'the anti-nautch movement' (a campaign against 'lewd' female dance performances) as a means of attaining the goal of 'social purity' for India. The other 'purifying' advances which many caste associations championed were the remarriage of widows, the raising of the age of consent, and the abolition of temple prostitution.[36]

By 1909 the National Social Conference had also endorsed what it referred to as uplift for India's 'depressed classes', meaning primarily the so-called untouchables. This was an issue picked up from the repertoire of the Arya Samaj and certain of the other important Hindu 'revivalist' organisations which had been involving themselves in campaigns of religious conversion or *shuddhi* (literally 'purification') and so-called social uplift for low-caste groups as a means of restoring both the size and the ethnological vigour of the Hindu nation. This issue of how those of 'impure' origin were to be treated, both by the nation at large and by the reformist personally, remained the most

---

[35] Srinivas's term Sanskritisation captures important aspects of this, but as has been argued by Carroll and others, it does not fully convey the array of themes and strategies involved, notably both the influence of Western moral conventions, and the lordly varna norms popularised both before and during the colonial period, as was seen in Chapters 1 and 2.

[36] *ISR* 3 Jan 1909: 210; on other areas of controversy, notably debates about the permissibility of overseas travel for the 'twice-born', see, for example, Conlon 1977: 147–67.

problematic area of all in these debates about the meaning of caste for the Hindu nation.[37]

On this issue the Conference 'reformists' started from the premise that Indians did possess absolute standards of 'purity, utility [and] reason' against which to test their customary behaviour. The degradation of the 'depressed' was defined as a product of backward custom which did not bear examination in the light of civilised morality. What was needed was decisive 'public feeling' against 'the grossly unfair notion' of stigmatising the 'depressed' as degraded and untouchable.[38] But here too the reformist risked being vilified as an enemy of the nation and its Hindu faith. If there was indecency in proposing female education and widow marriage for people of 'good' blood, how much more shocking to tell pious and dharmically correct Hindus that they had moral and spiritual obligations to the 'lascivious', 'carrion-eating' Chamar or Holeya.

On this issue in particular then, many reformists emphasised all-embracing bonds of pious Hindu faith rather than scientific 'modernity'. In 1909, the Social Conference approved a resolution calling on their supporters to endorse the seeking out of so-called converts, meaning people of 'unclean' caste who had become adherents of Christianity, Islam and Sikhism, so that they could be 'readmitted' to their 'old faith'.[39] What was meant by 'old faith' was of course Hinduism, the 'true' faith of the Indian homeland. Here then 'reformists' were representing themselves as protectors of a truer and deeper Hinduism than that of narrow-minded 'caste elders' and other 'tradition-minded' authorities. It was 'caste-bound prejudice' which they defined as the great despoiler of Indian faith and nationhood, in this case through resistance to the readmission of much-needed returnees to the Hindu 'fold'. Furthermore, on this as on other points, 'reformists' were careful to say that their goals had sanction in the 'Sanatan Dharm' (literally 'the eternal religion') of the Vedas. In this they were clearly echoing the Brahmanical language which their readers would have recognised from the polemics of the many organisations which used this term *sanatan dharm* as a call to propagate 'orthodox' Brahmanical ritual and other expressions of Hindu faith in the modern world.[40]

[37] Jones 1976; *ISR* 3 Jan 1909: 212.
[38] *ISR* 3 Jan 1909: 211–12; 23 May 1909: 449.
[39] *ISR* 3 Jan 1909: 212–13.
[40] *ISR* 3 Jan 1909: 207.

HINDU NATIONALISTS AND THE DEFENCE
OF CASTE

As has already been seen, not all Hindu 'reformists' treated the solidarities of caste as a bar to national progress. The views summarised under the second of the three positions listed above (p. 155), that is, the 'golden chain' view (extolling caste as varna, an ideological bond of moral solidarities), were endorsed by thinkers from much the same English-speaking urban milieu as the anti-caste 'reformists'. But those at this end of the 'modernising' spectrum saw the nationalist's role as one of guardianship for a threatened but still glorious national culture.

These thinkers' calls for uplift and pan-Indian solidarity therefore invoked a much more militant vision of exclusive Hindu nationhood. They too were convinced that the phenomenon of caste raised 'public' issues for Indians to address in the quest for national purification and advancement, and thus they too spoke from impersonal platforms in the hope of creating what they called a new public feeling among their audience. These were also commentators who borrowed from the language of Western science and social theory. But their speeches and writings placed even greater emphasis on pride in race, blood and nationality, and so they were much less inclined towards piecemeal 'liberalisation' or 'Westernisation' of the social order. And while these anti-'reformists' too deplored certain features of caste in contemporary Indian social life, they insisted that caste in its true form was essential to the 'genius' of Hinduism, and was therefore something positive and uniquely Indian, an inheritance of high moral values from the national past.

For the thinkers who belong in this second category, caste in this 'true' sense was not divisive and pernicious, as was claimed by 'modernising' social reformers. On the contrary, these were cultural revivalists who rejected the 'reformist' view of varna as an affliction which had despoiled the liberties of a once-free people. The line taken by these far more conservative commentators was that the ancient ideology of varna was the product of a free people exercising dynamic political will.

One of the leading proponents of this view was Jogendra Nath Bhattacharya. Writing in 1896, Bhattacharya declared that the varna scheme had been forged as 'an act of large-hearted statesmanship' which had set up ideal models of conduct and morality for a diverse and conflict-prone population. Bhattacharya's book *Hindu Castes and Sects* was one of the first modern anthropological treatises to be produced by an Indian scholar. A graduate of Calcutta University, he acquired renown as president of the Bengal Brahman Sabha, a 'modern'-style caste association which claimed to represent the Bengal region's numerous and socially differentiated Brahman populations. He was also head of the Nadia College of Pandits, a survivor of several such institutions in the north Indian pilgrimage centres; the College purported to give authoritative judgements on matters of Hindu 'tradition'.

Bhattacharya was thus a prime example of the articulate 'modern man' who embraced assertive nationalist ideals, yet spoke from the platform of a 'modern' Hindu 'revivalist' organisation, not as a would-be caste reformer but as a passionate defender of established Brahmanical norms. Indeed, far from being a recipient of 'derivative' Western views and values, Bhattacharya's writings both echoed and reformulated older forms of learned debate and discourse. These were represented in the earlier part of the century by the many Hindu savants who countered the campaigns of evangelical missionaries by arguing that Christianity was a 'religion of trickery', and that the proper purposes of religion could only be accomplished on Indian soil by persons of appropriate varna.[41]

Bhattacharya's principal argument in defence of caste was the claim that, in ancient times, the creation of the human orders or varnas had brought great good to the peoples of the subcontinent: it had united them and taught them pious ideals, and it had provided the means of assimilating the 'foreign hordes' who had so often invaded the Hindu homeland.[42] Through the insights of India's ancient law-givers, Bhattacharya declared, the ideal of the learned Brahman had turned descendants of the early Aryan 'vedic singers' into 'one race under the name of Brahmans'. The 'several fighting clans' were similarly welded together around the valorous ideal of the Kshatriya, overcoming divisions and disparities to become 'one great family, under the name of Ksatriyas [*sic*] or Rajputs'.[43]

---

[41] See above, pp. 145–7; Young 1981.
[42] Bhattacharya 1896: 4.
[43] *Ibid.*: 6. As was seen in Chapter 3, these points are anticipated in G. M. Tagore's essay 'The Aryan polity' (Tagore 1863).

So, in the memorable phrase coined by Bhattacharya, caste in the form of the fourfold varna scheme was a 'golden chain' which Hindus had 'willingly placed on their necks, and which has fixed them to only that which is noble and praiseworthy'.[44] Therefore, far from being 'tyrannical' and 'cruel', caste had endowed Indians with selfless spiritual ideals and a concept of solidarity which had long united the subcontinent's separate 'races and clans'. According to Bhattacharya, these qualities had been apparent in the values of varna which had inspired Indians, including the leaders of the 1857 Rebellion, in the struggle against foreign rule.[45] Similar points were made by other Bengali thinkers of this period for whom caste was a path of virtue in a world of new and alarming disruptions to proper varna norms, and also to norms of 'proper' gender hierarchy.[46]

Bhattacharya's arguments had much in common with the published statements of Swami Vivekananda (1863–1902), arguably India's most important twentieth-century religious thinker. Vivekananda's pronouncements on caste are particularly noteworthy because his philosophy of national pride, social service and revived Hindu faith anticipated so much of Gandhi's thought. His writings condemned the oppressive treatment of so-called untouchables and other subordinate castes, but Vivekananda also echoed contemporary Western ethnological themes in his remarks about the natural differences of ability and character that separated persons of unlike varna.

Each caste has become, as it were, a separate racial element. If a man lives long enough in India, he will be able to tell from the features what caste a man belongs to. (*Works* VIII: 54)

Two different races mix and fuse, and out of them rises one strong distinct type. This tries to save itself from admixture, and here you see the beginning of caste. Look at the apple. The best specimens have been produced by crossing, but once crossed, we try to preserve the variety intact. (*Ibid.*: 274)

[Caste has its] bad side, [but] its benefits outweigh its disadvantages. (*Ibid.*: 242)

It is in the nature of society to form itself into groups ... Caste is a natural order; I can perform one duty in social life, and you another; you can govern a country, and I can mend a pair of old shoes, but that is no reason why you are greater than

[44] Bhattacharya 1896: 7.
[45] *Ibid.*: 5
[46] For example, the works of the Bengali littérateur Bankimchandra Chatterjee: see Raychaudhuri 1988: 152.

I, for can you mend my shoes? ... Caste is good. That is the only natural way of solving life. (*Ibid.*, III: 245–6)[47]

The fact that varna had come to be so widely identified with idealised patriotic virtues helps to explain why so many Indian thinkers proposed schemes of social and cultural regeneration which were to be realised through recruitment into purified varnas or mega-castes. These were moralists who held that caste had a place in the lives of modern Hindus, by which they meant that it could be remade as a bond of moral community at the national level. This vision of an India reborn around varna-like moral communities had wide appeal, particularly among adherents of the Arya Samaj and the other so-called 'theistic' spiritual movements to be discussed below.[48]

IDEALS OF THE MODERN CASTE HINDU

The same reverence for varna as a morally cohesive national bond was also implicit in the pronouncements of many 'modernising' caste association leaders. This led many theorists to subscribe to the third of the positions summarised above – the idealised corporation view – in which caste as jati was vested with moral messages for the modernising Hindu nation. This notion of named regional castes (jatis) as enlightened citizenries was attractive to nationalists such as Justice Ranade and to a number of other supporters of the National Social Conference, which annually confronted educated Indians with painful questions about the supposed ills of their society. Paramount among these was the problem of how to reconcile the claims of caste norms with their obligation as Hindus to realise the all-embracing 'genius of the nation'.[49] The views of these commentators, like those of Jogendra Nath Bhattacharya, should also be seen against the background of a growing array of so-called *jatimala* writings in Bengali and other vernacular languages. These treatises extolled conformity to rigorous norms of jati and varna hierarchy on both scriptural and 'scientific' grounds.[50]

[47] Vivekananda's writings (1989–92) also contain many anti-caste remarks; as for example the assertion that all forms of caste are 'bondage' (*Works*, VI: 320).
[48] This term was widely applied to such groups as the Arya Samaj, implying that such associations were manifestations of Hinduism in an advanced stage of evolutionary attainment.
[49] *ISR* 3 Jan 1909: 207; on this idea of castes as 'enlightened citizenries', see Inden 1990.
[50] Bandyopadhyay 1997: 18, 253 n. 46.

Whether they saw caste as a national problem or as a time-honoured moral code offering guidelines for the nation's uplift, those who used public platforms to define the significance of caste for contemporary Hindus regarded themselves as prophets of 'modernity', and were keen to show their awareness of Western racial theories and other manifestations of 'modern' science. A notable exemplar of these trends was the nationalist scholar and publisher Shridhar V. Ketkar (1884–1937). Ketkar urged Indians to take a 'scientific' approach to the analysis of caste, extolling the doctrine of four varnas, 'if properly understood', as 'a very healthy doctrine for any people'.[51] Yet he repudiated the idea of mutually antagonistic Aryan and Dravidian racial essences, and through an analysis of the *Institutes* of Manu, attacked those who '[sought] justification and maintenance of the caste-system' on the basis of the 'half-developed and hybrid [teachings of] ethnology'. He was particularly scathing about 'Aryan' Indians who claimed to be ethnologically superior to Tamils and other 'Dravidians': '[if] there are any people who are very proud of their pure Aryan blood, it is the black Bengalese of Mongoloid features ... It is amusing to observe that some ... [Bengalis] are now, since the [1904] Russo-Japanese war, quite willing to admit their racial connection with the Mongolian stock.'[52]

Once again it is important to see that these debates were much more than passive reflections of European orientalist scholarship and colonial data-collection. Those Indians who made caste a priority in debates about the ills of their society often based their arguments on the old forms of learned Hindu debate described at the beginning of this chapter. Even those who had assimilated the premises of Western race theory still tended to stress Hindu themes in ways which were definitely not characteristic of European writers. Such commentators

---

[51] Ketkar 1909–11, II: xxv.

[52] *Ibid.*, I: 79 n. 3, 78–82, 169–170. This scholar of Chitpavan Brahman origin studied in the USA with a scholarship from the Maharaja of Baroda; he received a PhD in sociology from Cornell University in 1911. Contrasting views were expressed by his contemporary Ramaprasad Chanda, an affiliate of the Bengal Literary Conference, who combined anthropometric techniques with Sanskritic textual scholarship. Chanda undertook a mass survey of Brahman skull measurements on behalf of the Ethnographical Survey of India, and constructed a racial classification of non-'Aryans' based on the nasal width statistics of '27 broad-nosed jungle tribes'; in his history of Indo-Aryans Chanda argued that the Buddha was racially Hindu and not 'Magian' as had recently been claimed by a German race scientist (Chanda 1916: ix, 1, 7, 79).

also cited a far greater range of Hindu textual materials than those which were known and used by European writers. This can be seen, in particular, in the widespread 'reformist' invocation of those Hindu Vedantist texts which criticised the teachings of the *purana* scriptures for their praise of elaborately involuted forms of caste differentiation. Thus these critiques of caste contributed to the shaping of twentieth-century nationalist ideologies in ways which cannot be dismissed as mere derivations from 'essentialising' European discourse. Indeed, these universalising views of caste – whether conceived of as a 'national' disability or a path to national regeneration – flatly contradicted many of the most sophisticated developments in late nineteeth- and early twentieth-century 'official' ethnography.

Both the enemies and the champions of caste in Indian life generally wrote as if the values they were critiquing comprised an inheritance of ageless Hindu tradition. In fact, however, the debates they were pursuing were a response to a world of alarming unpredictability. In this world of flux and insecurity, caste or castelike affinities were a comparatively new phenomenon for a substantial proportion of the Indian population. Self-styled modernisers were therefore confronting situations of extreme volatility in which the language and symbols of hierarchy and dharmic obligation were becoming more pervasive – and more systematically propounded across the subcontinent – than had been the case in earlier centuries.

As was seen in Chapter 1, the growing pervasiveness of 'caste' or caste-type affiliations and values, which can be observed across much of the subcontinent from the later eighteenth century onwards, was to a considerable extent a product of the volatile new institutions of the colonial state's 'restored' Hindu client kingdoms. All across the subcontinent, the effort to sustain and manage such sponsored 'Hindu' realms as Wodeyar Mysore and the Maratha-ruled dominions of Satara and Tanjore generated a vast literature in both English and the vernaculars. These works familiarised both the colonial authorities, and a later generation of Hindu 'modernisers', with norms that had hitherto been a matter of much more abstract or technical learned lore. The ideas dealt with in these debates emphasised impersonal and universal values of 'Hindu' piety. These fed directly into the notions of universal 'Hinduism' and 'Hindu nationhood' expressed by a wide range of polemicists and organised movements, ranging from the Arya Samaj and other 'modernising' revivalist organisations, to the

Dharma Sabhas and other would-be guardians of formal Brahmanical norms.[53]

There were many contradictions in the way this new public Hinduism had come to operate both within and beyond the sponsored Hindu realms, and many reasons why the sons of service and professional families in particular should be eager to engage in pious appeals of all kinds for an assault on spiritual impropriety and 'corruption', and thus for regeneration of 'Hindu' moral order. This can be readily seen from the wide range of universalising or 'theistic' teachings which were such a conspicuous feature of the urban 'public' arena during the later colonial period. In the eyes of the mainly young, male, English-speaking city-dwellers who dominated the various societies and fellowships devoted to spiritual and social renewal, both Hinduism and 'caste' were matters for agonising self-scrutiny, both personally and collectively. And the urgency of this was all the more pressing because of the fact that behaving as a 'Hindu', and conforming to 'caste' norms, were to many people still comparatively new, uncertain and bitterly contested phenomena throughout the subcontinent.[54]

The so-called Hindu revivalist movements of the late nineteenth and twentieth centuries had a profound impact on the 'modernising' critique of caste. The teachings of the Brahmo Samaj, the Arya Samaj and the Prarthana Samaj appealed to many of those who had been unsettled by the spectacle of sponsored colonial 'Hinduism' which had been emanating from the protected kingdoms, shrine centres and other focal points of uncertainty in the terrain of the 'modern' Hindu. These 'revivalist' organisations familiarised large numbers of Indians with an ideal of transcendent pious community which was far from being hostile to caste. On the contrary, while most of their adherents challenged the idea that the highest forms of knowledge and ritual expertise should be the preserve of a closed caste of Brahmans, they insisted that there could be no true Hindu piety without some form of revived or purified form of caste which would be based on a bond of idealised moral affinity rather than blood or birth.

The best known of these universalised spiritual ideologies was formulated by the Arya Samaj, whose founder, the Gujarati Brahman

---

[53] Mukherjee in Mukherjee and Leach 1970; Jones 1989: 95–102; and see Chapter 1 above.
[54] See O'Hanlon 1985: chs. 3–5; and Masselos 1974.

seer and social activist Swami Dayananda Saraswati (1824–83), defined the ideal basis for Hindu society as *varna vyavastha*, 'caste order'. His goal then was to endow the regenerated 'Aryan' nation with a scheme of purified varna classifications. Everyone was to read and know the sacred vedic scriptures, and none was to be debarred by birth or inherited unworthiness from knowledge of these texts. Those at the top of Dayananda's moral scheme were to be people who had attained learning and spiritual purity by personal attainment. Brahman birth was therefore of no account in this scheme, and indeed the Aryas' most aggressive polemics were directed against the claims of Brahmans to spiritual and moral superiority over other Hindus. But the Aryas' purified Hindu social order was still a hierarchy. It still rested on an ideal of collective moral affinities. It also continued to use the recognised symbols of varna identity, vesting its initiates with a sacred thread identical to the *suta*, which distinguished those of superior twice-born varna from the common mass of ritually inferior Shudras.[55]

The other newly formed fellowships of so-called 'theists' and 'liberal religionists' also used techniques of public declaration and recruitment to communicate ideals of transcendent divinity and all-embracing moral community. Groups such as the Manava Dharma Sabha, or Society for Human Religion (formed in Surat in about 1844), and the longer-lived Prarthana Samaj, or 'Society of Liberal Religionists' (which attracted its first adherents in Bombay, Poona and Ahmedabad between 1867 and 1871), also drew attention to caste as a burning issue in the lives of public-spirited nation-builders. This was often done by means which intentionally inverted the norms of ritual purity and commensality through which caste was manifested in the lives of so-called traditional Hindus.[56]

The favoured technique here was the staging of corporate food-sharing ceremonies which consciously married the rituals of *bhakti* congregationalism to the self-consciously 'modern' symbolism of the European-style public banquet. By the late nineteenth century, the reputations of many 'public men' (and sometimes women) were being made or lost on the basis of involvement in these functions. In 1892, for example, the co-founder and General Secretary of the National

---

[55] Saraswati 1975: 16, 77, 96–7; and see Jones 1976 and 1998.
[56] *ISR* 20 Sept 1908: 2, 44; see Masselos 1974: 83–5; O'Hanlon 1985: 97–100, 102, 113n, 221–2.

Social Conference, R. Raghunatha Rao, was denounced as a traitor to the 'reformist' cause and subjected to humiliating abuse in the *Indian Social Reformer* because he had evaded attendance at a controversial 'caste reform' dinner. This had been organised as a mark of legitimation for the remarriage of a widowed Hindu bride.[57]

Members of the Prarthana Samaj were expected to support key 'reformist' causes including widow remarriage, female education, the abolition of child marriage, and a more generalised aim which was referred to as the challenging of 'caste rules'. But their doctrines of 'Liberal Religion' did not preach outright 'castelessness'. Membership was not open to those of so-called untouchable birth.[58] The 'breaking of caste' was not a requirement for membership either, even though in 1906 the organisation set up an offshoot body which was devoted to the 'uplift' of untouchables. This venture was described in terms borrowed from evangelical Christian activist language as a 'Mission to the Depressed Classes'. Like many Western social work organisations, it founded schools and gave instruction in faith, hygiene and craft skills, thus providing a model for other groups involved in campaigns to 'elevate' those of low or impure caste status.[59]

Members of these organisations often found that the values and observances which constituted caste in their everyday social lives were sharply at odds with the ideals of their theistic faith. This was reformism at its most painful. Like similar associations elsewhere in India, the Prarthana Samaj was a public organisation in the sense that its adherents were expected to set standards of conduct and spirituality for the general population. Its precepts were communicated to this general audience from public platforms and in the 'reformist' press. But it proved extremely difficult to distinguish between the two separate domains of caste being identified here. At an impersonal level of conduct and formal commitment, the adherent's 'public' standards applied: all men were as one before a formless benign Creator; all men were brethren, and the 'depressed' were to be the beneficiaries of 'uplift'. But Prarthana Samajis were not told, for example, that their households must give up the services of sweepers, tonsurers and other

---

[57] *ISR* 26 May 1912: 459.

[58] Raval 1987: 145.

[59] *ISR* 20 Sept 1908: 25; an earlier Depressed Classes Mission had been founded in 1887 by a Chitrapur Saraswat lawyer, Kudmul Ranga Rao: see Conlon 1977: 148 and Ghugare 1983: 81–98.

untouchable specialists in the removal of ritually defined impurities. Here, in this second or parallel domain of caste, all Hindus were clearly not equal brethren. They were either pure or impure, within or beyond permissible social intercourse: to be served by caste barbers and other pollution-removers was to conform, in public, to the particularistic caste lifestyle prescribed for one's jati or 'sub-caste'.

So these advocates of liberal modernity were expected to make 'private' choices about matters which were essentially corporate and 'public' in the sense that they touched on other people's judgements about one's honour, or the acceptability of one's children as marriage partners. It was here that caste was to be defined as something that adherents might 'observe' if they so chose. But how was this choice to be exercised? How could individual conscience apply in matters which pitted the moral claims of one's jati against the modern morality of universalising pious fellowship? And, worse, once 'reformists' started making decisions about whether to deviate from their own particular caste norms in the matter of marrying off pre-pubescent daughters or attending widow-remarriages, there was the danger of denunciation in the press and in the public utterances of one's fellow 'progressives'.

It is no wonder that there were so many battles like the Raghunatha Rao controversy. The attempt to redefine standards of 'modern' Hindu morality around notions of personal choice and individual responsibility made it exceedingly difficult for 'reformists' to negotiate between the considerations of blood, honour and purity that governed their 'domestic' world, and the ideals of all-embracing fellowship that were supposed to be espoused on public platforms, in dealings with officialdom, and in the attempt to set abstract ethical standards for the revival of the Hindu moral order.[60]

HINDU 'MODERNISERS' AND THE RECONSTITUTION OF JATI AND VARNA

By the mid-nineteenth century it had already become common for the dilemmas of the modern Hindu to be played out in terms of caste. In the 1860s, Brahmo Samajis and other 'reformists' debated the propriety of wearing the sacred thread. In the early decades of the twentieth century, the question for aspiring Hindu nation-builders

[60] Compare Conlon 1977: 158–62.

was whether people of principle should wage a 'war against the caste-system' by refusing to provide the Census enumerators with data on their jati or varna identity.[61] And year after year, 'reformist' journals aired the anxieties of would-be reformists who were being asked to inflict the sanctions of so-called outcasting on spouse, children and other kin by sticking to publicly professed 'modern' principles on such questions as the marriage age of their daughters.[62]

Again and again, we see how would-be Hindu modernisers were much more ready to turn to the norms of varna than attempt to make themselves 'casteless' in the quest for purified national faith and community. Swami Dayananda had enjoined the wearing of the *suta* or sacred thread of the 'twice-born' as one of the 'signs of learning that distinguished the literate twice-born classes from the illiterate Shudras'.[63] From the late nineteenth century, both Arya Samaj members and followers of Swami Vivekenanda were encouraged to participate in public rites of incorporation which involved investiture with the sacred thread, and the imparting of the sacred formula known as the Gayatri Mantra.[64]

Jati affiliation too came to be portrayed in the 'modern' public arena as an expression of citizenship and spiritually informed nationality which had the potential to fulfil and regenerate the modern Hindu. In the late nineteenth and early twentieth centuries, aspiring nation-builders like Justice M. G. Ranade of the National Social Conference were well aware that the so-called tyranny of caste was regarded by ethnologists as a counter-evolutionary development. It was the creation of castes which had supposedly distorted the subcontinent's moral and political sensibilities, and had either retarded or permanently debarred Hindus from the attainment of nationhood.

In Ranade's time, the views of Western race theorists were regularly echoed in the Indian 'reformist' press. The theory of historic race conflicts was widely accepted by contributors to these journals as a factual picture of India's primordial past. As progressive men of science, they endorsed the mythical collisions of ancient light-skinned 'Aryans' and dark 'aborigines' as the 'cause of caste', rather than dharmic truth and divine will. For many self-styled Indian moder-

---

[61] *ISR* 8 Nov 1930: 137. See below, Chapter 6.
[62] *ISR* 29 Nov 1908: 145.
[63] Swami Dayananda Saraswati 1975: 475.
[64] Vivekenanda *Works* VII: 107–8.

nisers, this provided an attractively 'modern' means of justifying such goals as the fusion of sub-castes through intermarriage, and other desirable advances in national life as defined by the National Social Conference.

The effect of this can be seen in an essay published in 1908 by the Maharashtrian writer W. W. Nowangay, and later in a monograph by Nripendra Kumar Dutt, Professor of History at Hooghly College, Bengal. Both borrowed almost word for word from Hunter in his call for the adoption of a 'modern' understanding of caste:

Thus we see that the most important factors in the development of caste were the racial struggle between the fair-skinned Aryans and the dark-skinned non-Aryans ... These were aided by the superiority claimed by the priests and witch-doctors in all primitive societies ... and by the inherent disinclination of a man to marry outside his own folk, especially when there are racial or tribal differences involved.[65]

To my mind two things have been chiefly instrumental in the creation of castes. The one is the puerile ideas about personal holiness and purity and don't touchism in the matter of food ... The Brahmans who are a race kindred to the Parsees must have begun to spread the infection of their curious ideas to the non-Aryan races when they first came in contact with these in very ancient times; ... The second cause of caste was the hatred which the white-skinned Aryans felt for the black natives of India.[66]

Both Dutt and Nowangay therefore accepted conventional Western race theories insofar as they proclaimed 'pride of blood' and antipathy between fair- and dark-skinned races as universal facts of evolutionary history. Indeed, this even provided Nowangay with a 'scientific' explanation for the phenomenon of untouchability, which he saw as a product of 'real' events, meaning historic race conflicts, rather than inherent or divinely mandated deficiencies. Thus, he said, the 'hatred of the Aryans', and possibly the 'far more deadly hatred' which had been felt in primordial times by 'the Hindus of pure caste but mixed blood' for 'the dark aborigines of India', had reduced such peoples as 'Chandalas' to a state of degradation. It was this which explained the existence of an 'untouchable class', some of whom, 'on this rich and fruitful soil of India, were driven to share with carrion birds and carrion dogs the carcasses of dead cattle'.[67] Nevertheless, Nowangay

---

[65] Dutt 1969: 34–5, first publ. 1931.
[66] *ISR* 29 Nov 1908: 151. See Chapter 3 above.
[67] *ISR* 29 Nov 1908: 151.

managed to reconcile his nationalist principles with this ethnological view of caste. He argued that although innate and historic race pride or 'pride of complexion' had indeed given rise to this 'divided state of the Hindus', India's colonial conquerors had made matters far worse by encouraging high-caste Hindus to take 'false pride' in their claims of 'pure' Aryan blood.[68]

At the same time, some 'reformists' who saw Aryan race spirit as a real and positive force in Indian life actually made moves to put their theories into practice. Particularly notable here were the Bombay activists who constituted themselves in 1913 into an organisation calling itself the Aryan Brotherhood. This group aroused fierce controversy in the English and vernacular press by devising what was perhaps the ultimate expression of 'modernising' congregational food-sharing. This was a public 'intercaste dinner' at which '150 men and women dined together and publicly set at naught the barriers of castes and creeds'.[69] Of course in many ways both the idiom and the aim of this enterprise were distinctively 'modern' and Western. Yet the idea of achieving what the organisers called the 'fusion of the various castes and sub-castes into one homogenous Hindu race' by eating together, thus using the ceremonial sharing of food to transform bio-moral substance or identity, would certainly seem to be rooted in a dharmic or conventionally 'Indic' frame of reference. The compatibility of these views with equally conventional Hindu ideas about the low and unclean nature of 'untouchables' will be discussed in the final section of this chapter.

THE GLORIFICATION OF PATRIOTIC 'HINDU' JATI VALUES

In sharp contrast to these anti-caste 'Aryan' theorists, Justice Ranade was a Hindu 'reformist' who reached very different conclusions about the meaning of caste for the modern nation.[70] His view of Hindus as a 'chosen race' did not lead him to condemn the separations and divisions of jati as destructive of India's racial strengths. On the

---

[68] *ISR* 29 Nov 1908; on the competing claim that caste was a result of Muslim rule, which had supposedly 'degraded' the unified race consciousness of Hindu Aryans, see *ISR* 8 Dec 1913: 177 and Kaul 1937: 33, 36, 52.

[69] *ISR* 8 Dec 1913: 176; *ISR* 22 Dec 1912: 198; Farquhar 1967: 419–20.

[70] For further background see Johnson 1973: 88–95; Cashman 1975: 9–10, 54.

contrary, although he shared National Social Conference platforms with radical anti-caste 'reformists', he exemplifies the third of the schools of thought summarised above (p. 155): the jati or regionally specific caste group as an idealised corporation, hence a source of historic national achievement and future greatness.

Unlike Kaul and Nowangay, Ranade's view of race history thus exalted jati affiliation as a means by which Hindus had formerly realised their gift for selfless spirituality. Like other high-caste Pune and Bombay nationalists, he derived his moral message from the key episodes of pre-British Maratha suzerainty. This for him was a golden age which had provided a foretaste of nationhood for the whole subcontinent. Here too the case of the seventeenth-century Maratha dynast Shivaji is paradigmatic. This account portrays Shivaji as an heroic liberator who reshaped the disparate identities of caste in western India to form the basis of a harmonious 'national' culture. European ethnological conventions were thus neatly turned on their heads.[71] For Ranade, the subjects of Shivaji had acquired a consciousness of caste in which were embodied the ideal qualities of national purpose. The example of these sharers in the moral order of caste could therefore inspire the modern nation in its quest for spiritual and political liberation.[72]

Ranade saw the large regional meta-castes of his own day in much the same terms, that is, as dynamic moral communities whose members were taking exemplary initiatives under the aegis of their 'reformist' regional caste associations.[73] The activities of these bodies were cited by other commentators too as evidence that jatis were coming to behave as accountable corporations, subject to the judgements of 'modern' public opinion. Like the proselytising of the Arya Samaj and the public utterances of prominent social reformers, these associations' campaigns against alcohol consumption, 'lewd' marriage

[71] Just as Britons had purportedly achieved the evolutionary triumph of nationhood through successful race blending, Ranade saw the nationality of the Maratha 'race' as the product of a fruitful alliance between the Brahman's innate selflessness and piety, the Maratha's valour, and the inherent strengths of literate 'Prabhu' service people and pastoral 'Mavli' arms-bearers (Ranade 1900: 79–82, 184; compare O'Hanlon 1985: 17). There is no mention of 'untouchables' as sharers in Maratha nationhood.

[72] Ranade 1900: 70–9.

[73] For example, by fighting to establish the acceptability of sea voyages without the penalties of 'outcasting' and *prayaschitta* expiation rituals. Such 'clean-caste' people as Kayasthas were thus not to be seen as prisoners of 'dead tradition', even though British rule had 'enfeebled' the institutions through which Indians had formerly regulated themselves in the national interest (Ranade 1900: 278–9, 321).

HINDU MARATHA LADY

7. 'Hindu Maratha Lady'. Watercolour showing the elaborate devotional worship which had become popular in 'clean-caste' households by the late nineteenth century. From an album commemorating a royal visit to Bombay in 1905; the paintings are signed M. F. Pithawalla, each with a female subject identified by caste or 'community'.

177

entertainments and other so-called social impurities familiarised many Indians with the idea of one's caste as an endowment of collective morality which existed in an impersonal public domain. Its standards were therefore to be defined somewhere beyond the localised face-to-face community and the writ of caste 'elders' and ascetic preceptors, that is, by 'modern' men arriving at decisions within the 'modern' public media.

Furthermore, the collective morality to which these self-professed modernisers subscribed was conceived of as the corporate property of a given jati. This allowed some 'reformists' to reconcile their modern principles with older and more pervasive understandings of jati as a framework of obligations defining conduct in matters such as diet, dress and marriage choices. In this way the new mode of life proposed by these thinkers represented a synthesis of Western and indigenous Brahmanical values. Such campaigns within the nineteenth- and early twentieth-century caste associations derived in part from a European ethic of thrift and respectability, though this was substantially transformed through amalgamation with existing Hindu values of purity and moral restraint. These assertions of allegedly modern values were greeted with much enthusiasm in 'reformist' publications.[74]

What Ranade and his contemporaries in the National Social Conference sought to define as a national social philosophy for India thus emerged as an uneasy synthesis of pride in race, pride in the moral sensibilities of 'caste' and pride in cautiously 'progressive' social reformist sentiments. Across a wide spectrum of 'progressive' opinion, this came into focus in the years before the First World War as a view of jati and varna affiliation as something analogous to a liberal political thinker's definition of citizenship. This is why caste in this sense, meaning membership of a self-regulating moral community, was perceived by Ranade and other nationalists as a basis for national renewal in the modern age.

It is notable too that Indians with very different political views who had good reason to distance themselves from the 'reformists' and the modernising nationalist organisations nevertheless used the language of 'scientific' race theory in their attempts to portray themselves as Empire loyalists with an entitlement to privileged treatment from the colonial authorities. Such moves were particularly widespread at the

---

[74] *ISR* 13 Dec 1908: 170; 16 May 1909: 440; 7 Apr 1912: 379.

time of the First World War when the search for an expanded pool of military recruits produced a multitude of representations from those who wished to proclaim their fitness for army service on ethnological grounds. Thus a celebration of Rajput virtues commissioned in 1915 by the Maharaja of Udaipur eulogised the 'manful' race qualities displayed by the many Rajputs volunteering for the princely regiments which were being assimilated into the Indian Army at this time. The Great War, says this writer, was a 'dharmic' conflict in which both Britons and their fellow Aryans in India had a common stake. The author therefore identifies the 'Aryan' Hindu soldier's loyal service in defence of the Empire as a demonstration of India's political coming of age, with the Rajputs showing a commitment to 'justice, honour and dharma' in the global conflict against the German enemy on behalf of all Indians of Aryan heritage.[75]

THE 'MODERN' HINDU CRITIQUE OF UNTOUCHABILITY

What has been seen thus far is that, by the time of the First World War, caste was widely held to present nation-builders with an array of problems to be addressed through public debate and social activism. And since jati and varna were now being so widely identified as expressions of Aryan or Hindu 'race genius', many theorists sought to distinguish between supposedly good and bad manifestations of 'caste spirit', and exalted the idealised solidarities of the twice-born as the embodiment of national faith and a cohesive national morality.

So what did 'modernisers' actually do when called upon to take action in the public arena? Campaigns to 'uplift' the so-called depressed classes posed the greatest challenges to those trying to equip the nation with a modern understanding of caste. Such activists generally subscribed to liberal social theories which emphasised individual rights and capabilities. Ironically, however, proponents of 'uplift' schemes often expressed themselves at the same time in terms which took for granted an idealised opposition between pure and impure, propriety and impropriety, cleanliness and uncleanliness. These concerns implicitly affirmed notions of twice-born or high-caste purity and dominance. The only new element here was that such

---

[75] Seesodia 1915.

'modern' representations of dharmic order generalised Brahmanical notions of rank and hierarchy into an impersonal rhetoric of nationality and public obligation. In other words, the moral message of caste became a matter of defining standards of ideal 'national' conduct, rather than an expression of personal face-to-face relations, as between 'clean-caste' patron and 'untouchable' scavenger, waste-remover or tonsurer.

The many Indian commentators who pronounced on the issue of so-called caste reform were well aware of the moves made by British missionaries and officials to promote 'uplift' for those defined as members of depressed or backward castes. In the early nineteenth century, evangelical missionaries based in south India led campaigns to emancipate the unfree labourers whom they identified as members of 'slave' castes.[76] In the 1850s the colonial courts made inconclusive attempts to legislate against the social 'disabilities' imposed on those of ritually impure birth. By the 1880s, the authorities in some areas were making piecemeal moves to provide educational allowances for those deemed to be 'backward' or 'untouchable' in caste terms.[77]

The Empire's apologists regularly cited such policies as evidence of the progressive energies of British colonialism. Yet sensitive as they were to colonial commentators who attacked the 'degradation' of low-caste groups as a sign of India's moral and social 'decadence', it is not surprising that those who took part in early twentieth-century social critiques were slow to focus on untouchability in the quest for wrongs to right within the domain of caste. Here, too, we see a reflection of 'modern' theories about race and nationality. As was seen in Chapter 3, for much of the nineteenth century the broad and ill-defined category of the 'depressed' was held to include large numbers of 'tribes', 'aboriginals' and 'non-Aryan castes' who were outside the norms and boundaries of the Hindu 'nation'. All this began to change when Hindu nation-builders began to turn their public spotlight on the faith, morals and condition of the 'depressed classes'. In order to 'uplift' such people and make them worthy co-sharers in the moral order of the nation, well-meaning reformists called for initiatives to '[promote] education including cleanliness and morality' among these groups.[78]

---

[76] Kumar 1965; Saradomani 1973.
[77] Galanter 1984: 155.
[78] *ISR* 13 Dec 1908: 170; 16 May 1909: 440; 17 Apr 1912: 379.

The result of these appeals was that 'untouchables' too came to be subjected to tests of public respectability and moral worth. Such testing had hitherto been directed at the many 'clean'-caste groups which were being scrutinised in the reformist press for signs of corporate 'awakening'. As in the case of these high-ranking populations, the public critique of caste was transformed into a public critique of the 'depressed' and their place in the modern Hindu nation. Once introduced to new standards of 'social purity' and ordered conduct, those of the 'depressed' who retained supposedly unclean, immoral or improper lifestyles could be accused of wilfully letting down the honour of their community and nation. They too were told that they had obligations which had been defined on public platforms and in the debates of 'modernising' polemicists and social theorists. These were assertions of public morality and civilised 'national' norms which implicitly endorsed Brahmanical principles of purity and hierarchy, even though they were supposed to constitute a statement of 'casteless' ideals for an enlightened modern citizenry.

In 1895 the National Social Conference adopted a cautious resolution calling for the 'uplift' of India's 'pariahs and untouchables'. The call for a 'progressive' stance in regard to the 'depressed' or 'backward' classes was reaffirmed in equally vague terms at successive Conference sessions, but the reformist position on this aspect of caste persistently sidestepped the question of what it was that made certain classes of Indians 'depressed' or 'untouchable'. This is not surprising, since the 'modern' Hindu faced severe problems in defining the condition from which such people were to be 'raised up'. There was no very obvious way to widen the notion of caste as a golden chain or bond of free, enlightened citizenry to include those who were still widely deemed to be ritually and physically defiling to the rest of the Hindu nation.

Modernising Hindu theorists were also aware that there was still much uncertainty among European ethnologists about whether India was a homogeneous caste society, or a composite of casteless 'tribes', 'pre-Aryan' untouchables and 'caste-fettered' Hindu 'Aryans'. It is no wonder then that European ethnology transmitted contradictory messages to 'scientifically'-minded Indian reformists in this period. On the one hand, some Western sources dismissed untouchability as a simple reflection of deprived physical and material circumstances; only the occupations of these 'depressed' groups, or other material factors such as 'impure' diet, rendered them degraded and 'untouchable' in the eyes of those subscribing to the 'superstitions' and 'prejudices' of an 'Aryan' or Brahmanical value system. This had clearly influenced Nowangay's view of untouchability as a product of material deprivation and racial antipathy between Aryans and non-Aryans. Yet at the same time, these theories of India's so-called race history were based on a notion that the 'depressed' truly were different from other Indians, that they belonged to scientifically identifiable racial groups which were backward, inferior and uncivilised in comparison to other Indians.

It is true that for 'reformists' like Justice Sankaran Nair, the regenerative bonds of nationhood were available to all. There were no unbridgeable race differences within the Indian nation.[79] Even untouchables could be 'reunited' with their fellow Indians within a new national order of purified varna-like classes which would be based on individual worth and merit. Thus no-one, including the 'untouchable', possessed innate or immutable qualities either of varna or of degraded *avarna* status. Thanks to the British nation, which had 'raised up the down-trodden classes from ages of degradation' the idea had been implanted 'that the spirit within is divine and that the Pariah man develops into a Brahmin by education and training'.[80]

The Hindu nationalists who campaigned for educational and social 'uplift' for the untouchable or 'depressed' castes were particularly inclined to express the goal of so-called social reclamation for these groups as a matter of the utmost ethnological urgency. These schemes of 'uplift' first began to be widely advocated in the reformist press at a time when the Census was reporting an alarming decline in population growth among Hindus relative to Muslims, Sikhs and Christians. Tilak's Pune rival, G. K. Gokhale (1866–1915), was one of the many nationalists who portrayed the success of Muslim, Sikh and Christian proselytisers in attracting low-caste and 'untouchable' converts as a sign of Hindu weakness and racial decline. His social service venture, the Servants of India Society, was yet another movement devoted to the energising of national spirituality through constructive social work.[81] Gokhale therefore bemoaned the 'rigidity' of the 'caste

[79] *ISR* 3 Jan 1909: 209.
[80] *Ibid.* This was also a reference invoking those mythical personages whose piety and learning are rewarded with transformation from untouchability to Brahmanhood – notably Kapila, the superhuman sage-poet and legendary founder of the Samkhya system of Hindu philosophy.
[81] *ISR* 28.Feb.1909: 306.

system' and portrayed the 'emancipation' of the 'depressed' as a redemptive act that should be inherent in the principles of the modern nation-builder.[82]

The fear as expressed by Hindu nationalists on this matter was that other 'communities' had become stronger and more vigorous in evolutionary terms, with higher levels of female fertility and a healthier and more active 'race spirit'. This was the basis on which members of the Arya Samaj were enjoined to arrest the supposed decline of the Hindu nation by taking part in campaigns of *shuddhi* or reconversion so as to reclaim untouchable 'converts' who had been 'lost' to the Hindu nation through the missionary endeavours of these rival faiths.[83]

A number of other Hindu 'revivalist' organisations committed themselves to this cause on the same grounds. The Prarthana Samaj or society of 'liberal religionists' (see above, p. 170), which had been founded to promote ideals of transcendent divinity and all-embracing moral community for 'enlightened' Hindus, was one of the earliest of such movements to invite its members to commit themselves to the regeneration of the nation by joining the 'noble work' of uplift for the depressed.[84] At the other end of the spectrum was the Sons of India Order established by Mrs Annie Besant and other members of the Madras-based anti-colonial spiritualist movement known as Theosophy. The Sons of India were defenders of ancient Hindu moral truths who believed that untouchables could and should be educated in a 'modern' scientific spirit. Nevertheless, they also believed in building on the 'inherited aptitude' that they saw as residing in children of particular caste origins. They argued, for example, that the sons of those untouchable ritualists who specialised both in tonsuring and in bodily healing had innate skills which could be built on scientifically by training them in physiology and botanical lore.[85]

In fact though, whether they belonged to 'conservative' or ostensibly 'liberal' organisations, the architects of the new Hindu nation set much the same standards of propriety and civilised behaviour for the people they professed to be reclaiming. Like comparable social service societies in nineteenth-century Britain, the energies of the Depressed

---

[82] *Ibid.*
[83] Jones 1976: 129–35.
[84] *ISR* 13 Dec 1908.
[85] *ISR* 23 May 1909: 449.

Class Missions were primarily devoted to fighting drink, 'vice' and uncleanliness. But in their Indian manifestation these goals reflected a convergence of modern science with a synthesis of Victorian morality and established merchant/Bania and Brahman pious norms.

These activists made it clear that, to be accepted as worthy members of the Hindu nation, 'reclaimed' untouchables must become clean, sober and thrifty vegetarians, and adherents of purified Hindu faith. Such people were thus to behave in a way that conformed to the known codes of 'pure' dharmic social convention. In 1908, the 'reformist' K. Ranga Rao, Secretary of the Mangalore Depressed Classes Mission, was reported as having addressed a gathering of Panchama-Holeya untouchables in terms which left no doubt about his views of the inherent 'vices' and impurities that he was exhorting them to overcome:

It is not so much the ill treatment of the higher castes, but your own faults that have been the cause of your poverty and degradation ... Your habits of drunkenness, and your utter disregard for education, have made you a poor, degraded and despised people.[86]

Ranga Rao then reviled those Holeyas who complained about their exclusion from roads, government hospitals and other public places: 'If you do not or can not take advantage of the public offices as we do, it is your own fault ...' The truth, he said, 'is that your very sight is repulsive on account of your dirt and uncleanliness of person'. Furthermore, 'If higher caste people ever beat you, that is because you become abusive when drunk. Behave properly, be humble and polite but at the same time try to improve your condition.'[87]

This might appear to be the same message of cleanliness, thrift, temperance and deferential respectability that evangelical missionaries and social workers were addressing to working-class Britons in this period, as well as to potential Christian converts throughout the overseas Empires. But Ranga Rao did not really have a Christian social reformer's vision of self-help and moral uplift. His goals for the Holeya were explicitly linked to the values of a universalising purita- nical Hinduism which owed much to Brahmanical definitions of propriety, and which therefore retained a view of untouchables as beings steeped in filth and dissolute indulgence. Ranga Rao was thus

[86] *ISR* 18 Oct 1908: 78.
[87] *Ibid.*

speaking both as a pious 'Hindu', in the racial and ethnic sense in which the term was now being used, and as a modern-minded man of science. On this basis he clearly felt doubly equipped to tell the Holeya what they must do to advance and 'elevate' themselves, thus throwing off the stigma of their 'depressed' status. If they did not do these things, their untouchability was something which they would therefore retain because they *deserved* to do so.

One can clearly see in this the established Brahmanical view of untouchability as an innate characteristic derived from contact with unclean substances and improper foodstuffs, from indulgence in uncontained passions and carnality, and from proximity to the low and 'demonic' in its many other forms.[88] Yet, at the same time Ranga Rao's views about untouchables were given all the more force because they were based on a synthesis of 'scientific' theories and Brahmanical norms, in particular those conventions which identify untouchable status as a burden of sin derived from contamination and ritual impurity. Furthermore, his views should not be dismissed as unrepresentative of contemporary 'reformist' opinion. Ranga Rao was echoing themes that appear in the writings of 'progressive' Hindu nation-builders throughout India, and his remarks (or the *ISR*'s version of them) were being carried in one of India's most prestigious and widely read nationalist journals.

The views of Ranga Rao and many other comparable proponents of untouchable 'uplift' were easy to reconcile with the teachings of eugenicists and race theorists, whose writings had defined both the spiritual and the physiological attributes of advanced nations, and had made clear distinctions between healthy and unhealthy manifestations of appetite and psychic energy. In other words, building both on the claims of their so-called 'pure' national faith and on modern science, the modern Hindu nationalist had powerful incentives to take a coercive and hierarchical view of so-called untouchables, and indeed of anyone else – including Muslims – who could be seen as transgressing these notions of collective national virtue and propriety. Such

---

[88] Including many forms of 'popular' religion, especially those involving blood sacrifice. Both Indian and Western writing on 'unclean' castes emphasised these groups' 'degrading' livelihoods and supposed indulgence in alcohol, beef and carrion as sources of their 'untouchability'; much was made too of their supposed licentiousness and alleged descent from 'impure', i.e. intercaste, unions. The idea of contact with human death as the prime source of ritual contamination does not figure prominently in colonial ethnographies. See Randeria 1989; and Chapter 5, note 5.

attitudes could be justified on the grounds that the 'backward' practices of untouchables and other unenlightened people were a wilful violation of Hindu race genius, and a threat to the health and progress of the nation.

Furthermore, the ostensibly liberal views explored in this chapter drew added force from their compatibility with the attitudes of those who were still embracing so-called Sanskritising or 'traditional' caste values at this time.[89] These views came together most visibly around such issues as teetotalism and cow-protection, as well as abhorrence for meat-eaters and other violators of 'pure' sastric varna norms. Indeed, even at their most radical, the colonial intelligentsias' 'reformist' ideologies often converged with the ideals of cleanliness and purity that had been popularised as requirements of a goodly and pious 'caste Hindu life' under the rule of the 'Hinduising' rulers described in Chapter 2. Well into the twentieth century, these so-called dharmic ideals were still extremely powerful in most local societies, as will be seen in the next chapter, which will explore the continuing emphasis on thread investitures, 'purifying' marriage strategies, and other signs of worth, honour and status among a wide range of 'respectable' or 'clean'-caste commercial and landed groups. At the same time, many such people were also becoming aware of the debates described in this chapter, pointing to obvious contradictions between ideals of casteless national unity and those of a varna-revering defender of the Hindus' 'national' faith. These issues remained problematic and painful for Indian nationalists down to and even after Independence, not least because so many of the important economic changes of the nineteenth and early twentieth centuries were contributing to the hardening of caste boundaries in every region of the subcontinent. It is therefore these changes that the next chapter will explore.

[89] Even the liberal *Indian Social Reformer* published a eugenicist attack on one of the key 'reformist' goals, that of sub-caste intermarriage, alleging that the eventual result of this would be the mating of clean-caste Hindus with people of inferior 'stock', and hence the degeneration of the Hindu 'race' (*ISR* 14 Apr 1912: 387, 26 May 1912: 461, 485). For a Bengali version of eugenic caste theory, see 'An enquiry into ... the production of eugenic offspring', cited in Harris 1976: 17.

CHAPTER 5

THE EVERYDAY EXPERIENCE OF CASTE IN COLONIAL INDIA

INTRODUCTION

This chapter deals with the changing face of caste from the 1820s to the end of the nineteenth century. During this period, the colonial state acquired powers of coercion and surveillance which profoundly affected the lives of its Indian subjects. At the same time, the growth of population, the quest for revenues, and the combined priorities of commerce and military security placed massive pressure on India's physical environment. Forests were felled and their 'tribal' inhabitants disarmed and subordinated. Much remaining grassland was put to the plough, pitting graziers and warrior-pastoralists against the tiller, the settlement officer and the colonial policeman. Old agricultural and artisanal zones stagnated; others struggled to hold their own against the challenge of volatile new cash-crop economies. By mid-century, new roads, ports and railways nourished the increasing commercialisation of agriculture and commodity production, creating a demand for wage labour and specialised skills, and endowing both the growing cities and the countryside with the trappings of 'modernity'.

Like the telegraph, the press, and the stone-built jails, courthouses and residential cantonments in which the presence of colonial power was most apparent, these material transformations could be seen and experienced by almost all Indians. Increasingly, such people as the Bhil, the Kallar and even the Maratha could no longer retreat to terrain in which they were comparatively secure and lordly. Few buffers now remained between these former arms-bearing groups and the people with whom they were now competing for rights and resources. In these new circumstances, caste became the measure of the new pecking orders that called the Bhil or the Bhuinya a low squatter or dependent labourer, and defined the landowning or moneyed 'caste Hindu' as high, pure and superior. This period's massive environmental changes therefore gave tangible force to distinctions between ways of life which had not hitherto been systematically ranked, compared and standardised.

As was seen in Chapters 3 and 4, during the nineteenth century many thinkers came to classify the subcontinent's 'castes', 'tribes' and 'races' in terms that reversed or confused older definitions of worth and virtue. Citing both modern science and the supposed truths of purified religious faith, these new habits of thought disparaged the attributes of the lordly life. The man of prowess was now identified with wildness and profligacy; traditions of sobriety and industry, it was said, were the appropriate values for this new India of order and productive growth. These were not just the views of Western orientalists, even though their expression clearly served the needs of British officials who wished to represent themselves as protectors of the merchant and cultivator in a land that had only just been secured from the ravages of Pindari war-bands and other so-called predators.[1] For growing numbers of Indians as well as Britons, the thrifty husbandman, the pious man of commerce, and the chaste 'clean-caste' wife had become the subcontinent's ideal inhabitants; those with little worth in this domain of progress and virtuous modernity were, inevitably, the 'low' tribal, the 'turbulent' poligar clansman, the Gujar and Meo ex-pastoralist, and the 'parasitical' warrior-aristocrat.

In the 1820s, despite all that had occurred through the two-stage process of change described in Chapters 1 and 2, India was still not a homogeneous 'caste society'. Those people who had adopted some variant of a lordly or purity-conscious 'caste' life had generally managed to maximise the flexibility of these jati and varna norms. The boundaries between individual orders or classes were still open and ambiguous in the early decades of British expansion; the language of caste or castelike relationships still allowed for the great man who could reshape or disregard conventional marriage rules and dietary codes, and for the thrusting regional elite with the power to proclaim something new about their birth and moral attributes.

This openness and fluidity were much less apparent at the end of the nineteenth century, when many more Indians had embraced forms of caste that were significantly more formalised than those of their recent forebears. In this more fully colonial environment, it became common to invoke a Brahman's or pious merchant's standards of purity and refinement in situations where these had previously had only limited significance. Thus the life of the so-called caste Hindu

---

[1] For example, Malcolm 1832, I: 133; and see Guha 1996.

came increasingly to involve the assertion of heightened difference. In particular, this involved the growing force of what is being referred to in this work as the pollution barrier, that is the assertion of rigorous barriers between those of 'clean' caste, and those stigmatised as innately degraded, unclean or polluting. This became especially apparent in situations of conflict and uncertainty, where both lowly and exalted people found advantage in displaying markers of opposition to those of unlike and ritually inferior 'community'.

For Indians themselves, and not just for their external classifiers, caste categories came to be used in the nineteenth century in two distinct but complementary ways. On the one hand, they were a kind of defensive shorthand, a reflection of unsecured gains or losses. At the same time, they served as a device for confirming or initiating change, that is as a means to contest other people's advantages and proclaim virtue and distinctiveness in contentious circumstances. This chapter will ask how and why these more exclusive conceptions of caste became so widely adopted in the course of the nineteenth century. In particular, it will explore the central paradox of this more castelike social order: while colonial India's caste differences became widely spoken of as fixed essences of birth and rank, Indians kept finding ways to reshape and exploit them to meet conditions of change and insecurity.

This applied to people of widely varying degrees of wealth and power. Even more so than in the pre-colonial period, jati and varna ideals were used to coerce and dominate, especially as insecure rural elites found themselves struggling to maintain authority over tenant cultivators and dependent labourers. But for less advantaged people too, caste differences were not simply disabilities imposed from above. On the contrary, in many cases jati and varna ideologies offered a means of fighting off the effects of colonial intrusion, or of excluding, separating and subordinating even weaker groups of dependants or rivals in volatile and unpredictable environments.

So how precisely did this hardening of caste boundaries become so widespread by the early twentieth century? The answer proposed here will involve the tracing of yet another twofold sequence of change which follows on from the two-stage process described in Chapters 1 and 2. The first of the two trends to be discussed here tended to rigidify caste relationships in areas where 'community' ties had remained comparatively fluid and open even with the spread of the

Brahman and *bania*-merchant values described in the previous chapters. Broadly speaking, this involved areas where insecure landed elites attempted to cling to ideals of prowess and seigneurial high religion, often with a strong focus on the god Shiva and this deity's associated complex of deified heroes and royal warrior divinities.[2] The second set of trends involved more commercially dynamic regions where the religion of the Vishnu pantheon had tended to predominate even before the colonial period, and where, under British rule, both tillers and trading groups had much influence in promoting purity-conscious social codes which equated the pursuit of respectability and credit-worthiness with the exaltation of strict jati and varna norms.

LORDS OF LAND AND MANPOWER

To start with the first of these broad trends, those who were hit particularly hard by the economic and environmental changes of the nineteenth century were the people whom Eric Stokes called 'squireens', that is, the superior landholders who found themselves clinging to inherited lordships in India's most volatile agricultural regions. Members of these seigneurial groups had generally come to be known by the title Rajput or its regional equivalents. Whether their gains had been made in relatively recent times or over many centuries, patricians like this – and the upper 'peasants' who had come increasingly to emulate them – had already been inclined to embrace the marks of a Kshatriya-like way of life, particularly in regard to matters of marriage and the policing of blood-lines, and also through acts of 'kingly' beneficence. Now more than ever, as they found themselves squeezed and threatened by the unfavourable new circumstances of colonial rule, such people sought to enhance and expand on these elements of Kshatriya lordliness.

What was new in the nineteenth century, however, was that growing numbers of vulnerable patricians and their imitators tried to change their relationships with the large-scale labouring and petty cultivating groups who lived amongst them, exalting themselves as these people's *jajmans* (patrons), and claiming a right to demand servitude and deference from them as subordinated *kamins* or

[2] In some cases the Vishnu pantheon's hero-king Ram provided a similar focus, especially for 'peasant' groups with aspirations to this kind of Kshatriya-style lordliness.

8. Photograph taken at a royal marriage in the Maratha-ruled princely state of Dhar. The donor's label reads 'Ancient weapons carried by Mahrattas at Dhar, central India – H. H. the Maharaja of Dhar is one of the leading princes of India and belongs to the famous Mahratta race.'

balutedars (clients).[3] Much of this was done coercively, and in ways that introduced strict norms of hierarchy and pollution-consciousness into areas of life where they had not hitherto prevailed. These moves were often bitterly contested and did not altogether succeed. Yet they did make the purity-centred values and caste norms described by Dumont far more pervasive than had been the case even in the eighteenth century. Thus, far from being a universal feature of 'traditional' Indian life, caste in this form, as an array of regionally based schemes of ritual hierarchy, sprang in large part from the relatively recent experiences of colonial 'modernity'.

It is true, of course, that in past centuries most Indian regions contained small but distinctive populations who were known by titles which identified them as specialist service providers. This would include such groups as north India's Bhangi 'scavengers' and Nai barber-tonsurers, and the Vannan washermen of Malabar and Tamilnad. Like traders and other occupationally specialised groups, most of these tonsurers, carrion-removers and ordure-collectors possessed a comparatively strong sense of corporate identity. Unlike most traders and artisans, however, these lowly specialists regularly handled substances which are defined as pollution-transmitting and radically unclean in the ritual sense that is specific to Hindu varna theory.[4]

By the logic of so-called caste society, those who follow these occupations are inherently 'untouchable', defiling or unclean (*ashuddh*), even though the tasks they perform are indispensable to the purity-conscious 'caste Hindu'. India's widely shared reverence for the cow has made leather-working a particularly polluting way of life; distilling and fishing have also been widely thought of as defiling. Although both British and Indian social reformers characterised the handling of ordure and animal remains as the definitive 'untouchable' livelihoods, modern anthropologists have seen human death as a source of even greater pollution. Thus, through their association with the dangerous forces which surround the death of humans, such specialists as cremation-ground attendants and tonsurers of mourners

---

[3] This terminology was not in universal use either before or after the British conquest. For the debate about *jajmani* and *baluta* systems, see Kolenda 1967; Commander 1983; Fuller 1989; Good 1991.

[4] Deliège 1992. On the debate about whether 'untouchables' themselves accept these concepts of ritual impurity and defilement, or instead see their low status as a product of enforced servitude and poverty, see Introduction, note 9, p. 12.

are now widely identified as the most polluting and polluted of all 'untouchable' service-providers.[5]

In the old high-cultivation zones, especially in Malabar, deltaic Tamilnad and the eastern Gangetic plain, there were actually two distinct categories of lowly people. There were, first, the comparatively small groups of 'unclean' specialists described above. In addition, however, there were very much larger groups of dependent rural labourers. Those who fell into this second category too have come to be described as 'untouchable' (Harijan or Dalit in twentieth-century usage). These were the people who had come to be known collectively by such titles as Chamar, Chuhra and Mahar in the north and the Deccan, and as Paraiyan, Palla, Mala, Holeya and Cheruma in the south. In the south, these tillers of the lands of seigneurial wet-zone grandees were depicted by missionaries and colonial scholar-officials as slaves or near-slaves. Caste as a 'system' was held to designate these people too as permanently unclean and impure by virtue of the defiling labour which they performed, not as free labourers, but as providers of obligatory service to landed proprietors.[6]

In fact, however, much of this ritually defined subordination was a creation of relatively recent times, as will be seen below. Until well into the nineteenth century, many pastoral and 'tribal' domains were not yet fully penetrated by settled agriculture, and where there was expanding cultivation in these less fertile tracts it generally involved dry crops requiring few labourers apart from the smallholder's immediate 'peasant' kin. As was seen in Chapter 1, whether they were known as Jat, Kanbi, Kurmi or Kamma, people who 'touched the plough' in these dry-crop zones were commonly seen as non-patrician but not unclean. Many of these were the people whom the declining patricians tried to reduce to the status of dependent menials during the nineteenth and early twentieth centuries, invoking the logic of caste as

[5] Parry 1994; Randeria 1989. Some 'untouchable' service-providers performed both kinds of tasks, as in western India where, for men of Mahar caste, the occupation of hereditary village watchman is sometimes still combined with such duties as sweeping roads and carrying death notices. (See Zelliot 1970: 30; compare Nanjundayya and Iyer 1930, III: 324–5.)

[6] Bengal's largest rural labouring group became known as Chandel/Namasudra, and their Gujarat equivalent as Dubla/Halpati. Both were designated 'Depressed' or 'Scheduled' in twentieth-century ethnographic listings. Contemporary observers reported that neither was 'polluted' in the same sense as Holeyas, Chamars, Paraiyans and 'unclean' populations elsewhere. Both however came to be treated as ritually low and inferior to those of 'good' caste (*bhadralok* in Bengal; in Gujarati *ujliparaj*, superior or 'fair-skinned', as opposed to *kaliparaj* or 'black-visaged').

a means of legitimating their demands, and often receiving at least tacit support from the colonial authorities.

Initially, however, what these deference-seeking patricians were drawing on were ideas about impurity and menial status which applied to the much smaller groups of pollution-removing specialists, that is, to tonsurers, corpse- and carrion-handlers, and other purifiers. As ideals of seigneurial virtue spread more widely in the post-Mughal successor regimes, and came increasingly to emphasise Brahman-centred conventions of propriety and purity, there was growing demand for the services of these caste-specific pollution-removers with titles like Nai, Vannan, Bhangi and Dom. Even in the dry-zone tracts which had been only partially 'Brahmanised' by the state-building strategies of the eighteenth-century warrior-dynasts, there was a strong trend towards the use of such specialists. In the older high-cultivation areas too, indeed wherever there were concentrations of landed 'squireens', unclean menials of this kind came more and more to act as preservers of status and moral worth for households of patrons or *jajmans*, or for larger sections of the 'community' in areas of village-wide *baluta* schemes.

Some of these specialists' tasks, notably laundering and ordure-removing, were performed on a daily basis. Others filled needs arising at times of so-called life-crisis. Men of 'caste Hindu' origin still commonly have their hair sheared to dispel the powerful pollution (*sutak*) which is transmitted by a death within one's immediate kin-group; well into the twentieth century this task was still generally performed by hereditary specialist tonsurers of the type referred to above. By the principles of Brahmanical varna theory and the *sams-kara* cycle of life-stages, childbirth too releases both physical and intangible pollutions which must be dispelled by male and female purifiers from the barber and washerman jatis of a given locality.[7]

Many of these conventions were clearly widespread in past centuries, as is indicated in the early eighteenth-century Maratha documents which record the workings of village-wide *baluta* schemes. Elsewhere too, such conventions of caste-specific pollution-removing were

---

[7] On the distinction between the temporary impurity or inauspiciousness associated with birth and death, as opposed to the permanent uncleanliness attaching to those of low caste, see Parry 1994: 215–22; Raheja 1988b. Pollution-removing specialists are still found in most localities, though only rarely do they receive guaranteed payments from hereditary patrons or 'customary' shares of a locality's produce. See Breman 1974.

clearly known and followed. At the very least, this meant that people whom we would now call caste Hindus would be broadly aware of certain key sastric tenets. These would be the norms which hold that a truly civilised community is one that provides itself with dependent 'village servants' (*kamins*: also known by such regional terms as *prajas* and *ayagars*).[8] This for many anthropologists is the core of 'traditional' caste. On this basis, the ties between superior 'caste Hindus' and their dependent menials are based on caste logic; the services performed by tonsurers and other *kamins* are caste-specific and derive their meaning from the principles of purity and pollution.

These concepts were defined by Louis Dumont as inherently religious, and therefore antithetical to the values of modern economic rationality. Even today, while there are many areas where elaborate service networks are largely or entirely absent, some commentators would argue that where households or village-wide networks of patrons are served by Nais, Vannans and other cleansers and pollution-removers, the values of the market-place do not apply. In theory at least, *jajmans* are not expected to calculate the precise worth of the service-provider's activities, nor seek more cost-effective alternatives to the hereditary scavengers and tonsurers whose services they receive, often on an hereditary basis. In past centuries, such dependants supposedly had a fixed entitlement to food-grains and other necessities rather than receiving a cash wage. In reality, however, where one did find these ritualised service bonds they co-existed and overlapped with straightforwardly monetised exchanges of goods and labour.[9]

The lot of *kamin* or *balutedar* service-providers in past centuries has been widely portrayed as that of lowly but still protected sharers in the rituals and material assets of their home locality. These were clearly not benign or harmonious relationships: the nineteenth-century famine records show that untouchable village servants were among the first to perish in times of scarcity. Yet in more recent times, especially in the late nineteenth and twentieth centuries, those who had once been accustomed to a *kamin*'s limited entitlements generally found themselves far worse off when their former patrons gave up the

---

[8] Fuller 1989.
[9] Fuller 1989; Commander 1983; Kolenda 1967. On the mixture of ritualised and monetary forms of labour involving the small regional populations whose members were often cultivators but whose jati titles conveyed a tradition of specialist craft expertise (e.g. in north India Kumhar potters, Lohar blacksmiths, or Teli oil-pressers), see, for example, Bhattacharya 1992.

struggle to sustain these webs of rights and service, leaving former dependants to make their own way as unskilled workers in an ostensibly 'casteless' labour market.[10]

The rigidity and universality of *jajmani* and *baluta* have undoubtedly been overstated. Dumont and his followers have been sharply criticised for portraying these acts of ritualised pollution-removal as the cornerstone of all 'traditional' caste relationships; as was seen in Chapter 1, caste rank has often embodied far more than a simple opposition between the pure and the impure.[11] What is notable historically, however, is that there were many areas where conventions of caste-specific pollution-removing were widely embraced in the relatively recent past, especially in the seventeenth and eighteenth centuries as many aspiring Kshatriyas became more formally jati- and varna-conscious. Yet both in these locales and in those where landed and urban people had already been observing refined or clean-caste domestic practices over many centuries, the presence of small numbers of hereditary pollution-removers in their midst did not mean that the whole society deferred to a universal norm of purity and pollution. It was not even the case that all those deemed to be Hindus measured one another by caste criteria which disregarded all 'rational' considerations of wealth, power and individual attainment. The great change to be explored in this chapter then is the painful process by which insecure landed elites, and also many 'modern' city-dwellers, struggled to turn ever-larger groups of people, even members of the urban industrial workforce, into subordinated menials defined by these same criteria which had hitherto been applied primarily to the small specialist pollution-removing populations.

PATRICIANS INTO CASTE HINDUS

In orientalist reportage, the dependent status of unclean menial groups was defined by superior landed people in terms of the sexual availability of their womenfolk. According to nineteenth-century missionaries and anti-caste polemicists, both men and women from client labouring populations were expected to appear before lordly or *savarna* thread-wearers in the bare-bosomed garb of suppliants, and

---

[10] Breman 1974.
[11] Marx took much the same view of the 'traditional' economy of Indian villages.

to use a special language of self-abnegation when speaking to those they served. Where landed groups had adopted more Brahmanical styles of lordliness, these accounts also said that those of unclean birth contaminated water and foodstuffs by touch and were therefore banned from wells used by their superiors; residential hamlets were far removed from those of the non-polluting. Even the shadow of a so-called untouchable was held to be ritually defiling. The Malabar and Konkan regions were said to be so strict in caste matters that the lowest groups were unseeable as well as untouchable, wearing bells, on pain of death, to warn others of their approach.[12]

Some of this may have been orientalist invention, but in other cases much of what was reported as the experience of untouchability is undoubtedly real, but also comparatively modern in origin. This is not to say that caste ideologies were a fabrication of colonial officials and orientalists, though as was seen in previous chapters, colonial debates and data-collecting did affect the way in which both Indians and Europeans conceptualised jati and varna. From the early nineteenth century, these developments in ideology continued to intersect with the direct experience of environmental and economic change. So it was as colonial subjects with anxieties about the preservation of status and economic advantage that Indians came to sharpen boundaries of rank which had in the past been far more fluid and ambiguous. As will be seen below, this was especially true of areas where patrician elites were losing their power and prestige, and where armed 'tribals' and other comparatively un-castelike groups were being transformed into populations of dependent labourers and sharecroppers.

So how did caste come to be reshaped in these turbulent environments? Until well into the nineteenth century, even twice-born 'squireens' of Brahman birth generally subscribed to ideals of king-like power and mastery in their dealings with dependent labourers rather than a rigid pollution barrier. This can be seen, for example, in the fertile agrarian plains of southern Gujarat, where tightly-knit landed elites had been formed by clusters of *lokika* or non-priestly Brahmans. These were the people who came to be known by the caste title Anavil; many such families also used the title Desai which implied a heritage of privileged service and proprietorship under the Marathas.

[12] Kumar 1992; and see, for example, Buchanan's observations of 1801 (Buchanan 1870, II: 67) and Sarkar 1985.

As was noted in Chapter 1, their Vellala and Brahman equivalents in the south Indian high-cultivation zones called themselves *mirasidar*, a comparatively modern term meaning co-parcenary titleholder and designated revenue-payer.[13]

In the early days of Company rule, these rural grandees still lived lives of conspicuous lordliness which distinguished them from both the ordinary non-elite 'peasant' cultivator and the lowly labouring populations. To be an an Anavil or *mirasidar* landowner was by definition to command retainers, that is, to live among servile dependants who tilled their master's soil and received the means of subsistence from his hand. Even well into the nineteenth century, this area's large agrarian population was bound together by just such webs of patronage and dependence. The lands of a typical Anavil Desai would be tilled by household farm-servants whose displays of deference confirmed the status of their patron-proprietor. Most of these receivers of the big man's largesse were known by the jati title Dubla, and also as Halis, a term implying service and maintenance ties which were perpetuated through the institution of hereditary debt-bondage or *halipratha*.[14]

The lot of such dependants was not enviable; in their dealings with the big Anavil lord or one of his many regional counterparts, the client bond-servant undoubtedly met much coercion and brutality. At the same time, their lot had been significantly different in the days when the rural patricians still wielded power without serious challenges from the colonial state and the new circumstances of the colonial market-economy. Even in the early Company period the life of a Dubla, Mahar or Paraiyan tended to be more that of an ambivalently viewed royal retainer than a modern 'untouchable'. There was commonly a ritual side to these people's labour. During local festivals the Paraiyan drummed or carried ceremonial emblems; he and his regional counterparts had special access to the fierce goddesses and deified human heroes whose powers were both fearful and indispensable to the wider society.

So, like the martial peoples of the hills and forests, these dependent groups were courted and sometimes feared by the rent-receiving Rajput, Anavil or Tamil Vellala mirasidar. When he danced, trumpeted

[13] Breman 1985; Ludden 1985: 84–94.
[14] Breman 1985; and see Breman 1992 on the adoption of the twentieth-century Gandhian euphemism 'Halpati' for this group.

or exorcised, the Mahar's or Dubla's glorification of his patron made him something akin to the landowner's humble subject, and therefore a distant but still active co-sharer in the big man's realm. Whether he needed labourers, emblem bearers or supernatural intermediaries, the 'squireen' made use of his Mahars or Dublas in ways that affirmed his prowess and potency. Therefore, until well into the nineteenth century and sometimes far later, the priority for these patrician groups was to have an imposing establishment of subjects, and not a parade of ritually degraded menials who were indistinguishable from village scavengers and other specialist pollution-removers.

In Bengal too, yet another version of the lordly culture described in Chapter 1 had become entrenched in regions of high population density and intensive agricultural production. By the early nineteenth century much of central and east Bengal had become dominated by a rural gentry (widely referred to as *bhadralok*, lit. 'good people') which contained many Brahmans, most notably those who followed the distinctive marriage practices known as kulinism. As in the case of Gujarat's patrician Desais, Bengal's landed rent-receivers had come to exercise seigneurial authority over populations of tillers and field labourers – although in contrast to Gujarat's big groups of bonded plough-servants, Bengal's dependent labouring and tenant groups included many Muslims, as well as non-Muslim servile groups to whom such demeaning titles as Bagdi, Bauri and Chandal came to be applied.[15]

The equivalents in rice-growing south Bihar were the big proprietary lords whom the region's Muslim rulers had termed *maliks*, and the dependent groups of so-called bond-servants who came to be known by the general term *kamia*, meaning service-provider, and also by the more specific jati title Bhuinya. Even in relatively recent times, these people's forebears did not slot into a neat order of fixed hierarchical caste relationships. The origins of the *malik* families were extremely mixed, and the groups whom the colonial ethnographers defined as members of hereditary labouring castes were also of diverse ancestry. Many of these *kamias* or Bhuinyas were clearly of 'tribal' and pastoralist origin; their arms-bearing forebears would have been assimilated, often forcibly, into expanding zones of settled agriculture under the rule of the revenue-hungry Mughal and post-Mughal rulers.

---

[15] Bose 1986; Ray 1984.

At the time of the British conquest, their relationships with the landed *malik* lords were still complex and open-ended, and had not yet been simplified down to that of the labouring bond-servant with an obligation to provide menial service for a landholding superior.[16]

In eastern Gangetic Hindustan, there were yet more high-farming zones where superior rent-receivers could claim to have been following a life of lordly refinement for many centuries. Here the established patricians included many co-parcenors from 'secular' or *lokika* Brahman groupings such as the Kanyakubjas and Sarjuparins of Awadh; these areas also contained clusters of landed Rajputs. Other Gangetic 'squireens' belonged to the north Indian status group known as Bhumihar, who had achieved a somewhat ambiguous entitlement to be regarded as Brahmans under the patronage of eighteenth-century rulers and their local deputies. In addition, some of upper India's high-farming localities contained sizable groups of elite landed Muslims; landed families of scribal and service origin who used the jati title Kayastha had also come to be included among the proprietary 'squireen' populations. In southern Awadh, eastern NWP, and much of Bihar, non-labouring gentry groups lived in tightly-knit enclaves among much larger populations of non-elite 'peasants' and labouring people. These other groupings included 'untouchable' Chamars and newly recruited 'tribal' labourers, as well as non-elite tilling and cattle-keeping people who came to be known by such titles as Kurmi, Koeri and Goala/Ahir. In earlier centuries, and under less insecure circumstances, these proprietary people had not made such clear-cut distinctions between themselves and those of servile or ritually inferior status. Even in the early colonial period, such categories as Jat, Koli or Kurmi constituted a very broad continuum, shading only very imprecisely into that of the 'lordly' Rajput or Bhumihar. Thus, even with the increasing spread of Brahmanical norms and values, the moral order of the widow-remarrying tiller was not yet fully distinct from that of the non-widow-remarrying 'kingly' jajman.

All this had greatly changed by the mid-nineteenth century, by which time very large numbers of people had come to experience quite a different manifestation of caste. This involved a widespread assimilation of sober *bania*-merchant or Brahman-centred norms and values

---

[16] Prakash 1990a: 34–81; on a similar influx of 'tribal' Santal and Rajbansi (initially known as Koch and Paliya) labourers into areas of expanding cultivation in north Bengal, see Bose 1986: 12.

among landed people who had not previously embraced them. These changes manifested themselves through a growing emphasis on the pollution barrier, and an insistence on the radical differentiation between those who were and those who were not defined as high, clean and superior in jati and varna terms. The sources of this transformation were complex and numerous, but paramount among them were the social and economic changes which embroiled a high proportion of the subcontinent's landed elites in fierce struggles against declining fortune and status. These struggles entered India's historical record quite directly. From about 1840, the travails of these embittered lords began to make their mark on the record of the subcontinent's turbulent political history. Above all, their struggles to retain power and status lay behind the Mutiny-Rebellion of 1857. They then continued to play a major role in the increasingly violent disputes that culminated in the large-scale anti-landlord 'peasant movements' of the early twentieth century.

The troubles of the old rural patricians can be traced to the period between about 1820 and 1840 when stagnant market conditions depressed the commercial value of agricultural land across the sub-continent. This was just at the time when the East India Company's provincial administrations were demanding what were often unrealistically high rates of revenue from these landed groups.[17] Either individually or collectively, the colonial authorities reclassified these families of rent-receivers as landowners with tightly defined obligations of regularly assessed payment under the colonial land settlement systems. During the early decades of the century, East India Company officials devised comparatively effective means of enforcement through the courts. Throughout the depression period of the 1820s and 1830s, these procedures were widely used against proprietors who had hitherto been able to evade or 'default' on revenue payments without serious threat of losing privileged landholding rights. Subsequently, in the middle decades of the century, there were two contrasting trends in India's agrarian regions. Previously marginal areas took off as zones of newly profitable 'peasant' agriculture, advantaging non-elite tilling groups, who were known by such titles as Jat in western NWP and Gounder in Coimbatore. There was also an intensification of agriculture in such areas as Tanjore, Gangetic Bihar

---

[17] Stokes 1978; Breman 1985: 108–9.

and eastern UP. These densely settled riverine locales became zones of agricultural 'involution', meaning that they were afflicted by volatile market conditions, rapid population growth and escalating social unrest.[18]

The result of these trends was that when agricultural prices and incomes began to rise after mid-century, the old landed elites were left trying to maintain their distinctiveness as people who scorned the plough and commanded retainers, at a time when they were becoming ever more badly placed to assert this kind of lordliness. Those who might naturally have turned to the commercial labour market found that the hiring of agricultural labourers had become prohibitively expensive. So what was a man of honour to do? In Gangetic Hindustan the ideal situation, long established by the practices of East India Company military recruitment, was for a family of appropriate descent to send its sons into the ranks of the Bengal Army. From the mid-eighteenth century, the Company's military authorities had systematically encouraged this trend. In the hope of keeping its soldiers loyal to their 'salt', a concept which was widely understood by arms-bearing people as a bond of pride and dedicated allegiance to their commanders, the Bengal Army had adopted elaborate techniques of selection and regimental ritual. These were designed to establish an explicitly high-caste identity for the army's regular regiments through the adoption of distinctly Brahman-centred marks of honour for serving sepoys, thus making service in the Bengal infantry regiments a cherished proof of honourable origins for its superior 'peasant' soldiers.[19]

Here then, we do see a British initiative which fostered (but did not create) a more formally Brahmanical sense of caste among key groups in the society. These Bengal Army recruits could expect to be provided with a 'pure' vegetarian diet while on active service, and their commanders appointed Brahman ritualists as the equivalent of military chaplains to Brahman and Rajput soldiers. Even when their sepoys went on pilgrimage to the Hindu holy places and had dealings with such arbiters of status as bathing-ghat priests and genealogical recorders (*pandas*), the Bengal Army took steps to identify its ranks as the preserve of superior 'twice-born' men. These guarantees were particu-

[18] See, for example, Guha 1985, especially ch. 5; on the concept of agricultural involution see Geertz 1974.
[19] Alavi 1995; Kolff 1990.

larly prized by recruits whose origins would not otherwise have been thought of as exalted or pure by Brahmanical standards. This was especially important for soldiers of Bhumihar Brahman descent whose distinctive 'caste' identity was largely created through military service, and then confirmed by the forms of continuous 'social spending' which defined a man and his kin as superior and lordly.[20]

By the 1840s, the Bengal Army was becoming wary of its old-style patrician soldiery and was beginning on grounds of both cost and reliability to seek recruits who were thought to be more amenable to 'modern' discipline. These included men of Sikh Jat origin from the disbanded forces of the former Punjab kingdom, and also many so-called Dogras from the Himalayan hill states whose claims of 'pure' Rajput origin were hotly disputed by the groups which had hitherto predominated in the Bengal Army. After the 1857 Mutiny-Rebellion, the search for 'simpler' classes of recruits without so-called 'social pretensions', 'caste prejudices' and 'disagreeable hindustani airs' led to large-scale recruitment among those whom the colonial authorities had come to call the martial races.[21] The favoured populations here included supposedly 'casteless' Pathans of the northwest frontier, as well as Gurkhas from Nepal.

These threats to the Company's former clients came at just the moment when soldiering was providing a crucial boost to cash-hungry landed families. By mid-century, a large proportion of upper India's non-labouring 'squireens' had come to depend on service incomes to finance their lavish wedding celebrations and all the other critical marks of their lordly lifestyles. These attacks on the sepoy-gentry groups' privileged livelihoods led directly to the most testing crisis of early Indian colonialism. Fearful of losing the means to sustain these costly norms, it was the landed Rajputs and Brahman 'Pandeys' of the Bengal Army who began and sustained the great Mutiny-Rebellion of 1857.

In the longer term, the chief consequence of these developments with regard to caste was a widespread hardening of boundaries between the superior landed groups and those deemed to be low and 'impure' in caste terms. Those worst hit by this trend were the non-elite rural labouring groups. Given their reduced incomes and the

[20] Alavi 1995.
[21] Balfour 1873, IV: R31; Alavi 1995; Omissi 1994: 31–2, 53.

rising cost of hired labour, the retention of paid field servants was becoming highly problematic for the Hindustan soldiering elites. The situation was much the same for the superior non-martial gentry groups in Bengal, Gujarat and Tamilnad. Certainly there were large-scale proprietors who fared comparatively well in these changing political and economic circumstances. Seigneurial ways and values often survived even after Independence among the descendants of these more favoured landed groups, as in the case of the 'kingly' Telugu *dora* lords described in Chapter 8. Yet in most areas, there were far larger numbers of petty 'squireens' with poorer lands and smaller holdings who now found that they possessed only one critical asset with which to stave off the escalating insecurities emanating from unfavourable revenue settlements and volatile market trends. This was the possibility of coercing those who could plausibly be identified as menials with an innate obligation to toil and serve. It was in these enounters that the logic of rigidly differentiated jati and varna rankings came to be invoked with particular severity.

From the mid-nineteenth century, patrician landowners in the old high-cultivation zones made moves to mark out and dominate populations of tied or subservient tenants, labourers and other inferior retainers. The symbols of caste featured strongly in these initiatives, even – indeed especially – where such demands had clear-cut economic value. In most cases, what the seigneurial groups were seeking to obtain was unpaid labour, often referred to as *begar*, or dues in kind (*rasad*), from those whom they deemed to be of servile birth.[22]

In some instances these were attempts to stave off decline by reinvigorating or intensifying existing forms of customary service. Elsewhere these were wholly novel demands, many being imposed on 'clean' tillers and cattle-keepers like the Ram- and Krishna-loving Koeris, Kurmis and Ahirs who were discussed in Chapter 2. In either case, these calls were buttressed with appeals to Sanskritic varna theory and Brahmanical caste convention. What the patrician groups were claiming was that to be landed, and to use a 'twice-born' caste title like Bhumihar or Rajput, was to hold a divinely mandated right to exact dues and deference from those of lowly caste origin. In south India – where Tamil *mirasidars* and Andhra rice-land proprietors were becoming more assertive in their dealings with labouring Paraiyans

---

[22] Pinch 1996: 126; Chaudhuri 1979: 349; Dhanagare 1986: 113.

and Pallas in Tamilnad, and Malas and Madigas in the Telugu country – insecure co-parcenors were increasingly inclined to address these labouring groups in terms which conveyed connotations of unclean or *avarna* status. Similar trends can be seen in relations between proprietors in upper India and their Chamar field servants. At the same time, Kurmi and Goala/Ahir tillers who held tenancies from these 'squireens' found themselves being identified as Shudras, that is, as people who were mandated to serve those of the superior Kshatriya and Brahman varnas.[23]

As they made these moves to subordinate 'unclean' labourers, the lordly groups came increasingly to represent themselves as defenders of correct dharmic standards. Domestic norms became more conspicuously Brahmanical, with many seigneurial households taking on a more elaborate range of services from the specialist pollution-removers. Restrictive marriage conventions also became more widespread; proprietary people came increasingly to adopt forms of alliance which had formerly typified only the most exalted princely houses. Patricians claiming Rajput origin were especially insistent that those who claimed to share their blood must reject alliances with the herding and 'tribal' groups whom their forebears had often accepted as bride-givers. These, it was said, were the practices of 'pure' lineages who were scrupulous about the preservation of blood-lines, and were thus entitled to demand deference and service from inferior 'peasant' groups. According to many missionaries and social reformers, these moves were also associated with the increased incidence of female infanticide, which was widely reported on at this time as the great evil of Rajput domestic life.[24]

CLEAN-CASTE FAITH AND AGRARIAN CONFLICT

These developments of the mid- to late nineteenth century represented a real shift in both the language and lived reality of rural social life.

[23] Bengal was often described as being without rigorous forms of untouchability, though colonial observers noted that in the later nineteenth century elite landed groups became increasingly insistent about the 'impurity' of 'Chandala'/Namasudra labourers. See Bandyopadhyay 1997.

[24] For example, Sherring 1872: 119–20, and see Kasturi 1994. As with other proprietary groups, not all those identifying themselves as Rajputs embraced these exacting norms; only some lineages opted for the 'best' or purest marriage strategies. For an anthropological account of this diversity in the definition of 'correct' Rajput marriage conventions, see Parry 1979: 221–46.

Seigneurial families who had once defined their honourable status primarily in terms of secure landed rights, and in upper India through privileged military service, now buttressed demands for service and *rasad* dues by imposing codes of ritual servility onto a growing array of landless farm servants and former 'tribal' share-croppers who had not previously been bracketed with 'untouchable' pollution-removers. Even smallholders and labourers of comparatively 'good' caste found themselves in this position, especially as more modestly placed landed groups began to pursue the same strategies as the more exalted fortress-dwelling Bhumihars and other rural grandees. Indeed it was often comparatively humble 'dwija' (high-caste) landowners who had the most to gain by trying to place non-elite cultivators, including those of comparatively 'clean' status, on a footing much like that of tonsurers and other *kamin*-type service-providers.

Here too, colonial policy was important though not all-powerful. In the south, colonial officials actually invented traditions of obligatory labour for those whom they defined as low in caste terms.[25] In the north, the provisions of new property legislation, including the Awadh Rent Act of 1868, conferred rights on 'squireen' revenue payers which were not confirmed for share-cropping tenants and dependent labouring groups. In later decades, as agricultural prices rose, many 'twice-born' landlords began to treat these distinctions in law as a licence to demand *begar* and *rasad* (or their regional equivalents) from those who laboured or held land under them. Those pressed in this way included many so-called middling peasants whom the struggling landed groups sought to designate as ritually impure and therefore innately menial, meaning that such people's caste status was to be defined as an inherited quality of servitude.[26]

In the later nineteenth century, this so-called *begar* question provoked one of north India's increasingly persistent waves of agrarian unrest. These outbreaks were centred in the old high-farming zones of Awadh, where non-elite cultivating groups attempted to fight off the coercive service demands of their 'twice-born' rent-receivers. The rise in agricultural prices which affected much of India from the late 1870s to the 1920s placed even greater pressure on these old proprietary groups. Predictably enough, their response was to inten-

---

[25] See Ludden 1985: 82.
[26] Metcalf 1979: 216–29.

sify demands for 'caste'-based dues and services from share-cropping tenants and labouring groups. Here too, as in western India, claims and counter-claims involving landlords on the one hand and tenants or labourers on the other were hard to enforce and therefore all the more bitterly fought over. These conflicts strongly influenced the way in which jati and varna came to be experienced in the nineteenth century. Indeed wherever India's agricultural economies were affected by slumps, surges and insecurities of livelihood and entitlement, these manifestations of caste became ever more pervasive in the lives of rural people.

With rather uneven support from the colonial authorities, as well as initiatives taken through movements of regionally based devotional religion, these *begar* and *rasad* impositions provoked widespread resistance among those whom the gentry landowners were trying to identify as low-caste and servile. With some notable exceptions, the groups who tried to fight off these pressures did so by invoking their own versions of jati and varna logic. This then was the context in which the modern experience of caste hierarchy and an all-pervading pollution barrier came into being in areas which had hitherto been only partially caste-like or 'Brahmanised'.[27]

The continuing spread of devotional religious movements had a profound impact on the non-elite tillers who were trying to fight off the claims of the gentry groups. In the Gangetic north, the claims of the worthy 'peasant' often became focused on the worship of the Vaishnavite deities, most notably through ethical teachings associated with the Hindi devotional text known as the *Ramcharitmanas*. In some areas, especially in Bengal and the Malabar coast, certain forms of purified Islamic teaching conveyed this same message, portraying the claims of local landed elites as iniquitous and ungodly. Where the patrician proprietary elites were Brahmans or other high-caste Hindus, these struggles with a predominantly Muslim tenant or labouring population inevitably made for a closing of ranks on both sides of this divide, with embattled landlords joining hands around a more assertive ideal of caste purity, and their former dependants asserting themselves in the name of a militantly 'Islamic' community.[28]

The monotheist or purified Hindu faith which was communicated

[27] *Ibid.*: 220 n. 68; 229.
[28] Dhanagare 1986: 119; Sengupta 1979; Lutgendorf 1989; Ahmed 1981.

in north India by the anti-Brahmanical proselytisers of the Arya Samaj had an equally powerful appeal to many non-elite rural groups. From the late nineteenth century Jat identity in particular came to be firmed up around the sober and pious Arya version of Hindu faith. To be Jat and Arya was thus to be radically different from the lowly – that is, from Chamars and other 'untouchables' – as well as from those who had hitherto claimed elite proprietary status, meaning Rajputs and lordly landowning Brahmans. In western India's newly commercialised black-soil cotton tracts, Arya Samaj proselytisers also helped to persuade prosperous 'peasant' landowners to purify their domestic practices, and to adopt the jati title Patidar in preference to Kanbi, with its connotations of undiscriminating marriage conventions and other coarse 'bhabha' (rustic) ways.[29]

For their part, the struggling seigneurial groups frequently claimed that the powers they were seeking to exercise over dependent labourers were of ancient origin, and that they were sanctioned in Hindu scripture as correct and righteous for the man of power in his capacity as upholder of dharmic propriety. In reality, these landed people were trying to take advantage of the fact that colonial India was coming to contain more and more people who were defining both themselves and others on the basis of an increasingly stark division between clean and unclean birth. Many of these so-called polluting groups were the non-patrician 'peasants' and field labourers described above. Others were newly marginalised forest people who had lost their privileged relationships with the Maratha dynasts and other rulers, but who were still without a settled niche in the village-based agrarian economies. When these people sold such skills as they had to the expanding agrarian populations, they were disparaged by the British as 'gypsies' and criminal predators. They were also despised as uncivilised vermin-handlers by the status-conscious village people for whom they trapped snakes, hunted game or collected forest produce.[30]

These battles over caste-specific dues and statuses set the scene for the emergence of the so-called peasant movements which took root in many areas from the time of the First World War. In the north, these outbreaks often took the form of anti-landlord activism involving

[29] Pradhan 1966: 40–2; Datta 1997; Breman 1985: 95.
[30] Crooke 1907: 72–5; Cox n.d.: 212, 234–6, 240–4; Skaria 1992.

bodies known as Kisan Sabhas (tillers' assemblies). Those involved were primarily land-hungry or landless rural groups with such titles as Kurmi or Ahir, which were indicative of non-proprietary origins. These protests were not confined to the members of any one caste, and those who took part commonly professed a sense of generalised 'middle peasant' solidarity. Yet far from dissolving the importance of jati and varna, both the organisation and the rhetoric of these movements built directly on heightened awareness of caste, identifying the tiller's enemies as 'twice-born' oppressors who espoused false Brahmanical values, and exalting the *kisan* as a worthy 'caste reformer' whose heritage as a Kurmi, Ahir or Yadav (Goala) was that of the noble Kshatriya and not the inglorious Shudra.[31]

These forms of activism generally had a millenarian or liberationist religious element, often being led or inspired by what colonial intelligence files referred to in the 1920s and 1930s as 'political *sadhus*' (Hindu mendicants). The most prominent of these politically active holy men, including the Awadh 'peasant' advocate Baba Ramchandra and Bihar's Swami Sahajanand Saraswati, had ties to established Hindu monastic orders with strong traditions of divinely sanctioned arms-bearing. Both drew on regional devotional traditions associated with the gods of the Vishnu pantheon. These activist monks also called on the non-elite cultivators who 'touched the plough' to deny that they were Shudras, and to see themselves as thread-wearing Kshatriyas and heirs of noble vedic Aryans.[32]

In Gangetic Bihar and eastern Uttar Pradesh (UP), where the rustic cults of the god-king Ram and the cow-loving Krishna were already strong, pious '*kisans*' responded eagerly to the idea that they and not the Brahman or Rajput were true exemplars of devotion and *dharma*, and that through these gods of peasant virtue the Kurmi or Ahir was empowered to assert an ideal of 'community' and assertive moral mandate. Such norms were to be fulfilled in ways that were linked to the anxieties of the land-hungry *kisan* with a fragile new prosperity to protect. The region's petty proprietors were therefore addressed by polemicists who exhorted them to better themselves and their 'communities' by protecting the cow and cultivating codes of Ram-like manliness which exalted soldier-like assertiveness for men and seclu-

---

[31] Pinch 1996; Dhanagare 1986.
[32] Pinch 1996: 11–12, 131–4; Hauser 1991–2, 1994.

sion for female kin. Donning the sacred thread of the twice-born was equally important in these campaigns, as was resistance to the landed Brahman or Rajput 'squireens' who were pressing for *begar* and *rasad* dues.[33]

THE SEIGNEURS AND THEIR CREDITORS

To turn now to the second set of changes referred to at the start of this chapter, the other great influence in this age of rigidifying caste barriers was the exaltation of pious purity by men of the pen and the ledger. As was seen in the first two chapters, the age of military fiscalism had generally been good for some though not all members of India's lordly landed groups, even in areas where its commercialised forms of statecraft had created new opportunities for men of commercial acumen, and for those with expertise in the associated skills of priestcraft and record-keeping. In the later nineteenth century there was a pervasive shift in the relative strength of the landed and the moneyed. In the more legalistic and bureaucratised environment which was fostered by colonial rule, these interpenetrating worlds of commerce, statecraft and landed privilege were pulling apart. The new winners in these situations typically had such jati titles as Marwari, Agarwal, Oswal and Chettiar, these being designations for the relatively small but powerful banking and trading populations who had earlier been allies and dependants of the big landed magnates and lesser squireen groups.

In many volatile agrarian regions, commercial men were becoming conspicuous as creditors of hard-pressed seigneurial people. These people of *bania* or trader-banker background relished the prestige they were acquiring from acts of pious largesse and the adoption of purity-conscious domestic standards. Such practices inspired widespread emulation on the part of non-elite landed groups (see below, pp. 221–5). The free-spending rent-receiver therefore found himself surrounded by people who disparaged his way of life and exalted the attributes of merchants and rustics. Of particular concern here was the fact that so many colonial commentators had taken to expressing hostility towards 'unproductive' proprietary people, proclaiming that the patrician elites were 'fast losing ground' to more vigorous peasant

[33] Pinch 1996.

9. Photograph sent to the colonial anthropologist J. H. Hutton, with a contemporary label identifying the sitter by occupation and 'community': 'India: Udaipur, Street Banker – Marwari Baniya'.

and commercial populations, and dismissing landed Rajputs in particular as a corrupted and 'down-going race', trying vainly to maintain their 'failing rule'.[34]

By the mid-nineteenth century, influential revenue specialists were reporting that they could tell the caste of a landed man by simply glancing at his crops. In the north, these observers claimed, a field of 'second-rate barley' would belong to a Rajput or Brahman who took pride in shunning the plough and secluding his womenfolk. Such a man was to be blamed for his own decline, fecklessly mortgaging and then selling off his lands to maintain his unproductive dependants. By the same logic, a flourishing field of wheat would belong to a non-twice-born tiller, wheat being a crop requiring skill and enterprise on the part of the cultivator. These, said such commentators as Denzil Ibbetson and E. A. H. Blunt, were the qualities of the non-patrician 'peasant' – the thrifty Jat or canny Kurmi in upper India, Marathas and Kanbis in the west, Kammas, Reddis or Lingayats in the south, upwardly mobile Mahishyas in Bengal. Similar virtues would be found among the smaller market-gardening populations, these being the people known as Koeris in Hindustan, or the skilled but low-status Shanar palmyra cultivators of Tamilnad. A man from this so-called yeoman background, a *khedut* or *kisan*, was reputed to maximise the use of his own family labour force (women as well as men), so as never to leave his lands 'to the mercy of hirelings'.[35]

If tillers of this sort fell into debt, the blame must attach to the money-lending *bania* (merchant), and not the worthy Jat or Kurmi. In the later nineteenth century, this thinking led colonial officials to try to protect Sikh Jats and the other non-elite 'peasants' whom they now favoured as military recruits by advocating legislation against so-called land alienation. This was the new official term for the acquisition of debtors' land titles by members of the so-called non-agrarian castes. In many troubled areas these moves were bitterly frustrating to members of newly prosperous commercial and professional families who identified themselves as Khatri, Agarwal or Arora by birth. In the urban Punjab particularly, people like this became the backbone of the early Congress, and one can see why these crudely caste-centred colonial policies helped to popularise the new anti-colonial nationalisms of the

---

[34] Sherring 1872, quoted in Campbell n.d.: 119.
[35] Blunt 1969: 264; Oldham 1876 Pt II: 92, 105.

late nineteenth and early twentieth centuries. These then were much more than matters of ephemeral colonial 'discourse'; among Indians too, lordliness was coming to be viewed as a dubious quality compared with the values of containment, restraint and ordered sobriety.

THE ADVANCE OF THE MERCHANT-VAISHYA

But where exactly did these assertively caste-conscious Indians find their new models of jati and varna? The answer to this is to be found in the milieu of the entrepreneur and commodity producer rather than that of the patrician landholder. While the nineteenth century brought insecurity to many proprietary landed groups, it was also an era of real if sporadic gains for men of literate and commercial livelihoods. It was through contact with these people that many Indians – including struggling gentry landholders – acquired a fuller knowledge of hierarchical caste conventions.

As was seen in Chapter 2, both priestly and secular (*lokika*) Brahmans, as well as people from 'clean-caste' commercial and service backgrounds, were thrust into new positions of power through increasing monetisation, specialised commodity production, and the spread of complex revenue operations under the post-Mughal 'successor' regimes. In the initial phase of colonial conquest, all sorts of self-made traders and specialist money-handlers were able to consolidate the hold they had gained over state and military finance. Despite intermittent attempts by the British to stop them, many then went on to enhance their power in rural regions by buying up land rights from Rajput or Brahman 'squireens' and other indebted proprietary groups in the agrarian depression of the 1830s.[36]

These moneyed people were referred to in the regional vernaculars as *mahajans*, *banias* or *saukars*. These terms were often used interchangeably for followers of commercial callings; the Tamil usage *chetti* or *chettiar* had the same connotations in the south. In the conditions of the nineteenth-century colonial economy, with its heavy revenue-taking and volatile commodity exports, native banking and trading houses were placed at a profound disadvantage compared with British-run firms. Nevertheless, the comparatively successful members

[36] C. Bayly 1988: 154.

10. Photograph labelled 'Rajput', probably also for use by Hutton in a wartime propaganda pamphlet on Indian racial 'types'.

of these merchant-*mahajan* populations became figures of great importance during the nineteenth century. As a result, an increasingly wide array of imitators and clients looked to the trading groups as models of piety and dharmic conduct in both town and countryside.

Of course there were many Parsis, Jains, Muslims and even Christian converts among the specialist commercial grandees. But when one looks at the trading groups who identified themselves as 'caste Hindus', those who came to exemplify the superior 'caste' standards of so-called *bania* or *mahajan-saukar* culture often had comparatively humble backgrounds. This was particularly true of the traders who had exploited new fiscal opportunities at the point of contact with military finance. In the seventeenth and eighteenth centuries when regional rulers were still highly flexible in their deference to jati and varna conventions, some self-made commercial magnates equipped themselves with highly un-*bania*-like accoutrements, including armies, harems and aggressive political aspirations.[37]

The emergence of a strong sense of caste among these *bania* groups is a relatively recent development, even though such people rapidly came to represent themselves as embodiments of ancient Hindu orthodoxy. Yet even in the mid-nineteenth century, many big traders, especially those with established links to the European colonial powers, still emphasised a 'kingly' model of honour and authority. These commercial groups' marks of lordliness were often endorsed by official *sanad*, or declaration, as the hereditary rights of the *mahajan* or 'big man' families who first held them.[38] After the British conquest, these models of officially sanctioned 'caste' leadership spread even more widely. This was especially notable in the south, where British officials encouraged specialist artisan populations to adopt similar conventions, vesting authority over the 'community' in so-called *panchayats* or councils of caste notables. By the end of the nineteenth century, colonial ethnographers were reporting that such people as fisherfolk and artisans possessed age-old institutions through which 'traditional' caste elders resolved disputes about both trade and domestic morality.[39]

---

[37] Including south India's Telugu-speaking Komati merchants. See Subrahmanyam 1990: 298–342.
[38] S. Bayly 1989: 336–7; Rudner 1994; also Laidlaw 1995: 89–119 on the interplay of kingly Rajput and pacific *bania*-style ideals of identity among urban commercial Jains.
[39] Blunt 1969: 104–31.

Until the early decades of the nineteenth century, south India's convention of so-called left-hand/right-hand caste groupings was still being invoked in the turbulent coastal towns of the Tamil and Telugu country by local 'big men' in circumstances of keen commercial competition. A man who did this while also endowing temples or other pious institutions would stand a good chance of enhancing his stature as a big Komati or Chettiar *mahajan* trader. Both local people and colonial officials recognised the prominent commercial magnates of the left and right as 'kinglike' men of power over these localities' comparatively humble artisanal and labouring populations.[40] This exaltation of magnate traders thus had the effect of fostering a fiction of community or collective affinity among people who were often of disparate backgrounds and had only recently come together to claim common caste affinity in the new commercial entrepôts. But the fiction of caste allegiance and deference to 'royal' caste headmen rapidly became a reality both within and beyond these localities. This tended to happen more and more as newly affiliated families acquired common assets, and then found that they could often protect these by enhancing their bonds of caste affinity.

THE INTERNAL LOGIC OF THE MERCHANT'S PURITY

These groups of 'community'-conscious trading specialists soon found advantage in adjusting their *mahajan* pretensions towards increasingly purity-conscious or dharmic ideals. This can be seen in the commercial towns of Bengal and Gangetic Hindustan, where Hindu trading people had begun to reject the lordly ways of life which they now associated with these regions' former Urdu-speaking nawabi aristocracies. By the early nineteenth century, these groups were turning instead to 'Hindu-ness', which they understood as the adoption of Brahmanically defined strictness in marriage and household custom. Many also proclaimed these new bonds by attaching themselves to purist campaigning organisations such as Bengal's Dharma Sabha.

Such people were often strongly influenced by new movements and organisations which had come to promote a very different model of piety and virtue for the man of means. From Nadia, Prayag (Alla-

---

[40] Brimnes 1996.

habad), Banaras and the other fast-growing centres of pilgrimage and dharmic priestly ritual, the great corporations of ascetics and genealogical recorders (*pandas*) were sending out representatives with a mandate to enlist more worshippers into their networks of pilgrimage and devotional adherence. In addition to trading and literate service people, these quests for new constituents attracted many 'tribals' and non-twice-born cultivators towards ways of life which emphasised classically defined versions of 'caste' custom.[41]

The self-made commercial people may well have been aware that sastric texts often portray handlers of money and goods as little more than Shudras, and certainly not as persons of quality. So in Bengal, as elsewhere, these pious movements appealed strongly to those struggling to establish their respectability and credit-worthiness in competitive environments. From the late eighteenth century there was a marked trend for newly established commercial people to abjure meat and alcohol, and to embrace the other forms of austerity that were associated with a pure or Brahmanical way of life. In some extreme cases, this included moves to proclaim the virtues of *sati* (the immolation of widows). The debates that were generated around these issues set the tone for much of Bengal's so-called orthodox Hindu revivalism for the rest of the nineteenth century.[42]

Similar moves were made by mobile trading people from the north and west, including those who came to be known by the title Marwari, this being originally no more than a regional designation for trading migrants from Marwar in Rajasthan. By the early twentieth century, however, these clusters of rich commercial people had become widely known as embodiments of distinctive *bania*-merchant culture. The name Marwari acquired pejorative connotations for many Indians, evoking images of rapacity in commerce, and a lifestyle of self-interested merit-making and ostentation. These stereotypes have been applied to many of India's other commercial groups too, both today and in the past.[43]

Among these people, too, it was the more prominent personalities among town-based commmercial populations who were able to advance themselves in this new race for honour and social endorse-

---

[41] These movements have also been seen as subversive of caste norms. See Chatterjee 1989; also Chatterji 1994: 42.

[42] Sangari and Vaid 1989.

[43] Timberg 1978; compare Laidlaw 1995: 87–119; Hardiman 1996.

ment. Newly established merchants signalled their commitment to dharmic correctness in ways that were readily recognisable to others. As in the case of the old rent-receiving populations, the making of scrupulous marriages became a critical strategy here. The urban trader-*bania*s rapidly became known as keen recorders of genealogical information.[44]

When such families extended their operations by despatching close kin to distant trading centres, they knew that both marriage and commercial connections would be denied them unless suspicious scrutineers could be shown that they were of suitably 'clean' and respectable status. What was being tested in these encounters was a composite notion of good credit, good conduct and good 'blood', meaning acceptability in marital terms. These were all expressions of the same rigorous standards of worth and value which made marriage ties an asset for traders in much the same sense as their stock of goods and their reputation for honest dealing. Indeed the 'big man'-*mahajan* often found himself under relentless pressure, aware that his own and his firm's stock of honour and credit-worthiness could rapidly dwindle away if he or his household relaxed the forms of conduct which signalled a commitment to dharmic propriety. And, although the considerations here were often those of the individual entrepreneur or tightly-knit family firm, such people's anxieties about advantage, honour and substance were coming to be expressed in terms of correct 'caste' practice.

Those who embraced these norms generally subscribed to the versions of *ahimsa* austerity which told the man of means to consign his wealth to meritorious purposes. Acts of conspicuous piety were therefore popular among the big urban traders. Such people achieved renown as patrons of temples and rituals, especially those glorifying the non-bloodtaking gods, often though not invariably Vaishnavite, whose cults are now thought of as the key features of puranic 'high' Hinduism. Banaras commercial families recorded these pious works in business ledgers (*bahi khattas*) as legitimate capital expenditures, that is, as transactions which underpinned their honour and credit-worthiness.[45]

In both the north and the south, *bania-mahajan* merchant families

---

[44] Rudner 1994; Sherring 1872: 287.
[45] Rudner 1994; C. Bayly 1983: 178–82, 377.

further proclaimed their commitment to these ideals through the endowment of hospices (*goshalas*) for the mass feeding of cows. Some *bania*-style ways of life are notable too for their exaltation of the Brahman; more widespread however is veneration of the cow. In puranic Hindu tradition, both cows and Brahmans sanctify by their acceptance of pious offerings. Ideally, all Brahmans are strict vegetarians and teetotallers who abstain from sensual indulgence and life-taking. The cow too is a pacific herbivore, appearing in the Hindu epics and *purana* texts as *kamadhenu*, the nurturer and wish-fulfiller; by exemplifying an ideal of nurturing divinity, it too is an embodiment of rectitude and purity for the 'caste Hindu'.[46]

These were powerful considerations for the many *mahajan*-merchants who had been taking over from the warrior dynasts and other declining men of prowess as patrons of temples, monastic foundations (*maths*), and religious festivals. The emergence of trader-bankers as patrons of the Ramlila, the great festival of Ram at Banaras, is a notable example of this trend.[47] In towns such as Surat and Ahmedabad, there was an established tradition by the early nineteenth century by which men of commerce endowed substantial shelters for a whole host of grain-eating creatures. The most spectacular of these are the intricately carved wooden bird-feeding towers which still survive in these western cities. There were other pious donors who favoured more surprising recipients of benefaction, including colonies of gift-receiving rats and insects. Far from being seen as vermin, these were reportedly cherished creatures, fed in their designated shelters on suitably 'pure' diets of grain and vegetable matter.[48]

By the later nineteenth century, it was the cause of militant cow protection that became the greatest of all rallying points for 'communities' professing the values of the pious *ahimsa* non-blood-spiller. To revere and champion mother cow became a mark of merit not just for Brahmans and those who could induce Brahmans to serve them as ritualists, but also for those from urban commercial backgrounds and even respectable 'peasants'. These were often people in a position to embrace the grand merchant-*mahajan*'s vision of dharmic correctness.

[46] van der Veer 1994: 87–92. Those following strict dharmic codes may reject foods resembling animate life; for example, banning beetroot for its bloody colour, and tomatoes and cucumbers because of their seeds and fleshiness.

[47] Freitag 1989.

[48] Burnes 1834; Lodrick 1981.

Where the Brahman himself might consider these newly prosperous tillers or traders too low to accept as patrons, or such people were influenced by anti-Brahman sectarian doctrines, they could choose the cow instead as a focus for their piety.

Although some *mahajan-saukars* were strongly influenced by the Jain and Zoroastrian Parsi faiths, especially in Rajasthan and Gujarat, elsewhere the new *bania* elites sought to establish themselves as leaders of a self-consciously 'Hindu' social order, giving their own favourable meaning to the conventions of the textual varna tradition. These norms were either implicitly or explicitly defined in ways which came to exclude both Muslims and untouchables from the realm of pious civility over which the *bania* claimed leadersip. Many who had come to be known by such *saukar* merchant designations as Agarwal, Oswal, Seth and Marwari found inspiration in the expanding networks of Vishnu-worshipping sectarian faith. By the early nineteenth century, the teachings of north India's Vallabhacharya ascetics, also known as Goswami gurus, were providing large numbers of these merchant lineages with a new corporate focus.[49] Far from advocating casteless forms of devotion, these gurus exalted the ideal of the Kshatriya-like benefactor who fulfils the scriptural norms of *dharma* (righteous order or moral obligation) through acts of conspicuous piety. However, the Goswamis also made it clear that the rich merchant was a welcome provider of largesse, thus allowing the *bania-saukars* to challenge the notion of the merchant as lowly Shudra.

These ideas became especially important in the north and west, where bankers, brokers and money-lenders had been seeking to establish a twofold assertion of honour and status. First, they wanted it known that their attributes were those of the Vaishya – the notional third class in conventional varna theory. But they also maintained that Vaishyas were much closer to the two other superior classes (the Brahman and the Kshatriya) than to lowly Shudra commoners. More and more it was these trends of faith and social aspiration among the moneyed and trading groups which pushed the pious 'caste Hindu' towards a more pollution-conscious and often militantly anti-Muslim understanding of jati and varna.

---

[49] Peabody 1991; Bennett 1990.

THE VAISHYA MODEL AND URBANISING 'PEASANTS'

These ideals of the *mahajan-bania* way of life were taken to increasingly distant places during the nineteenth century. The expanding if unreliable opportunities of the colonial economy led Gujarati and Deccani Vaniyas, Tamil Chettiars, and Hindustan Oswals, Marwaris and Agarwals to areas where struggling cash-crop producers required cash advances to finance their revenue payments and labour costs. These money-lenders and commodity brokers thus set standards of 'caste Hindu' life in such regions as the remote hills and jungles of central India and in the fertile Deccan plains which had hitherto seen little of the temple-building zeal and puritan strictness of the vegetarian, teetotal, merchant household.[50]

By mid-century, the norms of the *bania-mahajan* were being actively embraced by many non-elite peasants in the richer cash-crop zones. Such emulation was especially common among the Patidar cotton-growers whose gains in the volatile Gujarat cash-crop economy involved close contact with big *saukar-mahajan* traders, especially those of Ahmedabad and other market towns. Here as elsewhere, the piety and domestic decorum which have come to be associated with upwardly mobile cultivators, indeed the Patidar's definition of caste itself, was taken in large part from the example of the big cotton and grain merchants who dominated these centres of Vishnu-worshipping *bania* culture.[51]

In these cash-crop tracts, it was now so-called rich peasants rather than just the old landed proprietary groups who identified themselves as persons of substance through the pursuit of complex and costly marriage strategies. To be 'pure' in these terms also came to involve the identification of some other set of toiling 'impure' people as one's own special lowly dependants. This was done by many of the north Indian Jat cultivators who responded enthusiastically to anti-Brahmanical Arya Samaj teachings in the later nineteenth century, as was seen above. These were 'middle peasants' who had hitherto made little use of Brahmans and had not worn the sacred thread. Now, reversing

---

[50] Commercial groups like southern Tamilnad's Paravas, Muslim *maraikkaiyars* and Nattukottai Chettiars established their guild-like investment networks as far afield as Burma, Malaya and French-ruled Indochina.
[51] Pocock 1972.

the established conventions of Jat life, many of them sought out Chamar 'untouchables' as plough-servants, and had themselves invested with the sacred thread at Arya Samaj purification ceremonies. Like their Kanbi-Patidar counterparts in central and southern Gujarat, they also redefined permissible marriage alliances so as to rule out the practice of liaisons with women from groups which were now being deemed too low for the breeding of 'true' Jat offspring.[52]

By the early twentieth century, colonial officials regularly aired the view that the sturdy non-elite cultivators they had once admired were becoming enervated and corrupted by this aping of patrician ways, lording it over servile labourers instead of tilling the soil themselves as their forebears had done. Yet the new trends seemed irreversible. Among the grander Patidars, a group known by the 'untouchable' title Dhed began to be used not just as agrarian labourers but as a client class singled out for special largesse in imitation of *bania*-style meritorious gift-giving. These acts of merit-making took the form of nightly house-to-house supplication: such benefactions were still being made in the rural localities visited by the anthropologist David Pocock in the 1960s.[53]

All these changes had a powerful effect on people's perceptions of one another across newly formalised caste boundaries. After mid-century, as more Indians came into contact with the towns and new village bases of migrant *banias* and *saukars*, the aspects of urban living that impressed them most were those which emphasised group solidarities. These were generally painful and contentious experiences; indeed in the colonial period it was the pacific urban or village Hindu, even more than the old rural proprietary groups, who was to be found contending for collective rights and honour in an aggressively caste-centred way.

Among the most fiercely contested terrain in these encounters was that of India's fast-growing industrial localities. Colonial Asia's rapid urbanisation created a wide range of social problems, and by the later nineteenth century many commercial and manufacturing cities had become turbulent and riot-prone. This trend was most marked in

---

[52] Datta 1997; Pradhan 1966; Crooke 1890: 95; compare Breman 1985: 85. (On the Aryas, see above, Chapter 4.)

[53] Pocock 1972: 17, 49; Breman 1985: 89–91; compare Bailey 1960: 151. Modern Dalit activists regard such titles as Chamar and Dhed as demeaning and have attempted to have their use officially outlawed.

centres with growing populations of mill workers, especially Bombay, Calcutta and Ahmedabad. There were also deep tensions in the scores of smaller ports, mill towns and mining centres which had to absorb great inflows of factory, railway and dock labourers, not to mention the growing armies of clerks, storemen and other low-level 'white-collar' workers whose skills were equally necessary to the expanding new urban workplaces.

In one sense these were all caste-free occupations which were unlike the ritualised exchanges of 'traditional' *jajman–kamin* relationships. However, in many cases, bonds of jati or birth-group actually tightened in these volatile environments. Many mill hands, especially those from comparatively open-ended 'peasant' backgrounds, found that they could best negotiate new relationships with foremen and labour recruiters by proclaiming their affiliation to headmen or *talaivans*, and by giving allegiance to newly established caste shrines and other tokens of shared community life. The growing numbers of overseas plantation labourers too were often recruited through intensi-fied 'caste' networks.[54]

More established townsfolk often feared and resisted the arrival of new migrants and new ways of life. From the early decades of the nineteenth century, Calcutta's lively world of literary satires and popular Kalighat painting built directly on the uneasiness of this urban milieu; one of the persistent themes in these art forms was that of caste norms overturned and low-caste people subverting the proprieties of *dharma*.[55] It was much the same in the south, where caste-specific demarcation disputes became a widespread feature of urban life. Formerly quiet shrine and market centres were notably prone to such disturbances. Like the Gujarat Patidars, in past centuries many of the Tamil country's superior landowners had regarded towns as privileged zones of sanctity where they could dramatise their 'pure' Brahmanical values by patronising temples and festivals and building impressive townhouses. Under the British, many of these localities acquired new functions as the sites of hospitals, courts and *cutcheries* (administrative offices). In the early nineteenth century, the colonial authorities generally accepted that even in 'modern' civic spaces it was important to preserve the honour of so-called clean-caste groups by protecting

---

[54] S. Bayly 1989: 371–8; Chandavarkar 1994.
[55] Chatterji 1994: 158; Guha-Thakurta 1992: 18–27.

them from contact with their ritual inferiors. It was a shock then for those of 'pure' caste to find that from mid-century many colonial officials were calling for high-caste residential streets and procession routes to be forcibly thrown open as public thoroughfares.[56]

The idea of making 'respectable' or 'pure' people rub shoulders with the 'unclean' was deeply threatening, especially to the many struggling patrician groups whose claims of worth and merit were now far from secure. The anthropologist T. C. Hodson reported in 1934 that such fears had actually given rise to mental disorders among susceptible high-caste groups. These nervous outbreaks he said were reflected in a particular vein of apocalyptic utterance that had reportedly become current in western India. The example he quoted evoked an eclectic but recognisable idea of Kaliyug, the Hindu scriptural idea of decadent and disordered times: 'The gods have gone to the hills; the saints have gone to Mecca. Under English rule the Dheds [a low 'untouchable' caste] ... hit and slap us.'[57]

In many cases though, it was missionaries and their low-caste converts, many of whom were from newly prosperous entrepreneurial groups like the Tamil Shanar/Nadars, who made the most provocative moves in these urban confrontations. In the far south this sensitive issue of 'sacred space' provoked outbreaks of violence from the 1840s until well into the twentieth century. The famous south Indian temple entry campaigns, which drew Gandhi's support in the 1920s, were merely a projection of these long-running regional conflicts onto the wider stage of nationalist political activism.

Many commentators have interpreted such conflict as an attack on caste 'tyranny'. Yet far from obliterating the consciousness of varna and jati norms, these campaigns generally attracted missionaries' low-caste adherents precisely because rights of access to roads and temple precincts were known marks of superior caste, and were therefore highly desirable in this era of enhanced jati and varna values. Even in the north, where Hindu–Muslim tension was far more common than caste 'honours' disputes, press coverage of these conflicts led some

---

[56] S. Bayly 1989: 445–52; Frykenberg 1982. These disputes resembled earlier right-hand/left-hand conflicts but carried on long after the disappearance of this more localised form of south Indian 'honours' dispute.

[57] *Congrès International des Sciences Anthropologiques et Ethnologiques. Compte-rendu de la première session* (London) 1934: 33.

polemicists to complain that Hindus of 'clean' caste were being menaced by an insurgent or purity-hating underclass.

If the colonial cities were volatile places, so too were the rural cash-crop zones where so many commercial families had established themselves. Whether they were migrant entrepreneurs or uneasy partners of the colonial revenue-taker and commodity producer, every nuance of the merchant *bania-saukar*'s personal behaviour could be scrutinised by potential bride-takers, business contacts and other arbiters of personal and family fortune.[58] Even before the nineteenth century, the marking off of territory had become a sensitive matter in this regard. At the time of the Company's initial expansion, men of commerce began building opulent joint-family houses in hybrid Indo-European styles which served to dramatise their new gains, particularly by drawing attention to their triumphs in the marriage market.[59] By mid-century, as they found themselves living in proximity to ever more ritually polluting people, further safeguards became necessary: to this concern to map out kin ties through household layout was added a growing insistence on being served at home by an appropriate array of *kamin*-like pollution-removers.

CASTE SUBORDINATION AND URBANISING LABOUR

Paradoxically, however, the forging of more rigid concepts of pollution and untouchability was not primarily a reflection of 'traditional' household practices. The most important of these changes in nineteenth-century caste life were pushed forward in a far more modern and impersonal arena, that is, within the military cantonments and urban industrial workplaces. As was seen above, after mid-century the decline of old-style artisanal and agrarian employment brought large numbers of non-elite migrants into the ports and industrial towns. Many of these were newly marginalised practitioners of 'unclean' village trades, especially the smiths, tanners and potters whom the wider world knew as Kumhar, Lohar, Chamar and so on. Although their occupations were quite skilled compared with those

[58] See Parry 1994: 114 on the modern caste Hindu's view of life as a continuous fight 'against impenetrable chaos and disintegration'.
[59] For Gujarat, see Pocock 1972; in Banaras too, many bankers' fortress-like residences were laid out as bastions of inward-turning 'pure' values.

of field labourers, such workers were usually too poorly capitalised to compete with suppliers of cheap industrial products. Moving to the cities, leather workers generally became low-paid labourers in such industries as tanning and boot-making. In colonial hospitals and medical colleges, many of the north Indian funerary specialists known as Doms were employed as mortuary attendants and dissecting-room assistants. In textile production too, mill hands were often from the groups which had come to be identified as 'impure' or unclean.[60]

These newcomers encountered very different conditions from those which had previously defined the meaning of caste in their lives. In the villages, formerly open-ended labour and tenancy relationships were still being turned into 'caste'-based service bonds. As was seen above, for both field labourers and the more specialised artisanal groups, this had the effect of eroding what remained of their entitlements as protected if often harshly treated retainers of 'kingly' *jajmans* (patrons). Paradoxically, when they entered the industrial workplace, such people as the Bhangi, Chamar and Mahar became subject to caste conventions which were often more potent and 'essentialising' than the norms of the 'traditional' village.

Untouchability as we now know it is thus very largely a product of colonial modernity, taking shape against a background of new economic opportunities including recruitment to the mills, docks and Public Works Departments, and to the labour corps which supported both the British and sepoy regiments. The nature of casual labour in the factories, ship-yards and brick kilns also tended to enhance the power of the pollution barrier. In all these settings, people who were known by such titles as Chamar, Mahar and Dom were not likely to become detached from the 'caste Hindu' norms which had come to define them as lowly and unclean. Quite the reverse in fact, as life in the modern workplaces so often reinforced the 'untouchable''s low status.

The modern experience of untouchability was further shaped by the other main area of employment for these urban migrants, which was in domestic labour and 'scavenging'. This was the arena in which the Paraiyan, Bhangi or Mahar found new classes of patrons and employers among the rapidly growing populations of city-based trading

---

[60] Arnold 1993: 5; Briggs 1920: 226–8.

people. There were also the newly prosperous people of superior 'peasant' origin who modelled their new residences on those of the *bania-mahajans*, and the literate specialists who had been forming themselves into tightly-knit caste groupings in the scramble for clerical and service employment, using such titles as Kayastha and Prabhu.

All these clean-caste groups used the services of the 'impure' in ways which greatly heightened the significance both of using and of being a so-called untouchable. As was seen above, the functioning of the 'modern' city's affluent clean-caste households – indeed their very viability as domains of order and respectability – had become dependent on the enactment of ever more elaborate acts of ablution and purification. This in turn created a growing demand for launderers and night-soil removers, and for such other specialists as the Kahar kitchen purifiers who apply cow dung as a cleansing agent in areas of special sensitivity in 'pure' family residences.

The result for those whose forebears had been rural labourers and 'plough-servants' was that increasing numbers of people now had incentives to identify them in simpler and more rigid caste terms than in past centuries, that is, as menials whose domain was that of pollution and ritual impurity. Again this was a trend that was enhanced though not created by the policies and material conditions of British rule. Although not all of these employment opportunities were explicitly pollution-related, wherever such big recruiters as the dam- and railway-builders created work-camps for construction gangs, Bhangis and other people of the acknowledged 'scavenger' jatis were brought in to serve as specialist waste-removers. Much the same was done when the epidemics of the later nineteenth and twentieth centuries prompted the colonial medical establishment to set new standards of hygiene for Indian towns. In this period the fear of disease spreading to the cantonments and white 'civil lines' from the Indian 'Black-Towns' led officials to recruit ever-larger numbers of municipal street-cleaners; these of course came largely from the so-called scavenger communities.[61]

The colonial army too became a large-scale employer of untouchables; no encampment was complete without its complement of barracks 'sweepers', regimental Dhobis (washermen) and other caste-specific labourers. Furthermore, the military was India's greatest

[61] Gooptu 1997: 887; Searle-Chatterjee 1981.

consumer of meat and leather, greatly enhancing the demand for specialist carcase-handlers and cobblers. As far as orientalist thought was concerned, well into the twentieth century British officials had widely diverging views about precisely which tribes or castes to classify as 'martial' and therefore suitable for military recruitment. They were in no doubt, however, that only such 'communities' as Mahars, Chamars and Bhangis could or would supply the cities and garrisons with street-sweepers, carrion-removers and leather-workers.

Indians experienced these views and policies as a notably 'modern' and 'scientific' consensus. Even with the adoption of Western plumbing, both Europeans and Indians still drew their household 'sweepers' from the ranks of those defined in caste terms as appropriate pollution-removers. Thus, while paying lip-service to ideals of pragmatic 'modernity', white expatriates reproduced many of the conventions of purity and ritualised cleansing within their own households. Contemporary manuals on home management instructed the wives of British officers and civil servants to recruit domestic servants of the 'correct' caste origin. Certainly no European or Indian establishment would have been able to induce non-'untouchables' to take employment as providers of 'impure' household labour. This was the case too in Western-style hotels and railway stations where the hygiene-conscious modern public was known to demand 'modern' standards of sanitation. Here too, the cleaning of bathrooms was and still is the province of the smartly uniformed 'sweeper', still generally a man of Harijan/'untouchable' origin in khaki shorts and singlet. It is in this guise, with his cleaning brushes and night-soil baskets, that the 'untouchable' is most commonly depicted in the illustrated ethnographies of the late nineteenth and early twentieth centuries. These photographic images of the uniformed sweeper or scavenger as representative 'specimens' of the Chamar, Bhangi or Dom contributed very powerfully to the perpetuation of modern untouchability.[62]

These views and practices should not be seen as mere products of invented colonial caste categories. Many of the ritual and 'scientific' manifestations of untouchability described above have persisted in post-Independence India because they have continued to suit those who have been able to reconcile their notions of modernity with the

---

[62] See Pinney 1990a. On this and other points concerning the making of modern untouchability there is much valuable material in Mendelsohn and Vicziany 1998 (see esp. pp. 88–9); their important study reached me after this volume went to press.

existence of 'unclean' toilers and pollution-removers in their midst. Even in the 1990s, hotel and household 'sweepers' commonly appear for duty in uniforms closely resembling those provided for such workers 100 years ago. Of course these were not the only service groups in colonial India who were marked out by the wearing of standardised semi-martial garb. The badge and uniform of the government 'peon', railwayman and post-office worker were also distinctive markers of livelihoods which came to be associated with ordered scientific 'modernity'. But of those who came to be subjected to this process, so-called untouchables were and still are more vulnerable than other Indians to a form of officially certified 'essentialisation' which links menial occupations with a concept of inherent caste essences.

'UNTOUCHABLES' AND 'RESISTANCE'

These then were the changes in colonial life which involved large numbers of Indians in more strictly defined caste relations by the end of the nineteenth century. But did those who found themselves defined as *avarna* or untouchable see the logic of the pollution barrier as a 'disability', and if so did they make systematic attempts to contest these norms? The campaigns of evangelical missionaries and other humanitarian reformers certainly exposed some members of these groups to a view of caste as a system of oppressions and injustices. The *shuddhi* or reconversion campaigns of the Arya Samaj and other Hindu uplift organisations also familiarised many low-status groups with anti-Brahmanical views. Certainly neither the missionaries nor such people as the clean-caste adherents of the Arya Samaj behaved as if the pollution barrier was a fantasy or irrelevance in everyday life.

In fact, despite the humble nature of their toil, to be employed as a municipal scavenger or barracks sweeper was a real boost to the fortunes of many people identified with the big 'unclean' servile populations – Mahars and Chamars especially. In the twentieth century, the small but vocal groups of educated and politically active 'untouchables' generally came from families who had distanced themselves from the lot of the poorer and humbler labourers and pollution-removers through such employment.[63]

---

[63] Mahar 1972.

On the other hand, most 'untouchable' labourers, leather workers and other members of the 'unclean' remained poor and illiterate. It was almost always the 'clean' man who owned the enterprises in which they laboured; the untouchable benefited only to a very limited extent from being associated with the power of the mills, the railways, the military and the other installations of the 'modern' economy. As far as caste was concerned, these developments served above all to firm up the 'untouchable''s corporate identity in terms which proclaimed for all to see that the Chamar, Mahar or Paraiyan was by nature a being who was distinct from all others, with these views being recognised and endorsed by the 'modern' representatives of the colonial state.

Furthermore, many of the conflicts that the missionaries and other commentators called anti-caste protests were assertions of the upwardly mobile, not of the lowliest untouchables. As has already been seen, this was the case in south India, where it was commercially successful Shanar/Nadars who contested for enhanced ritual honours by adopting the ceremonial attributes of 'kingliness' in marriages and other life-cycle rituals. The winners in these disputes referred to the gains they had made as victories for 'the Pillaimar', the 'Nadars' or even all 'Shudras' of a given locality – in other words, as a triumph for those of like jati or varna against their collective enemies. Thus, even though the necessary leadership and finance generally came from small groups of well-off individuals, in these situations gain and loss did come to be spoken of in the language of 'community' and collective will.[64]

Even those involved in so-called caste movements among people of very low ritual status had little choice but to try to readjust their symbolic status in regard to the pollution barrier, rather than repudiating notions of purity and pollution altogether. This was the case even in the many situations where so-called caste uplift became closely intertwined with the anti-colonial movements of the pre-First World War *swadeshi* era, and with the politics of militant 'peasant' unrest in India's most turbulent rural regions.

A case in point was the so-called sweepers who were known by the jati title Bhuinmali in east Bengal's jute-growing Mymensingh district.

---

[64] On comparable north Indian entrepreneurial groups with low-status oil-pressing and distilling backgrounds (Telis and Kalwar/Jaiswals) see Bailey 1957; C. Bayly 1983: 340, 373.

As R. L. Chakraborty has shown, this group, some of whose members had made modest economic gains during the nineteenth century, had hitherto been considered too unclean to be served by the specialist 'napit' barber-purifiers who provided ritual tonsuring to those of higher caste. In 1910, at a time of increasing conflict in this region between Hindu landlords and their Muslim tenantry, Bhuinmali activists organised a militant 'uplift' agitation, using the press and other 'modern' publicity techniques to press high-caste landlords to agree that persons of Bhuinmali origin were henceforth to be entitled to be tonsured by barber 'napits'.[65]

Surprising though it may seem, this campaign against the 'disabilities' of a low Hindu caste received strong backing from local Muslims. For the region's Muslims, this so-called caste movement offered a welcome opportunity to find points of division within the Hindu 'community' whose struggling landed elites had hitherto tried to shore up their supremacy in rural politics through a combination of economic claims and ritual assertions over low-caste client groups. This provocative claim that the Hindu 'community' had an inner fracture line dividing the 'clean' groups from those of low or untouchable caste was to become an increasingly potent feature of Indian politics both before and after Independence.

More specifically, the actions of these Bhuinmali campaigners anticipated the strategies employed from the 1920s onwards in B. R. Ambedkar's pan-Indian campaigns on behalf of the 'Depressed Classes' (untouchables). (See below, Chapter 6.) Furthermore, those involved in these movements had little choice but to frame their arguments and strategies around the conventions of 'caste society'. Groups like the Bhuinmalis certainly showed little sign of repudiating the varna and jati norms that gave meaning to the activities of ritual tonsurers.

Historians of India's so-called 'subalterns' have portrayed such initiatives as assertions of anti-authoritarian 'resistance', especially when they took the form of collective action by low-caste or 'tribal' people against landlords, money-lenders, or agents of the colonial state. In fact, few of these battles involving 'tribal' and 'low-caste' campaigners were attempts to disavow caste as a system of perceived oppressions and discriminatory practices. In most cases, far from

---

[65] Chakraborty 1994.

embracing anti-hierarchical 'castelessness', these were attempts by people in comparatively advantaged circumstances to take over the conventions of purity and hierarchy and then turn them to their advantage. In these situations, the differences between so-called Sanskritising movements on the one hand, and initiatives of so-called anticaste resistance on the other, were extremely limited.[66]

Thus, if these were instances of 'resistance', they certainly did not erase jati and varna values from the experience of either high- or lowcaste people. Caste did become a reality for large numbers of Indians in the nineteenth century. In all sorts of environments, in the forests of Bengal and the far north, in the hills and remote upland dry zones of the Deccan as well as much of the far south, the gods, garments and dietary habits of the 'pure' provided models for emulation among people not hitherto much concerned with standards of Brahmanical or *bania*-style piety and rectitude.

As we have seen, two distinct models of 'caste society' had come into operation in the centuries immediately preceding the British conquest, with a leading role being played by the rulers of the precolonial period. Even before the 1820s, these trends had made Indians increasingly deferential to the norms of jati and varna, though not yet generally inclined to favour the Brahman-*bania* model of caste over that of the man of prowess. As this chapter has shown, however, the continuing impact of rapid economic change and colonial legislation during the later nineteenth century had the effect of spreading a dual array of purity and hierarchy ideals much more widely throughout the society. Both for declining lordly groups and for advancing merchant and 'peasant' populations, the colonial period confirmed the advantages of insisting, both defensively and assertively, on precise degrees of embodied virtue and 'purity' in one's dealings with clients, creditors, officials and potential marriage partners. It was in this context that the leaders of the mass nationalist movements of the twentieth century found themselves needing to define their attitudes to caste and its place in a 'modern' social and political order.

---

[66] As illustrated by the low-caste devotional Satnami sect. See Babb 1972; Gooptu 1997.

CHAPTER 6

CASTE DEBATE AND THE EMERGENCE OF GANDHIAN NATIONALISM

INTRODUCTION

By the early twentieth century, caste had acquired real meaning in the lives of most if not all Indians. It was still too diverse and fluid a phenomenon to be thought of as a single all-powerful 'system'. Nevertheless, the concept of the pollution barrier and the Brahmanical ideal of purity were familiar to more people in the subcontinent than had been the case in past centuries. These strong though still disparate jati and varna norms had taken shape against a background of complex economic and political change. In addition, even for the poor and uneducated, these experiences of caste often reflected the themes of regional and pan-Indian controversies in the 'modern' public arena. Furthermore, as the power of the state continued to grow, manifestations of caste in the more intimate areas of everyday life came increasingly to reflect an awareness of what the law-courts and the bureaucracies might say or do. This could hardly have been otherwise since government had acquired the authority to define entire 'communities' as criminals, and to stigmatise other named caste groups as practitioners of 'primitive' marriage customs which made them too lowly in jati and varna terms to be recruited into the colonial army.

Today, through the workings of law, administration and even the university system, the state still plays a large role in sustaining the reality of caste, even though the Indian Republic has experienced fifty years as a mass electoral democracy with an egalitarian or 'secular' Constitution. Both this chapter and the next therefore concentrate on the laws and powers of the Indian state from the pre-Independence period to the 1990s. This chapter explores attempts by Gandhi and the other key political figures of the twentieth century to forge viable constitutional arrangements in a society where divisions of caste and ethno-religious community were seen both as national 'essences' and, simultaneously, as impediments to modern nationhood. Chapter 7 will then discuss the provisions of the 1950 Constitution, and the events in more recent times which have made 'reservations' – meaning public welfare provisions for so-called Backward Castes – a bitterly divisive issue in Indian politics. Thus, the focus of Chapters 6 and 7 will be official debate and policy-making; Chapter 8 returns to the practical realities of caste in twentieth-century economic and social life, and Chapter 9 explores the controversial phenomenon of so-called 'caste war'.

CASTE AND THE MODERN NATION

Constitutional politics developed in India against a background of debates and power struggles in which both Indians and Britons treated caste as a natural unit of electoral allegiance. By the time of the First World War, India had more Western-educated 'native gentlemen' than any other colonial society. From mid-century British officials paid anxious attention to these politically active intelligentsias, and to the proliferating voluntary associations which came together in 1885 to form the Indian National Congress. The anglophone lawyers, officials and journalists who dominated these bodies claimed to speak for the 'public' at large, rather than specific castes or communities. They expressed themselves in a language of universal rights and citizenship which was clearly at odds with the stereotype of a caste-fettered India where nationhood was unattainable. Even so, many officials insisted on the importance of caste as a hidden but critical factor in these developments. The all-India decennial Census monitored the expansion of English education, especially in the old Maratha centres and the Gangetic north, as well as in the Presidency capitals. The Census takers attached particular importance to the castes of university students. Much was made of the unsurprising fact that these came primarily from the Brahman and other specialist service groups with a tradition of literacy and occupational mobility.[1]

Caste featured just as strongly in the concerns of the official panels which met from the 1880s to investigate provincial education and government service recruitment. These bodies too placed much emphasis on the fact that it was largely members of the same literate groups who secured clerical and administrative posts in the provincial

---

[1] Brahmans in the south and west; Kayasths, Khattris and Muslims of *ashraf* (gentry) background in the Gangetic north, and members of the Hindu *bhadralok* (Brahmans, Kayasthas and Baidyas) in Bengal.

bureaucracies. This was widely held to have made many district cutcheries a preserve of corrupt single-caste networks. To the alarm of the '*dwija*' (high-caste) witnesses who appeared before the panels, there were calls now for strict recruitment quotas to break the power of so-called Brahman or Kayastha official 'cliques'. (See below, pp. 239–43.) The most outspoken of these Indian contributors therefore argued that the government's white-collar recruitment policies should specifically exclude those of low caste on grounds of their unsuitable 'manners and habits'. Others cited ethnological and eugenic arguments to the same effect: 'As horses of good breed only are selected for Cavalry Regiments, so preference should be given to men of good families ...'[2]

When the first organs of elective local self-government were formed in the 1880s under the provisions of the so-called Ripon Reforms, many officials noted that members of the same groups were in a position to dominate decision-making in the newly enhanced municipalities. This was only a limited constitutional experiment, with minimal powers being vested in tiny local electorates; in 1909 the first moves were made to extend the electoral principle to the provincial legislative councils. Hesitant as they were, these measures aroused fierce opposition. Such ultra-conservatives as Sir James Fergusson (Governor of Bombay, 1880–5) accused the scheme's Liberal architects of pandering to conspiratorial forces which he said were always present beneath the surface of Indian society.[3]

These seditious energies were held to derive their power from the tight webs of caste affinity which were supposed to be particularly dangerous among Brahmans. A case in point for Fergusson was Pune, capital of the eighteenth-century Peshwas. Here professional men of Chitpavan origin, as well as members of other Marathi-speaking Brahman service families, had become the dominant force in an array of publishing concerns and regional political associations which were highly assertive in their demands for faster public service promotions and other goals dear to the anglophone 'gentlemen'.

In Fergusson's view and that of his predecessor Sir Richard Temple,

---

[2] Bhai Jawahir Singh of the Lahore Guru Singh Sabha, and Munshi Diwan Chand of the Sialkot Municipal Committee, to Punjab Public Services Comm, vol. 1: *Proceedings of the Public Services Commission* Sections 1–3 Calcutta, 1887; compare Frykenberg 1965. In Madras, attempts were made to restrict Brahman entry to the civilian services as early as the 1850s, as noted in the *Report of the [1980] Backward Classes Commission* II: 147.

[3] Seal 1968: 159–60.

it was deeply undesirable to put electoral power into these people's hands. Regardless of any apparent Westernisation, they all supposedly shared a mental and moral make-up which was dynamic and advanced in ethnological terms, even 'nationalistic'. Nevertheless, these inherited qualities were said to make Chitpavans and other Maharashtrian Brahmans eternally dangerous to the Raj. Their collective racial heritage predisposed them to hunger for their lost political dominance. Long after the 1857 Rebellion, the modern Maratha Brahmans' corporate drives were still held to be manifested in a collective consciousness of the power which their forebears had attained under the Peshwas.[4]

Thus, said Fergusson, it was they – 'the agitating Brahmin class' – who were behind the call for self-government in his presidency; the members of this 'ambitious Brahmin party' were unappeasable and would never be fit to exercise power responsibly.[5] The true nature of these groups, said fearful Bombay officials, had been revealed in 1879 in the response of the region's politically active intelligentsia to the actions of W. B. Phadke, a Chitpavan ex-government clerk from Pune who was praised in the Brahman-run Deccan newspapers as a Hindu patriot in the tradition of the great dynast Shivaji when he organised an armed band from the Ramoshi 'criminal tribe', and plundered a series of Deccan villages. 'Nothing that we do now, by way of education, emolument, or advancement in the public service, at all *satisfies* the Chitpawuns [Chitpavans]', Temple declared in 1879.[6]

With the coming of mass public activism to Indian politics, these fears intensified. Officials saw conspiratorial caste sentiment as the catalyst behind the agitations that swept much of north India at the time of the violent Cow Protection outbreaks of the 1890s, and again in the anti-colonial Swadeshi ('home industry') agitations of 1905–10. This was the period when Pune's 'Extremist' Congress leader B. G. Tilak transformed the great urban *melas* (festivals) honouring both Shivaji and the regional deity Ganpati into expressions of militantly anti-Muslim and anti-colonial protest.[7] Tilak was known to be a Chitpavan like most other Pune nationalists, including his 'Moderate'

---

[4] Johnson 1973: 53; compare Ternan 1869: 15 on the Maratha Brahman 'Pandits' of Jaloun allegedly '[preaching] extermination of the British' in 1857.

[5] Seal 1968: 159.

[6] *Ibid.*: 234–5; Johnson 1973: 64.

[7] Ganpati is the Maharashtrian form of the elephant-headed Shaivite god Ganesh. See Cashman 1975: 75–122; Johnson 1973: 84–90; Courtright 1985: 188–201.

rival Gokhale; much was made of Tilak's links with revolutionary nationalists from Bengal, most of whom were of *bhadralok* background.

Informers employed to gather intelligence for the Bombay police were assiduous in collecting information about Tilak's *melas*. These reports represented Tilak as an exceptionally dangerous subversive because of his alleged access to the webs of secret communication which supposedly united the Presidency's 'orthodox Brahmans'. As in the early nineteenth century, when Jonathan Duncan and other influential officials debated the supposed menace of 'Brahman government', Tilak and his Brahman nationalist contemporaries were widely portrayed as seditious fanatics with a mission to install 'Brahman rule' in the subcontinent. Madras too came to be seen as a domain of conspiratorial Brahmans with dangerous links to Theosophy, the American-born cultural revivalist movement which had a strong influence on anti-colonial activists in both Ceylon and south India.[8]

Caste then had come to be seen by many commentators as a force pervading the 'modern' Indian world, and with some justice. From the 1880s, the hundreds of organisations which called themselves caste associations or caste conferences acquired sizable memberships, and were accorded much attention in official reportage as well as the Indian-owned vernacular and English press. Through these and other voluntary associations, many members of India's 'respectable' elites had mastered the forms of public institutional life which the British had brought to the Asian empire. The value of these quasi-Western constitutional practices lay in the wide range of themes and goals which they could communicate, both to the colonial authorities and to other Indians. Thus the same 'public men' who could be heard propounding ideals of nationhood and Aryan racial bonds through the organs of the Indian National Congress and the Hindu revivalist organisations, were often equally at home on the platforms of associations which pointed to regional jatis and caste clusters as repositories of shared moral identity.

Many of these organisations had real resources and influence, even though their messages were often greatly at variance with the everyday reality of caste. In the years before the First World War, one of the largest of these ventures – the NWP's Kayastha Pathsala – acquired

---

[8] Johnson 1973: 86, 99, 100; compare Irschick 1969: 101–22; Baker 1976a.

everyday reality of caste. In the years before the First World War, one of the largest of these ventures – the NWP's Kayastha Pathsala – acquired extensive assets including schools, property holdings and a publishing house; it had also become an important meeting ground for nationalist campaigners. As in the case of other caste organisations, the Pathsala leaders' claims about the primordial affinity of all Kayasthas were decidedly overblown; even this comparatively well-defined group was still more of an ambiguous status category than a 'community'. Furthermore, in common with other caste associations, the Pathsala's membership was an uneasy amalgam of pious conservatives and anglophone professional men with 'reformist' sympathies. These Western-educated affiliates often found themselves at odds with fellow members who disapproved of such standard 'reformist' goals as female education, the remarriage of widows and the abolition of child marriage. What the more conservative members wanted these bodies to support often looked decidedly 'backward' by these standards: the spread of Vedic knowledge and Brahmaniscd domestic norms, and the abandonment of lordly indulgences including meat-eating, alcohol consumption and the sponsorship of 'lewd' wedding entertainments.[9]

Despite all these inconsistencies, however, a significant proportion of people calling themselves Kayastha still found it worth their while to pay attention to the Pathsala; much the same was true for their Chitpavan and other counterparts. This was in part because of the scale of their endowments and resources. It was also the case that both modernising 'reformists' and their opponents could so readily endorse such goals as the expunging of so-called 'social indecency'. These and similar causes could be seen both as expressions of traditionally Vedic or 'Brahmanical' values and at the same time as proofs of the kind of evolutionary progress that many orientalists now expected any 'community' to display if its members were to be deemed worthy of trust and preferment in the public arena.[10]

We saw earlier that it was common for both Indian commentators and British officials to hail the caste conferences' activities as expressions of progressive 'caste spirit'. Furthermore, colonial officials came to treat the 'native gentlemen' who acted as their chairmen and

[9] C. Bayly 1975: 31, 163–6; and see Carroll 1978.
[10] Conlon 1977: 138–67; Carroll 1978. For an original and illuminating approach to 'caste reform', see Arunima 1996.

government for Indians. The electoral constituencies which were established through the implementation of the 1882 Ripon Reforms and the 1909 Morley–Minto Reforms were defined on the basis of collective interest or 'community', rather than a Western-style principle of one person, one vote.

THE MODERNITY OF NON-BRAHMAN 'CASTE SPIRIT'

This was the context in which so-called non-Brahmanism emerged as a political force uniting activists from a mixed array of service, commercial groups and superior 'clean'-caste/*sat-sudra* 'peasant' groups in the Madras and Bombay Presidencies. These were the regions where the provincial administrations were most fearful of alleged Brahman conspiracies. This made their officials particularly keen to foster the supposed spirit of anti-Brahmanism as a counterweight to the voice of 'Brahman subversives' in the newly enhanced municipal and provincial councils. In Madras this strategy resulted in the creation of the Justice Party, whose leaders formed this Presidency's first Indian ministry under the 1919 dyarchy Constitution.[11]

This Madras-based organisation had been founded in 1916 in close collaboration with colonial scholar-officials. The organisation had no real party structure at the time when the new voters who had been enfranchised under the Montagu–Chelmsford 'dyarchy' Constitution went to the polls in 1920. Few of the candidates who won seats in this election were affiliates of Justice; the Madras authorities nevertheless deemed virtually every victorious non-Congress candidate who was not of Brahman birth to be a winner on behalf of the non-Brahman 'party'.[12]

There are close parallels here with the origins of the Bombay Presidency's Non-Brahman Association, which was founded in 1920 with sponsorship from the Maratha ruler Shahu Chhatrapati of Kolhapur state. This Kolhapur dynast, who claimed direct succession from the original Maratha state-builder Shivaji, was closely associated with the 'Depressed Class' leader B. R. Ambedkar. He was also an Arya Samaj adherent, a leading backer of Maharashtrian social 'uplift'

---

[11] On the 1920–6 Justice Ministry, see Baker 1976.
[12] Baker 1976: 30–8.

causes, and an early supporter of the move to create separate electoral constituencies for non-Brahmans.[13]

The term non-Brahmanism was thus an invention of the colonial political arena. Both in Bombay and in the south, those who called themselves non-Brahmans were generally allies in short-lived political coalitions rather than members of an authentic ritual or moral community. Princely 'non-Brahmans' like Shahu Chhatrapati injected a strong element of lordly varna-consciousness into these organisations' activities, most notably through their sponsorship of thread-investiture ceremonies for Marathas and other 'non-Brahmans' who joined their campaigns for formal recognition as 'dwijas' of the Kshatriya varna.[14] At the same time, these groups did use slogans and symbols reflecting satirical or hostile views of Brahmans which were common in many regional folk cultures as well as 'modern' Hindu revivalist teachings. Furthermore, those who claimed leadership of the two non-Brahman organisations continued to make these views ever more widely known when their parties held power at provincial level in the 1920s and 1930s.

In south India especially, growing literacy in the vernaculars also helped to spread awareness of regional identities which were often conceived in terms of resistance to Brahmans. Through school textbooks as well as temple worship, Tamil-speakers were familiarised with tales of pious kings and warrior heroes exemplifying Tamil 'peasant' solidarities in the face of alien invasion. Even the widely disseminated Ram epic acquired a distinctive south Indian twist, with the hero-king's demonic enemy Ravana becoming the heroic centre of the story in the popular Tamil version of the story. In these areas, an amalgam of devotional *bhakti* faith and appropriated Western ethnological theories were conspicuous in the pronouncements of polemicists who denounced Brahmans as the descendants of alien Aryan conquerors. Such writings further proclaimed that south India's Brahmans were still conspiring to oppress the region's primordial 'sons of the soil', these groups being defined as a race by virtue of their Dravidian linguistic heritage and their supposed traditions of worthy 'peasant' virtue.[15]

Maharashtra, too, generated a Maratha-led *bahujan-samaj* ('community of the majority') campaign which seems to have had authentic

---

[13] Omvedt 1976: 184–5.
[14] *Ibid.*: 130.
[15] Balfour 1873, IV: R60; see Washbrook 1990: 215.

popular roots. Its adherents vied with Tilak and other Brahman nationalists for the right to annex Shivaji as their heroic exemplar. In the mid-1920s the politics of the Pune municipal council were dominated by battles over the staging of rival Brahman and non-Brahman Shivaji *melas* (festivals), as well as clashes aroused by proposals to erect a municipal statue of the anti-Brahman moralist Jyotirao Govindrao Phule (1827–90).[16]

In encouraging the growth of 'non-Brahman' political organisations, the Madras and Bombay authorities claimed that they were recognising a force that had long been active among 'progressive' elements in these societies. In support of this they pointed to the initiatives being taken by Hindu princes and other notables from these areas' more 'virile' caste groups, representing such figures as brave modernisers attempting to 'un-shackle' Hindu minds by challenging 'Brahman tyranny'.[17]

By the early twentieth century, these developments had the effect of bringing Hindu-ruled princely states into the political limelight, as rulers of Jat, Maratha and south Indian ex-poligar lineage discovered that there were valuable gains to be made by proclaiming themselves leaders of notional non-Brahman constituencies. This was an important new role for these dynasts. It was particularly attractive as a means of professing loyalist anti-Congress sentiments, thus denying the charges of decadence and political unreliability that had come to be so widely levelled against all such 'feudal' lineages. The problem here was that the attempt to be an exemplar of supra-regional Jat or Kallar 'uplift' could be hard to reconcile with the more traditional princely claim to be lord of all 'communities' within a single pluralistic realm. Even so, the raja of Bharatpur sought to establish himself as the accepted leader of all Hindustan Jats by glorifying the pilgrimage complex at Pushkar as a site of distinctive Jat piety and by endowing schools and pilgrims' hostels for the uplift of the Jat 'community'.[18]

Even more importantly, the heirs to important Maratha-ruled

---

[16] Omvedt 1976: 3–5, 236–7; Gore 1989: 65; O'Hanlon 1985.

[17] The non-Brahman movements split in the 1930s; members of lower-ranking 'clean'-caste groups adopted the term 'backward' to distinguish themselves from so-called forward or upper non-Brahman groups whose members had previously dominated these organisations. On the Madras Provincial Backward Classes League (formed 1934) see Galanter 1984: 36; Saraswathi 1974; Ramaswamy 1978.

[18] As of 1881 the princely states had a population of about 56 million out of a total of 256 million for the subcontinent.

princedoms identified themselves with the cause of Maratha *bahujan-samaj*, persuading both officials and Indian commentators to see their long-running attempts to claw back revenues from lordly Brahman feudatory lineages as assertions of spiritual and social liberation on behalf of all Marathas and/or even all 'non-Brahmans'. The most successful of these campaigns was waged by the Kolhapur ruler, Shahu Chhatrapati. As was seen above, Shahu Chhatrapati was an early sponsor of the Bombay Non-Brahman Association. Within his home state, this Maratha dynast set a pattern which has endured into the 1990s when he embarked on a campaign to relieve the so-called backwardness of his realm's 'non-Brahman' subjects. This again was taken primarily to mean those of superior clean-caste 'peasant' birth, i.e. Marathas.

These peoples' backwardness was supposedly reflected in the same occupational and educational imbalances that were made much of in north India in the case of Muslims. In Kolhapur the alleged disadvantage for which relief was sought was the preponderance of Brahmans in schools and public service posts. In 1902 the Kolhapur ruler adopted one of the earliest examples of an official caste-based 'reservations' scheme, decreeing that 50 per cent of all administrative vacancies were to be reserved for those of 'non-Brahman' birth. A similar measure had been enacted in Mysore state in 1895. The idea that such quotas were the best means of righting the ancient wrongs of disadvantaged 'communities' was to become one of the key legacies of this period's new constituency-based political activism.[19]

In the years before and after the First World War, the proceedings of the provincial Public Service and Education Commissions continued to be dominated by these issues. These bodies received thousands of representations which blamed the purported injustices of the 'backward' on the conspiracies of 'oppressive' Brahmans and other 'Aryan' elites. Wartime service was the other critical element here. While 'subversive' Congressmen involved themselves in the great wartime Home Rule League agitations, self-styled representatives of some of the big 'peasant'-*kisan* populations exerted themselves to have their castes deemed eligible for army service. Where such campaigns were successful, the entry of such people as Kolis into the ranks of the

---

[19] The Kolhapur ruler also financed educational schemes and other philanthropic ventures for 'backward' groups. See O'Hanlon 1985; Johnson 1973: 102–7; Omvedt 1994. On Mysore's 1895 state-wide 'reservations' scheme, which was preceded in 1874 by attempts to implement 'Backward Class' quotas for police recruitment, see Singh 1982: 80–1.

officially recognised 'martial races' was hailed as a landmark of collective caste uplift.[20]

Economic uncertainties for wage labourers and commodity producers continued to be important here. For vulnerable landed and labouring groups, both the slump which followed the First World War and the disaster of the 1930s Depression demonstrated powerfully that claims of caste difference could provide a crucial margin of advantage in times of distress. Even in the big anti-landlord agitations of the 1920s and 1930s, calls for relief and justice in the name of specific caste groups were widespread, appearing with great persistence alongside the more generalised appeals for class-based *kisankhedut* or 'peasant' and 'tenant' rights and interests. Thus, the large-scale *kisan* or tiller agitations that engulfed the southern Awadh region in 1920–2 were largely organised around the caste 'elders' councils' (*panchayats*) of the larger 'middle peasant' cultivating castes. This mostly involved tillers of Kurmi origin, even though the leaders of these protests claimed to represent a general 'peasant' constituency extending far beyond that of any one rural caste cluster.[21]

The superior Gujarati tillers who had come to call themselves Patidars were yet another broad regional cultivating group who made much of the kin ties and prestigious ritual solidarities of jati. An early stage in this process can be seen in the success of those Patidar cash-crop farmers who came to dominate much of southern Gujarat's rich cotton-growing land during the later nineteenth century. This they achieved at the expense of dependent labouring populations; the colonial officials had furthered their interests by applying the provisions of the Criminal Tribes Acts to the region's so-called predator groups, thus forcibly transforming them into a tied labour pool for 'worthy' cultivators.[22] It was these Patidar landowners' descendants who achieved renown as 'peasant' nationalists by attaching themselves to the Indian National Congress's first great campaigns of rural non-cooperation, the Kheda agitation of 1918 and the Bardoli *satyagrahas* (civil protests) of 1921 and 1928.[23]

Thus, appeals to jati and varna often permeated the organisation of both rural and urban 'resistance', as well as instances of so-called

---

[20] Parry 1979: 119; Gore 1989: 62.
[21] Dhanagare 1986: 111–19.
[22] Pocock 1972: 29–30.
[23] Hardiman 1981; Dhanagare 1986: 88–109; Breman 1985: 79–99.

collaboration with the colonial state. Furthermore, by the time the 1935 Government of India Act expanded provincial electorates to include a substantial proportion of non-elite smallholders, politically active Indians generally accepted as a matter of course that the solidarities of caste were relevant and indeed fundamental to the electoral process. When provincial nationalists moved out into the countryside from their more familiar urban bases they talked about the nation and 'peasant' uplift, but their attempts to mobilise these new electorates inevitably referred to the concerns and 'essences' or moral affinities of specific caste groups. This was certainly how the electoral process was reported, again supporting the widely shared view that caste affinities had an important place in modern politics. This is hardly surprising given the proliferation of educational trusts and other voluntary associations claiming to represent specific jatis and varnas; by the 1930s, the symbols and solidarities of caste had definitely come to permeate both the language and the organisation of Indian political life.

CASTE AND THE NATIONALIST IDEAL

Against this background, it is not surprising that references to jati and varna have continued to loom large in Indian political life in the period since Independence. The founders of the Indian Republic were notably ambivalent about caste. The 1950 Constitution's celebrated commitment to casteless egalitarianism was prefigured in one of the major documents of the nationalist 'freedom struggle', the Indian National Congress's 1931 Karachi Resolution. No mention of caste appears in this text, which was formulated around ideals of democratic politics and modernising economic development by the Congress's leading proponent of 'secular' nationalism, Jawaharlal Nehru.

Throughout the 1930s and 1940s, Nehru and his Congress Socialist allies expressed their concept of the Indian nation in these casteless and egalitarian terms. So too did the 'reformists' of the *Indian Social Reformer* who in 1930 denounced the government's caste listings as divisive tools of imperialism, and urged their readers not to provide the Census enumerators with details of their varna and jati.[24] The

---

[24] *ISR* 20 Sept 1930: 47; 1 Nov 1930: 138. On the avoidance of caste references by such organisations as the all-India Kisan Sabha (founded 1936), see Omvedt 1994: 180.

radical Congressman 'Netaji' Subhas Chandra Bose was equally insistent that the birth of a new India presupposed 'a new society based on principles of equality and justice', declaring himself a 'firm believer in the abolition of caste'. Prefiguring his later commitment to a militarised version of the anti-colonial struggle in armed alliance with Germany and Japan, Bose declared in 1930 that no Indian should be denied the privilege of bearing arms for his nation on grounds of caste origin.[25]

Yet even among the educated and politically active, these were minority views. In the pre-Independence decades politicians of widely differing allegiances made caste a central reference point in their writings and electoral strategies. The Unionist Party, which came to power as the representative of substantial landed interests in the Punjab in 1937, was widely regarded as a predominantly Jat and Muslim organisation and regularly expressed its position as being 'against Brahmans and banias [members of trading castes]'.[26] Caste loomed equally large for bodies pressing the interests of the Hindu 'community' against what they represented as the divisive campaigns of self-styled 'depressed class' movements, these being the various organisations promoting separate political goals on behalf of *avarna* or 'untouchable' populations, and in some cases the so-called tribals.

In the Punjab and Bengal, these fears focused on proposed constitutional schemes which threatened to tilt the balance in these provinces' legislative assemblies in favour of representatives of the Muslims and other non-Hindu 'communities'. Thus Bengal's Hindu landlords (*zamindars*) and other adherents of the militant Hindu Mahasabha organisation took the lead in promoting programmes of so-called caste consolidation, through which 'tribals' and untouchables were to be induced to declare their allegiance to the Hindu 'community'. Here, as elsewhere, far from telling their listeners not to respond to the Census's caste and 'community' questions, these Hindu supremacist campaigners actively encouraged 'tribals' and members of low-ranking rural labouring and cultivating groups such as Rajbanshis and

---

[25] *ISR* 18 Oct 1930: 110; on Bose's calls for intercommunal and intercaste 'interdining' in his anti-colonial fighting force, the Indian National Army, see Thorne 1985: 270; also Bose 1946: 9–10, 319.

[26] The Punjab's Unionists received support from the province's Adi-Dharm movement (the term *adi* being used to mean original or primordial) which represented so-called untouchables as the descendants of a dispossessed native race. See below, and Omvedt 1994: 179.

Chandel/Namasudras to identify themselves to the Census officials as Hindus of thread-wearing Kshatriya varna so as to swell the numbers of those returned as members of Bengal's Hindu 'community' in the provinicial Census returns.[27]

Furthermore, for many pre-Independence congressmen, the so-called disabilities of those who were classified as low or 'backward' in caste terms were anything but an irrelevance to the modern nationalist's goals. The 1950 Constitution gave the state an explicit obligation to ameliorate disadvantage among those who were referred to as the nation's 'weaker sections', meaning 'tribals' and untouchables. It was these populations for whom the colonial bureaucracy coined the terms 'Scheduled Castes' and 'Scheduled Tribes', with the intention of defining those who were to receive these special forms of protection and 'uplift'.[28] The question to be explored at this point is the significance which caste held for Congress leaders and their important rivals in the interwar years, that is, in the period when the exercise of state power was transformed by the growth of the electoral arena, and the emergence of 'modern' mass agitational protest.

As we have already seen, many early nationalists hoped to separate 'reformist' aims from the goals which the Congress embraced in its official political campaigns. In the years before the First World War, however, many aspiring social reformers began to speak for the cause of so-called Adi-Dravida ('original Dravidian') entitlements in the south, and the parallel claims of the Adi-Dharm movement in the Gangetic north. The leaders of both movements argued that those identified in colonial ethnographies as 'slave castes' and 'pariahs' were racially distinct from the so-called Aryan peoples of their home regions, and that they were these areas' only true 'sons of the soil', meaning that they were descended from their primordial inhabitants. In these campaigns, much was made of ethnological theories which held that such 'depressed' populations as Madras Paraiyans and Gangetic Chamars deserved compensation and 'uplift' because their ancestors had suffered at the hands of Aryan invaders who had killed their kings and stolen their lands.[29]

---

[27] Thus confirming a 'Sanskritising' trend which had been developing among these groups since the early part of the century: compare Pinch 1996; and see Chatterji 1994: 192–200.

[28] The struggle to define and identify these groups, and to devise corporate measures for their benefit, will be discussed in Chapter 7.

[29] See above, pp. 157–8; also Juergensmeyer 1982.

Furthermore, under strong pressure from such bodies as the Depressed Classes Conference, which met in 1917 under the chairmanship of the 'reformist' Congressman N. G. Chandavarkar, the Indian National Congress issued its first cautious declarations on the amelioration of caste 'disabilities'. The provisions of the Congress's 1917 Resolution on Untouchability, which called for social justice for members of the 'suppressed', 'submerged' or 'Depressed Classes', were reaffirmed in the Congress's 1920 Resolution on Non-cooperation. The importance of this document, which was intended to cement Hindu–Muslim unity in anticipation of the first major all-India campaign of nationalist protest – the 1921–2 Non-Cooperation Campaign – made its use of 'reformist' phrasing particularly notable. So too did the fact that the resolution committed the Congress to make the removal of the so-called Depressed Classes' 'disabilities' a major nationalist priority.[30]

These were both highly qualified declarations which portrayed the problem of the 'depressed' as a matter requiring voluntary 'religious' solutions. The idea was that those whom the Congress's 1920 Resolution referred to as 'the religious heads' and other 'leading Hindus' should make 'special efforts' to reform Hinduism in the matter of its treatment of the so-called 'suppressed classes'. There was no emphasis on legislation or other state action; the problem to be solved was expressed as the need to rid *Hinduism* of the 'reproach of untouchability'.[31]

In the 1920s, Gandhi and other prominent Congressmen pursued a variety of 'religious' solutions to what they had come to identify as the problem of the Depressed castes and tribes. Gandhians established special *ashrams* (teaching and spiritual centres) for members of the serf-like Gujarat field labouring population known as Dubla/Halpatis. These *ashrams* taught the Gandhian virtues of temperance and spinning through popular devotional hymns (*bhajans*), though some activists, notably the leading Congressman Vallabhai Patel, told Halpatis that it was their dharmic duty to serve their Patidar masters without attempting to break their bonds of inherited servitude.[32]

---

[30] Zelliot 1988: 183; Keer 1981: 35; on V. R. Shinde (1873–1944) the radical Bombay Prarthana Samaj 'theist' who founded the Depressed Classes Mission in 1906, see Ghugare 1983.
[31] Zelliot 1988: 185.
[32] Breman 1985: 137–40.

Similarly, in the old *girasia* chiefdoms of the southern Gujarat hinterland, Gandhian workers founded another set of Swaraj ('Self-Rule') *ashrams* among populations of Bhils and other so-called tribals whose jungle terrain had been penetrated by Parsi and high-caste Hindu distillers and money-lenders. This Gandhian initiative again used *bhajan* hymns to try to popularise temperance, vegetarianism and other norms of 'pure' caste Hindu life among these groups, encouraging them too to take on a new name – Adivasi ('original people'). This rapidly became the preferred Gandhian term for all the groups which the colonial ethnographers had called tribals or aboriginals. These moves were associated with the adoption of traditions of hierarchical rank and purity-consciousness among many so-called tribal populations.[33]

In this period Gandhians looked above all to the Hindu temples as the domain in which to attack the 'evil' aspects of caste and untouchability. They therefore made much of agitations involving newly prosperous Ezhavas (ex-toddy tappers) on the Malabar coast and 'depressed' groups in the Marathi-speaking regions of Bombay Presidency. These widely publicised conflicts at Vaikam in Travancore in 1924–5 and at two Maharashtra temples in 1929–30 came to be referred to as temple entry campaigns. Basically these originated as conventional local 'honours' disputes, with would-be worshippers striving for tokens of precedence and ranked affiliation within the domain of a powerful regional divinity.

However, in this period of vehement debate about the meaning of nationhood and indigenous social 'reform', self-styled progressives were quick to identify these clashes with more edifying goals and ideals. Beginning with the Vaikam campaign, these battles over access to Hindu temple precincts and processional routes were taken up by advocates of national 'uplift' as symbolic tests of low-caste advancement. Although Gandhi soon lost faith in these agitations because of their 'unsound atmosphere' and use of force, at least some participants took on the garb and slogans of nationalist *satyagrahis* or Gandhian freedom fighters. These campaigners took pains to invoke a standardised terminology of 'temple entry', and attracted much publicity when they told the world that they were engaged in a liberation

---

[33] Hardiman 1981; Breman 1985: 169; compare Burghart and Cantlie 1985: 134–57. On *girasia* warrior lordships, see Chapter 1.

struggle against the forces of 'Brahmanism' and 'upper-caste oppression'.[34]

By the 1920s the English expressions 'untouchable' and 'untouchability' were in widespread use as terms for the quality of collective uncleanliness that had come to be routinely referred to as a universal feature of the caste system. Gandhi's writings on Indian social and moral topics were particularly influential in this regard. His publications of the 1920s and 1930s contain passionate polemics about the doctrine of untouchability as a 'horrible and terrible' stain on the Hindu faith, an 'evil' and an 'insult to religion and humanity'. 'Surely', he wrote in January 1926, 'judgement will be pronounced against Hinduism, if we as a body do not rise as one man against this social and religious atrocity.' Eight years later, to the distress of such prominent nationalists as the Bengali littérateur Rabindranath Tagore, Gandhi publicly described the 1934 Bihar earthquake as divine retribution for the sin of untouchability.[35]

Gandhi's insistence on 'religious' solutions to the problem of untouchability lay behind his adoption of the neologism Harijan (usually translated as 'child of God') as a replacement for such terms as 'suppressed' or 'backward classes'. Hari is a popular Vaishnavite title for the Supreme God, and this association with *bhakti* devotional themes was intended to counter the stereotype of the 'untouchable' as licentious carrion-eater and blood-spiller. The term has been widely employed since the 1930s, though in recent times its use has been condemned by self-styled representatives of low-caste groups. Their complaint is that it identifies so-called Harijans with the submissive self-surrender of the *bhakti* devotee, thus representing them as infantile beings in need of the civilising hand of their betters. Today the word is still used in official and academic writing, though not in everyday vernacular speech. Since the 1970s, many campaigners have sought to replace it with the coinage Dalit ('the oppressed'), which has connotations of modernity and militant class struggle rather than pious self-effacement.[36]

---

[34] Menon 1994: 80–3; Zelliot 1988: 187, 1992: 10–11.

[35] *Young India* Jan. 1926, quoted in Iyer 1986, I: 486; Pande 1985, II: 268. On the spread of the English terms 'untouchable' and 'untouchability', both apparently in general use from about 1909, see Galanter 1984: 25 nn. 19–21. The Madras 'reformist' K. Natarajan was an early user of the term, as was the American-educated Maharashtrian ethnographer Sridhar V. Ketkar: see above, Chapter 4, and O'Hanlon 1985.

[36] Gupta 1985: 30–1; on modern use of the term Dalit, see for example Randeria 1989:

CASTE, SOCIETY AND POLITICS IN INDIA

The Harijan Sevak Sangh ('Servants of Untouchables Society') was founded by Gandhi and his close associates in 1932 as a means of deepening the nationalist movement's commitment to the cause of 'redeeming' India's so-called suppressed classes. But, like the old pre-1914 regional Depressed Class Missions, the organisation was deeply ambivalent in its understanding of untouchability. The Gandhians who ran the Harijan Sevak Sangh were initially of 'clean' caste origin. Their goal was to instil habits of cleanliness and propriety in their untouchable beneficiaries, and to wean them from toddy-drinking, carrion-eating and unseemly sexual indulgences.[37]

What Gandhi's critics have found objectionable is the assumption that so-called Harijans needed to be 'uplifted' or 'civilised' because they were indeed unclean and immoral by righteous Hindu standards. This is precisely what many 'reformists' had said in the 1900s and were still saying a generation later. As a youthful Bihar Congress activist in the early 1930s, the veteran Harijan politician Jagjivan Ram objected vehemently to what he called 'give-up-meat-wine-and-develop-cleanliness lectures' addressed to the 'depressed' by high-caste social reformers.[38] Looked at from this vantage point, the Gandhian version of low-caste uplift was merely an updating of what the Ramanandi gurus and other devotional preceptors had said in the eighteenth and early nineteenth centuries. This was, in effect: abjure sin, adopt our pious brand of ascetic purity, offer yourself in humble submission to our preceptorship, and you will be admitted on sufferance to our mystical communion.

Furthermore, the Gandhian message was that untouchables could be 'redeemed' only through mild and tractable behaviour. However unjustly treated, the Harijan should be an unworldly lover of god and nation, selflessly setting aside concerns of revenge or personal advancement in the higher cause of Hindu unity and national redemption. Apart from Harijan, the term which Gandhi used most often when referring to the characteristics of the ideal 'untouchable' was the Gujarati caste name Bhangi. In Gandhi's lifetime, this title was most

171 n. 1; for earlier use of the term by such pre-Independence 'uplift' campaigners as the Bihar monk-activist Swami Sahajanand, see Hauser 1994: 81–2; also Census of the United Provinces 1931, Report: 552.

[37] Iyer 1986, I: 427, 438; Zelliot 1988, 1996: 105, 170.

[38] Having perpetrated 'unparalleled atrocities' on those who were 'once [their] equal in culture and attainments [and] having degraded them into servile sub-humans', these campaigners' pronouncements '[added] insult to injury'. (Ram 1980: 45).

commonly used as a designation for hereditary household waste-removers. To use this regional jati name for untouchables in general was to portray the self-effacing domestic 'sweeper' with his meek posture and emblematic basket and brushes as an archetype for all of India's 'depressed' populations.[39]

The idealised Bhangi was certainly supposed to be an exemplar of the virtues which the Harijan Sevak Sangh was charged with spreading among the 'depressed'. Underlying this was the classically Gandhian goal of instilling the virtues of the worthy 'uplifted' Bhangi in the nation at large. For readers of the nationalist and 'reformist' press, this Bhangi stereotype offered a vision of the godly and humble untouchable as an instinctive Gandhian, that is, a goodly and dutiful toiler bringing the benefits of cleansing humble service to his home community, and through it to the whole nation.[40]

This emphasis on sacrifice and devotion in the life of the Bhangi led neatly back to the purposes of the Harijan Sevak Sangh. This organisation had been intended as a spiritual enterprise rather than a political pressure group. As such, its concerns were as much for the redemption of clean-caste Gandhians as for the 'uplift' of the 'depressed'. Its public statements therefore conveyed the message that the redeemed untouchable should be humbly grateful on two counts: first, for having been remade physically and morally into a clean vegetarian teetotaller; and secondly, for being allowed to act as an instrument of repentance and spiritual cleansing for the high-caste benefactors who had 'uplifted' him (her).

Although Gandhi campaigned to make the eradication of untouchability a crusade for the pious Hindu, until the 1940s he continued to exalt the principle of varna as an egalitarian 'law of life' which was indivisible from the Hindu faith. Providing it was purged of the 'sinful' belief in untouchability, the principle of varna order (*varnashramadharma*) was to be understood as divine and moral.[41] In the 1920s, his defence of varna drew heavily on the evolutionist themes which were still so widely endorsed by 'modern' science and social

---

[39] Zelliot 1988: 185.
[40] In the 1940s Gandhi called for full repudiation of caste rather than his earlier goal of a purified caste order purged of untouchability; his vision of India as a perfected all-Bhangi utopia was characteristically quixotic: '... finally there will be only one caste, known by the beautiful name Bhangi, that is to say, the reformer or remover of dirt'. (Quoted in Galanter 1984: 37.)
[41] Iyer 1986, II: 538–9, 595.

theory. He therefore argued that karmic notions of rebirth and inherited varna identity were truths endorsed by contemporary ethnological teachings:

In accepting the fourfold division, I am simply accepting the laws of Nature, taking for granted what is inherent in human nature, and the law of heredity. We are born with some of the traits of our parents. The fact that a human being is born only in the human species shows that some characteristics, i.e. caste, are determined by birth.[42]

Gandhi's evolutionist account of caste did not deny the element of free will: at least some 'inherited characteristics' could be 'reformed', he maintained, thus placing the onus on the individual to uplift himself spiritually and to correct social wrongs. Even so, '[it] is not possible in one birth entirely to undo the results of our past doings, and in the light of it, it is in every way right and proper to regard him as a *Brahmin* who is born of *Brahmin* parents'. So Gandhi declared that while 'a man's caste is no matter for pride', and 'no superiority attaches to any of the four [varna] divisions', it would be 'an idle short-cut' to discard the positive ideals which the varna system enshrined. 'A *Brahmin* may by doing the deeds of a *Sudra* become a *Sudra* in this very birth, but the world loses nothing in continuing to treat him as a *Brahmin*.'[43]

By the 1930s Gandhi's ethnological borrowings had acquired an overlay of Marxist theory. He thus pronounced the varna system to be 'ethical as well as economic. It recognises the influence of previous lives and of heredity.'[44] In its 'true' form varna did not promote crude inequalities of class or social rank: '... the idea of superiority or inferiority is wholly repugnant to it [the varna system]'.[45] Varna thus properly conceived 'is no man-made institution but the law of life universally governing the human family. Fulfillment of the law would make life livable, would spread peace and content [*sic*], end all clashes and conflicts, put an end to starvation and pauperisation, solve the problems of population and even end disease and suffering.'[46] And again: 'All *varnas* are equal, for the community depends no less on one than another.'[47]

---

[42] *Young India* 21 Jan 1926, in Iyer 1986, II: 22.
[43] *Ibid.*
[44] *Ibid.*: 601.
[45] *Ibid.*
[46] *Ibid.* 1987, III: 562
[47] *Ibid.*

Elsewhere Gandhi defined 'the law of *varna*' as meaning that 'everyone shall follow as a matter of *dharma* – duty – the hereditary calling of his forefathers, in so far as it is not inconsistent with fundamental ethics. He will earn his livelihood by following that calling. He may not hoard riches, but devote the balance for the good of the people.'[48] Gandhi's claim then was that the materialism of striving class-based Western societies derived from a far more pernicious principle of human order than that of *varnashramadharma*:

The beauty of the caste system is that it does not base itself upon distinctions of wealth [and] possessions . . .

. . . the spirit behind caste is not one of arrogant superiority, it is the classification of a different system of self-culture. It is true to the principle of heredity.[49]

Similar views about varna as the path to a socialist utopia were expressed by other Gandhians as well. In 1937, for example, a contributor to the *Congress Socialist* newspaper extolled the principles of varna as a manifestation of 'ancient scientific socialism' which, if restored to their 'pristine purity', could remedy the social ills of India and the entire world.[50]

THE DEPRESSED CLASSES AND THEIR CHAMPIONS

Naturally those who were in a position to shape the goals and language of Indian nationalism were mostly of high-caste origin, and mostly though not exclusively male. With the exception of Jagjivan Ram, until well into the twentieth century few if any members of the provincial Congress committees were of 'tribal' or low-caste origin. Brahman Congressmen outnumbered those of other castes by a considerable margin. Those who were not of Brahman birth came largely from the commercial and service jatis; even the many cash-crop producers who joined the Congress during the 1930s Depression had generally embraced the dharmic notions espoused by Aryas and purity-centred commercial groups.[51]

By the 1920s, scholar-officials and aspiring 'reformists' had come to

---

[48] *Ibid.*: 563.
[49] Gandhi, 'Caste v. class', quoted in Gupta 1985: 72.
[50] *ISR* 4 Sept 1937: 11; compare Chatterji 1994: 39–40.
[51] McLane 1977: 63.

use the catch-all term 'depressed' for anyone who was deemed in anthropological sources or everyday practice to be inherently low or polluting in the eyes of 'clean-caste' Hindus. Those who were 'depressed' were assumed to be deprived in material terms, and proponents of special aid to these groups saw the ritual and material forms of their so-called disabilities as being inextricably linked. From the early writings of Ambedkar to the most recent speeches of campaigning 'Dalit' activists, it has been persistently argued that India's so-called untouchables and tribals are by definition poorer and more disadvantaged than other Indians because the injustices inherent in caste have made this so.

These notions have been contested over the past fifty years on the grounds that their underlying principles are crude and ahistorical, that they do not reflect the dynamism and fluidity of the Indian social order, and that to identify caste as the cause of deprivation creates an excuse for denying benefits to materially disadvantaged non-Hindus. Even so, the theory of caste-based corporate backwardness has remained central to the Indian government's policies of uplift for the disadvantaged (see below, Chapter 7).

It might be assumed that the early activists who claimed to speak for the 'depressed' would be inclined to make common cause under a shared umbrella of disability or dharmic impurity. This was the rationale of such organisations as Ambedkar's Depressed Classes Federation (founded in 1930 and relaunched as the All-India Scheduled Caste Federation in 1942). But for those who expected the 'depressed' throughout India to join hands in the public arena, it was perplexing that so many members of these low-ranking *avarna* groups were concerned to define *other* 'impure' people as lower or more polluted than they were themselves. Thus, newly 'advanced' Mahars in Bombay Presidency used the courts and the press to assert that they were ritually superior to other Marathi-speaking untouchables, most notably to those known by the jati title Mahang. Bodies of Telugu-speaking Malas and Madigas had been contesting for marks of 'honour' and ritual precedence in the northern Madras districts since the 1880s, and similar status conflicts were being waged by many other untouchable and near-untouchable groups.[52]

---

[52] See Punalekar 1985.

Many of these battles were associated with missionary-led regional 'uplift' campaigns, and with new employment opportunities for these groups. As was noted above, the most widely recognised examples of this were the modest economic and educational gains made by Mahars in Bombay Presidency and Nadar/Shanars in the Tamil country. These conflicts were often violent, and they were certainly far from being a manifestation of collective low-caste militancy against the 'pure'.

The 1919 Government of India Act gave formal constitutional recognition to these 'suppressed' peoples; under its provisions, one out of the fourteen non-official nominated members of the Central Legislative Assembly was to be a representative of the so-called Depressed Classes, and the provincial legislatures were also required to have a fixed proportion of Depressed Class members. Even so, in this period the designation 'Depressed' had become notably problematic in 'Aryan' north India, where many contributors to nationalist and reformist debate argued that only in the far south – a land of dark-skinned 'aboriginals' and 'Dravidians' – did one find truly 'depressed' peoples.

By the early 1930s would-be representatives of north India's 'untouchables' commonly took the view that 'Depressed' was a term for south Indian groups like Paraiyans and Holeyas who were supposedly in a special class of their own, having been identified by both Western ethnologists and 'modern' Hindus as unclean, degraded and culpably 'impure'. As a result, activists such as S. D. Singh Chaurasia, a Lucknow campaigner associated with the United Provinces Hindu Backward Classes League (founded 1929), pressed for the use of a less demeaning euphemism for so-called untouchables. What Chaurasia and others hoped to find was a term that would somehow embrace all those of very low ritual status for purposes of public protest. At the same time they wished to signal that the 'untouchability' of the north Indian Chamar or Mahar was less degrading than that of the truly 'depressed'. By this was meant the Holeya or Paraiyan whose extreme lowness was so widely and insidiously seen by both Indians and Europeans as a consequence of sin, debauchery or 'degenerate' racial origins.[53]

[53] See Galanter 1984: 158.

In the 1930s the designations most often chosen by these would-be untouchable spokesmen were 'Backward Classes' or 'Hindu Backward Classes'. This implied that at some level the ethnologists and Hindu revivalists were right to stigmatise the 'low' south Indian Paraiyan or Holeya as a specially 'degraded' being whose so-called untouchability was of a different quality from that of the north Indian Mahar or Chamar. These decisions about terminology therefore introduced even more ambiguity into the problem of how 'caste' and 'race' were to be understood by would-be social reformers, Hindu nationalists and colonial officials. Was there one caste system or many? Were all Indians part of a shared 'Hindu' caste order? Were 'untouchables' to be defined as a single pan-Indian class of the 'impure', and if so on what basis were such people as north India's Chamar 'spokesmen' seeking to distance themselves from so-called depressed 'non-Aryans' such as Paraiyans and other 'degenerated non-Dwijas'?[54]

AMBEDKAR AND THE 'ANNIHILATION OF CASTE'

During the 1930s, a number of India's legislative assemblies debated and, in some cases, enacted modest anti-untouchability measures, most notably the Madras Presidency's 1938 Removal of Civil Disabilities Act, and Bombay's 1939 Harijan Temple Worship Act. Far from being greeted with acclaim by the 'modern' men who sat as members of these bodies, such initiatives evoked some notably fierce opposition, especially in areas where 'Hindu' political interests were held to be threatened by militant non-Brahman or Depressed Class activism. Joya Chatterji notes that in Bengal every Hindu member of the Central Legislative Assembly spoke out against an Untouchability Abolition Bill which went before it in 1933; some openly declared that they regarded untouchables as innately unworthy beings who could never 'come up' to the standard of clean-caste Hindus.[55]

Even in the face of these unabashedly 'Manuvadi' views, there were still deep divisions between those politicians who viewed untouch-

---

[54] For official use of the term Backward Classes dating back to the 1880s, see Galanter 1984: 154–8. Since Independence, Backward or Other Backward Classes has become a term for non-elite groups who would insist that they are not of impure or untouchable descent. See below, Chapter 7.

[55] Chatterji 1994: 40.

ability as a 'stain' on Indian faith and culture.[56] The key counterblast to the Gandhian view of caste came from B. R. Ambedkar (1891–1956), India's first Western-educated and professionally qualified 'untouchable'. Ambedkar came from a family of rural Mahars from the Ratnagiri region. Like other occupationally mobile Mahars from this part of the Konkan, many of Ambedkar's relations had achieved modest prosperity through service in the Bombay army; the family also had a tradition of adherence to the Kabirpanthi devotional movement.[57]

This *bhakti* sect (*sampradaya*), which cultivated ecstatic devotion to the person and teachings of the humble weaver-saint Kabir, left its imprint not just on Ambedkar and his kin but on a significant proportion of the region's Mahar population. Indeed, by the end of the nineteenth century, Ambedkar's home area was one of those regions in which a combination of new economic opportunities and inspirational religious teaching had endowed certain untouchables or near-untouchables with an unusual sense of cohesion, and a capacity to acquire new skills and resources. In the early nineteenth century Gujarat's Swami Narayan movement had fostered a similar 'self-help' ethos among ex-'predator' pastoralists of Koli descent. By mid-century, Christian missionaries in Madras Presidency and the Punjab were claiming the credit for inspiring such people as Tamil Shanars and 'backward' groups in the Punjab with a similar spirit of self-advancement.

In 1917, having completed a Ph.D. at Columbia University under the pioneering sociologists Alexander Goldenweiser and E. R. A. Seligman, Ambedkar returned to India where he joined the Bombay Bar, lectured at the Government Law College and served as a Bombay provincial legislator. By the late 1920s his speeches and publications on the wrongs of the 'Backward' classes had made him one of the most prominent public activists in the subcontinent. Ambedkar was a keen advocate of forcible 'temple entry' as well as the adoption of the sacred thread and other tokens of 'clean-caste' birth which were forbidden to so-called untouchables by the precepts of formal varna theory. In such works as *The Annihilation of Caste*

---

[56] The pejorative term Manuvadi is now used by 'Dalit' activists to refer to belief in 'dharmic' caste norms and ideas of low-caste sinfulness and inferiority, as prescribed in the *Institutes* of the mythical sage Manu. See below, Chapter 9.

[57] Keer 1981: 8–9; Gokhale 1990: 226; Zelliot 1996: 312.

11. Dr B. R. Ambedkar (1891–1956), champion of the 'depressed classes' and an outspoken opponent of Mahatma Gandhi on caste issues.

(1936) he took a radically un-Gandhian view of 'uplift' for those demeaned by what he called the poison of Brahmanism.[58] One of his most vehement polemics, *What Congress and Gandhi have done to the Untouchables* (1945) was a bitter denunciation of the Mahatma and his allies as enemies of the 'depressed'.[59] As to the 'golden chain' notion that caste could operate as a system of high-minded ethics and pious ideals, Ambedkar was scathing:

The effects of caste on the ethics of the Hindus is simply deplorable. Caste has killed public spirit. Caste has destroyed the sense of public charity. Caste has made public opinion impossible. A Hindu's public is his caste. His responsibility is only to his caste. His loyalty is restricted only to his caste. Virtue has become caste-ridden and morality has become caste-bound. There is no sympathy to the deserving. There is no appreciation of the meritorious.[60]

In 1927 Ambedkar caused a sensation when he dramatised his campaign against 'Brahmanism' and 'caste oppression' by publicly burning a copy of the *Manusmrti*, that is, the so-called *Institutes of Manu*. As we saw above, this work had been widely represented by both Western and Indian commentators as the defining code or schema of Brahmanical Hinduism.[61] Ambedkar's controversial gesture thus reflected both a lawyer's and an 'orientalist''s view of the power of texts rather than custom or individual will to shape human behaviour. At the same time, this gesture of wiping out the codified word was an attack on the values of those pious Hindus for whom sacred writings were embodiments of divinity. Ambedkar's opponents were therefore quick to portray him as a would-be destroyer of Hinduism itself, a view to which he contributed by describing his goal

[58] Zelliot 1988: 192–3, 1992: 10–11; Juergensmeyer 1982: 39; Ambedkar 1936: 99. Ambedkar was denied permission to deliver this polemic as an address to an Arya Samaj offshoot body, the Society for the Abolition of Caste (Jat Pat Todak Mandal, founded 1922). Like the scholar and social reformer Shridhar V. Ketkar, Ambedkar's studies had been financed by the Maharaja of Baroda, a keen princely advocate of the 'non-Brahman' cause.

[59] Invited to give evidence to the 1928 Simon Commission (Indian Statutory Commission on constitutional reform), Ambedkar asserted his controversial view that the 'Depressed Classes' should not be treated electorally as part of the 'Hindu community'. Asked by the panel whether his forebears were 'pre-Aryan', he replied 'Well, I do not know. That is a view.' (Moon 1982, II: 465.)

[60] Ambedkar 1936: 63.

[61] Ambedkar said he had burned the *Manusmrti* as a 'symbol of the injustice under which we have been crushed for centuries' (Keer 1981: 105–6; Lokhande 1982: 31). Yet he also argued that early Hindu scriptures did not propound untouchability; this he saw as a development arising from struggles between Buddhism, propagated originally under the great dynast and law-giver Asoka, and the faith of 'Brahmanism' which he associated with the rise of the Hindu Gupta dynasty in the fourth century AD (Ambedkar 1948: 121, 144–55).

as that of relieving Hindus from their 'thraldom to the Shastras', and by declaring:

What is called Religion by the Hindus is nothing but a multitude of commands and prohibitions ... Under it there is no loyalty to ideals, there is only conformity to commands ... I have no hesitation in saying that such a religion must be destroyed ...[62]

So, for both Gandhi and Ambedkar – who together with Nehru must rank as the subcontinent's most important twentieth-century politicians – caste in general and untouchability in particular were real and problematic facts of Indian life. Of course as key contributors to the 'modern' Indian's understanding of caste, Ambedkar and Gandhi reached very different conclusions as to what if anything the state could or should do about the plight of the 'depressed'. But neither left his contemporaries in any doubt that for them this plight was real, and to be regarded as a matter of deep reproach to the faith of professing Hindus. Also, both clearly subscribed to the view that it was the business of modern nationalist leaders to use the vocabulary of caste to define and address social issues. Both took it for granted that in the political arena a leader should address named 'communities' as embodiments of shared descent and moral identity. Neither dismissed caste as an ethnographic invention or self-serving 'colonial' fantasy. Here they were both at odds with Nehru and his fellow 'secular' nationalists who saw no need to treat caste as a political problem, or to prescribe special measures to ameliorate caste 'disability'.

These debates had a critical impact on the last great devolutionary measure to be implemented under the Raj. This was the 1935 Government of India Act in which the colonial authorities confirmed the principle of special electoral representation for minority religious 'communities'. The 1935 Act more than trebled the size of the Indian electorate and granted full provincial autonomy to elected Indian ministries. In other words, the colonial state was now willing to allow more power than ever before to be exercised through the operations of elected representative assemblies in each of the eleven provinces of British India. With the electoral stakes now so much higher than they had been under previous constitutional schemes, the question of who precisely was to be classified as members of the Hindu and Muslim 'communities' acquired more significance than ever before. And it was

[62] Ambedkar 1936: 87–8.

at this point, at a critical moment of political conflict and growing economic distress, that the key figure of Ambedkar came to the fore with a bid for separate electorates for untouchable or 'backward class' populations.

For Hindu nationalists this ploy aroused deep fears that the colonial state would cease to count the very sizable numbers of untouchables or 'backward classes' in determining the size of India's 'Hindu' population. These groups were thought to number between 50 and 60 million out of a total population of about 350 million in British India. To subtract them from the population on which the provinces' Hindu electoral representation was calculated would make a critical difference to the subcontinent's electoral arithmetic, particularly in Bengal and the Punjab where the balance between Hindu and Muslim was so close.[63]

Indeed, with the Census figures now indicating lower birth rates for Hindus than for other religious 'communities', it was widely thought that this move might actually overturn the Hindu electoral majority in many areas of British India, and would certainly undercut Congress's claim to represent the entire Hindu 'nation'. These fears prompted the Hindu Mahasabha and other Hindu revivalist and supremacist organisations to intensify their recruitment drives among untouchables and 'tribals'. Whether formally converted to other faiths or not, these were people whom Arya Samaj leaders and other Hindu activists now particularly wished to claim as Hindus. As was seen above, these organisations sought to achieve this by vesting such people with what were regarded as incontestable marks of 'Hindu' identity, meaning the sacred thread and a recognised set of jati and varna titles.[64]

Ambedkar was well placed to take electoral advantage of these developments. As self-made champion of the 'suppressed', he rejected the Gandhian argument that Harijans should subordinate their cause to that of the nation's unity. In a celebrated address at Nagpur in 1930, Ambedkar created yet another sensation by referring to India's untouchables as 'slaves of slaves', meaning that they were doubly oppressed as victims of both caste and colonial rule. For the 'unclean',

[63] Especially at a time when the all-India Census returns showed that the subcontinent's non-Hindu populations were apparently growing at a faster rate than the Hindu 'community'.

[64] As has been seen above, many members of these groups had been engaging in 'Sanskritic' thread-adoptions or 'Kshatriyazation' moves in their own right: see, for example, Pinch 1996.

he said on numerous occasions, Hinduism itself was a form of imperialism, and the goals of nationalists were meaningless unless they committed themselves to liberate the 'depressed' from this dual tyranny.[65]

Ambedkar's standing as chief spokesman for the 'depressed' was endorsed by the colonial authorities with his appointment as a delegate to the first Indo-British Round Table Conference, which was convened in 1930 to deliberate further constitutional change for India. At the second Round Table Conference in 1931 Ambedkar made his crucial demand for separate 'untouchable' (or Depressed Class) electorates. This was bitterly contested by the Congress leadership, including those who represented themselves as defenders of corporate 'Hindu' interests. In 1932, Gandhi and Ambedkar agreed on a compromise constitutional package, the so-called Pune (Poona) Pact. This arrangement, essentially a victory for Ambedkar, did away with the principle of separate 'untouchable' electorates. Yet while it kept caste Hindus and the so-called Depressed Classes together in the same electorates, the new system reserved a proportion of special seats in the provincial assemblies for 'depressed' candidates.

The provisions of this Pune Pact became the basis of the other key landmark of pre-war nationalist politics, the Communal Award of 1932. This agreement, which assigned a fixed number of seats in each province's legislative assembly both to members of the religious minorities and to the Depressed Classes (henceforth the 'Scheduled' Castes and Tribes), paved the way for the Government of India Act of 1935. Its link with past practice was that it preserved the principle of special electoral representation for Muslims (as embodied in the 1909 Morley–Minto Reforms). Its key innovation was the new move – reflecting Ambedkar's qualified victory over Gandhi and the Congress – to create separate electoral representation (on the Pune Pact principle of special candidates' seats) for 'communities' which were to be defined on the basis of tribal and low-caste identity, rather than faith or 'nationhood'.

It was at this point that the colonial authorities set up the intricate machinery of listing or 'Scheduling' for the new special caste-based

---

[65] 'The British have an Empire. So have the Hindus. For is not Hinduism a form of imperialism and are not the Untouchables a subject race owing their allegiance, and servitude to their Hindu Master?' *Gandhi and the emancipation of the untouchables* Bombay 1943: 65–6 (quoted in Shankardass 1982: 244).

constituencies. This mammoth exercise was undertaken in 1936. Its aim was to identify and list every so-called depressed 'community' in each province where the 1935 Act applied so as to work out how many special candidates' seats to reserve for the 'depressed' (i.e. 'tribals' and 'untouchables') in its provincial legislatures. Initially nearly 400 'untouchable' populations were listed, together with scores of so-called 'tribal' communities. These were the original Scheduled populations of British India.[66]

THE LOGIC OF CASTE IN THE
PRE-INDEPENDENCE YEARS

By the time of Independence, then, the usages of caste had become firmly established as electoral assets. More Indians too had reason to embrace jati and varna bonds as sources of advantage in situations of material insecurity. The economic and social pressures of the later nineteenth century had encouraged significant numbers of people to exploit the local face-to-face relations of jati and varna. These trends carried on from the 1920s into the Depression era of the 1930s. This, of course, was a period of deep economic distress. Yet it was also a time of rapid industrialisation and physical mobility, with many returning migrant labourers and other victims of collapsing cash-crop economies competing for livelihoods in the fast-growing industrial towns. It was in these settings that many poor urban labourers began to propound new syncretistic myths of caste origin and new forms of 'neo-*bhakti*' devotional faith which glorified shared bonds of 'community' as a heritage of oppression transcended.[67]

In these volatile environments, it was not just the weak and deprived who sought to hedge themselves round with more tightly defined jati and varna identities. For those of comparatively privileged social background, this period saw the compilation of a great multitude of all-India caste directories, not by the colonial state, but by Indians themselves. These volumes were intended for the use of a given 'community' and contained extensive listings of individuals and families, and their achievements in business or the professions. Such directories were most commonly commissioned on behalf of commer-

[66] Joshi 1940: 291 n. 1.
[67] Gooptu 1997.

cial groups, but they were popular too among members of the old Brahman and Kayastha-type service groups.

Caste bonds proved their worth in other ways too, both in the 1930s and in wartime. Many new caste associations and caste conferences were founded in this period. These bodies promoted a variety of practical schemes in addition to community directories, most notably the establishment of hostels for students and other jati or sub-caste members residing away from home. Here the important stimuli were the continuing expansion of education, urban employment, and long-distance road and rail communications. As a result, the constant refrain of self-styled caste leaders, which was widely acted on in this period, was that the 'community' must show progressive values by taking responsibility for the needs of the many young single men who were now working or studying in unfamiliar towns and cities. This meant ensuring that these young people were not led astray by urban temptations, that they had suitable food and respectable lodgings; often they received scholarships and other forms of material support.

These were all developments which were tending to make the experience of caste an increasingly forceful part of everyday reality, not merely in regard to marriage ties and other immediate face-to-face contacts, but in concrete practical actions which were being taken at the supra-local or all-India level. Yet the final point to make about the period from the 1910s to the late 1930s is the importance of the revolution in the public rhetoric surrounding caste. This was promoted above all by Gandhi, and by Gandhi's key antagonist on caste issues, B. R. Ambedkar.

These two men's far-reaching pronouncements arose in a context where caste issues had already been widely commented on by such organisations as the Arya Samaj and the 'traditional' Hindu *sanatan dharm* ('orthodox religion') networks. The Arya Samaj's ambivalent position on caste has already been discussed. Its adherents' treatment of caste and the nation tended to emphasise shared Aryan or 'Hindu' bonds and to de-emphasise caste, though, as was noted in Chapter 5, many of the Hindustan tillers who identified themselves as Jat tended to interpret the Arya message as a validation of their own distinctive caste virtues. By contrast, *sanatan dharm* supporters of 'orthodox' Hinduism promoted a purified version of caste as a structure of complementary essences which would ultimately strengthen the nation. It was primarily this tradition on which Gandhi built, but with

264

the one critical exception that he came to view untouchability as a truly unacceptable expression of caste values.

It was Nehru's 'secular' vision of social modernity that shaped the Constitution of independent India. Yet the other two traditions have retained considerable power as well: first, the Gandhian goal of a modified and purified caste system, and, secondly, set against this, the Ambedkarite view, which has found its most recent expression in the assertiveness of the militant Dalit movements. These complexities and contradictions were all carried forward into the social welfare policies of the newly independent Indian republic.

CHAPTER 7

STATE POLICY AND 'RESERVATIONS': THE POLITICISATION OF CASTE-BASED SOCIAL WELFARE SCHEMES

INTRODUCTION

By the time the new Republic's 'secular' Constitution was being drafted, the claims of caste were active though not necessarily decisive elements in the domains of work, worship and politics. Both before and during the colonial period, this shift towards a predominantly castelike social order occurred through the economic and political changes which were described in previous chapters. New trends in ideology were also important here, particularly the initiatives of nationalists and social reformers, as well as the writings of Western orientalists.

Having concentrated in Chapter 6 on the role of the pre-Independence electoral arena, this chapter explores the moves made by jurists, politicians and government agencies in the decades after 1947. For most of this period, the Republic's official institutions were directed to use their powers in inherently contradictory ways. On the one hand, they were to promote the making of a 'modern' casteless India. Yet simultaneously, they were to accept the reality of caste in fulfilling the state's other key modernising goal, that of relieving so-called 'disability' by improving the lot of the 'depressed'.

This chapter therefore has a dual focus. First, it will discuss the provisions of the 1950 Constitution in regard to low-caste 'uplift'. Secondly, it attempts to interpret the battles over caste-based regional welfare schemes ('reservations') which have been an explosive feature of Indian politics in the years since Independence. The emphasis here will be on government and party politics in the forty-year period when the public sector commanded a high proportion of the country's resources, when the state was still a major employer, and when state agencies still retained the massive regulatory powers with which they had been vested after Independence.

266

In theory at least, what government did and said about caste should have begun to lose its significance from the mid-1980s. It was from this point that attempts were made to improve India's poor post-Independence economic performance by scaling down the country's elaborate planning and regulatory apparatus (the so-called 'permit Raj'), and by encouraging the growth of a market-orientated private sector. It might have been expected that the state would rapidly lose its ascendancy both as an employer and as an arbiter of social change, especially after 1991 when a balance of payments crisis prompted further 'liberalisation' with loan support from the World Bank and the International Monetary Fund.

From this point at least, then, the country should, in theory, have seen significant reductions in bureaucracy and public expenditure. This, together with industrial growth, a decline in public-sector employment and rapid growth in private-sector education, might have cut to a minimum the numbers of Indians with a direct interest in such matters as caste quotas in state-run universities and overstaffed public-sector enterprises. In reality, however, so-called liberalisation has been a slow and hesitant process which has not rapidly reduced the public sector's overall share of GDP (still an estimated 45 per cent in 1993, and probably not much less in the late 1990s).[1]

Furthermore, while the fear of large-scale losses in both jobs and public subsidies generated fierce debate and conflict – much of it framed in caste-specific language – neither of these initiatives gave priority to industrial privatisation or deregulation of the labour market. Significant social change did occur in this period, most notably the growth of a mass consumer market; this so-called new middle class reportedly numbered as many as 100 to 200 million by the early 1990s. Yet, well into the 'liberalisation' era, there have been indications that the claims of caste have actually grown stronger in important areas of Indian life.[2] Particularly in certain types of labour recruitment, the growth of the private sector seems to have perpetuated or even enhanced the relevance of jati identities. Certainly in the

---

[1] Cassen and Joshi 1995: 211; also Joshi and Little 1996: 173–85, on the slow and limited reduction of the public sector's share of GDP (as of 1992–3) compared with 1970–1 and 1980–1, particularly in such sensitive labour-intensive areas as the railways and loss-making mills.

[2] Compare Srinivas 1996.

late 1990s, considerations of caste have shown little sign of disappearing from either the public or the private domain.

CASTE AND THE 1950 CONSTITUTION

The Republic's founding principle of secularism ruled out the possibility that India would follow the path of such countries as Ireland and Pakistan: despite the efforts of contemporary Hindu supremacist organisations, no one religion has yet been singled out as a constitutionally defined national faith. Thus, in keeping with Jawaharlal Nehru's vision of India as a casteless and egalitarian nation state, the 1950 Constitution was framed around a concept of what it calls the fundamental rights of citizenship.[3]

These rights are deemed to inhere in the individual, rather than in castes or ethno-religious 'communities'. The 1950 Constitution therefore requires the state to treat all citizens equally, without regard to birth, gender or religious affinity, and it makes no attempt to define a cultural basis for Indian nationhood. Consequently, it contains no references to Brahmans, gods, sacred scriptures or concepts of ritual purity, thus apparently ignoring virtually everything that a modern anthropologist would define as fundamental to both caste and Hinduism. The one significant exception to this is the Constitution's reference to cow protection (Article 48). This was included against the wishes of Nehru and his fellow 'secularists'; the courts have given state governments limited powers to ban cow slaughter, and some regional cow protection acts have indeed been implemented in response to campaigns by Hindu supremacists.[4]

Yet paradoxically, this predominantly 'secular' Constitution does require state agencies to recognise the existence of caste through its provisions for what is called the special care and advancement of untouchables and tribals (or Harijans and Adivasis; in administrative language, the Scheduled Castes and Tribes). It does so in two distinct ways. First, Articles 15 and 17 endorse the old reformist view of caste as a structure of corporate 'disability' which subjugates the 'unclean' or 'untouchable' by subjecting them to the forms of physical exclusion described by generations of ethnographers and social activists. These

---

[3] For a penetrating account of the Nehruvian legacy, see Khilnani 1997.
[4] Jaffrelot 1996: 164, 205.

exclusions are specifically addressed in the Constitution. The famous Article 17 on untouchability declares:

'Untouchability' is abolished and its practice in any form is forbidden. The enforcement of any disability arising out of 'Untouchability' shall be an offence punishable in accordance with law.

Article 15 tackles 'disability' by embracing the language of pre-Independence anti-untouchability campaigners:

No citizen shall, on grounds only of religion, race, caste, sex ... be subject to any disability, liability, restriction or condition with regard to – (a) access to shops, public restaurants, hotels and places of public entertainment; or (b) the use of wells, tanks, bathing ghats, roads and places of public resort maintained ... out of State funds or dedicated to the use of the general public. (Article 15: 2)

Secondly, under its much-debated Article 46, the goal of advancing the position of the country's so-called 'weaker sections' is to be pursued collectively, that is, by providing special benefits for those classes of citizens who are deemed to be socially and materially disadvantaged by virtue of either 'tribal' or low-caste birth. This Article declares:

The State shall promote with special care the educational and economic interests of the weaker sections of the people, and, in particular, of the Scheduled Castes and the Scheduled Tribes, and shall protect them from social injustice and all forms of exploitation.[5]

In addition, there are references in the Constitution to an undefined wider category of 'depressed' or 'socially and educationally backward classes of citizens'. The identity of these groups – the 'other backward classes', in a much-cited phrase coined by Nehru – is left unclear; only the Scheduled, i.e. untouchables and tribals, are specifically singled out in these provisions. This ambiguity in relation to the 'other backwards' has been a critical issue in national and state-level politics since the late 1960s, as will be seen below.

Apart then from this imprecision in regard to 'backwards', the clear implication of these provisions was that with the avowed intention of correcting inherited deprivation, the state was required to treat both caste and tribal identity as authentic facts of Indian life, thus in this sense disregarding the Constitution's commitment to equality and

[5] On the implications of these provisions, see Basu 1982 and especially Galanter 1984: this chapter's account of caste-based compensatory discrimination policies draws extensively on Galanter's valuable study.

individualism. It is clear too that official welfare measures for the 'weak' and the 'backward' were to be administered collectively to those whose forebears had been the victims of so-called caste disability. Whatever their personal circumstances, those of Brahman and other 'forward communities' were deemed ineligible for these schemes. Instead of individualised means tests, such benefits were to be allocated through forms of elaborate official taxonomising which are still in force today. These require state agencies to decide which regional 'tribes' and 'castes' are in need of official 'uplift', and to dispense their benefits accordingly. Such measures of so-called compensatory discrimination – and in particular, the allocation of university places and public-service appointments on the basis of community quotas rather than strict competitive merit – would be termed affirmative action or positive discrimination in the West.

Although in recent times some of these provisions have been extended to members of non-Hindu regional minorities, this system has generally been based on an idea of fixed and inflexible boundaries between Hinduism and other Indian faiths. Caste and its 'disabilities' were seen as the features of a monolithic 'Hindu' world; by this definition, adherents of so-called convert faiths had no need for redress of shared 'disability'. This was a crude and unreal picture of both caste and religious or 'communal' affiliation, but its stark simplicities have proved very enduring in the years since Independence.

So how did the Constitution come to this ambivalent position, recognising the logic of caste in its undertaking to fight 'social injustice' and advance the 'weak', while otherwise denying its relevance to the citizens of a democratic nation-state? As we have seen, the influence of B. R. Ambedkar was the critical factor here. Despite Ambedkar's many years of opposition to Congress, Nehru chose this advocate of electoral and material compensation for the 'depressed' as his first Law Minister. Ambedkar therefore played a central role in the drafting of the 1950 Constitution, particularly the provisions covering untouchability and uplift for the 'weak'.

This provision paved the way for legislation against so-called caste disabilities, and an all-India Untouchability (Offences) Act came into effect in 1955. Its language echoed attempts by pre-Independence jurists to establish workable legal principles to apply in the area of social advancement for the 'unclean'. The Republic's judges found it as difficult as their colonial predecessors had done to define exactly what it was that this law had criminalised, and which groups it was to protect and 'uplift'. Its provisions were certainly not intended to ban the use of specialist household and funerary pollution-removers, even though by most anthropological definitions such people must be regarded as unclean and collectively 'untouchable' in the eyes of the patrons or *jajmans* whom they serve. Nor was the Act taken to mean that individuals would be prosecuted for undertaking rituals of cleansing if inadvertently touched by the hand or shadow of a Harijan. On the other hand, it was clear that the Act outlawed those practices which featured in pre-Independence reformist polemics, most notably the exclusion of known 'untouchables' from village wells, schools, eating houses and other sensitive gathering places. Some state-level legislatures have even made it an offence to refer to people by such terms as Dhed, still a widely known 'untouchable' caste title in Gujarat.[6]

Enforcement in this area has proved extremely difficult, however, and the courts tended to interpret the provisions of the Untouchability Act in relatively narrow terms. This was true too of its successor, which was enacted under a title which did not mention caste or untouchability. This new law, the Protection of Civil Rights Act, echoed what was seen to be the more modern terminology of American social justice legislation. Even so, the intention was still to criminalise overt forms of injustice against those of Harijan or 'unclean' birth. This was therefore an area of constitutional provision which told Indians that caste was real, and that the modern state has an obligation to protect its citizens from forms of disability which were unique to caste as a 'system'.[7]

This view of caste as an unjust reality of Indian life can be seen too in the Constitution's other main pronouncements on social uplift for the deprived. First, there are the all-important measures concerning reservations or 'affirmative action' quotas in public employment, as well as privileged access to higher education for members of the 'backward classes'. The recipients of these benefits too are defined in terms of community, that is, as members of the so-called Scheduled

---

[6] Randeria 1989: 174 n. 7.

[7] On the ineffectiveness of the 1955 Act, see Department of Social Welfare 1969 *Report of the Committee on Untouchability*: 42–81; and for a trenchant critique of these provisions see Béteille 1981.

Castes and Tribes. Secondly, Articles 330 and 332 make special electoral provision for these groups. This is paradoxical since the Republic based its political system on universal adult suffrage in place of the highly restricted franchises of the 1919 and 1935 Government of India Acts. Even so, independent India has preserved the colonial principle of separate representation for 'communities' which are deemed to need special protection and 'uplift'. A further irony here has been the invoking of the Nehruvian ideal of secularism so as to exclude adherents of the minority religions from these provisions. Separate electorates for Muslims and other minority religious groups were abolished at Independence. Only members of the Scheduled Castes and Scheduled Tribes (and also women) were included in the new schemes of compensatory electoral weighting which reserved a proportion of state and central legislative assembly seats for representatives of these groups. Adherents of other 'conversion' religions, including the Ambedkarite neo-Buddhists (but not Sikh 'untouchables'), were also excluded from these schemes.[8]

During the 1950s the Republic vested power in bureaucratic state agencies with a brief to attack injustice and social 'backwardness'. Such key officials as the Commissioner for Scheduled Castes and Tribes were well versed in the theories of planning and development which had become influential in both India and the West during the Second World War. On paper at least, tens of millions of Indians have been provided for since Independence by central and state-level schemes which have organised land redistribution, loan allocations and a host of other official programmes so as to give special preference to those of tribal and Harijan-'untouchable' origin.[9]

[8] The 1980 Mandal Commission Report accepted that there were 'backward' castes or castelike groups among Muslims and other non-Hindus, but reaffirmed the long-standing orientalist view that only in Hinduism is caste inherent to the faith, other religions being fundamentally 'egalitarian in outlook'. See Desai et al. 1985: 69. On Ambedkarite Buddhists see pp. 281–2 below. Articles 330 and 332 create special seats for Scheduled Castes and Tribes in both the national parliament and the state assemblies, with the numbers of seats to reflect their proportion of the overall population.

[9] For further details see the 1969 Report of the Government of India Committee on Untouchability. Shukla and Verma (1993) show a massive imbalance in outlay under the central government's aid schemes for Scheduled populations; until the 1960s the Scheduled Tribes were allocated far more under each Five-Year Plan's aid and uplift schemes than the much larger populations of Scheduled Castes (untouchables). But while bureaucratic rigidities and other failings greatly limited the effects of this expenditure, the earmarking of large sums for such programmes as business and agricultural loans for members of Scheduled Tribes and Castes (nearly 80 and 83 million rupees respectively under the seventh Five-Year Plan) certainly drew attention to the 'community'- or caste-based categories being used to

Yet for all their modernising goals and strategies, these agencies inherited much of their language and procedure from the administrative operations of the Raj. Their strategies often reflected the socially conservative thinking of the early Indian social reformers, and of the colonial policemen and military recruiters who dealt with Indians on a basis of shared racial and moral essences, rather than individual rights under the law. Even the Republic's first Commissioner for Scheduled Castes and Tribes expressed much the same views as the 'uplift' campaigners of the early 1900s, characterising Harijans as 'lazy in mind and body and callous to [their] own condition', and deploring their supposed reluctance to educate their children.[10]

In certain areas the new Republic did take steps to overturn this 'essentialising' logic. After Independence important Hindu temples such as those at Pandharpur in Maharashtra and Guruvayur in Kerala were declared open to Harijans. In addition, the courts made piecemeal moves to abolish the regional pass laws and collective penal sanctions which had been devised for use against so-called criminal tribes and castes.[11] There were rulings too against the use of preferential caste quotas in military and police recruitment, and attempts to ban the exclusion of would-be service recruits who had hitherto been defined as 'non-martial' by virtue of their caste or 'tribal' origin. From 1951 the Census of India abandoned most of the operations which had hitherto used caste and 'tribe' as units of enumeration in the collection of regional and all-India population statistics.[12]

Even today, though, law and public policy are anything but 'casteless'. The Indian Army has fought off attempts to abolish its pre-Independence Sikh, Jat, Rajput and Dogra regiments, and in most so-called 'mixed-class' regiments it has refused to mix recruits of different caste within the individual companies that comprise a battalion.[13]

redress deprivation. (The 1981 Census recorded population figures of 105 million for the Scheduled Castes and 52 million for 'tribals' out of a total population of 710 million.)

[10] Commissioner's *Report* for 1951, quoted in Massey 1995: 58–9; compare Chapter 4, p. 184, above.

[11] Congress campaigned before Independence against the 1911 Criminal Tribes Act. The Act was repealed in 1947, though its replacement, the 1948 Habitual Offenders Act (its title echoing that of Britain's nineteenth-century Habitual Criminals Act), retained features of the old 'community'-based colonial legislation. The term 'criminal tribes' remained in use well after Independence. See Arnold 1986: 221, 262 nn. 135–6; Nigam 1990: 155–6; Ghurye 1963: 14–15.

[12] Galanter 1994: 164 n. 46, 170–1 n. 78.

[13] Rosen 1996: 208–12.

Similarly, Indian penal sanctions are now directed against individuals, and the law no longer criminalises entire 'communities'. Yet it is still common for officials and politicians to utter pronouncements about the predatory 'otherness' of such people as Kolis, Gujars and 'tribals'. Furthermore, even though the Census of India had greatly reduced its compilation of caste-based statistics, officials in other areas of government continued to insist on the state's need for 'scientific' data on the names, occupations and regional rank orderings of the country's 'tribal' and caste 'communities'.

Without such information, the new republic would have had no means of carrying out its mammoth task of identifying those who were to receive electoral and welfare benefits for the 'depressed'. Given the de-emphasis on caste in the Census, those charged with implementing the reservations policies simply took over much of the existing colonial data. In most cases officials used the same lists and statistical tables that had been compiled in 1936 under the provisions of the 1935 Government of India Act.[14] Thus a whole new generation of post-Independence officials became schooled in both the jargon and the techniques used in distinguishing 'Upper Shudras' from 'Twice-Born', 'Lower Shudra' and 'Scheduled' caste groups.

Since Independence, officials and academics have had much to say about the flaws and inconsistencies in these procedures. In the Punjab, for example, those identified as members of the Khatik caste were deemed eligible for Scheduled Caste benefits. Yet, in neighbouring Uttar Pradesh, this same 'community', whose members were described as low-status goat-butchers and produce-sellers by colonial ethnographers, was classed as 'forward' rather than 'backward'.[15] Yet for all their anomalies and contradictions, these classifications have proved remarkably long-lived. Attempts have been made to prune the listings, as in 1965 when an all-India investigatory committee recommended 'de-Scheduling' several of the broadest regional Harijan 'communities' including Chamars, Mahars and Bengal Rajbanshis. The panel argued that in all these groups there was now a sizable proportion of individuals and families who had advanced themselves economically and educationally, and that as a result their 'communities' should no longer be treated as collectively backward. Yet so great have been the

[14] This had granted special electoral representation to members of so-called Scheduled Castes and Backward Tribes (Galanter 1994: 130, 148).
[15] Galanter 1994: 141; Radhakrishnan in Srinivas 1996; Rao 1981: 50–1, 344–5.

vested interests associated with the system that representatives of 'Scheduled' populations have fought and generally won their battles against such proposals.[16]

Even in the Census itself, the old traditions of official ethnographic reportage were far from dead in the post-Independence era. Although enumerators no longer compiled statistical tables based on respondents' caste affiliations, the Census authorities still made much of caste in their subsidiary descriptive reports, as for example in the 400 village survey monographs which were a feature of the 1961 all-India Census. The volumes of *Ethnographic Notes* which were produced for the 1971 Census were even more remarkable for their deployment of 'orientalist' caste stereotypes:

The Pulayans look generally dirty. It is doubtful whether they take bath [*sic*] even once a week.

The social rank of the Kolhatis is very low ... They eat ... the flesh of carrion, and are addicted to strong drink ... The Dukkar Kolhatis are reported to be inveterate criminals and are vigilantly watched by the police.[17]

All manner of oddities have resulted from the recycling of colonial caste categories. In one case dating from the 1950s, local Census returns for occupational distribution puzzled a visiting American statistician by showing an improbably high level of manufacturing employment in an exceptionally deprived agricultural region. It turned out that the enumerators had entered their respondents according to the 'traditional' occupations associated with their caste titles, thus listing impossibly large numbers of people as 'manufacturers' because they used names which had conventional associations with distilling, tanning and wood-working; in fact, as for similar people all over India, virtually everyone thus entered was an agricultural labourer.[18]

Central government has also continued to sponsor the operations of H. H. Risley's brainchild, the Anthropological Survey of India. In the late 1990s this same body was still overseeing a massive exercise in caste-based data-collection – the *People of India* project – with

---

[16] Galanter 1994: 127–8, 136–8. On the judiciary's use of data from the colonial *Castes and Tribes* volumes in cases where both groups and individuals have contested exclusion from the Scheduled Caste listings, see Rao 1981: 50–1.

[17] *Census of India 1971*. Series 19: Tamil Nadu. Part VB, Schedule C – *Ethnographic Notes*, I: 79 and II: 70. For an account of the use of caste listings and other caste material in studies sponsored by the Census authorities, see Padmanabha 1981.

[18] Schwartzberg 1981.

funding from that key embodiment of Nehruvian development ideals, the Indian Planning Commission. From its inception in 1985 this project's aim has been to draw up what it calls anthropological profiles of 4,635 named castes and tribal 'communities'. Its methods have included the large-scale testing of DNA samples, with researchers using the molecular typing techniques employed in human genome-mapping projects in an attempt to identify differences between individual castes and 'tribes' at the most fundamental level, that of their genetic make-up.

Thus this apparently ultra-modern aspect of the *People of India* project is rooted in a belief in the reality of caste as a matter of profound biochemical differentiations. Furthermore, a very consider-able part of the 600 contributors' efforts has been given over to anthropometric measuring exercises using the favoured human head-form survey techniques of Risley's day, including the compilation of nose-width and skull-size tables for individual 'tribal' and caste 'communities'. Far from telling Indians that caste and tribe are colonial fabrications or an irrelevance to the country's development concerns, the project's contributors therefore treat caste norms – including untouchability – as universal and permanent. Indeed, several entries in the project's mammoth alphabetical glossaries are virtually indistin-guishable from those of the old colonial *Castes and Tribes* volumes. Readers are told that as a composite 'type', the Scheduled Castes have 'relatively broad noses'; Chamars, says another entry, are characterised by 'a long, narrow head shape and a long, moderately broad nasal shape'.[19]

The use of caste-based reservations for purposes of social 'uplift' has been widely contested over the past fifty years. Critics say that this strategy rests on concepts of collective deprivation which are crude and ahistorical, and that it promotes a view of Muslims and other non-

---

[19] Singh 1992, 1995: 302; and especially Singh *et al.* 1994, which presents the project's massive compilation of statistics on 'biological variation' between India's castes and tribes. See C. Pinney in *THES* 2 Sept 1994: 22, and Bates 1995, especially p. 248 n. 51. Foreshadowing this project was the large-scale analysis of blood samples undertaken by Indian and British anthropologists in the 1940s in attempts to determine which blood types were characteristic of individual castes and 'tribes'. See Karve and Dandekar 1948. On the uncritical use by other modern social scientists of Victorian ethnological terms and methods, see Chattopadhyaya 1973. Also Mishra *et al.* 1996, reporting on the use of cognitive psychological techniques to rank and classify Bihar 'tribals': this study treats individual 'tribes' as separate units for analysis, scoring their members in tests intended to measure each 'tribe''s levels of 'psychological differentiation' and individual 'autonomy'.

Hindus as being in some way unworthy of the state's protection.[20] The system has been challenged too on the grounds that the caste-name lists and other data used in these exercises repeat many of the errors and contradictions of the old colonial ethnographic inventories. A particular complaint is that the caste designations appearing on the Scheduled Tribe and Caste lists include many which refer to the broadest and most generalised regional status groupings, and certainly not to homogeneous 'communities' with an inheritance of uniform 'disability'.

Indeed, it is widely acknowledged that not every Chamar or Paraiyan is equally 'deprived', that so-called backwardness is not confined to untouchables and tribals, and that even those of Brahman birth may be poor and ill-educated. Above all, say the critics, caste-based 'uplift' schemes have precisely the opposite effect of what they were intended to achieve: far from expunging the evils of caste, they create incentives for Indians to affirm their caste origins since aid-seekers must proclaim ritually inferior birth in order to qualify.

Furthermore, the much-debated theory of the 'creamy layer' holds that these quota schemes do not direct aid to those who are truly needy. This expressive term refers to the few comparatively well-off families who are generally said to be found among all but the lowliest Scheduled 'communities', usually as a result of a previous generation's educational and economic advances. Typical examples here would be the families of both Phule and Ambedkar, whose immediate forebears were notably better off than other low-caste Maharashtrians, or the near-untouchable oil-pressing and distilling groups who were 'up-lifted' through involvement with evangelical missionaries, or success in commodity production. Such comparatively prosperous people and their descendants have tended to be the main beneficiaries of the Republic's post-Independence welfare provisions. Therefore, say the critics, reservations schemes which do not use means tests to exclude this 'creamy layer' will never succeed in improving the lot of the truly 'backward' and 'deprived'.[21]

Even in the 1990s such criticisms are still vigorously refuted on the grounds that the handicap of 'Scheduled' birth involves forms of disadvantage which are unique to those of low-caste origin. In

---

[20] Galanter 1984: 165–7.
[21] See I. P. Desai 'Should caste be the basis for recognising backwardness?' in Desai *et al.* 1985: 61–101.

particular, the system's defenders maintain that those of Brahman or Rajput parentage are far likelier than a Chandela, Dom or Bhil to have well-off kinfolk to aid them in times of need. Those championing reservations also deny that these schemes preserve and strengthen caste consciousness. Thus, when those of Chamar or Dom birth exploit the reservations process they do not truly think of themselves as Doms and Chamars: caste consciousness is just a device, a 'ladder' by which the individual climbs out of a 'social cul-de-sac'; having done so the ladder is then 'kicked away'.[22]

The debates on this topic have been all the more vehement because both before and after Independence, some campaigners have linked these apparently sound and rational anti-reservations arguments to assertions that the 'depressed' are poor and backward by divine mandate or personal deficiency, and therefore have no claim on the state's limited resources. The thought that government action might in some way give credence to these views has been particularly alarming to defenders of the Nehruvian 'secular' tradition. Much has been said since the 1950s about the danger of perpetuating the very stratifications that the Republic's modernisers wished to expunge. The contradictions are still very clear to those on both sides of this debate: with one voice the Constitution declared untouchability an evil to be abolished, while with the other the resources of the modern state were being mobilised to determine its citizens' caste and 'tribal' origins. So even though the aim was to make the old 'reformist' goal of social uplift a task for the state, the world was not being told that caste was debarred from the language and procedures of government. It was therefore hard to see how these moves would encourage Indians to disregard jati and varna distinctions in their everyday lives.

RESERVATIONS AND THE ELECTORAL ARENA

It seems unlikely that the effect of these contradictions could ever have been confined to the domain of trivial bureaucratic anomaly. As soon as government created the machinery to provide named 'communities' with electoral and material assets, the way was open for reservations schemes to become an instrument of competitive party politics. All

---

[22] Parekh and Mitra 1990: 106–7. Much heated debate on this was generated by the publication of the 1980 Mandal Commission report on 'reservations' for the so-called Other Backward classes: see especially Kumar 1994, Upadhyaya 1992, Béteille 1981: 47–9.

that was required was a shift in the political arena of the sort which duly arrived in the late 1960s with a decline in the prestige and polling power of the ruling National Congress, and a scramble by the party's new regional rivals for the populist credentials which had hitherto been a major Congress asset. Once these developments raised the political profile of the so-called Other Backward Castes, the principle of caste-based welfare schemes rapidly lost its claim to be a politically neutral administrative tool, aimed solely at correcting injustice and relieving deprivation.

At Independence, official sources reported a figure of under 50 million for India's Scheduled Caste population, and about 25 million 'tribals' or Adivasis. Using figures from the 1951 Census of India, the all-India Scheduled Caste lists were revised in 1956 to include a total of 55.3 million people. Thus the benefits which had been devised to correct inherited 'backwardness' were intended initially to apply to little more than 20 per cent of the country's population.[23] The position changed dramatically as national and state-level politicians began pressing for the principle of caste-based public welfare provisions to be extended to a very much higher proportion of their potential supporters. By the 1960s, increasing gains were being made by those demanding extended reservations quotas for as much as 50 to 90 per cent of the country's inhabitants. These far more sweeping versions of 'compensatory discrimination' were closer to the goals of pre-Independence activists in the west and south; here non-Brahman or Backward Class campaigners had aimed to strip high-caste groups of their supposed advantages, rather than devising welfare benefits for a small deprived minority.

As was seen in Chapter 6, in 1921 the princely state of Mysore defined *every* 'community' except Brahmans as 'Backward', and created extensive educational reservations for these groups. After Independence, this region (part of Karnataka state after 1973) became an important battleground for pro- and anti-reservations campaigners. In the early 1950s the Mysore state government preserved the region's policy of defining everyone in the state except Brahmans as 'Backward'. When the High Court declared these provisions unconstitu-

---

[23] The figures for 1951 put the Scheduled Castes at 14 per cent of the total population, and Scheduled Tribes at 6 per cent. The 1941 Census of undivided India reported an untouchable population of 48.8 million, or 19 per cent of those classed as 'Hindus', and 12.6 per cent of the total population (Galanter 1984: 130–1, 169).

tional in 1958, the state compiled a list identifying all 'backward' communities by name. This process of classification covered over 90 per cent of the population; after prolonged court battles the state government reluctantly reduced this proportion to 74 per cent, and thereby significantly reduced the numbers of people eligible for reservations.[24]

Even in the 1950s, when educational and employment reservations in regions other than the south were restricted to relatively small numbers of so-called Scheduled Castes and Tribes, these measures had still been electorally significant. Although it was Ambedkar who had first proclaimed separate electoral identity for those of 'unclean' descent, Congress became the main beneficiary of this strategy after Independence. As inheritor of Gandhi's mantle and Nehru's 'secular' credentials, and with its own nationally known Harijan politician, Jagjivan Ram, operating as an effective counterweight to Ambedkar, Congress consistently attracted more untouchable voters than any other party.[25]

This does not mean that Indian voters have lacked the ability to make 'modern' electoral decisions, or that they have opted for particular parties or candidates on the basis of 'traditional' caste and religious solidarities. But the presumed affinities of tribe, caste and religion have nevertheless been regularly invoked in the electoral arena. Old-style caste associations remained active in many areas after Independence, most notably in Bihar where, in the 1950s, self-styled leaders of the Ahir-Yadav 'community' used the platforms of the Yadav Mahasabha and all-India Yadav Youth League to utter vigorous though initially unsuccessful demands for the extension of electoral concessions to members of the non-Harijan 'backward castes'.[26]

Even when events would seem to suggest otherwise, as in the case of Congress's landslide 1984 victory following the assassination of Indira Gandhi, political commentators have assumed that 'community' will invariably play a role in determining the outcome of elections. In

---

[24] See Galanter 1984: 178, 223–6. Since the 1960s a figure of 85 per cent has been widely cited by organisations claiming to represent the deprived, this being the proportion of the population that they wish to identify as either 'untouchables', 'tribals', non-elite 'Other Backwards', or members of the religious minorities.

[25] On Congress's ascendancy under Nehru, attributed by many to its state-level leaders' skill in allying with notables commanding local caste and community 'vote banks' (whose members could be relied upon to follow their lead at election time), see Brass 1990.

[26] Frankel 'Caste, land and dominance in Bihar' in Frankel and Rao 1989, I: 46–132.

the 1990s the major Indian newspapers still carry election reports with such headlines as:

Poll scene – Advantage Laloo Yadav [the incumbent Chief Minister of Bihar]: fight on caste lines

[Gujarat] – Tribals hold the key for both Congress and BJP

Mulayam [UP's Chief Minister] makes a dent in Jat stronghold[27]

In the era of Nehru and Patel, however, even India's most celebrated post-Independence champion of the 'depressed' was unable to challenge Congress by building on the caste factor. In 1956 Ambedkar made one last move to turn the country's untouchables into an all-India constituency under his leadership. When his Scheduled Caste Federation fared poorly in the post-Independence elections, he made the move that had long been foreshadowed in his attacks on Brahmanical values. Ambedkar had flirted since the 1920s with the idea of renouncing Hinduism altogether. When he finally initiated his celebrated campaign of mass religious conversion for untouchables, he chose Buddhism, a faith of authentically south Asian origin which he believed to be caste-free and egalitarian in its teachings. Ambedkar therefore appealed to all Indians of untouchable or *avarna* origin to abandon whatever variant of Hindu faith they followed, and above all to stop identifying themselves as Hindus for electoral purposes.[28]

There was a substantial response to this campaign in Ambedkar's Marathi-speaking home region, and in some parts of the northern Hindi belt. Many adherents elevated Ambedkar himself to a status of semi-divine preceptorship. The spread of this neo-Buddhist faith attracted fierce criticism from Hindu supremacists, especially from the paramilitary Rashtriya Swayamsevak Sangh (RSS) and its allies. These were still comparatively small and marginal groups in the 1950s, though even in this period they were capable of mounting energetic propaganda campaigns. RSS supporters therefore made much of the neo-Buddhist phenomenon because it suited their strategy of dramatising the need to 'save Hinduism' from such instances of 'denationalisation' as mass Christian conversions among insurgent 'tribals' in Nagaland and south Bihar (Jharkhand).[29]

---

[27] *Hindu* Int. Edn 19 Nov. 1994: 12; 11 Feb. 1995: 3. (On the Hindu supremacist BJP or Bharatiya Janata Party, see below, pp. 297–303.)

[28] Zelliot 1996; Keer 1981; Omvedt 1994.

[29] Jaffrelot 1996: 164.

Although the 1961 Census of India reported a total of over 3 million neo-Buddhist converts, the movement never acquired an all-India following, developing instead as a bond of cult-like affiliation among small groups of comparatively prosperous Maharashtra Mahars and UP Chamars. The movement thus reinforced distinctions of rank and jati identity rather than transcending or erasing them. The neo-Buddhists have never overcome these limitations, and their networks did not become a focus for 'Scheduled Caste' political solidarity in the country at large. Thus, unlike the radical neo-Buddhist sects of south-east Asia, the Ambedkarites' potential as a home-grown source of liberation theology or millenarian political mobilisation has never been effectively realised.[30]

The formation of this movement therefore did not stop Congress from holding the broad middle ground in Indian politics for the first twenty years after Independence. Under both Nehru and his successor L. B. Shastri (Prime Minister 1964–6), Congress continued to win electoral support from both the religious minorities and the deprived, however defined. In most regions the party was also solidly backed by big landowners and businessmen, as well as English-educated public servants and urban professionals. Under this regime of moderate socialists and Nehruvian industrialisers, state agencies sent out contradictory but not provocative signals about jati and varna. The message here was that caste was something which a modernising, 'secular' government had to take into account in some though not all of its operations. Yet while caste-based welfare provisions had been inserted into the Constitution, voters could reasonably conclude that these would have no radical or politically explosive effects.

During the 1960s, this political balance began to disintegrate with the rise of assertive new rurally based electoral coalitions. In the 1967 general election Congress was returned to power with a significantly reduced share of the national vote compared with the first three polls after Independence. Even greater upheavals occurred at state level in the 1967 elections, most notably in UP, where the country's biggest regional electorate ejected Congress from power for the first time since Independence. UP voters turned instead to an array of populist 'peasant' organisations, which were grouped together in 1969 as the

---

[30] The 1981 Census reported a figure of only 4.7 million Indian Buddhists, with a growth rate lower than that of Hindus. Zelliot 1996: 222–63; see Lynch 1969.

BKD (Bharatiya Kranti Dal or Indian Revolution Party), and from 1974 as the BLD (Bharatiya Lok Dal or Indian People's Party). This movement's founder and leader, the former Congress politician Charan Singh, made much of his non-elite rural origins, drawing particular attention to his Jat background, and cultivating a charismatic platform style through which he portrayed himself as champion of the rustic 'little man'.

This proved an effective ploy with voters who identified themselves with the big Hindustan cultivator jatis, that is, tillers claiming 'respectable' Jat, Kurmi and Ahir-Yadav antecedents. The BKD/BLD thus framed its message as a composite of caste, class and 'communal' themes, addressing its potential adherents as the wronged and worthy '*lok*' or 'masses', meaning people whose needs as small-scale capitalists, as pious Hindus, and as members of 'Forward' or clean-caste non-elite 'communities' had supposedly been disregarded under twenty years of Congress rule.[31]

Continuing into the early 1970s, big gains were made in other states too by agrarian-based anti-Congress coalitions – the DMK and AIDMK in Tamilnad, the Akali Dal in Punjab, the Telugu Desam in Andhra Pradesh, and the leftist parties which came to prominence in Kerala and Bengal. Gujarat and Bihar too were swept by charismatic 'people's' agitations, most notably that of the old Gandhian Jayaprakash Narayan, who preached a millenarian message of non-Red revolution or 'people's power' (*jan shakti*) in the Bihar countryside.

All these movements claimed to speak for small-scale owner-cultivators. A high proportion of these so-called 'bullock capitalists' had come to feel deeply betrayed by post-Independence Congress governments whose Nehruvian industrialising strategies are now widely seen to have done real damage to this sector of the country's regional agrarian economies. As a result, these were people for whom the old Congress leadership could be convincingly demonised as a tool of Westernised urban plutocrats and other self-serving anti-'peasant' interests. It was time, said Charan Singh and the other new populists, for 'small men' to assert themselves against the swollen state agencies that had kept grain prices low and agricultural input costs high. There were promises too to attack the corrupt party bosses and

---

[31] Brass 1985, 1990; Hasan 'Class and caste' in Hasan *et al.* 1989: 256–69. The BLD's coalition partners also included the largely urban-based Hindu supremacist movement known as the Jan Sangh.

city-based bureaucrats who had denied other benefits – especially caste-based job quotas and educational reservations – to the sturdy non-English-speaking middling-caste *'kisan'* or son-of-the-soil. As early as 1947, Charan Singh had called for educational and employment reservations of up to 60 per cent for the 'sons of cultivators', arguing that the country's clean-caste tillers were its only true producers of wealth; in 1956 he presided over the first all-India Backward Classes Conference, a landmark in the emergence of the reservations-conscious *kisan*-power militancy of the post-Independence period.[32]

'PEASANTS' AND 'BACKWARD CASTES'

These manifestations of so-called 'new agrarianism' had an explosive effect on Indian politics following the officially sponsored drive towards high-yield capitalist agriculture under the American-backed Green Revolution schemes of the mid to late 1960s. The effect of this 'new agrarian' militancy was to lead both the anti-Congress parties (including the Hindu supremacist Jan Sangh and its allies) and the reborn Congress of Nehru's daughter, Indira Gandhi, to try to outbid one another in the electoral arena by mounting emotive populist appeals to the Indian 'masses'.[33]

Jati and varna themes received much emphasis in these pronouncements. It was in this period that the old broad-based Congress of Gandhi, Nehru and Patel became widely spoken of as a tool of narrow 'community'-based interest groups. The term that journalists and academics coined for this phenomenon was KHAM, an acronym for Kshatriyas, Harijans, Adivasis ('tribals') and Muslims. What this conveys is the crude but broadly accurate observation that once Congress leaders in key agricultural regions – most notably in the Hindi heartland states of UP, Rajasthan and Haryana – could no longer appeal to voters as the party of the whole nation, they began to target their electoral appeal towards the two extremes of the economic and social spectrum.

Clearly Muslims, Harijans and Adivasis or 'tribals', the 'HAM' voters, continued to be thought of as natural Congress voters because

[32] Hasan 'Caste and class' in Hasan *et al.* 1989: 257.
[33] On calls by Hindu supremacist activists for distribution of land to low castes and tribals, see Jaffrelot 1996: 240.

Congress was the party of 'secularism' and so-called protective discrimination for the deprived. The 'K' in the acronym stood for Kshatriyas, this being a reference to the elite landowners who in the Gangetic north were typically of Rajput or Bhumihar origin. Such people had allegedly been won over as Congress voters when the party signalled to them that its ruling state ministries were willing to favour their economic interests by suspending or relaxing the land ceiling laws. These Nehruvian quasi-socialist enactments of the early post-Independence years had supposedly paved the way for large-scale transfers of land to the rural poor by setting limits on the size of individual property holdings.[34]

This then was the position in the years immediately preceding Mrs Gandhi's 22-month period of dictatorship (the so-called Emergency of 1975–7). The populist goals espoused by both Congress and its 'new agrarian' opponents had come to be expressed in terms which covertly signalled the importance of jati and varna classifications to anyone who could be thought of as wronged or deprived. From virtually all points on the political spectrum, voters were being told to see caste bonds both as an asset and as a means by which others had hitherto been able to advance themselves unfairly.

The exercise of state power therefore played a major role in the linking of caste with the phenomenon of mass 'kisan' (peasant) mobilisation. This is apparent in the events which followed Indira Gandhi's successful bid to neutralise the Congress's old-style power brokers, beginning in 1970 with the launch of a pan-Indian populist initiative in alliance with the Communist Party of India. This campaign, with its slogan *'gharibi hatao'* ('away with poverty'), was a showcase for Mrs Gandhi's claim to be a land-reformer and fearless people's advocate independent of traditional party allegiances. The pledges which she made in the run-up to her remodelled Congress party's 1971 general election victory held out a promise of quick economic windfalls for those who were marked out by the scheduling process. To these groups in particular, that is, to populations classed by the state as tribals and untouchables, Mrs Gandhi and her supporters offered a vision of aggressive and personalised champion-ship. Radicalism and muscle were to replace old-style parliamentary procedures; new welfare and land redistribution schemes were to be

---

[34] Brass 1990; Kohli 1987; Frankel 1978; Frankel and Rao 1989–90.

financed with cash raised by party activists dealing directly with *nouveaux riches* rural contractors and the other new allies whom the Congress sought to cultivate at this time.[35]

All this was deeply unsettling to many clean-caste 'peasants'. With what its rivals kept calling a Brahman-led and 'KHAM'-based Congress now making populist overtures to shady businessmen, militant untouchables and Muslims, there seemed to be good reason for non-'scheduled' smallholders to mount their own confrontational 'people's' agitations. By now virtually every political party had come to portray its rivals as enemies to be debunked through mass resistance and 'peasant' or 'people's' activism. It was against this background that caste-based reservations were transformed into a contentious though fragmentary spoils system. In the era of *'gharibi hatao'*, politicians came to treat educational and employment quotas as electoral assets, persistently raising the stakes at election time by promising larger quota allocations to important groups of voters.[36]

The move that made all this possible was the invention by central policy-makers of that giant new category of the collectively deprived, the so-called Other Backward Classes, commonly abbreviated as OBC. This move held out a chance of preferential welfare provisions to the millions who were neither 'tribal' nor 'untouchable', but who could now harbour hopes that they too would be classed as victims of corporate disadvantage. In theory, when it came to the mechanics of listing, counting and naming, these 'Other Backwards' should have been all but impossible to identify. How was one to say whether any given non-elite *sat-sudra* 'community' was more or less 'backward' than another? Clearly the 'Other Backwards' would prove to be people of even more disparate livelihoods, statuses and economic circumstances than the country's 'scheduled' populations.

Yet it was equally clear that the major winners in the new OBC benefits lottery would be the great multitude of smallholders who saw themselves, and were seen by others, as non-elite 'peasants' (*kisan-kheduts*) of 'clean-caste' origin. More specifically, these were predominantly people whose forebears had been generalised about by both

---

[35] Kohli 1987; Brass 1990.

[36] See Kohli 1987 on the use of such strategies by Devraj Urs, Chief Minister of Karnataka (1972–80), a state with long-running reservations battles between those claiming to represent its two major 'non-Brahman' populations, the Vokkaligas and Lingayats.

British and Indian commentators in the colonial period as 'the Jats', 'the Kanbis', 'the Kammas', and so on.

In other words these were rural 'caste Hindus' whose consciousness of caste ties now had at least two contradictory dimensions. In marriage and other ritual matters, distinctions between so-called sub-castes or other ranked subdivisions within a given mega-jati cluster still retained much power; in these contexts one Jat, Kanbi or Kamma was definitely not the same as all others. (See below, Chapter 8.) Yet at the same time, for such purposes as the battle to claim state welfare entitlements for 'OBCs', the reverse was now true, especially in areas which were still dominated by people identifying themselves with one of the big rustic 'kisan' jati clusters. In such regions it was widely recognised that there were real gains to be made through the framing of appeals to one's fellow clean-caste 'peasants' in precisely these terms: 'we the Jats', 'we the Kanbis', 'we the Kammas'.[37]

The other crucial factor here was the creation from 1956 of the new linguistically defined state boundaries which were drawn up so that individual states became zones of high numerical concentration for the members of only one (or at most two or three) of the broad *sat-sudra* 'peasant' jati blocs. In Bihar, these numerically predominant culti-vating populations are those whose members use the titles Koiri, Kurmi and Ahir-Yadav. Their counterparts in Karnataka are Vokka-ligas and Lingayats; in Haryana and Gujarat the equivalent 'commu-nities' are Jat and Kanbi-Patidar, while in Andhra most clean-caste 'peasants' identify themselves as Kammas or Reddis.

This trend made the Indian states an ideal arena in which politicians could advance themselves by addressing constituencies of the 'back-ward' on the basis of shared caste identity. Once 'mobilised' and encouraged to assert themselves in concert with others of like kind, these were 'communities' which by virtue of their large numbers and comparative prosperity were far better placed than those of tribal and untouchable origin to make their will felt in the electoral arena. These then were people with the ability to shape the new regionally administered quota schemes for their own advantage.[38]

---

[37] Brass and Robinson 1987; Yadav 1994; Rao 'Conceptual issues' in Frankel and Rao 1989, I: 21–45.

[38] Brass 1990: 206–7. Bihar was separated off from Bengal largely in response to demands from caste associations representing Hindi-speaking Kayastha professional men for a state where non-Bengalis could achieve political control.

It was the very slipperiness of the new OBC category that made it so attractive to voters and party leaders. Here there would be no pollution barrier to refer to, dubious as this itself was as a test of who should be deemed collectively backward or deprived. We have seen that the concept of caste-defined backwardness already had an established pedigree in Indian political life. From the late 1940s there were calls for aid to the so-called 'Other Backwards' (meaning primarily non-Harijan 'peasant' groups) from spokesmen for the fragmented Bombay and Madras non-Brahman movements. There had been no formal 'non-Brahman' organisations of this kind in the Hindi-speaking north. But in these regions too, there were attempts after Independence to give political expression to the assertions of 'peasant' Vaishnavism which had led smallholders of Ram- and Krishna-loving Kurmi and Ahir-Yadav origin to don the sacred thread as self-styled Kshatriyas.[39] One of the more notable organisations of this kind was the Bihar Backward Classes Federation which was founded in 1947 under the leadership of the millenarian populist R. L. Chandapuri. The all-India Backward Classes Federation was formed in 1950; by 1954 there were fourteen organised bodies campaigning for special rights and reservations for India's non-untouchable 'Backward' populations at both regional and pan-Indian level.[40]

The claim of these aspiring representatives of the 'Other Backwards' was that social and material 'backwardness' was not just an affliction of untouchables and so-called tribals. On the contrary, as bearers of titles denoting 'clean' non-proprietary caste origin, self-professed spokesmen for these groups argued that their 'communities' too had been collectively demeaned over the centuries by the pretensions of the pure Brahman and the 'lordly' Rajput. They too were educationally and materially deprived; they too should be entitled to state aid to compensate for these historic 'disabilities'.

There were few signs at Independence that central government would ever move to extend so-called protective preference devices to anyone other than the Scheduled Castes and Tribes. Yet there was one official arena which did exist as a focus for this notion of compensatory state aid for non-untouchables. The 1950 Constitution had provided for the creation of a special Backward Classes Commission

[39] Also traditions of Jat-dominated anti-Brahman sentiment propounded by the Arya Samaj. See Pinch 1996.
[40] Galanter 1984: 162 n. 44.

with an ambiguous brief of investigation and policy-drafting on behalf of the 'socially and educationally backward'.[41] This was generally taken to mean that the country should have some kind of all-India panel with the power to aid those who were part of Nehru's problematic category of the non-tribal and non-untouchable 'Other Backwards'.

The question here was whether to depart from past precedent in defining the recipients of this aid. Some commentators hoped to exclude the reference point of caste altogether in this case, arguing that too many of the truly 'backward' would miss out on benefits unless it was recognised that deprivation was not confined to particular named 'communities'. However in 1953, when central government moved to appoint and brief this special panel for the so-called Other Backward Classes, proponents of the old caste-centred 'reformist' logic prevailed. In 1954, the anthropologist N. K. Bose, formerly Gandhi's secretary and later Commissioner for Scheduled Castes and Tribes, declared that the guiding principle of the newly constituted Backward Classes Commission was '... the desire and will of the Indian nation to do away with the hierarchy of caste and of its consequent social discrimination, and [to] prepare the ground for full social equality'.[42]

Here then was an official agency mandated to apply caste-based notions of collective disability to a very much larger proportion of the population than the 20 per cent who were already covered by the scheduling process. Between 1953 and 1955, this eleven-member Backward Classes Commission struggled with the daunting task of creating a master list of the country's non-tribal and non-untouchable 'backward' populations, ultimately producing a catalogue naming 2,399 'communities' as collective victims of so-called backwardness. This was thought at the time to represent a total of 116 million people, or about 32 per cent of the population. If one adds to this the Scheduled Castes and Scheduled Tribes, who were thought to comprise another 14 and 6 per cent respectively, the Commission's logic had thereby deemed over half the Indian population to be deserving of the state's 'special care' on grounds of their low-caste or tribal origins.

---

[41] Article 340, *Constitution of India*.
[42] Quoted in Galanter 1984: 169 n. 69. Article 340: 1 provides for the appointment of a Commission 'to investigate the conditions of the socially and educationally backward classes ... and the difficulties under which they labour and to make recommendations as to the steps that should be taken ... to remove such difficulties and to improve their condition ...'

By this same logic, virtually every other Indian was deemed to belong to a new category, that of the 'Forward Communities'.[43]

Although the 'new agrarian' populists of the 1960s and 1970s were far more assertive in their expressions of class-conscious anti-'Forward' sentiments, such people as Tamilnad Brahmans could see the threatening implications of these moves. In states like Tamil Nadu, 'peasant' *sat-sudras* greatly outnumbered Brahmans and other 'Forwards'. So there was much to fear if central or state governments were to be empowered to treat those belonging to so-called elite castes as unworthy oppressors, defining upper-caste origin as a mark of unfair material advantage, and squeezing 'Forwards' out of universities and public service posts in preference to those who could call themselves Other Backwards.[44]

Even louder alarm bells sounded when the 1953–6 Commission turned to what it conceived as its next task, which was to offer specific solutions to the problem of 'backwardness'. Its report recommended unheard-of reservations targets for 'Backwards': quotas of up to 70 per cent in medical and technical colleges, and reservations in government service posts ranging from 25 per cent of senior government posts to 40 per cent at lower levels.[45]

This would have been provocative enough, but more was to come. One of the country's most divisive post-Independence political controversies first made itself felt at the all-India level when yet another panel, the 1978–80 Backward Classes Commission (or B. P. Mandal Commission), revived the idea of centrally enforced education and employment quotas for 'OBCs'. Through these proposals for really large-scale caste-based social engineering, this panel provoked a violent pan-Indian outcry which had profound effects on both state-level and all-India politics. But the earlier 1953–6 Commission decided to offer an even more radical cure for inequality and deprivation than preferential quotas in education and employment. Its majority report recommended massive intervention in the agricultural economy through a system of rural price supports, as well as protection for smallholders on insecure tenancies and large-scale land redistribution.[46] In other

[43] Galanter 1984: 154–87.
[44] Washbrook 'Caste, class and dominance' in Frankel and Rao 1989, I: 204–64.
[45] Galanter 1984: 172.
[46] 1953–5 Backward Classes Commission (K. Kalelkar, Chairman), *Report* (repr. 1983), I: 65–75.

words, once the 'backward' were identified, the state was called upon to fulfil its duty to protect and advance the so-called weaker sections by launching a wholesale attack on the inequalities of the agrarian economy.

This logic was crude but not ill-founded. It was indeed the case that insecure tenures and other forms of agrarian deprivation were and still are most pervasive among those who are 'unclean' in ritual terms. But the rush to quash the report was hardly surprising since the Commissioners were proposing measures which would have transformed the nature of rural property-holding throughout the country. Under Nehru and his immediate successors, India's development programmes were based on principles of gradual income redistribution, not radical agrarian restructuring. So it is not surprising that when it issued its final report in 1956, Congress ministers denounced the Commission and dismissed its recommendations. Even the Commission's chairman repudiated its findings, as did four of its other ten members. The only surviving element of the Commission's original aims was a decision to vest state governments – but not the central administration – with the power to establish their own Backward Classes Commissions and listings mechanisms should they so desire.

THE MOVE TO UNIVERSAL 'BACKWARDNESS'

So would there really have been a new age of casteless prosperity for all if the Commissioners had had their way? Clearly what they had in mind was far more in the way of aid for the 'weaker sections' than the piecemeal welfare provisions that were put in train from the 1950s onwards. It is therefore possible that caste would have come to mean less for many Indians if the state had somehow made it less easy to equate low caste status with extreme deprivation. On the other hand, forced seizures of property would certainly have been resisted by the landed, including better-off members of low castes. Agrarian society would thus have become more rather than less volatile, with rural populations becoming all the more inclined to express economic and social division as a god-given mandate distinguishing the clean and worthy from their inferiors.

In fact, post-Independence governments have had no intention of tackling 'backwardness' by attacking rural property-owners. Although the Constitution guaranteed aid for the 'weak', the shelving of the first Backward Classes Commission report left central government with a requirement to do this only for the Scheduled 'communities'. As of the early 1960s, the state was therefore in an oddly contradictory position, acting as guardian and listing agency for comparatively small numbers of these tribes and very low castes, while holding simultaneously that it was 'casteist' and undemocratic to do the same for so-called Other Backwards.

During the 1960s the state governments became arenas in which the advocates of preferences for 'Other Backwards' began to make rapid gains. As state-level politicians began to see the potential gains to be made through the new assertiveness of turbulent 'peasant' populations, individual state governments began to act on their power to create state-level lists of non-untouchable and non-tribal 'Backwards'. By the early 1970s, a total of twenty-six regionally based Backward Classes Commissions had been empanelled. As was noted above, the most influential of these were in the southern states where regional 'backward class' or 'non-Brahman' goals had been espoused since the colonial period. Tamil Nadu's DMK, political heirs to the anti-Brahman ideologies of the Madras Justice Party, came to power in the state in 1967. The DMK's key electoral pledge was a commitment to 'destroy' caste; once in power, however, it erected an edifice of caste-based welfare provisions which perpetuated the use of jati- and varna-based classifications in state politics.[47]

Amid much controversy, these state-level Backward Classes Commissions assembled voluminous bodies of data. Their reports contained elaborate accounts of the occupations, incomes, education and social standing of thousands of named 'communities', the vast majority of whom had titles and occupational traditions implying *sat-sudra* 'peasant' origin. These exercises thus set in train a systematic revival of the reservations principle at the regional level; this in turn prepared the ground for the 1978–80 pan-Indian Mandal Commission which called for giant 'OBC' quotas across the whole country.

The new state-level commissions made much of the involvement of eminent Indian social scientists in their operations, claiming that this

---

[47] For details see Sivaramayya 1996: 221; on Gujarat's state-level panel, the so-called Baxi or Bakshi Commission appointed in 1972, see Desai 'Should caste . . .' in Desai 1985; on the DMK, see Barnett 1976; Washbrook in Frankel and Rao 1989, I: 204–64.

made their data far more reliable and sophisticated than that of the old colonial listings. In later years some at least of these academics condemned both the methods and the conclusions of these exercises, noting particularly the use of questionnaires which were either offensive or incomprehensible to informants.[48]

At the time, however, the state panels were widely believed when they said they had dealt with the problems identified by critics of earlier and cruder reservations schemes. Above all, the enumerators now claimed that they could stop caste-based preferences from becoming self-perpetuating. Social and material 'progress' could be recognised and tabulated, they said; by applying appropriate tests it would be possible to exclude well-off sections of a caste from the OBC registers, or to remove whole communities once their members had achieved significant gains in schooling and living standards, thus solving the much-debated problem of the 'creamy layer'.[49]

In reality, few if any members of a listed 'community' are ever willingly reclassified, especially in those states where the so-called Forwards consist largely of 'Aryan' groups (i.e. Brahmans) who have been vilified since the days of the pre-Independence non-Brahman movements as aliens and oppressors. The gains to be made in this area are so significant that the descendants of people who campaigned as recently as the 1940s and 1950s for recognition as Kshatriyas have been fighting in the last thirty years to remain on the lists of low-status 'backwards'. In effect it is only 'communities' without political muscle who can be made to forfeit their quota entitlements.

In fact, this entire enterprise has turned on political muscle. Its defenders have made much of its progressive goals and methodologies, but the people who have made real gains through the OBC reservations process since the 1970s have been those who can claim membership of the large-scale 'middle peasant' caste clusters. The big state-level reservations battles have involved attempts by the self-proclaimed spokesmen for such groups as the Lingayat and Vokkaliga 'communities' to exclude their state's rival 'kisan' clusters from the OBC listings. Those who have gained comparatively little from the process are the members of truly low-status non-Harijan groups – the small

---

[48] Desai p. 69 in Desai *et al.*1985.
[49] Some states introduced means tests to exclude the comparatively well-off 'creamy layer' sections from these provisions; despite repeated challenges, the principle was upheld under the Supreme Court's controversial 1993 Mandal judgement (Sivaramayya 1996: 232–4).

'backward' specialist populations associated with 'traditional' service or artisanal occupations.[50]

THE MANDAL COMMISSION

By the mid-1970s most of the state-level Backward Class commissions had reported their findings. In such states as Tamil Nadu and Karnataka the ruling ministries made moves to fix startlingly high OBC quotas in education and public employment. In these regions, it had therefore become official policy to place the majority of the population in the category of those entitled to preferential protection and welfare provisions by virtue of being 'backward', 'tribal' or 'untouchable'.

It was against this background that a key moment of opportunity arrived for aspiring 'peasant' populists. In 1977 a fragile alliance was forged between Charan Singh's BLD (Indian People's Party, the party of the *lok* or 'peasant masses'), the Hindu supremacist Jan Sangh and an array of other uneasy allies including such influential Congress defectors as the veteran Scheduled Caste leader Jagjivan Ram.[51] These anti-Congress activists engineered the victory of the unstable Janata coalition government that came to power after the dissolution of Mrs Gandhi's 1975–7 'Emergency', during which the country was ruled by authoritarian decree.

Even at this point, although the electorate had temporarily turned against Congress, voters still did not subdivide themselves into reliable caste-based 'vote banks'. On the other hand, voters clearly did understand the references to jati and varna which politicians now routinely built into their populist appeals. This was a weapon that the 1977–9 Janata government needed to deploy to compensate for its inability to bring about the promised peasant millennium of cheap power, low-cost inputs and subsidised crop prices. Once again there was no question of forced title transfers or other radical measures to aid the small owner-cultivator at the expense of the big landowner. Indeed all that the ruling Janata coalition could promise was to 'empower' tillers and other worthy members of the *lok*, that is, to end the dominance of

---

[50] See, for example, Kaul 1993, Kohli 1987 and Manor 1989 on Karnataka where battles in the 1960s and 1970s over the inclusion of 'peasant' Vokkaligas and Lingayats in the Backward Class listings yielded disproportionate gains for these 'clean-caste' groups, at the expense of smaller middling-status jati clusters with a weaker voice in state-level politics.

[51] The Janata coalition leaders also included Bihar's rustic millenarian Jayaprakash Narayan. On the collapse of Janata see Brass 1985: 17.

elite non-'peasant' Nehruvians in public life. These people were understood to be almost exclusively of high-caste origin. This 'empowerment' was to be achieved, said Janata leaders, by enlarging corporate reservations quotas to include the bulk of the non-elite clean-caste 'peasantry'. In other words, the welfare of the *kisan* 'masses' would be guaranteed by reserving educational places and government posts for those who supposedly possessed true insight into the needs of the common man.[52]

So Janata's panacea for rural distress was caste-based reservations for 'Other Backwards'. This meant that central government would be pledged to take action by enumerating these people too, with the aim of setting uniform national quotas for them, just as in the case of the Scheduled Castes and Tribes. In 1978, twenty-three years after the shelving of its predecessor's report, a new all-India Backward Classes Commission was convened.

This controversial new body was placed under the chairmanship of B. P. Mandal, a Bihar politician of Yadav-Ahir 'peasant' background. Its brief was to establish a formula to be used throughout the country in the task of reserving posts in central and state governments for so-called OBCs.[53] The Commission's report, submitted in 1980, greatly extended the criteria defining caste-based 'backwardness'. Its new listings thus placed a total of 3,248 'communities' in the OBC category, that is 350 million people or 54.4 per cent of the country's population. On this basis, the commission's much-debated statement of policy recommended an unprecedented increase in public-sector reservations, calling for employment quotas of 27 per cent for 'Other Backwards', plus an additional 22.5 per cent for Scheduled Castes and Tribes.

Even before the report appeared, some Janata-controlled state governments had anticipated the Commission's findings by rushing through their own greatly expanded reservations schemes. This is not surprising: in many states, those who were well placed to seek power as exponents of the 'new agrarianism' were precisely those who could claim to speak on behalf of big aggrieved 'peasant' populations. The

---

[52] Brass 1990; Rudolph and Rudolph 1987.

[53] Like the 1953–5 Kalelkar Commission, this 1978–80 Backward Class Commission was advised by an official Panel of Experts. This included the veteran sociologist M. N. Srinivas (see p. 13, n. 11); while critical of the Commission's findings and their political consequences, Srinivas has argued both for the reality of caste as a force in Indian life and for its complexity and dynamism. Srinivas 1996: ix–xxxviii; see also Desai 1985: 65.

higher the quotas for OBCs and Scheduled groups, the more these state-level schemes looked to those on the outside like a device to isolate and punish those defined as high-caste (and to reward party supporters), rather than a means of 'uplifting' the deprived. These moves provoked widespread violence, most notably in Bihar which had taken especially vigorous steps to increase OBC reservations.[54]

Congress returned to power in 1979; like its predecessor of the 1950s, the Mandal Commission's report was shelved and its recommendations left in abeyance at the all-India level. State-level reservations battles remained widespread however, most notably in the politically volatile south where increased OBC quotas served as a favoured 'vote-catching device' in the words of one disapproving leftist journal.[55]

'MANDIR' AND MANDAL: CASTE AND FAITH IN THE POLITICS OF THE 1980s

Against this background of political and ideological controversy, the turbulent politics of the 1980s and 1990s persistently linked expressions of militant 'people's power' to the logic of jati and varna. The collapse of the short-lived Janata government in 1979 was followed by yet another wave of farmers' or 'kisan'-power agitations. In the Deccan and the far south, and among plains-dwellers in the Punjab, Haryana and western UP, the militant successors to the Janata era's 'new agrarian' tradition recruited large memberships, and staged mass public agitations against government agricultural policies.[56]

Many analysts regard these campaigns of the 1980s as assertions of progressive 'people's power', and in some cases as manifestations of a 'postmodern' trend of worldwide environmentally and gender-conscious anti-materialism. More realistically, other observers have seen India's 'new agrarians' and their successors as conservative, market-orientated capitalist farmers (individualistic 'kulaks' in old-style Marxist jargon) whose campaigns have been wrongly characterised as the struggles of the deserving class-conscious 'peasant' masses. Within India, there has been general acknowledgement on

---

[54] Bose 1985a: 182.
[55] *EPW* 6 Sept. 1986: 1574. For a penetrating analysis of this period, see Bose and Jalal 1998: 211–26.
[56] Brass 1994; Rudolph and Rudolph 1987.

both sides of this debate that such battles do in fact reflect experiences of deeply felt 'peasant' distress. Furthermore, attempts to explain these upheavals have made much of these militant *kisans*' supposed bonds of 'community feeling', and of the sense of caste which has been widely said to have played a central role in both defining and dividing those who have taken part in these battles.[57]

Attempts to discern the workings of a 'caste factor' have been prominent, too, in debates about the other key political development of the 1980s and 1990s, this being the rise of the Hindu supremacist BJP (the Bharatiya Janata or Indian People's Party) founded in 1980. The goal of the BJP and its allied organisations of the so-called 'family of the *sangh*' or Sangh Parivar was and is the promotion of *Hindutva* or 'Hindu-ness'.[58]

Proponents of this cause subscribe to a doctrine of authoritarian ultra-chauvinism in which a militant and exclusive understanding of Hindu faith is defined as the core of Indian nationhood. Its expressions of hostility to Muslims draw explicitly on the supremacist racial ideologies of the pre-Independence era. From its inception, the BJP identified itself with the militant campaign to build a *mandir* (a Hindu temple) on the now notorious site that is reputed to be the birthplace of the god Ram, and which, until its destruction by Hindu supremacists in 1992, was occupied by a sixteenth-century mosque, the Babri Masjid. The BJP's struggle to assert its brand of combative Hindu nationalism against both the 'secular' Congress, and the leftist parties which espouse 'Mandalite' reservations schemes, has given rise to the label 'Mandir vs. Mandal' for the politics of the post-1980 period.

By the mid-1980s, the BJP had become a major national rival to the Congress; over the next decade it fared best in the north, though it made fruitful alliances with regional parties in the Punjab and Maharashtra, and acquired considerable support in the south. In the 1996 general elections, the BJP and its allies actually out-polled the declining Congress party and became the largest political grouping in the national parliament. A short-lived BJP government was formed at this time but lost power almost immediately to an anti-BJP coalition

---

[57] Brass 1994.
[58] Together with the BJP, this Sangh Parivar confederation includes the paramilitary RSS or Rashtriya Swayamsevak Sangh, literally 'Association of National Volunteers' (founded 1925), and the RSS's offshoot the VHP (Vishva Hindu Parishad or 'World Hindu Council') founded in 1964. See van der Veer 1994; Jaffrelot 1996; Hasan 1994.

of leftist and regional parties, the United Front, to which Congress first gave its support and then withdrew it. In the resulting 1998 elections the BJP out-polled the Congress even more decisively.

In the large, poor and turbulent northern states especially, prominent members of the 1996–7 anti-BJP United Front coalition included a number of parties propounding explicitly caste-based goals and recruitment strategies. The most important of these were the Samajwadi Party (SP) which presented itself as the party of OBC interests, and the Bahujan Samaj Party (BSP) which campaigned for the 'empowerment' of Dalits (ex-untouchables).

The Hindu supremacist organisations have remained vocal and powerful in Indian politics, however. The BJP has attracted a far wider range of supporters than its Hindu nationalist predecessors, making much of the unrest which afflicted the country under 'secular' governments, as well as the alleged failures of both Congress and its leftist rivals to deal effectively with foreign enemies, particularly Muslim-dominated Pakistan. At the same time, the Hindu supremacists have appealed strongly to 'Forward' voters who feared that they would lose out under so-called Mandalite reservations schemes. BJP leaders offered a vision of a state purged of quasi-Marxist 'secularism', and therefore no longer inclined to 'pander' to the so-called depressed groups. This meant not only Muslims, but also militant Harijans or 'Dalits'.

It is notable that these new proponents of 'Hindutva' have tended to invert the old pre-Independence stereotype of the Muslim 'other'. Unlike the Hindu extremists of the nineteenth and early twentieth centuries, few BJP adherents revile Muslims as an oppressive 'feudal' elite. On the contrary, the 'Sangh Parivar' has tapped into the fears of a broad and insecure stratum of the country's fast-growing middle class by characterising Muslims as members of a turbulent and potentially seditious underclass. In this respect, Hindutva ideologues see Muslims as sharing the same dangerous qualities which they attribute to activist non-Muslim Dalit/untouchables. In their eyes both groups have been wrongly protected and 'pampered', both by Congress and by the pro-reservations caste-based SP and BSP parties which, by the late 1980s, had become the BJP's chief rivals in the northern states.

Yet the BJP has been ambivalent in its use of caste language. Its leaders have denounced old-style Congress 'secularism' as well as 'Mandalite' social welfare schemes, denouncing preference quotas for 'unworthy' minorities and low-caste groups as opportunist devices that have divided the nation and lowered the country's educational and professional standards.[59] But while repudiating the logic of 'secularism' and caste-based reservations schemes, the BJP's leaders hoped to throw off the Brahmans-only label that had dogged older Hindu supremacist organisations, most notably its controversial paramilitary ally and parent organisation, the RSS. Hindutva activists therefore tell non-elite 'peasants' and even 'backwards' that they have an important place in the 'Hindu nation'; in 1994 the RSS's controlling council made a great point of its decision to install its first-ever 'non-Brahman' supreme leader or Sarsanghchalak.[60]

Furthermore, the Hindu supremacists have told individual 'communities' that their caste heritage embodies a special obligation to be faithful to the cause of Hindu nationhood. Since the aggressive values of Hindutva have been popularised around the veneration of Vishnu in his manifestation as the righteous divine warrior and ruler Ram, this appeal to caste has been most insistent in regions with a strong tradition of Vaishnavite 'peasant' assertiveness. In Bihar, for example, where the leftist 'Mandalite' politician Laloo Prasad Yadav successfully opposed the BJP in the late 1980s by espousing the cause of high reservations quotas for 'OBC' groups, Hindutva activists reviled their pro-reservations opponents as betrayers of the Yadav heritage, which before Independence had become focused on rustic Kshatriya ideals and the Vaishnavite cults of Ram and Krishna.[61]

Hindutva activists also argued that people of so-called tribal and non-Muslim 'Dalit' origin should embrace the cause of Hindutva, claiming that Hindu nationhood could and should attract everyone who could conceivably be classified as a Hindu by blood and descent. In areas of eastern Gujarat containing large populations of impoverished 'tribals', BJP politicians began in 1989 to try to win both 'Scheduled Caste' and 'Scheduled Tribe' voters away from Congress by presenting themselves as protectors of non-Muslim 'Dalits' against the oppression they were allegedly suffering at the hands of Muslim officials and landowners. This has been one of many regions where

---

[59] *EPW* 6 Sept. 1986: 1573; and see Omvedt 'Kanshi Ram and the BSP' in Sharma 1994: 153–69.
[60] Rajendra Singh, a physics professor from Allahabad University, widely described in the Indian press as a UP 'Kshatriya' (*Frontline* 8 April 1994: 129–30).
[61] Pinch 1996.

Hindu supremacists have sought to portray themselves as champions of so-called Backwards as well as unifiers of the nation. Unlike their 'secular' pro-reservations enemies, the BJP's vision of 'Hindu-ness' purports to offer all true Indians a chance to be co-sharers in the common Hindu heritage whether they are 'tribal' or Harijan, 'backward' or high-caste, and without the divisive and supposedly 'casteist' device of reservations quotas.

Other Hindutva campaigners, however, have signalled a very different view of caste as a feature of the 'Hindu nation'. Their views recall those of the Hindu supremacists of the 1930s who dismissed moves to relieve so-called Harijan disability as a device to give undeserved privileges to the 'unworthy', that is, to those who in their eyes were low in caste terms because they bore a burden of sin from past lives.[62] This would seem to be the implication of the call made by Hindutva activists in the 1990s for the scrapping of the 1950 'secular' Constitution, and its replacement with a new political order based on principles derived from the divine 'laws' of Manu. Some Sangh supporters have even been quoted as saying that under a Hindutva regime the state should take constitutional steps to endorse the supremacy of Brahmans.

This is in sharp contrast to the gestures of pro-'Dalit' conciliation made by some Hindu supremacists who have publicly praised the 'Dalit' hero Ambedkar. In doing this they have had to disregard Ambdekar's famous repudiation of Hinduism, exalting him instead as a lover of the nation who shared their own antipathy to the 'secularism' of Gandhi and the Congress. But as of the mid-1990s, there are still strong anti-'Dalit' and anti-Mandalite themes in Hindutva propaganda, especially in regard to the alleged damage being done to the nation's educational standards by schemes which reduce or even abolish qualifying marks in public college entrance examinations for OBCs and 'Scheduled' (Harijan and 'tribal') candidates. Thus, says one sneering witticism, beware the 'Backward' with an unearned medical qualification: his degree certificates conceal his lack of 'merit', and his hapless patient will awake to find his eye removed instead of his tooth.[63]

[62] See Chapter 6, above.
[63] *EPW* 6 Sept. 1986: 1573; for coverage of the 'relaxed standards' policy in medical and other college admissions, see e.g. *Hindu* Int. Edn 22 Oct. 1994: 3, and 1 Mar. 1997: 1 on the Supreme Court's quashing of the UP government's abolition of qualifying pass marks for Scheduled and 'OBC' medical college entrants.

CASTE IN THE ELECTORAL ARENA
IN THE 1990S

Not surprisingly, all this has evoked uneven and inconsistent responses from both low- and higher-caste voters. But it has certainly helped to keep the concept of caste as prominent in the debate about Hinduism and nationhood as it was when these issues were being debated by Indian 'reformists' in the decades before and after the First World War.

In December 1989, a successor party to Janata – the Janata Dal – achieved power as the leading element in a national coalition government which rapidly came under pressure from another self-styled defender of the rustic 'little man'. This was the '*kisan*' leader Devi Lal, who, like Charan Singh, had made his name as a self-styled spokesman for the Hindi belt's Jat and 'OBC' populations. Soon after the elections, this Haryana-based activist threatened to destabilise the fragile ruling coalition by staging a giant rally of militant 'peasants' in the country's capital. In response, the Janata Dal prime minister, V. P. Singh, announced plans to implement the Mandal Commission's moribund recommendations for greatly expanded OBC reservations in education and public service appointments. This move, which would have reserved 27 per cent of government posts for OBCs, in addition to the 22.5 per cent already reserved for Harijan/untouchables and Adivasi/tribals, provoked violent resistance in many parts of the country, most notably a series of widely publicised self-immolations by high-caste student protestors.

In 1992 India's Supreme Court issued a controversial ruling – the so-called Mandal judgement – which set a maximum figure of 50 per cent for all state-level reservations schemes, thus challenging the much higher quotas that had either been proposed or were already in effect in many parts of the country. This set off a battle about whether states with much higher quotas should have special exemptions from this ceiling, leaving Tamil Nadu at 69 per cent for example, and Karnataka at 68 per cent. Calls by the pro-reservations parties to give every state the freedom to set its own quotas were fiercely opposed by both the Communist CPI(M) party and the BJP. In 1994 one of the chief advocates of high OBC and Scheduled reservations quotas, Bihar's leftist Chief Minister Laloo Prasad Yadav, proposed that the state should push its reservations up to a staggering 80 per cent. In neighbouring UP, the SP/BSP coalition proposed a comparatively low reservations quota of 27 per cent, but the reactions from the move's opponents within the state were equally fierce.[64]

Indeed, for much of the 1990s, Uttar Pradesh was the scene of successive political upsets with profound if confusing implications for the country at large. In 1993, in the first elections following the central government's dismissal of the state's Hindu supremacist BJP ministry, a hitherto unthinkable partnership between the regionally based, leftist parties, the SP and the BSP, defeated both the Congress and the pro-Hindutva BJP. Each of the two winning parties had represented itself to UP's state-level electorate as champions of the 'deprived'.[65] But, as was seen above, far from dismissing caste as an irrelevance to the plight of the disadvantaged, both the SP and the BSP appealed to voters in terms that focused on the binding power of jati and varna, or more precisely on the interests that voters were being told they shared as members of, respectively, non-elite 'peasant'/OBC castes (SP) and Scheduled or Harijan/Dalit populations (BSP).

The remarkable thing about this 1993 electoral alliance in UP was that previously the SP and the BSP had appealed to voters as embodiments of two mutually irreconcilable populations of the 'deprived'. Up to this point, OBC and Dalit voters had been thought of as eternal rivals in the bitterly competitive politics of 'Mandalism'. Yet here they were, in apparent harmony, successfully bringing down the Hindu supremacist 'Mandirites' of the BJP. Then yet another upset occurred in UP: a mere four years later, the same two pro-reservations 'Mandalite' parties had become rivals again. This in itself was unsurprising. What startled many commentators was that the Brahman- and 'clean-caste'-dominated BJP then joined hands with the Harijan/Dalit-led BSP as part of its strategy of allying with regionally based anti-Congress parties. Given that the BJP was and still is widely identified as an anti-reservations party dominated by Brahmans and other high-caste Hindus, this move would seem very hard to reconcile with the Dalit-based and pro-reservations BSP leadership's outspoken hostility to so-called Manuvadi elites.

While this era of Mandal–Mandir politics may therefore seem

---

[64] See coverage in *Hindu*, for example, Int. Edn 17 Sept. 1994: 3 and 20 Aug. 1994.
[65] Several BJP state governments were dissolved in the wake of the 1992–3 Ayodhya crisis. See 'After Ayodhya', *South Asia – Special Issue* 17, 1994.

ideologically incoherent and even downright baffling, the striking constant in these developments has been the persistence of caste themes at virtually every stage in the period's complex electoral manoeuvres. For the foreseeable future it is certainly difficult to imagine their disappearance, or even a serious attempt by politicians and their supporters to make the political arena truly 'casteless'.

FUTURE POLITICAL PROSPECTS

In the late 1990s, party leaders and aspiring candidates from virtually every political party now routinely take a stand on the issue of reservations in the prelude to local and pan-Indian elections. And given the apparently unstoppable trend towards ever-larger caste-based benefits quotas, it would be electoral suicide for any party, even the anti-'Mandalite' BJP, to propose the outright abolition of caste-based reservations. For example, even in 1992 – a year of sustained assertiveness by Hindutva activists – press reports indicated that the Hindu supremacist BJP leader, L. K. Advani, would say no more in public than that his party was opposed to any measure expanding on that year's Supreme Court ruling which declared that caste-based 'total reservations' would stay at 50 per cent of state populations.

In fact, state-level election manifestos routinely feature competing pledges to expand the reservations system far beyond the old arenas of college admissions quotas and public service posts. In 1994, the Congress party's appeal to the Karnataka state electorate was couched almost exclusively in caste-based terms. Its manifesto contained a promise to grant land and free student accommodation to members of the Scheduled Tribes and Castes, as well as an 'action plan' to direct benefits to the state's 'Other Backward' castes. At the all-India level, in 1995 the Congress called for an amendment to the Constitution expanding the principle of reservations to cover job promotions as well as recruitment quotas for members of Scheduled and 'OBC' populations.[66]

Since Independence then, jati and varna categories have been given concrete meaning in law, development policy and academic debate. Both in bureaucratic practice and in the electoral arena, those with the

---

[66] *Hindu* Int. Edn 12 Nov. 1994: 3; Srinivas 1996: xxix.

power to affect public policy have treated caste as a powerful if problematic reality of everyday life. In this respect, the Indian state has played a crucial role in both initiating and confirming these trends. Despite the country's limited moves toward deregulation and economic 'liberalisation', the range of resources or 'life-chances' being distributed through state action has not been substantially decreased. Indeed, if anything, the element of caste-based reservations or quotas within this still sizable state sector has grown in size and importance since the early 1980s. Both politicians and electorates have therefore had powerful incentives to champion schemes which allocate rewards and opportunities on a caste-specific basis.

The news media, too, have played a central role in this process, taking it for granted in accounts of the country's competitive party system that a significant part of the electorate will take note of so-called caste factors when they vote. So even though caste has persistently failed to act as a safe predictor of individual electoral choice, the dubious concept of the 'vote bank' still refuses to die: state and national elections continue to be analyzed in terms of the 'Jat vote' or the 'Brahman vote'. Few if any politicians behave as if the majority of Indian voters are casteless embodiments of free will; appeals to class interests or communal solidarities almost always contain at least a covert reference to the bonds of caste, if only as a form of conspiratorial cohesiveness ascribed to others. In a political system that treats caste as 'real', the party that champions the right 'communities' stands a good chance of out-polling its rivals, particularly if it can offer some plausible gain in the reservations race.

The electoral system has therefore adjusted to the potential of caste to act as a 'modern' man's prop and credit source by apparently facilitating the creation of caste-based 'vote banks' where none had formerly existed. In the 1980s, Paul Brass found rural constituencies in UP where for the richer 'bullock capitalists' it made good sense to invest surplus cash in local party politics. This was apparently done by ploughing the profits of commercial farming into crude cash-for-votes schemes. Payments were fixed and graded by caste: such and such a sum for the allegiance of one jati's voters, a higher rate for members of another whose members were richer and more numerous.[67]

There has been strong pressure on state governments to reconsider

---

[67] Brass and Robinson 1987: 340–1.

the original post-Independence provisions which excluded non-Hindus from the reservation process. As of the 1990s, the position differed from state to state, but there have been moves to extend the definitions of 'backwardness' to include members of the religious minorities. In October 1994 the Kerala state government decided to include the state's entire Muslim population in the OBC category, thus making them eligible for employment reservations and other benefits. To do this, the government adopted the simple device of classifying all Kerala Muslims as Mappilas, that is, as members of the one named non-Hindu 'community' that had originally been placed on the OBC register.[68]

The Indian state is certainly not all-powerful, and the moves it has made in regard to caste, reservations and the amelioration of social and economic 'backwardness' have been anything but consistent or decisive. Nevertheless, both the 1950 Constitution and the country's more recent social justice schemes have confirmed much that the colonial planners and policy-makers had established in areas where they too regarded jati and varna as powerful realities of Indian life. Indeed, now that so many vested interests are bound up with the workings of reservations quotas and appeals to caste-defined electoral constituencies, it is hard to believe that the language of Indian politics will ever be purged of its references to 'scheduling', OBCs, Dalits, KHAMs, Backwards, Forwards, Manuvadi elites, and all the other caste-related categories and slogans. Yet the complex and often contradictory reality of caste in contemporary India is far from being a product of law and political action on their own. It is these further dimensions of modern-day caste experience that the next chapter seeks to explain.

[68] *Hindu* Int. Edn 5 Nov. 1994: 13.

CHAPTER 8

CASTE IN THE EVERYDAY LIFE
OF INDEPENDENT INDIA

INTRODUCTION

Having seen that the modern Indian state has been anything but caste-free in its language and actions, the focus now returns to the domain of family, locality and personal perception. Today, as in the colonial period, the claims of caste still extend well beyond the conventions of public policy and the electoral arena. Yet it is equally clear that these norms have been significantly affected by the many changes which have transformed Indian life and thought in the years since Independence. The aim of Chapters 8 and 9 will be to ask what altered meanings Indians have come to attach to these aspects of jati and varna, exploring those areas of contemporary experience in which assertions of caste logic have had appeal for both the insecure and the advantaged.

There are two distinct though overlapping manifestations of caste to be pursued here. The first, to be explored in this chapter, concerns caste consciousness as it has been manifested in surprising though generally uncontentious forms, most notably where we see conventions of jati and varna difference retaining their power in the modern workplace and in the thinking of educated city-dwellers. The second, to be explored in Chapter 9, is a far more sensitive matter in modern India: the persistence and extreme violence of the so-called caste war outbreaks which have received much sensational coverage since the 1970s.

In both of these areas, a particular conception of caste identity has come to the fore, especially among people who see themselves as informed and modern-minded. In its treatment of caste as something in the nature of an ethnicity or nationality, it draws on themes which were present in many of the earlier reform or uplift movements discussed in previous chapters, but with an enhanced tendency towards rivalry and antagonism in dealings with other jati and varna 'communities'. It is this which has made many contemporary caste interactions appear very different from the networks of interdependency or structural opposition described in the classic ethnographies of the post-Independence era.[1]

This exclusive or ethnicity-like view of jati and varna rests on a notion of caste as an urgent moral mandate, that is, as a bond of collective virtues and obligations on the basis of which public-spirited people should take decisive action when they hear the call to arms. These appeals have had ramifications far beyond the realm of family and locality; in the cases to be discussed here, the public arena and the supra-local political stage have played a major role. Thus the reality of caste for modern Indians still springs from interactions between the concerns of the parochial face-to-face locality, and an awareness of debates and events in the domain of regional and national politics.

Caste is certainly not the only basis on which Indians have professed bonds of common entitlement and disability in their home localities, and in their dealings with external authority. Since the 1950s, cross-cutting affinities of faith, class and ethno-linguistic identity have often had a more direct and lasting impact on both local and national life than the claims of anti-Brahmanism, or Harijan 'uplift', or so-called caste reform movements.[2] Yet since Independence, large numbers of Indians have found advantage in presenting themselves to state agencies as members of named regional jatis or wider multi-caste groupings, claiming either a shared inheritance of superior worth and virtue, or a history of injustice at the hands of Forward or high-caste 'oppressors'.

Furthermore, references to jati and varna have almost always come into play at some level when more generalised forms of mobilisation have occurred, even among those who claim to speak on public platforms in the name of a Hindu or Aryan 'community', or as Dalits, or peasant *kisans*, or as heirs to a supposedly suppressed regional culture – that of the Kannada-speakers or Tamil-Dravidians, for example.[3] At the very least, the idea of promoting allegiance among people of like caste has come to be invoked in public speech as a way of imputing backward social attitudes to others. Thus 'we' are the ones with a legitimate claim to solidarity; it is always 'they' – one's unworthy rivals – who are given to so-called 'casteism' or 'casteist' values and actions.

[1] For example, Leach 1971, esp. pp. 1–10.
[2] Pinch 1996.
[3] Washbrook 1989; Barnett 1976.

These two English neologisms are invariably used pejoratively. Since Independence, politicians from virtually every mainstream party and ideological tradition have routinely attacked their opponents for making 'casteist' appeals to the electorate. Indeed, until recently, the one point on which conservative Hindu nationalists, Nehruvian 'secularists' and revolutionary Marxists have generally agreed is in their rejection of the old pre-Independence concept of the 'golden chain'. (See Chapter 4.) Yet there can be little doubt that for many modern Indians the idea of pride in caste as an expression of selfless virtue has undergone a real revival. A much-debated example of this trend would be the campaigners for Hindu self-assertion in Rajasthan who, in 1987, publicly glorified *sati* (widow-burning) as a supposed manifestation of noble Rajput values. And while it would be wrong to exaggerate the importance of this one case, both this chapter and the next will seek to explain why such appeals have become increasingly intelligible and attractive in recent years. The aim here will be to ask why caste has come to operate for so many Indians in the manner of an 'imagined community', that is, as a bond of idealised allegiance answering needs which both in India and elsewhere have been more widely associated with the claims of two other forms of supra-local attachment – the modern nation and the ethno-religious 'community'.[4]

THE INSECURITIES OF THE MODERN ENVIRONMENT

While some commentators have portrayed Western academics as being excessively preoccupied with caste, few would deny that jati and varna conventions have remained active and visible in the post-Independence period.[5] In the 1970s it was widely argued that these had come to differ in striking ways from more 'traditional' expressions of caste ideology, and that awareness of caste had undergone a particularly

---

[4] On 'casteism', see for example the Indian Conference on Social Work's *Report on Casteism and Removal of Untouchability* (1955), cited in Sheth 1979: 188 n. 10. On *sati*, see Unnithan 114–15 in Searle-Chatterjee and Sharma 1994; Hawley in Hawley 1994: 9; and Oldenberg in Hawley 1994: 105.

[5] See the important overview provided in Fuller 1996, esp. pp. 1–31. For a critique of academic writing on caste see Appadurai 1986; for a contrasting view, see Jagjivam Ram 1980, esp. ch. 58, 'Casteless society – a dream'.

profound change in the arena of the modern workplace and the modern nation-state.

The term 'substantialisation', originally coined by Dumont, was employed here. The aim was to explain why caste was still so evidently a force in Indian life, while being understood in ways which were so often at odds with the principles of 'traditional' caste. Thus the puzzle that users of these terms hoped to resolve can be summed up as follows. On the one hand, so-called traditional caste values had been widely portrayed as the props of an immobile, other-worldly, fatalistic and backward-looking social order. Yet on the other hand, it has been those identifying themselves as modern people living in a world of individuality and active agency who have often been most inclined to exalt caste solidarities as embodiments of progressive contemporary values.[6]

For Dumont the traditional caste Hindu had no inviolable caste 'substance'. The essence of caste resided in the structured opposition between ranked groups which perceived one another both hierarchically and holistically. Each caste Hindu shared a particular caste lifestyle; one's own particular *dharma* or code of conduct was distinct from that of other caste groups, but this was a basis on which relations between hierarchically ranked castes and sub-castes were structured. Without fulfilling *dharma* in this interactive sense, with its emphasis on differentiations between ranked sub-castes or *gotras*, one could not be or remain a Bhumihar, Vellala or Patidar. Fulfilling *dharma* was thus not simply a matter of living out the life to which one was born as heir to an innate and permanent Vellala or Patidar 'substance'. Instead, the leading of a 'dharmic' life required the so-called caste Hindu to work continually to maintain personal and collective purity. This was to be achieved in ways which required interactions between high and low or pure and impure caste groups, with those who ranked both higher and lower on this scale being bound together in this asymmetrical symbiosis.

The implication of this theory of substance and 'substantialisation' was that in so-called traditional caste society, all Patidars were not the same as other Patidars. On the contrary, the Patidar caste was an open-ended array of divergent sub-caste units – the 'superior' Leva

---

[6] This was not why Dumont originally employed the term. His intention was to indicate how modern 'politicised' caste differed from caste in its 'traditional' form, which for Dumont was interactive or relational rather than 'substantialised'.

sub-caste of Patidars being distinct and alien to those of 'lesser' Bhakta, Kadva or Matia sub-caste.[7] Furthermore, caste identity could be lost or forfeited, hence the formalised mechanisms of 'outcasting' which once featured so prominently in the colonial ethnographies.

As we have seen, most Indians did not become insistent on these minutely graded sub-caste barriers until relatively recent times. Yet purity-loving, 'holistic', gotra-conscious forms of caste identity had indeed become widespread by the end of the colonial period; it was these manifestations of jati and varna logic which Dumont and his contemporaries had called 'traditional'. What social scientists began to find in the 1960s and 1970s was that many Indians did seem after all to regard their identity as Bhumihars, Vellalas or Patidars as in some sense innate and immutable. It was this apparent shift to an idea of inherent and fixed caste substance or identity which anthropologists came to refer to as 'substantialisation'. This ingrained something that made one Bhumihar or Patidar now seemed to have the features of a fixed ethnicity or blood bond which harmonised with or overrode the sub-caste (gotra) as the primary unit of 'traditional' social affiliation.[8]

Of course, this shift to more modern or 'substantialised' experiences of caste has been anything but complete, with both variants often co-existing and overlapping in everyday life and thought. Nevertheless the differences between them are real and important. A number of influential studies have traced the origins of this 'modernised' or 'substance'-centred idea of caste to the 'modern' experiences of economic and political life both during and after the colonial period. It has been noted that these changes of perception were evident in the arguments of many nineteenth- and twentieth-century caste uplift movements. Many of these 'modern' organisations had promoted the goal of sub-caste fusion as a moral value in its own right. They had also argued that 'reformists' could flout dharmic convention by crossing the ocean or practising widow remarriage without losing the essential 'substance' that defined their caste identity.[9]

In the years after Independence, social scientists found further evidence of the spread of these modern-minded or 'substantialised' forms of caste consciousness. One key ethnography of the 1970s

---

[7] Breman 1984: 84.

[8] Compare Parry 1979 on the existence of Rajputs who come both above and below the line of 'dharmic' conformity.

[9] See Barnett 1977.

explored this trend in the experience of a particular supra-local 'clean-caste' jati, the Kontaikkattai Vellalas (KVs) of Tamil Nadu state.[10] When this study was undertaken by Barnett, those identifying themselves as KV/Kontaikkattais still claimed seigneurial origins and often held title to ancestral rice lands. But, as in other densely populated cash-crop regions, their much-subdivided holdings had become uneconomic, and many KVs had turned to employment in the region's turbulent mill towns. Far from making them indifferent to the claims of caste, Barnett found that these experiences fostered a sense of shared identity which defined all KVs regardless of sub-caste or occupation as heirs to an immutable essence or 'substance' which was unique to the entire jati. Being Kontaikkattai in this modern or 'substantialised' sense, therefore, did not depend on what members of particular kin groups or KV sub-castes might do or fail to do towards the preservation of personal or collective purity.[11]

At the same time, this study found KVs having to make difficult individual judgements about how and to what extent considerations of caste should apply in complex 'modern' situations, especially those involving interactions with Harijan-untouchables. One revealing vignette in Barnett's account has KV factory labourers debating whether to stage a walk-out in which they might have been joined by fellow workers of Harijan-untouchable background. None of them seems to have been in any doubt about the caste identity of their fellow workers. Furthermore, those discussing the strike proposal clearly found it natural to act as a joint decision-making unit on the basis of their shared KV jati origin. Some apparently felt that a multi-caste strike might be good strategy in this workplace; there was no suggestion that such an alliance might involve food-sharing or other polluting contacts across caste lines.

Yet there were KV workers who resisted the idea of joint action with Harijans precisely because these workers were of untouchable/ *avarna* origin like their own or their rural kinsmen's agricultural labourers. Others argued that KVs were inherently lords and leaders of men, and that in the factory environment it was therefore incumbent on them to act as leaders of all the strikers. With hindsight, the

---

[10] *Ibid.*

[11] Equally well documented is the trend towards the fusion or 'substantialisation' of the Karnataka cultivating groups who have come to be identified as members of the Vokkaliga 'community'. See Manor 1989; Kaul 1993.

key point here is the all-important power of the pollution barrier in the thinking of these 'clean-caste' workers. As has already been seen, even in the colonial period this increasingly compelling differentiation between those of 'clean' and 'unclean' caste had become the most powerful and enduring expression of 'modern' caste experience.[12]

BEYOND 'SUBSTANTIALISATION' – MARRIAGE AND THE DOMESTIC ARENA

The idea of caste as a real and forceful presence in contemporary environments is also conveyed in T. N. Madan's studies of Kashmiri Brahmans, though his work improves very considerably on formulations relying on a crude opposition between 'traditional' and modern or 'substantialised' forms of caste awareness. Madan's accounts of these Kashmiri Brahmans who use the title Pandit as a jati designation employ the two terms *qaum* (*quom*) and *zat*: both are commonly rendered into English as 'caste'. Kashmiris of Pandit birth, says Madan, conceive of themselves as a single *qaum*, that is, a people: a Kashmiri Pandit is born into this and no other *qaum*, and there is no other way to acquire Pandit identity. *Zat* is a regional variant on the word jati; all beings and entities possess a *zat* or essence, 'a product of physical and moral elements'.[13]

In humans, this innate and distinctive *zat* essence is the basis on which one defines those who are alien and therefore unmarriageable, though the affinity created by *zat* involves something more subtle than the mere biological fact of shared blood and kinship ties. Yet this quality of corporate caste essence, which is inborn in all members of a given jati, is simultaneously both innate and alterable, Madan says. It

---

[12] This aspect of 'caste Hindu' life and the continuing claims of the seigneurial model of caste are discussed in greater detail in this chapter and in Chapter 9. Again, though today a real and forceful element of Indian life, the pollution barrier is not being treated here as a static or ahistorical manifestation of caste values. (See above, Chapter 5.) New light will be shed on the often limited extent of caste consciousness in a variety of modern workplaces in Jonathan Parry's forthcoming study of north Indian factory environments. Among older works documenting the persistence of caste differentiations in 'modern' environments, Desai (1976) found untouchability exclusions being regularly practised in village *panchayat* (local government) meetings, as well as widespread exclusion of Harijan/untouchables from village wells. (Compare Anant 1972.) Khan 1980: 130 reports perpetuation of caste-specific residence patterns in the operation of government house-building schemes for the low-caste poor, and Gough (1989) notes resistance to the admission of untouchables to village schools in the 1980s.

[13] Madan 1992: 104.

can be lost altogether by an individual, as for example by marrying a Muslim. In everyday life it must therefore be sustained through proper dharmic conduct. Far from being immutable, one's ingrained *zat* essence can be 'refined' through appropriate effort, or corrupted through neglect of the dharmic duties that are correct for one's particular caste.[14]

Contemporary caste logic is thus decidedly not an expression of unchanging Indian cultural 'essences', though by the same token it is not mere orientalist fantasy, or a fiction of the modern public arena. And, although concepts of hierarchy, ritual purity and shared caste essence or *zat* still often underpin coercive class relations, they are not just an oppressor's charter. There is much controversy on these issues, but few academic specialists would dismiss caste as an irrelevance in modern India. Most though not all would accept that there is more to jati and varna than a simple structure of disability, even those who contend that it is primarily the effects of 'retarded capitalism' that have kept caste 'alive' in contemporary India.[15]

André Béteille has intervened decisively in these debates by arguing that for members of India's English-speaking administrative and professional intelligentsias, considerations of caste have ceased to be paramount in areas where even 'modern' people are commonly thought to defer to them. He notes this both in the making of marriages, and also in the strategies which anglophone city-dwellers adopt to advance the careers of their children. Of course, it must be remembered that in matters of marriage the English-speaking intelligentsias are often unlike other Indians. Nevertheless, these cosmopolitan English-speakers exercise a disproportionate effect on the country at large. As Béteille shows, their world has become a domain of individualised decision-making and concern for the small-scale family unit; these are definitely not milieux in which age-old caste codes are passively accepted and transmitted from generation to generation.[16]

Yet it is precisely in this world of dynamism and individual agency that we can still see large numbers of Indians for whom a complex mixture of seemingly 'traditional' and modern-day versions of caste

---

[14] *Ibid.*
[15] Alam 1989: 248; compare Ilaih 1996.
[16] Béteille 1986 and 1991a. But see too his treatment (Béteille 1992b) of the increasingly powerful influence of caste in political life, especially the expansion of 'distributive justice' schemes involving caste-based employment quotas in universities and other major public institutions.

norms have remained powerful. This is true both where people have made conscious choices in the matter, and also for those coerced and 'essentialised' by others through the language of jati and varna, as will be seen in Chapter 9 in the discussion of so-called 'caste wars'.

This interpenetration of caste concerns with apparently caste-free thought and behaviour is apparent throughout India's complex social terrain. Even in the most cosmopolitan professional households, where the values of 'secular' anti-'casteism' are ardently endorsed, everyday domestic service still commonly draws on caste-defined specialisms. When middle-class city-dwellers employ cooks and superior manservants (still known by the Anglo-Indian term bearer), these salaried employees would seem to have little in common with 'traditional' *kamins* or ritual dependants. Yet purity-consciousness in regard to food and kitchen areas still prevails to the extent that people of 'clean'-caste descent are unlikely to employ bearers and kitchen servants from anything other than 'clean'-caste backgrounds. By the same token, the cleaning of bathrooms – even in blocks of modern flats – will almost certainly be carried out by servants of Harijan/ 'Sweeper' background.

Similar complexities can be seen too in the moves made by the many members of India's expanding middle classes who arrange matches for their educated sons and daughters by advertising in the classified matrimonial columns of India's vernacular and English-language newspapers. In the late 1990s both the home and international editions of these journals still publish thousands of 'bride/ groom wanted' advertisements every week. Those placing these items include many non-Hindus, but in the most widely read anglophone dailies the great majority identify themselves as Hindus for whom the matching of caste and sub-caste (*gotra*) in marriage is a major priority.

This is done by those of high or 'clean' caste, as well as those at the bottom of the varna hierarchy. Some of these advertisements appear in separate sections headed 'Scheduled Caste/Scheduled Tribe', with families using such jati titles as Chamar to identify themselves, even though these have come to be regarded as pejorative and demeaning in other contexts. Typical of the 'matrimonial classifieds' to be found in the national dailies are the following:

Hindu Nadar wheatish [fair-skinned] ... slim pretty girl 25 yrs ... highly educated USA green card holder alliance invited from Broadminded USA settled boys of same caste. (*Hindu* 24 December 1994: 7)

314

Matrimonial Bride Wanted Hindu − Pallar, B.E. [degree qualification] ... Civil Engineer and Entrepreneur [age] 31/ [height] 163[cm]/ [salary Rs] 6000 seeks suitable bride. (*Hindu* 27 June 1995: 10)

Wanted − ... well educated and well placed bridegroom from Kalinga Vysya Community. For a Kalinga Vysya Telugu girl of Visakhapatnam. [Educational] Qualification: M.C.A ... Height: 162 cms. Age: 24 ..., good looking and of wheatish complexion, employed in a Computer Software Company. Father Senior Professor ... Swagotram: Mantrikula. Maternal Gotram: Srivatsala (we are not particular) ... (*Hindu* 18 January 1997: 11)

Sindhi Bhaiband [age] 41 [height] 64 [inches]; ... Divorced. Well settled. Business Japan ... Vegetarian Cool nature Sincere Seeks bride [age] 30–40 Hindu healthy cultured home-loving vegetarian. High caste family of moral Indian values. Full photo [and] Horoscope [required] ... (*Times of India* 14 December 1997: iii)

Alliance invited for well educated Chamar girl ... pure vegetarian, religious, Haryana based ... (*ibid.*: vii)

Alliance invited by an aristocratic, Brahmin, progressive, highly educated business family ... (*ibid.*: i)

Suitable Brahmin bride for handsome Sanadhya Brahmin boy ... completing Ph.D. (Physics) ... Write with biodata, photograph, horoscope ... (*ibid.*)

Suitable Rajput match for US citizen ... [*ibid.*: vii][17]

Clearly, some at least of these families would appear to have little difficulty in seeing caste both as a 'substantialised' ethnicity, and as a manifestation of 'traditional' sub-caste gradations. Yet in neither sense is caste the only concern here. Much emphasis is given to skin colour and general appearance, as well as parents' occupation and the spouse-seeker's current or potential earnings in a 'modern' profession. An entitlement to reside and work abroad is another valued asset. Advertisements may also signal comparatively 'modern' or 'cosmopolitan' attitudes by such phrases as 'broad-minded', 'caste no bar' and even '[groom must be] willing to respect girl's individuality and career ambition'.

What then about the apparent conflict between concern with caste and even sub-caste, which in a sense treats individuality as irrelevant to marriage choice, and the evident interest taken in determining the couple's astrological compatibility, which would seem to show just

---

[17] Nadar and Pallar are Tamil jati titles, both formerly conveying very low-caste rural origins. 'Green card' is a reference to a foreigner's certificate of entitlement to take employment in the United States. 'Wheatish' (or 'wheaten') is one of the skin-colour classifications used in colonial police reportage; this terminology is still widely employed today.

the opposite? Clearly many of these advertisements indicate that while a potential match must first be deemed suitable on caste grounds, tests must also be made of the couple's personal suitability; at this point individuality does come into play, with the comparing of horoscopes being widely seen as a reliable guide on this point.

At the same time, however, within some sections of India's expanding middle classes, there has been a trend for parents to downgrade 'traditional' caste considerations, and to give far greater priority to astrological calculations in matrimonial searches.[18] Even so, there can be little doubt that in these situations those of 'clean' caste will expect spouses to be of broadly 'respectable' origin, thus ruling out 'tribals' or low-castes, as well as Hindu–Muslim matches. Once this is determined, such families employ the complex *jyotish* (astrology) techniques which were perfected for use in temples and royal courts in past centuries. These are held to be mathematically rigorous and therefore 'scientific'. Furthermore, since such calculations are individualised, they are often perceived as being better suited to the spirit of a progressive modern nation than a concern for the specifics of jati and gotra. Yet, paradoxically, parents seeking a *jyotish* expert in these situations would rarely find one who does not descend from one of the tightly-knit specialist regional sub-castes (often though not invariably Brahmans) whose members deployed these techniques on behalf of rulers and other elites in the pre-colonial kingdoms. This is the case even for those contemporary astrologers who underline the modernity and precision of their art through the use of computer graphics and web sites on the Internet.

CASTE-SPECIFIC PURSUITS AND ENVIRONMENTS

Ironically, it is largely because of the complexity of these modern environments that so many Indians have found reason to turn to one or other of the contemporary forms of caste logic. This is clearly not just a matter of external coercion or state policy. Despite all that the politicians and the law-makers have done to make caste real for modern Indians, awareness of jati and varna distinctions has come from within as well as outside and above the local environment. It has been the pressures and insecurities of everyday life in both towns and

18 Compare Kemper 1979.

villages that have kept the sacred thread and the caste *purana* in widespread use across so much of the subcontinent. These experiences have also ensured that the distinction between the pure and the impure has remained a matter of importance to the ordinary householder, as well as the specialist temple priest or tonsurer.[19]

Thus, intertwined with awareness of what the politicians and the law-courts may say or do are judgements about the relevance of one's own and other people's caste origins to the more intimate concerns of life. The complex calculations that contribute to marriage choices, as well as decisions about food, dress and ritual observances, still provide many Indians with important challenges and opportunities through which they may negotiate standards of decorum and piety within the household or small-scale 'community'.

So what else has this entailed in a complex society which possessed so many 'modern' economic and cultural features – including a large and ostensibly 'secular' intelligentsia – even before the end of colonial rule? To whom do concepts of caste matter, and in what areas of social interaction? In past centuries, caste in its varied forms was as much a value system of the cities and long-distance commercial networks as of the supposedly parochial 'peasant' locality. Since Independence, massive population growth and rapid urbanisation have had very disparate effects on both regional cultures and livelihoods, though here again one cannot make simplistic distinctions between 'traditional' environments where caste ideals prevail and those of the 'modern' milieu where such conventions recede.

Over half the Indian population still live in the countryside, though the trend in densely settled agricultural regions has been for both the landless poor and descendants of the old rural elites to migrate to the towns. Those left on the land include significant numbers of large-scale commercial producers. These are characteristically the *sat-sudra* or non-elite 'middle peasants' who have been widely referred to as members of the 'dominant' landed castes. Yet in many grain-growing areas, agricultural productivity has improved just enough since the 1950s to sustain large numbers of petty owner-cultivators, the so-called 'dwarf-holders'. These are people who survive at extremely low levels of subsistence by maximising the output of tiny holdings, while competing for whatever low-paid wage labour these locales can

---

[19] Parry 1994; Fuller 1984.

provide. Official statistics indicate that these poor labourers and smallholders are still drawn disproportionately from the ex-untouchable or Scheduled castes. Furthermore, despite the emergence of a prosperous and educated 'creamy layer' element within many low-caste populations, overall these groups still reportedly have far lower average levels of income and literacy than Indians of 'clean'-caste origin.[20]

In the cities, sophisticated enclaves of computerised high-technology enterprise have come into being since the 1980s, most notably in the mushrooming 'silicon suburbs' of Bangalore, Delhi and Bombay. At the same time, both the expansion of education since Independence, and the growth of the public sector with its swollen bureaucracies and appetite for clerical labour, have intensified one of the other key trends of the later colonial period, this being the continuing growth of large, vocal and insecure populations of literate city-dwellers whose livelihoods derive primarily from 'modern' occupations. These office workers may seem well off compared with the much larger populations of unskilled labourers and rural smallholders. Nevertheless, they are a threat to the established intelligentsias. At the same time, their aspirations have often been frustrated as they and their children struggle to find employment in 'respectable' fields, that is, in teaching, administration and commerce, or in the technical and managerial professions for those with the most sought-after qualifications. These frustrations have kept the cities volatile and, as we will see in the final chapter, have interconnected with the tensions of the turbulent rural regions.[21]

Broadly speaking, the economies of big towns have tended to be unevenly split. On the one hand, there is generally an extensive domain of small-scale workshops and petty artisanal production. At the same time, most cities contain a volatile though often vigorous industrial sector. Even in the 1990s this sector of the urban economies is still dominated by the railways, mills and other inefficient old public

[20] On rural economies, see Washbrook 1989 and Tomlinson 1993: 73–91. Regional variations have been considerable, however, as shown for example in Mitra's (1992) contrasting accounts of Orissa and Gujarat. On economic differentials, Shukla and Verma (1993: ix) report that approximately half the members of officially recognised Scheduled Castes are agricultural labourers and one-quarter marginal or small farmers; they also show only half the rate of literacy among Scheduled Castes compared with that of clean-caste groups.

[21] See, for example, Washbrook's (1989) account of 'petit-bourgeoisification' in Tamil Nadu.

concerns employing large numbers of unskilled workers. In theory, caste is not a factor in recruitment or occupational choices in these environments. In reality, however, many towns still contain high concentrations of industrial and artisanal labourers whose occupations still have at least an indirect connection with their 'traditional' caste livelihoods. Jatav/Chamars and their regional equivalents still predominate in the urban leather-working trades and municipal sanitation services; the big textile-manufacturing towns, especially in western India, are also known for their high concentrations of Harijan/untouchable mill operatives.[22]

At the same time, the great pilgrimage places and all-India sacred centres (*puris*) – Banaras, Ayodhya and Madurai, together with Puri in Orissa and dozens of other much frequented shrine and pilgrimage locales – have all continued to sustain highly organised forms of commercial enterprise which are based around the marketing of specialist priestly expertise. Large numbers of ritualists, as well as purveyors of pilgrims' supplies (including sacred images and holy offerings, and also food, lodging and transport), all derive their livelihoods from servicing these shrines and their worshippers. Every year, these localities attract thousands or even millions of pilgrims of both low and high caste origin.[23] Those taking part include many prosperous and widely travelled 'modern' people as well as uneducated farmers and labourers. In many cases, ritual specialists have adopted the marketing techniques of Western-style retail catalogue businesses to sustain and expand their clienteles. A number of the great south Indian temples sell Shaivite sacred-ash parcels by post, publishing price lists for acts of worship which devotees can commission *in absentia*. Those taking advantage of these mail-order schemes do so on the understanding that a specialist of appropriate caste, usually a Brahman, will perform their chosen rituals.[24]

In north India, the needs of the modern worshipper are catered for with equal efficiency by the vigorous forms of commerce which

---

[22] Isaacs 1965: 55, 153; Lynch 1969: 207; Searle-Chatterjee 1981, 1994; Gagnik and Bhatt 1984.

[23] Parry 1994: 66.

[24] A leaflet issued by the Thirunallur temple in Tamil Nadu offers devotees *vibuti* (sacred ash) by return of post: '[those wishing] to perform poojas to Lord Saneeswara Bhagwan ... are requested to ... send [the prescribed amount] through M.O. [money order] ...'; charges range from Rs 32.50 for a year's 'simple *archana*' (ritual) performed monthly on the devotee's birth star day, to Rs 208 for a year's 'deluxe Sahashranama *archana*'.

sustain the hereditary Brahman pilgrimage priests (*pandas*) of the great Gangetic holy places. The highly commercialised livelihoods of these *pandas* are based on the receipt of cash fees (theoretically gifts, *dan*) for the performance of funerary rituals on behalf of the millions of pilgrims who use their services annually.[25]

For all their entrepreneurial features, these pilgrimage centres' specialised ritual occupations are still followed by members of specific named regional caste groups. As Jonathan Parry has shown, in Banaras men of Harijan-untouchable Dom birth predominate in the trade of funeral pyre attendants; members of an ambivalently regarded quasi-Brahman *jati*, the Mahabrahmans, follow yet another of the Banaras funerary callings, that of the officiating mortuary ritualist. Vrindavan, the great centre of pilgrimage and devotion to the god Krishna, further illustrates the intertwining of caste with the functional specialisms of the 'modern' city. One of Vrindavan's devotional specialities is the housing of thousands of destitute widows from Bengal and Upper India; these women fulfil the norms of high-caste dharmic life-cyle teachings by living out their days as practitioners of radical austerities in the town's vast purpose-built widows' *ashrams* (hospices).[26]

In other areas too, a significant proportion of the country's population has continued to follow the sort of artisanal, commercial and priestly occupations which in past centuries gave rise to unusually tight bonds of guildlike caste affiliation. Wherever such livelihoods exist today, there are all sorts of skills and commodities on offer that would have been recognisable in India's towns and villages a century or more ago. The specialists who purvey these goods and services include grand trader-bankers like the Nattukottai Chettiars of Tamil Nadu and north India's Oswals and Agarwals, as well as humble fishermen, ritualists and craftsmen.

---

[25] Parry 1994: 99. Commercial marriage bureaux embody yet another form of lucrative caste-conscious entrepreneurship; in big cities there is vigorous competition between matchmaking agencies which advertise their ability to provide 'state of the art' services to discriminating spouse-seekers 'of all castes and communities' (*Times of India* 14 Dec. 1997: VIII).

[26] On Mahabrahmans, see Parry 1994: 81; compare Randeria 1989 on the funerary role of Bhangis in Gujarat. Parry 1994: 91 notes that Punjabi and Bengali pilgrims support members of different named jatis as mortuary ritualists; compare Fuller 1984 on Madurai temple priests. See Searle-Chatterjee 1981: 13–14 on the high concentrations of untouchable 'sweepers' and other household pollution-removers in Banaras, where covert anti-Chamar 'temple entry' bans still prevailed in the 1970s.

These are all people who find that the connections they define through the conventions of jati and varna are still valuable assets. Indeed, in uncertain times, a wide range of 'modern' Indian businesses have continued to find that profit margins can be protected or enhanced by pooling assets and sharing information within established kin and caste networks. This is true of the descendant of so-called traditional merchants in Ahmedabad, Madras or Banaras who does business in a 'modern' computerised environment, but takes pains to preserve the trappings of a purity-conscious Vaishya lifestyle within his household, shunning meat and alcohol and maintaining a cow-shelter or bird-feeding platform as an expression of 'pure' *ahimsa* values. It is even characteristic of the thriving commercial expatriates in London or New York who use their wealth to commission histories of their 'community', and who send cash to the tutelary shrines or *maths* (preceptoral foundations) around which their ancestors originally defined their identity as Komatis, Lohanas or Agarwals.

None of this is consistent with the aims of the official planners of the 1950s and 1960s who favoured a socialist model for India's post-Independence development, and who therefore subordinated producers in the private sector to the regime of 'permit Raj'. The expectation was that India would thereby combine rapid economic growth with a move toward casteless egalitarianism. Yet, in the short term at least, these policies tended to preserve or even reinforce the differentials of caste in everyday life. In order to operate the system's quotas, licences and protective labour laws, both central and state government re-cruited far larger official bureaucracies than those of the colonial era. Not surprisingly, given the stringent educational qualifications required for senior posts in state service, those at the higher administrative levels remained predominantly of high-caste origin, just as they had done under British rule.

Today such people often lead 'secular' or even partially 'casteless' lives insofar as their food habits or marriage choices are concerned. It is harder though to visualise the disappearance of caste differentials in matters of middle-class education and occupation, even if the trend towards economic liberalisation eventually shifts more areas of employment into the private sector. Certainly in the 1990s, few Indians are in any doubt about the disproportionately small numbers of low-caste or 'backward class' officials in senior government service posts; the issue is still a matter of active public debate.

Furthermore, as M. N. Panini has shown, throughout the period of 'permit Raj', businesses in the private sector were far from caste-neutral in matters of employment and promotion. It was often the most competitive 'modern' entrepreneurs who found that their profits depended on being able to circumvent import quotas and other official restrictions. In these conditions, what businesses needed above all were docile workers and managers who could be relied on to preserve the firm's secrets. Such firms found that they could often achieve this by building on the experience of caste in its 'substantialised' form, that is, on the capacity of broadly homogenised jati and varna ties to become a basis for solidarity and preferment in the modern workplace.

This of course had been the aspect of caste which British officials had feared and exaggerated in their attempts to break so-called caste cliques in public service employment. Yet many post-Independence managers found that it was more advantageous in the conditions of 'permit Raj' to build on such ties of blood and 'community' in recruitment rather than on the apparently more rational criteria of individual skills and qualifications. More recently, the retreat from 'permit Raj' has certainly not led central or state governments to impose caste-specific reservations quotas on new private sector ventures. Yet the maintenance of 'community' allegiance in the workplace is still seen to make sound business sense in many areas, even under these conditions of so-called economic liberalisation.[27]

RURAL 'COMMUNITY' VALUES AND THE POWER
OF THE POLLUTION BARRIER

Above all, though, it has been the volatile fortunes of cultivating people that have kept many Indians alert to the nuances of caste. The bonds of shared 'community' have been most ardently proclaimed in environments where agrarian resources have been scarce, and where control of land and labour has proven contentious and unpredictable. This has been apparent in times of conflict involving the large 'middle peasant' populations who gained a powerful new voice in politics by rallying to the assertive *kisan*-power agrarianism of the 1970s and 1980s.

[27] Panini 1996.

The situation of these owner-cultivators has been far from secure, and very few of them can truly be described as members of 'dominant' landowning networks. As so-called bullock capitalists, the commodity-producing smallholders reaped uncertain benefits from the Green Revolution. These, above all, are the people who have regarded the language of caste as a means of minimising loss and adapting to uncertainty. Whether the community they claimed to constitute was known as Jat or Kapu, Patidar, Namasudra or Yadav-Ahir, these *kisan/khedut* 'peasant' populations have become increasingly inclined to assert a strong perception of their own and other people's caste endowments. Those who share their titles and marriage ties still tend to live in large homogeneous clusters. There are still sizable areas of western UP where virtually all the substantial tillers still call themselves Jat. Their 'clean-caste' counterparts in south India identify themselves as Gounders in Tamil Nadu's dry-grain Konku region, as Kammas and Reddis in the Telugu country, and as Vokkaligas and Lingayats in Karnataka. This concentrated numerical predominance has been widely identified as one of the great assets of so-called 'dominant castes'.

Anthropologists have often reported that these 'clean' non-lordly groups do not concern themselves with the sort of intricately graded ladders of precedence to be found in the deltaic south or the Anavil-dominated tracts of southern Gujarat. These are the places where Brahmans are far more numerous, and where complex 'transactional' pecking orders appear to be carefully worked out in a way that establishes a composite hierarchy among all the different high-, middling- and low-caste groups in a given locality.[28]

But if Jats or Kammas do not much care how they might be 'transactionally' ranked in relation to other middling non-elite groups, they will almost invariably be fiercely strict about the pollution barrier. This has become the norm even in regions like the Tamil country where 'peasants' contest virtually all forms of privilege and status, professing anti-hierarchical sentiments which echo the themes of regional *bhakti* spirituality as well as the populist egalitarianism of the non-Brahman and Dravidian supremacist movements. These are places where most other features of caste as a 'traditional' pan-Indian

---

[28] Marriot 1976; on the often qualified and uncertain nature of this 'dominance' see, for example, Beck 1972.

'system' are largely absent, but where the one point of consensus is the decisive 'otherness' of the Adi-Dravida or Jatav-Chamar.[29]

This sense of differentiation has had a powerful impact on the tactics used by rural people to cope with threats to their assets and livelihoods. Whether victim or victimiser, tenant or landlord, labourer or struggling 'bullock capitalist', those trying to sustain themselves in unsettled times would be unwise to disregard the gulf that divides those of 'unclean' descent from the non-polluting *sat-sudra*. The circumstances of rural life have created equally strong incentives for the householder who claims lordly Nayar, Rajput or Anavil Brahman descent to cling to his family's vestiges of superiority, and above all to insist that his children may not marry the kin of the plough-touching 'peasant'.

There are great diversities in all this, but distinctions of title, rank and corporate honour still matter, even in localities where those whose forebears were called Kolis and Koeris have taken to wearing the sacred thread and calling themselves twice-born Kshatriyas, where the Shanar or Kurmi have acquired as much land as the Rajput or Brahman, and where the so-called Sudras or Upper Backwards have long been worshipping bloodlessly and maintaining scrupulously 'pure' vegetarian households. The rituals of village life – marriage feasts, temple processions, *tamashas* (festive assemblies) to welcome visiting politicians – are still often orchestrated in ways that both contest and confirm local ranking schemes.

However fluid and variable these pecking orders may be, they do still operate in ways which distinguish the high from the low, and the clean from the unclean.[30] Marriages between people of substantially different caste background are still as rare in the countryside as they are in the cities. Furthermore, in both towns and 'nucleated' village settlements (the type of rural locality found in most areas of peninsular India), there are still older housing areas containing single-caste residential streets. These include the Brahman-only streets surrounding many Hindu temples, as well as the concentrations of impoverished Harijan-untouchables who still live apart from 'clean'-caste populations in their own separate hamlets and urban slum enclaves.[31]

Above all, in times of change and upheaval in the countryside, those

[29] As illustrated by Daniel 1984: 112.
[30] See, for example, Breman 1985: 146.
[31] Randeria 1989: 173; Daniel 1984: 111–13.

of different jati and varna have had good reason to consider the claims of caste before deciding on their objective 'class' interests. People of supposedly unclean or tribal descent have found since Independence that when they look for supporters in a struggle over tenancy rights or labour conditions, their natural allies will still be those of like 'kind' and 'community'. This is consistent with a wider trend that has been much commented on in recent years. Even where economic issues have contributed to mass regional 'mobilisations', appeals to either caste or ethno-religious community are now commonly held to have become more and more the dominant mode of Indian political activity since the 1960s.[32]

Thus, even where labour unions or militant agrarian organisations call for joint class-based alliances, untouchable Jatav-Chamars, Parai-yans or Dheds will generally discover, often painfully, that their situation is not the same as that of poor wage-labourers or dwarf-holders who can locate themselves on the other side of the pollution barrier. In times of strife, a locality's 'clean'-caste Ahir or Kanbi labourers and cultivators will probably still be inclined to distance themselves from lowly 'Dalit'/untouchables. Such poor non-untouch-ables will be likely to claim affinity with landed 'big men' of their own or similar caste origin, particularly where such potential allies include rich or educated individuals with connections outside the locality. This will be the case even in situations where, in 'rational' economic terms, the clean-caste tiller has more in common with the untouchable labourer or dwarf-holder.

Putting jati and varna first in these situations is a response to conditions in the here and now, and not a survival from the primordial past. As was seen in the case of the strike debate among the Kontaikattai Vellalas, 'clean' *sat-sudras* of modest means would have good 'rational' reasons not to risk a slim margin of advantage in insecure times by making common cause with people of untouchable descent. To do so might endanger valuable marriage and ritual connections with more powerful people of their own blood and 'kind' while simultaneously eroding the fragile profitability of ancestral landholdings. Indeed, even where such holdings seem to have little obvious economic value, there is still advantage in being seen in one's locality as a person of respectable proprietary stock. Above all, even in

32 Alam 1989: 237–8.

an ostensibly egalitarian age, such 'modern' people as Barnett's KV informants have continued to distinguish themselves from descendants of servile toilers and dependants.

CASTE AND THE OLD LORDS OF THE LAND

These appeals to a 'substantialised' or homogenising 'imagined community' of jati and varna have been sustained by two forces in particular. The first of these, the continuing power of the pollution barrier in most regions of the subcontinent, has already been discussed. The second is the continuing power and conspicuousness of grand 'feudal' landowners. In this case particularly, one can see how readily these 'substantialised' forms of caste have co-existed with ideals deriving from a more 'traditional' version of dharmic codes.

Not all patricians have found new livelihoods in the towns, and the lordly styles of life with which they are identified have certainly not disappeared from agrarian India. Many of these seigneurial groups have had to struggle to retain their symbolic and material assets, but their power in large areas of both the north and the south still signals to the wider society that 'good' blood is a desirable asset in a world of change and insecurity, even though its worth may have been significantly devalued by reservations and 'Mandalite' social justice schemes. But even fifty years after Independence, few Indians are surprised to find people who claim lordly warrior descent still trying to treat their field labourers as personal retainers, demanding sexual access to their women, and using force to exact *begar*-like service dues from them.

Militant 'Dalit' activists have attempted to challenge this kind of coercion. Yet it is notable that *begar* has remained a live issue in many areas of so-called caste war conflict.[33] Attempts to challenge *begar*-like practices have been frustrated by the fact that neither Nehruvian socialists nor *gharibi hatao* populists have persuaded all rural Indians that such claims are 'feudal' and illegitimate. The complex changes that have occurred in rural economic life since the 1940s have tended, at least for some struggling landed people, to lend credibility to the idea that there is righteousness and protection for the weak to be found when the big man exercises his lordly will.

For those who take this view, the 'feudal' landowner's seigneurial

---

[33] See Chapter 9. Hasan 'Class and caste' p. 266, in Hasan *et al.* 1989.

acts may be held to spring from something higher than one man's lusts or material interests. That something is an aspect of 'caste' (or *zat* as it has been understood in recent centuries), this being an ideal of order and predictable moral obligations. These ideals are still visibly rooted in recognition of the fragility of that order. Even today, ordinary conformist 'caste Hindus' have good reason to conceive of the environment in which they live as one of barely contained disharmonies. If danger and upheaval are the norms of everyday experience in both the supernatural and the material world, there will always be a need for the sword-wearing tribute-taker who is equipped to act as both usurper and orderer on behalf of the meek tiller and toiler.

It is at this point that the logic of caste often still takes shape, at least in part, as an exaltation of the man of prowess, rather than the 'pure' or ascetic Brahman or *bania*/merchant. In modern India, there are still many people who see the Kshatriya's mandate to dominate as a normal fact of life. Although much weakened in the colonial period, when the sturdy toiler came to be widely valued over the rapacious seigneur/ *girasidar*, there are many comparatively remote areas where the fortress-dwelling land-controllers survived long after Independence.

Well into the 1970s, the Telengana region on the Maharashtra– Andhra Pradesh borderlands contained one such group, a class of landlords known as *doras*. These were 'squireen' lords in the unmistakable tradition of the *girasi* rajas whose forebears had acquired their revenue-taking rights in past centuries through force of arms. At this time the *dora* families still lived in miniature forts which were known locally as *ghadis* or princely seats, a term evoking the rent-receiver's claims of martial power and kingliness. Even forty years on from the anti-*begar* campaigns of the colonial era, these 'little kings' were still reportedly exacting unpaid labour and dues in kind – usually sheep and other livestock – from untouchable labourers. *Doras* also reportedly made much of the seigneur's tradition of sexual dominance, claiming the right to deflower labourers' daughters on their wedding night, and taking over a dependant's wife when their own were pregnant.[34]

In Bihar and UP, as in many other regions, people of lordly background used false title transfers and other means to evade the anti-landlord legislation of the 1950s and 1960s. Even where big holdings

---

[34] C. V. Subba Rao 'Resurgence of peasant movement in Telengana' *EPW* 14 Nov. 1978: 1878–80; see also Ilaih 1996.

were reassigned, those confirmed as direct owners of land were not humble 'tillers': in much of the Gangetic plain, people of acknowledged Brahman, Rajput or Bhumihar descent remained the largest and most numerous owner-occupiers of arable land.[35] Elsewhere too in rural India, 'squireen' traditions of rank and honour were contested but never wholly expunged. Landed Bhumihars and Rajputs of *girasidar* origin were still visible to the wider society, and other rural people looked to them as models of honour and prowess who embodied in their diet, dress and worship the ideal of the worthy Kshatriya.

It is true, of course, that in the years before Independence, such people as Bihar Kurmis and other 'clean' *sat-sudras* embraced so-called caste reform movements which denied the superiority of the landed Rajput or Bhumihar grandees. But even these assertive 'peasants' were conscious of the refined seigneurial traditions associated with the grander proprietary groups. Many of them therefore insisted that their own virtues were lordly ones, in other words, that one could plough and still be an Aryan and a Kshatriya in the tradition of the royal warrior forebears of the divine Ram and Krishna.[36] It was often these lineages of non-lordly Jat, Kanbi or Kurmi descent who used the profits of both pre- and post-Independence cash-crop farming to sustain hitherto unaccustomed forms of squireen-style consumption and patronage. Increasing numbers of 'kisans' thus adopted the rich diet and lavish piety of the grandee households. Such people became particularly Kshatriya-like in their assertions of power and authority over 'tribal' or Harijan-untouchable dependants, as in the case of the Kanbi-Patidar landowners who had come to display these lordly pretensions in their dealings with the class of unfree client labourers known as Halis or 'bond-servants'.[37]

Examples of continuing fascination with the Kshatriya ideal abound, as can be seen in the many post-Independence publications which exalt the doings of individual named jatis. The production of these 'community' histories has been as active an industry in the late twentieth century as it was in the pre-Independence period.[38] As recently as 1988, a polemicist representing himself as an Oxford-trained Indian 'socio-historian' published an account of the supposed

[35] Brass and Robinson 1987; Frankel and Rao 1989–90; Rudolph and Rudolph 1987.
[36] Pinch 1996.
[37] Breman 1985.
[38] See, for example, Hardgrave 1969.

origins and heritage of north India's Khatris. Today, as in the past, those who call themselves Khatri favour the livelihoods of the pen and the ledger. In the colonial period, however, Khatri caste associations extolled the heritage of their 'community' as one of prowess and noble service (*seva*), claiming that their dharmic essence was that of the arms-bearing Kshatriya and therefore quite unlike that of the commercial Agarwals and other pacific Vaishyas. These same themes were recapitulated by the author of the 1988 text: the Khatris, 'one of the most acute, energetic, and remarkable race [*sic*] in India', are heirs to a glorious martial past, 'pure descendants of the old Vedic Kshatriyas'. The writer even tries to exalt Khatris above Rajputs, whose blood he considers 'impure', being supposedly mixed with that of 'inferior' Kols or 'aborigines': in his view only Khatris are 'true representatives of the Aryan nobility'.[39]

Kshatriya models of 'community' also loom large in the claims of those identified as Kolis in the Deccan and Upper India. Until the 1940s (and even later in some cases), to be known as a Koli was to be classed as a person of base criminal stock, hence ineligible for military and police recruitment.[40] This was deeply damaging to precariously placed Koli smallholders, for whom the sober Vaishya-style values of their Vaishnavising new-peasant forebears offered little real security in an uncertain market economy. People in this situation had often turned to soldiering to supplement declining incomes; many tillers of Koli descent now had reason to do this. They therefore took on what they viewed as a Rajput way of life, proclaiming kinship with true Kshatriyas, and thereby denying the stigma of lowliness attached to Koli origins.

In the decades since Independence there have been good reasons for the same people or their descendants to rally to the 'Mandalite' banner, seeking to be declared 'backward' and thus eligible for employment reservations and other preferences for 'OBCs'. And yet this did not wipe out that special regard for the lordly Rajput-like way of life that has remained prominent in debates about the rights and wrongs of landowners, tenants and labourers in contentious situations

[39] Puri 1988: 3, 78, 163, 166. The writer appeals to the Khatri 'race' to 'wake up' and cherish their heritage as 'followers of the Hindu Dharma Sastras' (5). Above all they should guard against 'hybridising', i.e. marrying non-Khatris (166). These views closely resemble those of pre-Independence race theorists (see Chapters 3–4). Compare Seth 1904.

[40] Parry 1979: 119.

in many parts of India. The state of Gujarat is a case in point here. Beginning soon after Independence, landed people in northern and central districts sought to oppose anti-zamindari and land-ceiling legislation through the operations of a pressure group calling itself the Gujarat Kshatriya Sabha. This body remained a powerful force in state politics until the late 1960s. It resurfaced as a promoter of 'Backward Class' interests in the 1980s, having originated as one of many organisations in different states using the language of caste-defined moral mandate to generate large-scale opposition to the logic of Nehruvian land-reform.[41]

The areas in which this idealised Kshatriya allegiance came to be invoked were those in which official land-ceiling schemes had been widely expected to advantage *sat-sudra* 'middle peasant' groups over the old lordly rent-receiving populations. The message of this organisation was that far from being feudal oppressors, the region's comparatively small number of landed Rajput lineages were part of a much larger array of deserving and honourable 'communities' who included the state's Koli population, together with other groups of armed pastoral and 'tribal' descent. This was ironic: in Gujarat those identified as Kolis were generally much poorer and far less 'Sanskritically' Hindu than the big Rajput landowners. In addition, Kolis had formerly been defined by those claiming both Rajput and Patidar identity as one of the 'wild' and unworthy groups whose women were no longer acceptable as partners for those of 'good' blood and lineage. Furthermore, in common with their Kallar-like ex-'predator' counterparts in other states, this was also a time when organisations claiming to represent Kolis as a 'community' were campaigning for their inclusion in the new state-level Backward Classes listings.

Yet the new Gujarat Kshatriya Sabha (GKS) organisation had much to gain by telling state officials that its campaign against land reform embodied the 'mobilisation' of this very wide range of ex-armsbearers in opposition to the 'kulak'/'rich-peasant' Kanbi-Patidars. In numerical terms, this self-proclaimed Kshatriya coalition claimed to represent as much as 40 per cent of the state's population, as opposed to the estimated 20 per cent who fell within the 'Kanbi-Patidar' category. These polemicists therefore argued that while it was acceptable for Kolis to exploit the reservations system if they wished, people of Koli

---

[41] Mitra 1992: 46.

birth should recognise that they and the region's Rajputs were all of martial stock, and therefore of like quality and heritage. This, ran the message, made them joint heirs with Rajputs to the *girasidar*'s turban and sword. They should all exalt the divinely sanctioned bond that divided righteous Kshatriyas from non-martial *kisan* groups; the Koli and the Rajput should see themselves as natural allies against the common 'peasant' enemy. These enemies, too, were identified in caste terms: they were the Patidars, to be reviled as commercial opportunists who had enriched themselves at the expense of worthy Kshatriyas through corrupt links with the Congress. These were unjust gains which the righteous Rajput and his worthy Koli ally had both a right and a duty to contest.[42]

THE PATRIOTIC 'MIDDLE PEASANT'

Here then we see one of the important regional manifestations of the trend described at the beginning of this chapter, that is, the shift towards a widely shared view of caste as a form of broadly homogenised ethnicity or 'imagined community' with powerful moral claims and entitlements. Since Independence, such views have been closely bound up with expressions of hostility towards the non-martial tiller; they have derived much of their bitterness from resentment of the 'middle-peasant''s supposed economic advantages. Equally salient, however, has been the fact that such people as Patidars have been so widely praised and courted in Indian public life. Since the 1930s, Gandhian nationalists have exalted the virtues of Indian villagers. Under Gandhi's influence, the productive 'son of the soil' became the Indian National Congress's image of the Indian *lok* or 'masses'. Here local values and concepts of 'community' (i.e. caste identities) have met and interacted with the great themes of the country's recent history.

David Pocock's classic anthropological studies revealed that the Gujarat *sat-sudra* peasants who had adopted the prestigious designation 'Patidar' distinguished themselves from humbler cultivators, notably Kanbis and Kolis, through the vigour with which they pursued schemes of competitive honour and marriage-making within their home regions. To be Patidar when these observations were made

---

[42] Shah 1990: 103–4; figures from Gould 1990: 365.

in the 1960s and 1970s was therefore to proclaim ancestral roots in a locality where 'good' marriageable Patidars were known to reside. By definition, this was not a place of dubious repute, meaning one in which the inhabitants were either Kanbi- or Koli-like in their living habits, giving bride-price instead of dowry, or performing blood sacrifice and openly consuming alcohol. In south India too there are comparable zones of high farming where the physical features of the village or 'native place' have been found to define and sustain the virtues of the sober, credit-worthy 'peasant'.[43]

As was seen in Chapter 5, in many cash-crop regions the origins of these ideals of the worthy 'peasant' way of life involved long-term success in commodity production, as well as adherence to devotional Vaishnavism, and the impact of overseas migration and colonial ethnographic stereotyping. As a result, the use of the superior 'peasant' jati title Patidar and its numerous regional equivalents has come to convey a message that is still widely recognised. This is a message of well-deserved gains achieved at the expense of thriftless people, meaning both the 'unclean' toiler and the girasi-like man of ease. This is certainly what Gandhians and Nehruvian modernisers have seen when looking at such people as the blood-spilling Koli and the swaggering, mustachioed Rajput: not valorous preservers of order, but hangovers from a bad 'feudal' past, and oppressors of the good, worthy son of the soil.

Furthermore, in the case of Gujarat it is widely known that 'peasants' of Patidar origin were among the earliest rural recruits to the anti-colonial 'freedom struggle'.[44] Therefore, the Patidar who celebrates his distinctive caste identity through the exaltation of sobriety and pacific Vaishnavism is in effect being a good son of the Gandhian nation. Those who knew and emulated the superior Patidar's version of 'peasant' conventions were widely idealised both before and after Independence as simple sages in homespun (Gandhian khadi), authentically rustic, but also responsive when called to the national cause. This message was reinforced by the fact that Vallabhai Patel, a leading figure in Nehru's cabinet and one of the most prominent Indian politicians of the twentieth century, was systematically represented in public life both as Patel the peasant 'khedut' and Patel the Patidar. The

---

[43] Pocock 1972, 1973; Daniel 1984.
[44] Hardiman 1981.

two were mutually reinforcing. It was a great asset to Congress that Patel, their 'Iron *Sirdar*', was so widely known to the electorate as an embodiment of 'peasant'/Patidar values. This idealisation of 'community' gave the impersonal force of nationhood a human face, the face of a 'peasant' with heroic strengths and virtues.[45]

Again though, the response to these messages reflected the intersection of local and external views of the caste Hindu's *dharma*. The ability to show that one is not of unknown or suspect origins is obviously of great importance in environments where long-distance migration has been common for many centuries, and where the unsettled mobile populations of raiders, 'tribals' and roaming pastoralists are known to have lived in uncomfortable proximity to the *satsudra* 'caste Hindu' peasant. Given the delicate gradations of honour and genealogy which, at least in the recent past, distinguished the superior 'son of the soil' from lowlier rural groups, it has clearly paid to advertise the trappings of 'peasant' virtue, that is, the virtue of the settled *kisan* whose gains are derived from stability and the meritorious use of his skill and acumen.

These considerations could even be made to accommodate the 'peasant''s familiarity with Gandhian social precepts. A willingness to encourage the remarriage of widows was an established test of progressive credentials, and, as good nationalists, a given clean-caste 'community' might therefore be expected to adjust accordingly. Yet an equally strong legacy of social and ideological changes in previous centuries was the pressure on superior men of the soil to treat widow marriage as a sign of lowly warrior-pastoralist descent. Here, though, the open-endedness of 'caste' values came readily to the rescue. The Patidar of modest means could say that the practices of the 'reform'-minded were appropriate only to those of the greatest wealth and standing within the 'community', indeed that it was unseemly for humbler people to go so far beyond the safety net of known everyday proprieties. To be a Gandhi is a goal unattainable by ordinary men: in real life very few could be expected to embrace the highest and most rarefied codes of propriety.[46]

---

[45] Breman 1985: 99, 136–7.
[46] Thus in villages visited by Pocock in the 1960s, one could be a meat-eating Patidar and a Patidar who worshipped blood-taking divinities. Here too conventions that might be proper for the 'superior' and affluent would have been signs of undue pretension in those of lesser means and status. Pocock 1972: 68–9; compare Parry 1979.

These then are 'caste Hindus' for whom caste identity has remained notably open-ended, despite the trend towards a more Brahmanical view of worth, order and purity in everyday life. Among Patidars and their counterparts in other rural areas, such standards will still leave room for doubt, for the need to prove oneself and one's kin as being of 'good' quality, and therefore unlike the thriftless meat-eater or servile toiler. In a world of material uncertainty, the match of every worthy 'peasant' remains a test of achievement and worth, and the parameters remain extremely wide, without fixed definitions of the behaviour that might secure a 'good' match, or a reputation for conformity to the superior version of a Patidar, Vellala or Jat way of life. On the contrary, the post-Independence Patidar or a Vellala was found to belong to a 'community' in the sense that he or she claimed an established caste title and a reputation for high moral endowments, but no body of universally shared custom, no uniform diet or rituals, no standard rate of marriage expenditure or period of death pollution.

Yet with all its variations and diversities, the everyday life of the caste-conscious 'peasant' has played a critical role in shaping the ways in which both rural and urban Indians have come to understand the phenomenon of caste. Anthropologists have found remarkable flexibility in these manifestations of modern caste life, and yet at the same time a notably clear understanding of what it means to belong to a worthy 'peasant' jati. This rests on a sense of affinity which is both open-ended and demanding in its consciousness of rank, and its claims of differentiation between those of superior and lesser blood.

The other element to stress here is how strongly this consciousness of 'substantialised' caste ideals has been reinforced by the rhetoric of the all-India political arena. The pervasiveness of claims about 'peasant' virtues as the values of modern patriotic Indians has kept alive a perception of certain modern or 'substantialised' forms of caste as a strong and valid force in national life. The sturdy Jat, the valorous Khatri and the humbly virtuous Chamar or Bhangi have all been repeatedly told that while some manifestations of jati and varna convention are bad, backward or 'casteist', it is nevertheless modern and progressive to identify with the heritage and entitlements of one's 'community'. It is by this means that the party boss may tell voters that he embodies the will and character of a 'community', and that by acting as their guardian or instrument he has thereby transcended considerations of career and personal gain.

As seen in Chapter 7, this is what the Janata leader Charan Singh did, communicating a message of strength and populist mission to his electorate by cultivating the image of Charan Singh the 'Jat' and Charan Singh the larger-than-life champion of the common man. The two interlocked all the more successfully because this use of familiar caste stereotypes left no doubt about who and what Charan Singh was opposing. In the 1977 electoral campaign he made much of the Janata caricature of Congress as a Brahman-run clique. And when his political rival the Gujarati ex-Congressman Morarji Desai was chosen to lead the fragile Janata coalition, Charan Singh bemoaned this as yet another unjust assertion of conspiratorial Brahmanism in Indian public life. Such charges are still both made and refuted in ways which convey to the electorate that caste is real, and that jati and varna identity have meaning in the modern environment as a source of collective entitlements and moral mandates.

CASTE CONVENTIONS IN EVERYDAY LIFE

Of course, these messages from the public arena did not of themselves keep caste conventions alive in the everyday world; indeed in many cases they have been contested by trends and messages which were far from favourable to those promoting the claims of caste-based 'community'. Yet, despite the great diversity of India's social and political experience since Independence, awareness of both 'substantialised' and 'traditional' jati and varna norms continues to be transmitted from one generation to another, subtly changing to accommodate new circumstances, and yet persistently recapitulating messages about the importance of preserving and perpetuating one's 'community'. These features of Indian life have been extensively documented in accounts of both town and village experience from the 1950s through to the 1990s.

In the anthropologist R. S. Khare's account of the typical north Indian 'hearth and home' (published in 1976), the forms of service enacted were far more elaborate than those of the urban households described at the beginning of this chapter. Among the 'twice-born' villagers whom he observed, Khare found women devoting great care to the supervision of specialist cooks, water-carriers and pollution-removers, each from a different named jati group. There were the Kahar, for example, whose occupational specialities have been reported since the colonial period as the carrying of palanquins (sedan chairs), the carrying of water, and the purification of household cooking areas with cow-dung.[47] These specialities all have important ritual connotations: palanquins are still widely used in marriages and other ceremonial occasions, and the milk and dung of cows have been employed for centuries as temple and household sanctifying substances. In the locales which Khare studied, the retention of specialised service-providers was still regarded as an act which defined thread-wearing Kanyakubja and Bhumihar Brahman householders as persons of worth and substance. Even families with experience of 'modern' consumer products chose to persist with these routines despite the availability of affordable labour-saving alternatives. Prosperous villagers ate 'Western-style' foods from factory-made chinaware which they washed with commercial detergents. Yet these households maintained a separate hearth equipped with brass and bronze vessels to be used for 'traditional' food; cleansing in this case was carried out with 'traditional' materials possessing ritual purifying properties.[48]

In many cases, superior thread-wearing villagers and low-status service groups have been equally determined to sustain such networks and conventions. This may seem surprising given the efforts of early twentieth-century 'caste reform' movements to persuade lowly specialists like the Kahar to repudiate ideas of collective ritual inferiority by insisting that their water-carrying services were merely a form of wage labour, to be freely entered into like any other.[49] Yet it is clear from modern anthropological evidence that people of Kahar birth often have little choice but to sustain themselves through the cleansing of twice-born hearths. This may well be the best livelihood available in areas where land and employment are scarce, even though such work defines the Kahar as a service-giver who contributes to other people's dharmic correctness, and therefore lower in *zat* essence than the householders who pay for his services.

In many other ways too, and despite all that the 'secular' Constitution has to say about the ideal of a casteless and classless India, the

---

[47] Khare 1976.
[48] *Ibid.*
[49] Pinch 1996: 111 discusses one such early polemic enjoining Kahars to see themselves as a population of noble Kshatriyas who were entitled to follow modern livelihoods carrying no connotations of ritualised clientage or dependency.

logic of rank and 'community' still pervades the etiquette of everyday life. In Tamilnad, cosmopolitan 'peasants' with long-standing experience of overseas migration and far-flung commercial interests were found in the 1980s to speak of themselves in 'fluid' terms as being shaped by the unique balance of essences that characterise the soil, air and water of their particular *ur* or natal locality.[50] And even in localities where the prosperous clean-caste 'peasant' has access to satellite television and the internet, Jat and Bhumihar parents may still teach their children to avoid the shadow and touch of the Chamar. The Thakur and the Kurmi might send their children to the same school, but will be unlikely to smoke together in the tea shop; and at the public watering-places which still supply so many rural households, the Thakur's wife will expect to fill her bucket ahead of women of lesser *sat-sudra* status.

Correct conduct often matters more than ever in these 'modern' environments, especially in the demands it places on women. A 'modern' woman's husband, sons and even unmarried daughters may well earn a wage in a multi-caste workplace. But even where women themselves are employed outside the home, it is still primarily the task of wives and mothers to counteract the inescapable pollutions which afflict their households by undergoing fasts and penances, and by supervising the cleansings, tonsurings and other rituals that identify the household with the conventions of their 'kind'. So the Hindu 'caste person' is not really man-in-society, if this is taken to mean a male whose existence is radically unlike that of the renouncer who transcends worldly ties of kin and caste. Now more than ever, respectability in caste terms may depend on what a household's women do on both of these fronts, meaning their activities as guardians of the family's jati and varna endowments, and also their periodic forays into the renouncer's way of life.

The conventions defining this kind of respectable caste lifestyle may be subtly or even openly subverted by 'Dalit' labourers and service-providers, in some cases through oral traditions which give a distinctive gloss to ideologies of hierarchy and pollution.[51] They can also be at least partly suspended in the appropriate context, for example in the

---

[50] Daniel 1984.
[51] Prakash 1990a, 1991.

ecstatic communion of pilgrims on the road to a Ganges bathing site or a great south Indian hill shrine.[52] This apparent castelessness is also a feature of the giant *melas* or worshippers' concourses that have become one of the hallmarks of contemporary devotional Hinduism. Yet on these occasions 'casteless' pilgrims commonly seek the services of Brahmans and hereditary ritualists from other named jati groups. Furthermore, as Parry has shown, there is generally a subtle interplay between the ascetic, renunciatory and apparently caste-denying or transcendent features of these pilgrimage experiences, and the elements which emphasise fulfilment of dharmic caste duty.[53] And whether alone or in a bus load of fellow villagers, the fasting barefoot pilgrim on the road to the shrines of Banaras or Sabirimalai follows conventions that only temporarily approximate to an ideal of caste-free unworldliness and renunciation. They apply when approaching an abode of divinity, but are not expected to dissolve the claims of caste in everyday town or village life. So these moments of wholly or partially casteless renunciation implicitly acknowledge the inescapability of worldly ties. Few would deny that there are claims of kin, blood and jati that must reassert themselves when the questing pilgrim returns to the life of the ordinary householder.[54]

Of course it is not just as a devotee that a villager or city-dweller can suspend the conventions of rank and 'community'. In a crowded bus or railway carriage the touch of an unknown Chamar or Paraiyan carries no lasting danger; and, of necessity, strangers address one another in neutral casteless language. On their home terrain, too, the Thakur landlord and Koiri ploughman may joke and share a cigarette in the fields, but when they re-enter their home village's streets the lower-caste man still uses formalised terms of deference to those of superior birth. He may even be expected to remove his shoes or shirt like a pious suppliant before entering the lanes where his thread-wearing superiors reside.[55]

These conventions allow for complex shadings and variations and may well reflect distinctions of wealth and power as well as birth. The

[52] Daniel 1984: 245–87; Gold 1988: 268–9, esp. n. 5; Karve 1988.
[53] Parry 1994; also works cited in note 52, above.
[54] Menon's study (1994: 40–61) provides a typology of regional temple worship in Kerala, with different types of festivals either confirming, challenging or disregarding 'traditional' caste hierarchies.
[55] See, for example, Deliège 1992, 1993.

village 'big man' of high caste will be spoken to more respectfully than a person of high caste who lacks means or strong local political affiliations. Even so, within those sensitive zones of 'hearth and home' where personal conduct and standards of household purity are closely scrutinised, it is widely expected that the Rajput speaks, dresses and behaves like a Rajput, and that he and his mustachioed kin will have a stake in policing the boundaries between those of different 'blood' or kind.

What then of the many recent studies which maintain that Indians of low or untouchable rank systematically deploy 'weapons of the weak' as a reaction against the conventions of a caste-based moral order? Clearly, everyday life and worship may sometimes provide the means by which members of the 'subaltern' classes can seek to contest or evade the principles of caste. This is what 'Dalits' are held to achieve when they use coded language to caricature the pretensions of the lordly, or when they build a critique of high-caste injustices into the cults of blood-taking goddesses and avenger divinities.[56] There are also forms of modern *bhakti* devotional faith which reshape the traditions of the Vaishnavite and Shaivite 'high gods', extolling the lowly Jatav/Chamar as a morally superior exemplar to the sinful caste Hindu.[57]

Yet if these are best seen as forms of 'resistance', such moves do not indicate unawareness of the conventions which make caste real and pervasive in rural society. Indeed, there is strong anthropological evidence to suggest that it is relatively low-ranking people, and not those who are usually thought of as purest and highest in varna terms, who are inclined to emphasise hierarchical caste logic in their everyday expressions of devotional faith.[58]

This would seem to be consistent with the findings of many fieldworkers about the enduring power of the pollution barrier for both high- and low-caste people throughout the country. Significantly, these researchers report that regardless of what the law and the Constitution have said about the abolition of untouchability, high or 'clean-caste' people respond very consistently when their views are probed about the status and identity of Harijan/Dalits, both in their localities and in the country at large. The findings here are that clean-

[56] Menon 1994; Lorenzen 1987.
[57] Khare 1984.
[58] Fuller 1988.

caste people generally regard all those whom they know to be of Harijan/untouchable origin as permanently polluted and unclean in ritual terms, without any further differentiation between them. On this basis it seems correct to argue that the paramount manifestation of caste in Indian life today is not so much the phenomenon of 'substantialisation' as it was reported on in the 1970s, but the distinction between those who can proclaim clean-caste origin and those whom higher-caste people can stigmatise as *avarna*, i.e. innately unclean and polluted.

Furthermore, it has been found that in contrast to this generalising view of untouchables, which appears to be widely shared by members of 'clean' castes, those who are known to belong to specific 'Scheduled' or 'Dalit' caste groups make a crucial distinction on this matter. These low-caste populations reportedly differentiate between the quality and nature of their own and other people's untouchability. It is members of *other* low-caste groups who are permanently and inherently polluted in the eyes of the north Gujarat Bhangi 'scavengers' and other 'unclean' informants who were studied by Shalini Randeria in the 1980s. 'Our' pollution, say these same Harijan/untouchables, is a consequence of having accidentally violated a known norm of dharmic conduct; 'our' uncleanliness is therefore reversible rather than innate and enduring.[59]

It is notable that in neither case do these Harijan/untouchables actually appear to question or reject the concept of ritual pollution itself. Nor is there evidence of a sense of common identity uniting those who belong to different 'unclean' or *avarna* jati groups.[60] Furthermore, even instances of so-called Dalit 'resistance' still commonly take their language and symbolism from the logic of caste. Thus, far from ignoring or repudiating the 'twice-born' man's distinctive caste markers, the militant Harijan makes a point of sporting upturned Rajput-style moustaches, knowing full well that such a signal is as recognisable and provocative in certain modern-day localities as it was in the days of the Raj.[61]

Despite the fact that ideas about the power and reality of caste,

---

[59] Randeria 1989; as noted in the Introduction, there has been much debate about whether members of low castes share or reject perceptions of their ritual inferiority.

[60] See, for example, Bose 1985b: 146 on the refusal by low-caste Mangs and Dhors to ally with Mahar victims of the 1978 'caste war' outbreaks (discussed in Chapter 9, below).

[61] Kamble 1981: 133.

pollution and untouchability are so widely shared in Indian society, 'caste society' should not be seen as static, unchanging and harmonious. Quite the contrary: without subscribing to a simplistic idea of India as a domain of universal high-caste oppression and Dalit 'resistance', one can see that in the India of the 1990s a significant proportion of regional and pan-Indian economic and social conflict has come to be bound up with claims of caste-based solidarity and moral mandate. It is this painful and controversial aspect of post-Independence caste life which the final chapter will explore.

CHAPTER 9

'CASTE WARS' AND THE MANDATE OF VIOLENCE

INTRODUCTION

Both today and in the past, the language and conventions of caste have proclaimed the value of absolute standards and proprieties, while accommodating uncertainty, change and conflict in both public and private life. While this has involved coercion as well as acts of 'resistance', Indians of many different backgrounds have found that both the exclusions and bonds of caste could help them to adapt and prosper in conditions of insecurity. This has been the case particularly for the struggling landed groups discussed in previous chapters. It has been evident above all where such people have moved to claim supremacy over lower-caste tenants and labourers, both in the nineteenth century and in the age of computerised communications, modern wage labour and mass electoral politics.

This chapter will focus on the second of the two manifestations of caste consciousness identified in Chapter 8 – the phenomenon of so-called caste war. In the decades of post-Independence 'new agrarianism' and its turbulent aftermath, appeals to both 'traditional' and 'substantialised' forms of caste solidarity have continued to put real power into the hands of those who feel wronged and insecure. This is nowhere more apparent than in the outbreaks of mass violence for which academics and journalists have coined such terms as 'caste war', 'caste feud', 'caste battle' and even 'caste genocide'. For all their crudeness these expressions are used by a wide range of commentators, including many leftists who might be expected to portray these confrontations as a story of casteless 'subaltern' solidarities and class conflicts.

What then is 'caste war'? Why has it been so widely accepted that caste can divide modern Indians to the point of systematic armed violence between those of high- and low-caste origin? Many social scientists have explored the local issues of tenancy, labour and landlessness which have underpinned these conflicts. Yet regardless of their political stance, most analysts are aware that class factors generally do not stand on their own in these situations. They know too that the rhetoric and organisation of those who make common cause in these outbreaks generally rest on the militantly exclusive or 'substantialised' perceptions of caste described in Chapter 8, that is, caste as a moral mandate which sanctions aggression against those of unlike *zat* or essence.

Predictably enough, these conflicts have also featured more 'traditional' expressions of caste, emphasising sub-caste hierarchy and multi-caste interdependencies of service and exchange. Indeed, so-called 'caste war' is one of the key areas of contemporary life in which these two fluid yet resilient variants of caste ideology have tended to intertwine and reinforce one another. Thus groups who share common interests as landlords, tenants or labourers often use both forms of caste language when they seek to recruit fighting allies. What has been said in such cases is, in effect, 'join us as Bhumihars, Jats or Kshatriyas; restore *dharma* by avenging the wrongs done to you by impure and unrighteous Dalits'.

In these troubled regions those who might otherwise stand together on a basis of shared material interest will therefore tend instead to give priority to considerations of caste. Poor Bhumihars will thus find it natural to join forces with rich Bhumihar landlords in attacks on 'Dalit' labourers or dwarf-holders whose economic circumstances are virtually indistinguishable from their own. Such alliances do not always prevail at the expense of more straightforwardly class-based mobilisations, but they have certainly been common enough to merit analysis.

THE TENSIONS OF THE COUNTRYSIDE

When commentators refer to the phenomenon of 'caste war', they generally have in mind the types of conflict that first began to be observed in both 'backward' and extensively commercialised agricultural regions during the late 1960s. One of the most widely reported of these early outbreaks was a grisly mass murder in the Tanjore (Thanjavur) region of the Tamilnad rice-belt, at a time of bitterly contested Communist-led labour agitation. This 1968 Kilvenmani massacre was one of the first such incidents to be reported in the pan-Indian news media in terms which cited caste as the decisive factor in the defining of both allies and opponents. As in the thousands of subsequent cases of this kind, this reportage emphasised the fact that the Kilvenmani victims were all rural labourers of ex-untouchable or Harijan descent; the perpetrators were allegedly agents of local 'caste Hindu' landowners.[1]

The area of Tanjore where this outbreak occurred still has a disproportionately large labouring population of untouchable/Harijan origin. Much has been written about the complex interplay of caste and class factors in such outbreaks. They have tended to occur in regions where deep hostilities were generated out of the adoption of high-yield 'Green Revolution' crop strains and the resulting commercialisation of smallholder grain production. As in other parts of India, better-off proprietors responded to the high cost of new cultivation inputs by mechanising their production, or by importing cheaper labourers from elsewhere.

Together with Kerala state, this was one of the few Indian regions with a tradition of rural Communist recruitment dating back to the 1940s, and thus a high degree of 'political consciousness' among a large group of people who were simultaneously very poor and very low in caste terms.[2] But the commentators who believe that much of India has been or is in the grip of 'caste feuds' have discerned similar polarisations – and a similar appeal to the presumed solidarities of jati and varna in times of economic insecurity – in a wide variety of other rural and urban regions. This has included areas where wealth has been more evenly distributed than in deltaic Tamilnad, and where regional caste 'systems' have apparently been far more open and fluid than those of the Kilvenmani area.

Thus, comparatively rich areas of Maharashtra, Karnataka, UP and Gujarat, as well as exceptionally deprived regions of Bihar and the dry-grain zones of Tamilnad, have all been badly hit by so-called caste war outbreaks since the 1970s. In these conflicts, it has been consistently reported that the battle lines have been drawn on the basis of 'community', meaning jati and varna divisions, or the newer umbrella categories of OBC ('Other Backwards') and Dalit ('the oppressed') – a term most commonly applied to Harijan/untouchables, though sometimes to 'tribals' and poor Muslims as well. Another widely used term in these confrontations is 'Manuvadi elite'. Like other pejorative

---

[1] Gough 1989: 186–9, 446–62, 527; Béteille 1996; Rudolph and Rudolph 1987: 378–87.
[2] Gough 1989: 446–62; compare Menon 1994.

phrases such as 'sons of Manu', this has become a blanket term for those who use the titles and symbols of ritually superior birth. In the populist polemics of UP's 'Dalit'-based BSP party, this generally means Brahmans and anyone else who can be held to have benefited unjustly from the teachings of *The Laws of Manu* and other dharmic texts.[3]

It is true that those involved in so-called caste wars since the 1960s have generally mixed the language of jati and varna with references to faith, class and nationality, defining themselves and their opponents not just as embodiments of caste-based 'community', but as landlords and tenants, capitalists and workers, oppressors and oppressed. In many such cases the caste factor has sometimes faded out completely, particularly in situations where the Hindu–Muslim divide has become a more compelling focus for local fears and enmities.

Nevertheless, so-called caste war is no mere orientalist fantasy. According to government figures, there were 40,000 anti-Harijan 'atrocities' between 1966 and 1976, this being the period of Indira Gandhi's so-called 'decade of development'. Another 17,000 such incidents were officially recorded for the nineteen months of Janata rule (March 1977–January 1980). Tamilnadu, Maharashtra, Gujarat and the Gangetic north Indian states have been the worst hit areas. In 1981 a total of 1,429 officially designated 'crimes against Harijans' were reported in UP, compared with only eight in Bengal and ninety-four in Kerala. From the mid-1980s to the late 1990s, accounts of such attacks remained a prominent feature of home affairs press coverage in many states including Tamilnadu, UP, Maharashtra and Gujarat. Worst of all has been Bihar, where as of January 1995 more people had reportedly died in 'caste war' outbreaks than in the whole of the six-year conflict between Muslim separatists and the Indian security forces in Kashmir.[4]

---

[3] 'Caste and caste oppression were invented by Manu, the son of a Brahmin' (*Frontline* news magazine interview with BSP spokeswoman, 11 March 1994: 13) For pre-1980 anti-untouchable outbreaks see Kamble 1981, documenting several hundred violent 'caste war' incidents occurring between 1947 and 1979 on the basis of regional newspaper reports. More recent 'caste war' attacks are regularly reported in the vernacular and English-language press: see Omvedt 1982: 9–37.

[4] Though see Brass 1997, especially pp. 128–76 on the selectiveness with which violent incidents may be reported and publicised as caste-based outbreaks. Figures from *EPW* 12 May 1979: 845; Alam 1989: 238; Hasan 'Class and caste', in Hasan *et al.* 1989: 269 n. 34. For anthropological interpretations of mass violence in south Asia, see Das 1990 and Tambiah 1996. And see Hawthorn 1984.

These bald statistics convey little on their own. What is evident is that in almost every part of India, conflicting assertions of organised 'kisan' power, landlord rights and Dalit protest have interacted with one another in ways which have tended to affirm the claims of caste. Most of these affirmations have emphasised the notion of the jati as a community of merit, worth and prowess, though Brahmanical concepts of varna have featured too in portrayals of the caste Hindu's 'Dalit' enemy as meritless, impure and anarchic.

Such appeals have been effective because they conjure up both the image and the reality of resources pooled and mobilised on behalf of a very broad array of allies: all 'Jats', all 'Rajputs' or 'Kshatriyas', all 'Dalits'. So at least for purposes of appealing to the state or fighting a named corporate enemy, large numbers of modern Indians have chosen to represent themselves as sharers in an exclusive bond of moral community, setting aside differentiations of rank and status which might still apply in other contexts.

Although its roots were in localised tensions within individual states and regions, by the early 1970s the 'caste feud' phenomenon had acquired a crucial all-India dimension. The context for this was the Naxalite panics which are still a feature of many troubled rural areas. (The term Naxalite refers to small groups of revolutionaries who attempted to wage Maoist-style 'class war' from rural bases in the Naxalbari region of West Bengal; the term has since been applied to many other regional conflicts involving both 'peasant' and 'tribal' militants.) Bihar has been particularly notorious as a zone of so-called Naxalite violence, especially in those areas which came to prominence through the depredations of paramilitary 'syndicates' known as *senas* or 'righteous armies'. When these organisations were formed in the 1970s, much of rural Bihar was experiencing a wave of tenant and labourers' agitations, with many violent attacks on landlords and other 'class enemies'. Police and other officials applied the label Naxalite to these militants, and the state government apparently cooperated with large landowners in the recruitment and training of anti-'Naxalite' self-defence units, the *senas*.[5]

In central and north Bihar, armed bodies with such titles as Bhumi Sena, Kuer Sena, Lorik Sena and Brahmharshi Sena were implicated in

---

[5] Many *senas* are said to have links through the police and local political bosses to rural 'dacoit' (criminal) gangs and the urban criminal underworld. Frankel 1989: 115–24.

attacks on localities containing real or imaginary insurgents. The term *sena* has strong devotional connotations, evoking the ideal of the Hindu warrior who fights for his lord in a spirit of selfless piety. Although their purpose was clearly to coerce and intimidate assertive tenants and labourers, these self-professed armies of the righteous represented themselves as defenders of caste-defined 'community' interests against the depredations of a low-caste 'Naxalite' enemy. The Brahmharshi Sena was thus widely recognised as a 'Bhumihar' militia. Although its key backers were clearly embattled landowners, this *sena*'s youthful fighters reputedly included the sons of both poor and prosperous rural families bearing arms together in the name of an embattled Bhumihar 'community'. The Lorik Sena and Samajvadi Shosit Sena both recruited from the Ahir-Yadav 'community', and the Patna region's much-feared Bhumi Sena drew its membership from youths of Kurmi origin. There was also an all-Rajput Kuer Sena which took its name from a famous hero of the 1857 Mutiny-Rebellion, Kuer or Kunwar Singh, a figure known in the Gangetic north as an embodiment of Rajput virtues and valour.[6]

The implication in all this was that *sena*s used violence in a worthy cause and were indifferent to personal gain: their fighters were righters of wrongs, and those whom they attacked were enemies of right-eousness. The use of the term *bhumi* by the Kurmi-based Bhumi Sena added a further dimension to these caste-centred appeals. What was being alluded to here was the cry of 'land to the tiller' which had been widely popularised in both the pre- and post-Independence periods by India's many regional peasant associations (*kisan samitis*). When these bodies called for redress on behalf of the sturdy son-of-the-soil or *bhumi*, they extolled the 'peasant' smallholder as a man of simple rustic virtue who had been deprived of primordial rights in land by devious outsiders.

The new forms of agrarian populism which became widespread in the 1970s evoked much the same ideal, identifying both the money-lender and the squireen landlord as enemies of this *bhumi* son-of-the-soil. Yet this still left ample scope for vilification of the Harijan or 'tribal' who had been encouraged to 'encroach' on the *bhumi*'s lands by the representatives of an allegedly corrupt and unjust state. So this Kurmi-dominated Bhumi paramilitary, like the armed groups who

---

[6] *EPW* 4 Jan. 1986: 15–18; 5 July 1986: 1146–7; 30 Aug. 1986: 1533; Frankel 1989: 122.

have claimed to speak for the interests of 'clean-caste' tillers in other states, were telling the world that their actions were divinely mandated. When its members burnt out a Harijan village, defiled its women and destroyed its crops, their justification was that they were an army called forth both by the state and by divine will to right the wrongs of those who had suffered at the hands of unworthy enemies, and that their claims to contested land and labour were inherently righteous.

None of this was or is an expression of 'primordial' caste sentiment. Nor can it be seen in crude terms as a creation of colonialism, though colonial experience is certainly relevant here. Present-day Indians would probably find the idea of 'caste war' less credible were it not for the legacy of both Indian and European ethnological theories, with their emphasis on claims of primordial loss and entitlement on the part of races and caste-based 'communities'. Yet such developments as the rise of the Bihar caste *senas* have been brought about primarily by contemporary experience. The critical factor here has been the recognition that there are real gains to be made by those who act on a vision of caste as a bond of entitlement and moral allegiance. As was seen in Chapter 7, such ideas had come to be widely endorsed by 'modern' politicians, and by the spokesmen for both 'peasant' and Kshatriya-model caste associations. In the cases cited here, it was insecure descendants of the old patrician landed groups who took the important initiatives.

Since the early 1970s, the activism of groups who call themselves Dalits has been the other central element in these confrontations. Many of their founders gave the new all-'Dalit' organisations intentionally provocative names. These include Maharashtra's Dalit Panthers, a name chosen in conscious imitation of American 'Black Power' militants, and the Bhumiheen Sangharsh Samiti ('the landless people's fighting front') which was formed in the late 1970s in one of the UP's most troubled rural regions by Chamar and other Harijan smallholders and landless labourers. Not surprisingly, those whom the militant tenants' and labourers' unions were calling their 'oppressors' claimed in response that appeals to shared Jatness or Rajputness were the landed man's best defence in troubled times.[7]

For landlords and non-Harijan tillers, it was especially alarming that these 'Dalit' activists were echoing the mixture of Gandhian and

[7] *EPW* 3 Feb. 1984: 184–6.

Marxist themes that had been invoked since the 1950s to justify new state policy initiatives. How then to counter this idea of the Dalit as heir to a superior moral mandate, and in a way that was calculated to impress politicians and planners at state and central government level? We have seen that by the early 1970s precariously placed landed people in several states had revived the institutional forms of the early twentieth-century caste associations (*samitis* and *sabhas*). In the past, the caste organisations which had spoken for 'peasant' jatis had told such people as Jats, Kurmis and Kammas that they had earned their comparative wealth and prestige by being pious and respectable, and by subduing 'uncivilised' people, meaning so-called tribals and Gujar-like 'predators'. Now these platforms were used to tell the hard-working Jat or Bhumihar that although he had safely survived the vagaries of the land-ceiling laws, his achievements and 'cultured' virtues were facing a new threat from refractory 'Dalits'.

In Gujarat this meant in particular the groups known as Dublas, who in this period were confronting clean-caste landowners with demands for more favourable tenancy and share-cropping arrange-ments, as well as cultivation rights on so-called waste and grazing land.[8] In Patidar *samiti* journals, the Dubla 'community' was reviled by name as a body of thriftless inferiors who were threatening the region's peace and productivity by evading their inherited mandate to labour and serve. Such militant 'Dalit' groups were therefore stigma-tised on two counts at once. They were reviled as 'Naxalite' insurgents fomenting sedition and criminality, and at the same time as enemies of caste order (*dharma*) to be fought by the righteous 'caste Hindu' with the weapons of community and moral mandate.[9]

THE MANDATE OF RIGHTEOUS VIOLENCE

There are obvious echoes in all this of the messages emanating from the 'smash poverty' campaigners and agrarian populists who exalted the wisdom and simplicity of the 'masses', and extolled the virtues of the peasant who knows when to invoke force in a righteous cause. Caste themes were prominent too in the mass farmers' rallies and

[8] As was seen in Chapter 5, the title Dubla refers to former 'tribals' whose ancestors were squeezed into the region's volatile commercial economy as so-called plough servants (*halpatis*).
[9] Breman 1985.

other assertions of 'peasant' power which transformed political life in the late 1970s in much of the south, as well as in Gujarat, Maharashtra and the Hindustan Green Revolution belt. This emphasis on the professed moral mandate of caste became even more conspicuous in the giant *rasta roko* (literally 'block the road') campaigns of the early 1980s. These involved the orchestration of vast rail and lorry convoys bringing the homespun-clad 'masses' to chant the message of *'kisan'* protest before the seats of state and national government. Well into the 1990s, in north India's volatile Green Revolution belt in particular, the ideal of shared jati virtues has continued to be much cited in displays of hostility to state policies and institutions which were held to embody the effeteness and un-Indian cosmopolitanism of Nehruvian Brahmans and other enemies of the 'people'.[10]

In the fertile plains tracts of western UP, the so-called mass mobilisations of commodity-producing smallholders have persistently been staged as celebrations of Jatness. This is a region where, even before the British conquest, a high proportion of productive land was in the hands of entrepreneurial grain-growers identifying themselves as Jat. At the so-called 'monster rallies' or mass 'peasant' assemblages of the late 1970s, those attending were addressed as sharers in the Jat 'community' tradition known as the *sarv-khap*, literally clan-territory assemblies. The *sarv-khap* was again invoked in UP by a new array of militant 'farmers' movements' which came to prominence in the Hindi-belt states in the 1980s. This has been most notable in the case of the Indian Peasants' Union or BKU (Bharatiya Kisan Union), widely characterised as being run by and for the Jat 'community' of UP, Punjab and Haryana.[11]

The ideal of *sarv-khap* clanship as a bond of allegiance and moral obligation has been widely identified as a 'traditional' characteristic of Jat social organisation. Colonial officials reported that clan-based Jat 'brotherhoods' supported one another with exceptional cohesiveness at the time of the 1857 Mutiny-Rebellion. This solidarity has been seen as deriving from schemes of time-honoured regional political jurisdiction and kin-based landholding (*bhaiachara* or 'brotherhood'

---

[10] Hasan 1994; Naik 1989: 100–12. In rural Gujarat, organisations staging 'peasant' agitations in the late 1980s were strongly criticised by rival groups for being too closely bound up with the interests of the Patidar 'community'. See Banaji 1994: 232.

[11] *EPW* 3 Feb. 1979: 184–5; Hasan 1994: 183; Hasan *et al.* 1989: Gill 1994: 205–7. On the *sarv-khap*, see Chapter 1, p. 37.

proprietorship).[12] Of course, it is possible that the power of the *sarv-khap* bond was much exaggerated by colonial ethnographers; certainly, clan-based Jat bride-exchange networks may have been more a caste reformist's ideal of enclosed or 'Sanskritising' marriage circles than a real feature of 'peasant'/*kisan* life. Yet, in the 1970s and 1980s tens of thousands of people did accept Jat 'community' summonses to the great '*kisan*' assemblages. Furthermore, those attending were reported to have been keenly receptive when told that they were heirs to a noble Jat heritage, and that to be summoned in the name of the Jat *sarv-khap* gave the force of righteous purpose to the community's goals and actions.

Such appeals have certainly been the signal for violent 'caste war' outbreaks, as in the case of the mass attacks on low-caste villages in the Kanjhawala region of UP in 1978. This was an area where landless labourers and dwarf-holders had been singled out to receive new holdings; these were to be taken from so-called 'surplus' land under the Janata government's policy of distributing cultivation leases to the rural poor. Local officials moved to implement this policy by transferring lands which had formerly been classed as grazing ground to the new leaseholders. It was widely known that most beneficiaries of the scheme would be of Jatav/Chamar origin, i.e. Harijan/untouchables. Both the Janata and Congress ministries implemented controversial schemes of this kind, with provision for landless members of the Scheduled Castes and Tribes to receive priority in the allocation of new leases.[13]

Existing owner-cultivators saw these schemes as threats to their fragile prosperity. In Kanjhawala, virtually all 'bullock capitalists' identified themselves as Jat; they were typical of the many plains-dwelling smallholders who had been poorly placed to exploit costly Green Revolution inputs. Marginal owner-occupiers of this kind generally possessed few assets apart from their 'clean-caste' status. Because such tillers can claim to possess a natural bond of blood with their better-off neighbours, officialdom has often turned a blind eye to their illicit use of tracts which appear on the record books as uncultivated 'waste' or grazing ground. This is the kind of situation that has made the issue of so-called waste, surplus or pasture lands especially sensitive in many areas, as for example in much of Gujarat,

---

[12] Stokes 1986: 129–42; Pradhan 1966.
[13] Hasan *et al.* 1989: 262.

Maharashtra and Bihar where otherwise vulnerable proprietors have evaded the land-ceiling restrictions by inducing officials to class part of their holdings as uncultivated or 'waste' terrain.[14]

In UP's 'caste war' zones, there were also pressures on richer Jat 'kisans'. Many of these areas were close enough to cities for poor villagers to take advantage of expanding urban employment prospects. This in turn encouraged those left on the land to bargain for higher wages. In areas like Kanjhawala virtually all the existing proprietary groups therefore had strong incentives to invoke Jatness as a bond of solidarity against this problematic local labour force, virtually all of whom were known to be Harijans and were thus being offered new cultivation leases. Richer farmers resented the lease schemes because they made their labourers even scarcer and costlier to employ, while turning others into potential competitors in the cash-crop market. Smaller 'bullock capitalists' were fearful of losing access to the so-called wastes. The outcome was the kind of systematic mass violence which was mobilised at 'monster rally' assemblages in the name of righteous Jat tillers preserving their 'traditional' land rights against usurpation by 'unvirtuous' Harijan-Chamars.[15]

Gujarat experienced comparable 'caste war' conflicts in 1981 after the Congress ministry launched a similar scheme, responding to the demands of 'Dalit' activists by pledging allocations of waste or surplus land to Dhed and Chamar untouchables. Smallholders of 'clean' Kanbi and Kadva Patidar origin blockaded and terrorised hamlets which they accused of harbouring 'Dalit' militants. Here too the spokesmen for local proprietors' interests reviled their opponents as ungodly revolutionaries whose challenges to clean-caste landowners sprang from their inherent baseness and impurity.[16]

It is this which has distinguished so-called 'caste war' from the agrarian conflicts of the colonial period. It is not that post-Independence India has been notably more violent than in the nineteenth or early twentieth centuries, when it was common for landowners to coerce and intimidate recalcitrant labourers and tenants, and to use the

---

[14] Kamble (1981) documents many such cases. See also Gagnik and Bhatt 1984.

[15] *EPW* 3 Feb. 1979: 184–6; Gill 1994: 207. See also Tambiah 1996 on the 1984 Delhi riots following the assassination of Indira Gandhi: rioters were widely identified in both caste and class terms, that is as predominantly Jat and Gujar ex-smallholders aggrieved about their poor compensation for lands near Delhi which had been swallowed up in urban expansion schemes.

[16] Gagnik and Bhatt 1984.

language of caste against them wherever this proved feasible. What has been different in recent times is that since the 1970s the ideals of the 'secular' nation-state have been regularly inverted by groups claiming to be under threat from the real or imagined aggression of militant 'Dalits'. This has allowed many of the victimisers to represent themselves both as victims and as embodiments of national virtue. Those claiming both patrician and non-elite kisan-khedut antecedents have thus encouraged others of their 'blood' and 'kind' to see themselves as sharers in a just cause, with both a right and a duty to punish the unworthy 'Dalit'/'Naxalite' whose actions have endangered both a specific clean-caste 'community' and the country at large. It has been on this basis that police forces and local newspapers have so often supported the victimisers rather than the victims in such attacks.

This can be seen most clearly in the violent outbreaks which engulfed much of Maharashtra in 1978, and again in 1985–6. The worst of these took place in the Marathwada region, which is yet another area where the spread of so-called Green Revolution cash crops enriched a minority of substantial 'clean-caste' landowners. These developments left poorer smallholders and labourers from the same non-polluting caste groups struggling to defend such small margins of advantage as they still possessed, often by insisting on the caste differentials separating them from 'unclean' populations, especially 'tribals' and those of Mahar origin.

In Maharashtra, Mahars are widely thought of as a 'community' which did especially well both before and after Independence through so-called caste 'uplift', and in particular through adherence to Ambedkarite Buddhism. In the region's largest city, Aurangabad, students of Mahar origin were known to be strongly represented among the growing population of Harijan/untouchable students and salaried graduates from whose ranks had come the founders and leading ideologues of the Dalit Panthers.[17] In the 1978 Marathwada riots, 'clean-caste' cultivators staged attacks on both Mahar and Bhil 'tribal' hamlet-dwellers, burning crops on lands which these labourers and dwarf-holders had allegedly 'encroached' upon.

Here too such clashes had their origins in schemes encouraging the rural poor to engage in the quasi-legal occupation of disputed 'waste' lands. And yet again there is evidence that ideals of dharmic order

[17] Punalekar 1985.

353

were widely cited, especially in attacks on villages with alleged Dalit Panther links. In these cases it was reported that 'clean-caste' farmers forced tonsurers and other ritual specialists to withhold purificatory services from 'encroachers' on the grounds that they had transgressed against righteous caste norms. Ambedkarite Buddhists were singled out for particularly aggressive treatment. The attackers burned oleographs of the Buddha and the Harijan hero B. R. Ambedkar, both still figures of veneration in areas of Ambedkarite neo-Buddhist conversion. In addition, those attacking so-called Dalits reportedly tried to reinstate the everyday manifestations of untouchability which had been singled out for eradication under the 1950 Constitution. These included exclusion from village wells, and the enforced use of separate cups in tea shops by villagers of known Harijan origin.[18]

Some commentators related the timing of these clashes to external events. Maharashtra's rural unrest in the 1980s has been linked to attempts by the Hindu supremacist Shiv Sena party to capitalise on its urban electoral successes in the 1985 elections by launching a drive for clean-caste 'kisan' support in the countryside. Like the Hindu supremacists of the late nineteenth and early twentieth centuries who gained a popular base through the use of Maharashtrian martial cult traditions, the Shiv Sena staged its mass rallies to coincide with the region's annual celebrations of Pola. This is a popular regional festival at which celebrants engage in the adornment and ritual feeding of cattle. Its rites are therefore in the tradition of cow-venerating muscular Hinduism which has come to be such an effective vehicle for the assertion of rustic score-settling populism. In the 1980s, Pola celebrations regularly became occasions at which gatherings of clean-caste 'peasants' shouted slogans reviling so-called Dalits. Those taking part reinforced the point by invoking the fierce *shakti* goddess Bhawani and also Shivaji the exemplar of valorous Hindu nationhood: both were hailed as embodiments of the righteousness which was supposedly under threat from unvirtuous 'Dalits'.[19]

---

[18] *EPW* 12 May 1979: 849–50; *EPW* 13 Dec. 1986: 2166. These were areas where government allocations of land to low-caste Ambedkarite Buddhist converts had provoked widespread violence in 1968–9. Kamble 1981: 97, 129; Shah 1985b: 117. During the so-called Emergency regime (1975–7), Congress leaders sought support from Harijan/untouchables by sponsoring mass filings of cases against high-caste farmers and landlords for violations of the Protection of Civil Rights Act. Punalekar 1985: 169.

[19] *EPW* 13 Dec. 1986: 2166; *Census of India 1961* vol. X: Part 7B *Maharashtra. Fairs and Festivals in Maharashtra*: 11–12.

THE MODERNITY OF THE 'CASTE WAR' TRADITION

In many of the most widely reported conflicts, 'caste war' violence has tended to feed back and forth between urban centres and the rural hinterlands from which towns like Banaras and Aurangabad draw many of their students and factory workers. Such outbreaks are not then to be seen as a reversion to the 'feudal' or 'traditional' past. 'Modern' institutions, especially the courts, the universities and the mass media, have figured prominently in the so-called caste feud phenomenon. In 1977 Maharashtra's state government sparked off a long-running controversy by announcing plans to rename the region's Marathwada university in honour of Ambedkar. This institution was typical of the many colleges and universities throughout the country which began in the 1970s to attract students from modestly prosperous rural families. As a result, such questions as who was to enter a place of higher learning, and even what name to give it, had become matters of debate among people who had hitherto had only a remote hope of educating their children beyond primary school.[20]

Since Independence, even Indians of 'peasant'/*kisan* background have become familiar with the idea that the nation's wellbeing and development gains can be measured in terms of its educational attainments. When anti-Mandal campaigners have resisted schemes to reserve college places for the deprived, they have often referred to the supposed destruction of 'merit', especially in cases where state governments have reduced or even abolished minimum admissions standards for so-called Backwards as a means of recruiting low-caste and 'tribal' candidates into medicine and other vocational courses.[21]

The Marathwada University controversy, with its background of both rural and urban social tensions, was thus the immediate catalyst for Maharashtra's 1978 'caste war' riots. These issues were once again

[20] This had originated as a demand issued by militants associated with the Dalit Panther movement. *EPW* 3 Feb. 1979: 185–6; 7–8 Feb. 1979: 223; 12 May 1979: 849; 13 Dec. 1986: 2166–7; Punalekar 1985: 158.

[21] *EPW* 6 Sept. 1986; Sivaramayya 1996. A major reference point in the so-called merit debate has been the series of judicial rulings on the issue of whether state medical colleges are entitled to set different qualifying entrance marks for admissions candidates: one formula was a 40% minimum score for Scheduled Castes, 30% for Scheduled Tribes, and 50% for general applicants. In 1982 the Supreme Court ruled unlawful a move to drop minimum entrance requirements altogether for Scheduled candidates. See Tharu and Niranjana 1996: 237–8; Upadhyaya 1992; Béteille 1992: 45–69; Kumar 1994.

in the forefront in western India's 1980, 1981 and 1985 urban 'caste war' agitations. Some of this period's worst outbreaks occurred in Gujarat, especially in Ahmedabad. This, too, is a city with large concentrations of clean-caste/*sat-sudra* students who reportedly played a leading role in 'caste feud' violence. A high proportion of these young people came from rural localities which had been the scene of clashes over yet another round of so-called surplus land allocations to landless 'Dalit'/untouchables.[22] Yet here as elsewhere, this new wave of conflict occurred primarily in an environment of urban modernity. Many of those attacked were 'Dalit' industrial workers engaged in strike action against conditions in the city's mills and factories. Nevertheless, these campaigns rapidly acquired a strong 'caste-war' complexion. As the unrest widened, 'clean-caste' student activists came to the fore, dramatising their opposition to so-called Mandalite social engineering policies by staging protests invoking the Gandhian tradition of mass popular resistance (*satyagraha*).

Two sets of symbols predominated in these agitations. One referred to the patriotic moral mandate of pre-Independence militant nationalism; the second invoked the modernising power of science and technology. Ahmedabad in particular was the scene of massive demonstrations at which students from medical colleges took a public oath to resist the state's reservations schemes, proclaiming that such policies weakened the nation's stock of educated brain-power. These protests featured the anointing of a commemorative statue of Gandhi with a ritual brow-mark (*tilak*) of fresh blood. An even more assertive message was conveyed by protesters dressed in operating theatre gowns who enacted mock surgical operations on a clay model of a human head. This was supposed to represent the skull of a 'Dalit' admissions candidate; to the delight of a jeering crowd the shattered fragments were shown to contain sawdust instead of a brain.[23]

All these events were reported with approval by the outspokenly anti-'Mandalite' local press. The 'modern' media have thus done much to keep these violent themes and images alive in the public arena. During the 1990s, the reach of international communications networks

---

[22] Parek and Mitra 1990: 90; Kamble 1981: 434–65; Baxi 1990.

[23] Gagnik and Bhatt 1984: 51; Parekh and Mitra 1990: 95–9; Bose 1985. Compare Searle-Chatterjee's account (1981: 13–14) of high-caste Banaras students staging a public ritual cleansing of a local 'freedom fighter's' statue which they said had been polluted by the touch of the Harijan politician Jagjivan Ram at an official unveiling ceremony.

spread very widely throughout India: between 1991 and 1997, some thirty satellite television channels began broadcasting across the country; US news magazines and other international publications are also widely available. Nevertheless, the country's own daily newspapers and illustrated weeklies are still a powerful force; some major journals even have home pages on the internet.

These regional publications tend to treat 'caste feuds' as an everyday fact of life, reporting regularly on such matters as the deployment of special police units to counter 'caste clashes' in alleged problem regions. Furthermore, such caste war 'atrocities' as UP's 1994 Shivpatia case and the December 1997 massacre of sixty-two Harijan/untouchable labourers in the village of Laxmanpur-Bathe in central Bihar have received lurid pictorial coverage in the newspapers and news magazines. These journals also regularly quote the assertive language of the public men (and women) who link confrontational social campaigns to the principle of *himsa*, that is, sanctified or divinely mandated violence. In many areas, those advocating the use of force either against or on behalf of so-called Manuvadi (upper caste) elites have become as widely known to newspaper readers as those who endorse the values of purity, constraint and non-violence (*ahimsa*).[24]

These accounts have placed particular emphasis on the defilement of women as a feature of so-called caste feuds. Sexual availability is still widely known as a 'proof' of lowliness in caste terms. Contrasted with the ostentatiously chaste Brahman or Vaishya, the standard stereotypes of 'community' still hold the low-caste Dhed, Chamar or 'tribal' to be unchaste and sexually incontinent, lacking both the moral and physical resources to preserve their women from other people's lusts. In this regard, what has been notable about 'caste war' incidents is that the rumours and media stories have been so universally persuasive when they convey the message that the difference between victims and victimisers in these situations is one of caste rather than class, faith or ethnolinguistic identity. Fearful people have found it all too easy to believe that it is murderous 'Dalits' who are on the march against

---

[24] The Shivpatia incident involved the brutalisation of a woman of low-caste Kanjar origin in a UP village where 'Dalits' had been in conflict with 'OBC' Kurmis. Another notorious incident, reported in 1994, involved a Rajasthan woman said to be of 'socially backward' Ramgariah origin and accused by villagers who were of mercantile Arora background of defiling a shrine. Even the electronic versions of daily newspapers report frequent 'caste clashes', as in the *Hindu*'s (internet) accounts of police actions in the turbulent Sivakasi area (26 April 1997).

them, or that 'the Thakurs', the paramilitary *senas* or the 'Manuvadi elites' are conspiring to bring dishonour and violent death to their vulnerable hamlets or urban residential enclaves.

The vernacular and English-language press have provided platforms for the 'worthy' peasant and landlord to strike cinematic avenger attitudes which reflect the machismo *himsa* message of 'Bollywood' thrillers, as well as the themes of older martial folk-cult traditions. In press interviews carried out after the 1993 elections which brought the SP/BSP coalition government to power in UP, prominent Indian news magazines carried interviews with men from 'Forward-caste' landed groups who were quoted as calling for a revival of the martial heritage of the Rajput patrician. One such article reported the comments of a Rajput village 'headman' (*pradhan*) who allegedly addressed the interviewer with a shotgun clutched pointedly across his knees. The Rajput reportedly tells the journalist 'I never used to have to do this [guard his lands from supposed 'Dalit' attackers] but now [following the SP/BSP's 1993 electoral victory] somehow everything is different. We Rajputs feel under attack, which is our own fault because instead of remaining warriors we allowed ourselves to become Banias [people of commerce] ...'[25]

Such views were held to be widely shared among landowners of Rajput origin at this time. Some of those interviewed reportedly spoke of their 'community' as having undergone a process of moral decline. Their 'people', they said, had lost their former ascendancy in the countryside because they had succumbed to the attractions of weak-kneed Gandhian teachings which had led them to embrace unwarlike commercial-caste '*bania*' values and livelihoods. Much was made in these reports of the ex-seigneurs' fears of the coming of an 'OBC-Dalit Raj' which would license vengeful anti-'Manuvadi' forces to seize their lands. It appears that new landlords' paramilitary organisations were recruited in these areas, as in the regions of Bihar where 'caste army' (*sena*) activity has been noted since the 1970s. Like their Bihar counterparts, these have reportedly used a neo-Marxist language of people's war: one such body in eastern UP was said to have called itself the Savarna Mukti Morcha, or 'Forward Caste Liberation Front'.[26]

---

[25] *Frontline* 11 Mar. 1994: 4.
[26] *Ibid.*; Bhambhri 1989: 84.

Bihar too apparently had a revival of paramilitary *sena* organisations in the 1990s. Among the most widely reported has been the Bhojpur region's Bhumihar-dominated Ranvir Sena or landlords' army which takes its name from yet another armed hero of the colonial era. Press reports have also made much of another north Indian organisation referred to as the Dalit Sena, an all-untouchable guerrilla group preaching a doctrine of Maoist people's war, and defining its enemies as landed clean-caste non-'Dalits' including Bhumihars, Rajputs and even 'peasant' Yadav-Ahirs.[27]

Once again the tensions of the towns and the countryside have intersected in these events, with much sympathy for the paramilitaries being expressed by educated and semi-educated youths in the big urban centres. As was noted above, large concentrations of first-generation students from rural backgrounds are to be found on the campuses of colleges and vocational institutions of the major north Indian cities. These vocal and politically active students often form caste-based enclaves within their colleges and technical institutions, boarding in residential student hostels which are run as exclusive 'community' foundations. In some localities, entire colleges have come to be associated with a particular caste group. Thus in 1994 – a year of widespread 'caste riots' in north India – students from 'Rajput-dominated' colleges in both Kanpur and Banaras reportedly played a central role in these outbreaks. In both cases the violence was said to be a response to the appearance of press stories about rural 'caste war' outbreaks in eastern UP where many of the students had their homes.[28]

CASTE STRIFE AND THE URBAN MIDDLE CLASSES

A further dimension of urban experience in recent years has been widespread fear and resentment of 'Mandalite' reservations schemes

---

[27] *Frontline* 11 Mar. 1994: 6; 26 Dec. 1997: 27–9; *Outlook* 15 Dec. 1997: 6–10. Dalit Sena units reportedly laid siege to 'class enemies' in their villages, held revolutionary People's Courts in the forests, and reviled the state's populist Chief Minister Laloo Prasad Yadav as a 'casteist' who used his power to promote the interests of his Yadav 'caste fellows', allegedly turning a blind eye to anti-Harijan 'atrocities'.

[28] The brother of a Rajput allegedly murdered in these clashes was reportedly a student in the college: press accounts said that student mobs sought to avenge 'community' honour by attacking 'dalit' and 'OBC' students and passers-by. *Frontline* 11 Mar. 1994: 5–6. On similar 'caste clusters' in urban colleges in Maharashtra, see Punalekar 1985: 156.

among urban families with a long tradition of professional training and white-collar public employment. Often there are painful contradictions in these attitudes. Those concerned may be northern Kayasthas or Tamilnad Brahmans by birth, or others from the sort of service or commercial background that gave rise in past centuries to India's formerly compact and secure English-speaking intelligentsias. Since the 1970s these people have watched the growth and diversification of the Indian middle classes with considerable alarm. The expansion of trade and industry, and the commercialisation of agriculture, have greatly increased the numbers of families who can aspire to equip their sons and often their daughters with law, engineering or medical degrees, or with the qualifications to sit the public service examinations.

The descendants of the old intelligentsias have been threatened on two fronts: by the new waves of ex-proprietary families who want their children to enter the universities and vocational colleges, and by members of thrusting 'peasant' groups and others of so-called Backward or Scheduled origin who are in a position to use the reservations system to achieve the same goal. This kind of urban English-speaking household will often have had no choice but to become acutely sensitive about the meaning of Kayastha, Khatri or Brahman birth for themselves and their children.

Whether justified or not, such people often fear that belonging to one of these 'Forward' castes or 'communities' may threaten or even negate their most cherished aspirations. During the 1990s, controversial court decisions and party political manoeuvres significantly reinforced these fears among members of these old cosmopolitan educated elites. The greatest blow here was the so-called 1992 Mandal judgement, in which the Indian Supreme Court upheld the principle of caste-based reservations in education and public service employment. This was followed by proposals from leaders of the Indian National Congress for an amendment to the Constitution introducing the principle of promotion quotas as well as recruitment reservations for members of the Scheduled Castes, Scheduled Tribes and OBC groups.[29]

This fear of being denied college places and administrative posts has been especially galling in households which would once have looked more or less automatically towards secure careers in the professions or

[29] Srinivas 1996: xxix.

government service. As Rekha Kaul has shown, some of those concerned have taken decisive action, as can be seen from the proliferation since the 1980s of so-called capitation fee colleges run by single-caste blocks of 'Forwards'. As private foundations, these are not subject to the reservations quotas imposed on state-run medical and engineering establishments. In states like Karnataka where, since the 1970s, the big clean-caste rural jati clusters like the Vokkaligas have been repeatedly dropped from and then returned to the OBC reservations listings, these private colleges appear to function both as profitable outlets for the investment capital of 'rich peasants' and as a means by which local notables can demonstrate philanthropic zeal to potential 'community' vote banks. At the same time, they offer higher-caste students the chance to apply for desirable college places without competition from those eligible for caste-based reservations.[30]

Equally striking are the operations of housing trusts run by Brahman-only caste associations. Such schemes have been established in Karnataka, for example, where high urban living-costs make it difficult for modestly placed 'twice-born' (upper caste or thread-wearing *'dwija'*) families to maintain 'respectable' household standards. In some cases, *varna* alone provides the basis for eligibility, with such undertakings opening their doors to anyone who can satisfactorily establish their Brahman birth, regardless of jati or sectarian tradition. One such trust reportedly requires those seeking loans to recite the sacred scriptural invocation known as the Gayatri Mantra and the name of their family's *gotra* (sub-caste or lineage cluster), such knowledge having been decided upon as a reliable test of Brahman origins.[31]

This persistence or reassertion of exclusive caste ties is all the more striking since in so many other ways the conventions of 'traditional' jati and varna norms have been significantly eroded for people with this kind of background. As was noted in Chapter 8, these trends have been most marked among educated English-speakers from the so-called Forward castes in Delhi and other major cities. Until recently this was a distinctive and confident world where the dominant voices were those of arts graduates and Indian Administrative Service 'batchmates' from the elite Delhi and Calcutta university colleges.

---

[30] Kaul 1993.
[31] Mitra 1994: 65–6.

These are people with family histories of public service and achievement in the liberal professions dating back to the pre-Independence period. Their forebears would normally include anglophone jurists, educators and 'freedom fighters' who read reformist newspapers in the early twentieth century and took a leading role in early debates about Hindu nationhood and social 'uplift'.

In these urbane circles, the favoured language has been 'secular', modernising and egalitarian, with a tendency to disparage 'feudal' survivals in Indian life, including the values and practices associated with 'casteism'. These then are educated men and women who are caught by the same contradictions embodied in the Indian Constitution, striving to be 'modern' and 'casteless' in many areas of their personal lives, while being forcibly reminded of the power of 'substantialised' or ethnicity-like jati and varna allegiances by the wider world, by the militancy of organised 'Dalits', and by alarming manifestations of 'caste war' in their troubled towns and rural hinterlands. In some cases such people have expressed public sympathy for the Hindu supremacist cause on the grounds that its adherents' opposition to 'Mandalism' is better for the nation than the recruitment of supposedly meritless people to the universities and the public services.

At the same time, many prosperous Indian expatriates in North America, western Europe and Australia have become keenly concerned with 'traditional' caste considerations. This is not surprising, given the uncertainties of immigrant life and the advantages to be gained even in ostensibly modern conditions by making much of available 'community' networks. As seekers of brides and grooms for their children, middle-class Indian expatriates (so-called NRIs, 'non-resident Indians') may resemble English-speaking Indian city-dwellers in stressing concern for income, education and astrological compatibility over the strict matching of jati and *gotra*. This, however, may reflect a confident awareness that the successful commercial or professional circles in which they move in London, New York or Sydney will contain few if any members of untouchable/Dalit caste groups.

These contradictions and complexities are nicely illustrated by the controversy that broke out in the 1990s over a violent and sexually explicit commercial cinema epic, *Bandit Queen*. The film is based on the life of India's best-known so-called 'outlaw', Phoolan Devi, an illiterate former gang leader from UP's famous *dacoit* (brigand) haven, the Chambal valley. In her trademark khakis and bandolier, Phoolan Devi has been both reviled and celebrated as an anti-establishment heroine since the 1970s. She was jailed on fifty murder charges in 1983, released eleven years later, and elected in 1996 to a seat in the national Parliament.

In 1994 Phoolan Devi filed suit against the makers of *Bandit Queen*, in which she is portrayed as an avenging 'Dalit' of lowly Mallah caste origin who turns to crime after being brutalised in youth by high-caste Thakurs. Many prominent artists and intellectuals expressed support for her attempt to suppress the film. Indian newspapers had her voicing her objections in language which any old-style Third World Marxist would applaud. One interviewer quoted her as having denounced the film, which was originally commissioned for British television, as a 'dangerous piece of caste hatred' which had been conceived 'to suit the perverted taste buds of imperialist Western mind [*sic*] which has been systematically brainwashed through ages to believe that all Indian maladies lie exclusively in its caste differences'.[32]

These claims provoked fierce debate, with defenders of the film arguing that its depiction of 'caste atrocities' was an effective and timely indictment of the 'Manuvadi system'. One of the artists and literati who took the opposing side, objecting particularly to the film's graphic rape and revenge scenes, was the outspoken journalist and screenwriter Arundhati Roy. Ironically, in 1997 Roy's widely acclaimed first novel, *The God of Small Things*, itself became the subject of legal action in the author's home state of Kerala, with the complainant alleging that the book's sex scenes, which involve a middle-class Malayali Christian woman and an 'untouchable' household servant, represent a danger to public morality.

There are important commentators who see trends such as the merging of sub-castes (*gotras*) or the marginalisation of caste considerations in middle-class marriages as a sign of the ending of caste itself, or of its transformation into a form of vestigial ethnic identity without the power and meaning of 'true' caste. But as earlier chapters have shown, so-called caste Hindus have for many centuries exhibited a consciousness of caste both in its more complex manifestations as a grid of intricately ranked status categories and in these wider agglomerative forms which were so powerfully shaped by external political

[32] *Hindu* Int. Edn 27 Aug. 1994: 6.

363

and economic changes. If anything, the experiences of the post-Independence period have tended to reinforce many manifestations of these disparate but interconnecting forms of caste. What may be happening now is the emergence of a greater gulf between matters of ritual caste consciousness, and the broader and more comprehensive forms of organised or ethnicity-like 'community'. This, however, is testimony to the constant reinvention by different generations of something which can still broadly be called caste, rather than to its disappearance.

CONCLUSION

This book began with an account of academic theories and debates, but it has argued throughout that no one model or explanatory formula can account for either the durability or the dynamism of caste. Indeed it has held that it requires the insights of both history and social anthropology to explore and interpret this contentious and multi-faceted element of Indian life.

Of course there have been other interdisciplinary studies of the subcontinent; these have inspired the methodology if not necessarily the conclusions of this work. Yet the fact remains that, for many historians of India, it has been difficult to relate the issues debated by anthropologists to the problems which they see in relation to caste, both in the distant past and in more recent times. So too for many anthropologists who, while acknowledging the fluidity of the Indian social order, have in some cases relied on oversimplified historical language in the attempt to identify its 'traditional', 'colonial' or 'modern' aspects.

It is not surprising then that the two disciplines sometimes seem far apart in their treatment of the subcontinent. Yet the two fields can and should be brought together, as has been done for so many other socially complex environments. As far as caste is concerned, striking things happen when we attach historical perspectives to the anthropologists' models. The principles identified by social scientists need no longer be taken as contradictory or mutually exclusive; nor need we opt for only one key theme in the analysis of caste, be this power, purity or orientalist constructions. What can be seen instead is a multidimensional story of changing and interpenetrating reference points. The making of caste society has involved a sequence of complex but intelligible changes in Indian life, most notably in the areas of religion, state power and the material environment. Taken together, the social scientists' divergent theoretical interpretations thus reflect the rich multiplicity and plurality of Indian life and thought, and in particular the capacity of Indians to respond with energy and resilience to the massive changes of the last two to three centuries.

The norms and conventions of caste have had a pervasive presence in the historical literature, and also in contemporary discourse. To ignore this, or to portray caste as a mere orientalist fabrication, would be the equivalent of trying to write about social change in modern Italy or the United States without serious discussion of faction and political corruption on the one hand, or race on the other. The comparable reference point for Britain would be class, and certainly no-one could credibly contend that class has been an unimportant factor in modern British life, or that the topic is an improper one for academic analysis.[1]

Even fifty years after Independence, caste has continued to be a major theme in Indian political debate. Of course far from defending its norms and values, many of those who make caste an issue in the electoral arena do so with the aim of denouncing it as a social evil or of attacking others for being backward-looking and 'casteist'. Yet there are few signs that references to caste are becoming less pervasive in contemporary politics. Furthermore, as Louis Dumont has shown, many aspects of contemporary caste life echo themes and principles to be found in classical Indian religion and scripture. In the West, neither race nor class can be related to any comparable body of codified texts and teachings.

This study has not argued that caste is the only or even the most important element of Indian life, let alone that caste as a 'system' has been the immutable core of Indian civilisation since ancient times. It does maintain that for all its diversity and its points of comparison with schemes of social differentiation to be found in other parts of the world, caste stands alone as a mode of thought and action. This distinctiveness is undeniable, even though caste certainly has much in common with other complex 'invented traditions', most notably those of nationhood and ethno-religious community. Indeed, India's nationalist and communal religious ideologies have both interacted with the ideas and experiences of caste, sometimes reinforcing their claims and sometimes challenging them, but never fully overriding or replacing them.

Caste is certainly not just a coded way of communicating or confirming differentials of power and wealth; nor are there decisive signs that its manifestations are on the verge of disappearing or

---

[1] For an important new historical treatment of class in Britain, see Cannadine 1998.

mutating into a 'modern' scheme of purely class-based social differences. It is true that the experience of caste has been both nourished and constrained by the forces which have affected and altered the class composition of India's regional societies, and also by the ideas of racial differentiation which have been a feature of both the colonial and post-Independence periods. Nevertheless, caste is not to be seen as a mere variant of the class or racial hierarchies prevailing in complex societies elsewhere. Its distinctive features can only be understood against the background of India's unique political and social experiences; the emphasis throughout has therefore been on changing patterns of statecraft, religion and economic life in comparatively recent times.[2]

The premise then has been that the phenomenon of caste in its many forms and variants has had far-reaching effects in the shaping of these political and social institutions. It was this which dictated the book's choice of questions. These were, first, what brought so many Indians within the pale of so-called caste society in the relatively recent past, that is, both in the centuries preceding the British conquest and in the era of colonial rule? Secondly, what made the ideals and experiences of caste life so fluid and yet so enduring as Indians experienced the transformations of the pre- and post-Independence periods? And finally, what has kept caste such an active and potent reference point in a society which is now so far removed from the world of the ancient scriptures, and even from that of the princes, peasants and empire-builders of the more recent past?

In relation to the first of these questions I have argued that the pale of caste society expanded in periods of rapid change and upheaval because its elements of both exclusion and open-ended fluidity could help so many people to advantage themselves in situations of either opportunity or uncertainty (or a combination of both). This led in turn to an emphasis on the resources and actions of the modern state.

---

[2] The arguments presented in this volume clearly do not support an oversimplified view of caste as a mere invention or fantasy of colonial orientalism. The emphasis here has been on the importance of Indian actions and initiatives, with a focus on pre-colonial states and rulers, and with British rule being seen as an active but far from all-powerful element in the making of caste society. Yet this is not to dismiss those more nuanced works which portray so-called orientalist constructions of caste as having subtle and far-reaching effects on Indian life and thought, and which treat Indian social commentators and politicians who regarded caste as 'real' (rather than a colonial fabrication or fantasy) as something more than passsive bearers or recipients of 'essentializing' Western thought. See Prakash 1990b, and works cited in Introduction, note 1.

Both under the British and in independent India, the Indian state has had a remarkable capacity to reinforce crucial elements of caste. This has occurred both through specific policies of social reform or caste-based 'uplift', and, much more broadly, in the many other areas of state action which have either intentionally or unintentionally contributed to the growth and perpetuation of so-called 'casteism' in its numerous modern forms. It has been, above all, the power of the pollution barrier that has been extended and reinforced in this way as a basis for the assertion of broad collective differentiations between those of superior and low or unclean caste. This has been the case even where the organs of state power have simultaneously exalted the principles of representative government and individual rights.

The book then tried to answer the third of these questions by arguing that, for all its importance, state action has been anything but an independent or all-powerful maker of caste experience in post-Independence India. This is especially apparent today when the intersecting effects of democratic politics, modern mass communications, expanding educational opportunities and economic 'globalisation' have worked to discredit the essentialisms of caste in the eyes of some. Yet these same forces have reinforced the value of caste for many other Indians who continue to find proof of the advantages they can derive from asserting both 'substantialised' and interactive or 'traditional' ideals of jati and varna.

To turn to the more detailed themes and arguments, the first half of the volume explored a range of far-reaching changes which were still underway long after the initial British conquest, arguing that the emergence of 'traditional' caste society was, in fact, a comparatively recent product of these transformations in Indian life and thought. The first two chapters traced the two-stage process by which an array of both lordly and Brahmanical or purity-centred ideals acquired importance in the lives of both the privileged and the weak. Focusing particularly on the eighteenth and early nineteenth centuries, the argument here was that these two points of reference offered a diverse but still recognisably castelike array of norms and strategies to those struggling for advantage in a variety of unpredictable circumstances.

The role of rulers and state power was a central element in these developments. This does not mean that dynasts and their elite retainers in the pre-British kingdoms somehow imposed hierarchical jati and varna norms on their hitherto casteless subjects. Indeed, recognisable versions of caste norms were certainly known and practised to a limited degree in some though not all regions of India many centuries before the age of the Mughals and their contemporaries.[3] Yet the formation of a far more caste-conscious social order took shape at a significantly later point, above all in the proliferating regional king-doms of the post-Mughal period. The spread of these jati- and varna-centred values was especially apparent in the dominions of the eclectic men of prowess of whom the seventeenth-century Maratha dynast Shivaji is the prime example. The pale of caste then expanded even more rapidly in the realms of the more socially exclusive rulers who exalted themselves as heirs to the scriptural varna ideal of the noble and pious warrior-dynast.

These, above all, were the men of power who set increasingly pervasive standards of dharmic correctness for other Indians, deferring to the pious values of their client merchant and service populations, and exalting norms of conduct which many anthropologists have portrayed as the core values of 'caste society'. Ironically, given the widely held modern view of caste as a scheme of religious values which are unique to the Hindu cultural tradition, non-Hindu as well as avowedly Hindu rulers played a dynamic role in this process. To rule was to name, order and classify; many of the regional community titles and other reference points of the modern caste 'system' were popularised through the usages of the great state-building lords and dynasts of the Mughal and post-Mughal periods.

Among the most notable features of this statecraft were the formal differentiations that came to signify both a ritual and an occupational distinction between the non-elite tiller who might be known as Kanbi, Jat or Kamma, and the sharer in martial lordship, epitomised by the Rajput seigneur with his mustachio and jewels, his virile pursuits, and his tradition of arms-bearing and privileged revenue-taking rights.

In many cases the religion of the high god Shiva provided a powerful focus for these groups' loose and flexible ideals of 'commu-nity'. Again, this was not a matter of imposition from above. Even for many unprivileged people there was clearly strong appeal and con-siderable practical advantage in being slotted into a known scheme of rank, which meant being defined as both symbolically and materially

---

[3] For a stimulating account of caste as a feature of ancient Indian society, see Thapar 1984.

superior to other groups of lowlier people, as well as being named as co-sharers, albeit at a humble level, in these schemes of royally sanctioned honour and status.

By the later eighteenth century, a powerful new element had entered the world of these dominion-builders. This trend derived from scriptural Hindu sources, these now being transformed and acted on as a far more widely known model for the actions of kings, and of their more powerful and commercially dynamic subjects. What was involved here was the spread of ideals which exalted personal purity, austerity and pious munificence, with the royal man of prowess now standing forth as embodiment and guarantor of a much more rigorous standard of dharmic correctness, both for his own kin and for his realm at large.

The popularisation of these hierarchical and purity-conscious social codes derived in large part from the growing power and wealth of the literate and moneyed specialists whose expertise had rapidly become indispensable to the rule of India's post-Mughal dynasts. The most important groups here were the priestly, ascetic and scribal Brahman specialists with expertise in record-keeping, commerce and ritual, together with purity-conscious merchants and trader-bankers, many of whom favoured caste-exalting traditions of Hindu devotion (*bhakti*) which focused on forms of the god Vishnu.

A wide range of both elite and non-elite Indians found advantage in embracing the traditions of dharmic piety which were favoured by these superior royal clients, proclaiming the purity of their persons and blood-lines through the adoption of rigorous marriage and dietary regulations, and prescribing strict codes of seclusion and modesty for their female kin. Increasingly too, those claiming 'twice-born' birth insisted on their absolute and divinely mandated superiority to small but important groups of unclean client service providers. The pollution-removing services of these tonsurers and other 'untouchable' specialists were seen increasingly as indispensable to the worth and status of those wishing to be seen as ritually pure or clean in the special sense which is specific to the scriptural theory of varna.

None of these developments enfeebled India's kings, or made the Brahman the sole point of reference in a world of all-powerful and immutable caste values. At the same time, the idea of 'Brahman raj', meaning a realm of widely shared dharmic norms such as those of the Brahman-feeding rulers of the Malabar coast or the Chitpavan

Peshwas of eighteenth-century Pune, was far from being an invention of the Brahman-fearing colonial imagination. Yet the claims of caste in these increasingly purity-conscious and hierarchical forms were not universally subscribed to even under British colonial rule. Anti-Brahmanical teachings continued to flourish among the adherents of many Hindu devotional sectarian traditions. For much of the nineteenth century, 'caste' life among many pastoral and non-elite cultivating groups remained far more open and fluid than that of the elite landed groups.

This same contrast applied to traders and other occupationally specialised populations for whom bonds of caste or caste-like allegiance had long fulfilled valuable guild-like functions in regard to the protection of special skills, resources and information. Well into the colonial period, 'caste' norms were still being actively forged around all three of the ideals of worth and community which were extolled in the sastric scriptures – these being the man of prowess, the service provider and the settled man of worth.

Despite these important areas of continuity, by the end of the nineteenth century both the experience and the ideology of caste had undergone far-reaching changes. These occurred both through the effects of British and Indian orientalist debate and through the massive upheavals that further transformed the politics and social life of the subcontinent. The most dramatic of these changes was the expansion and rigidification of the pollution barrier. As was seen in Chapter 5, the experience of untouchability as a widely shared 'disability' of large numbers of labouring, artisanal and service people was in many ways a real, if unintentional, creation of British rule.

The reasons for this were complex. The fact of India's subjection to a Western colonial regime was obviously of great importance here. Yet in many ways British rule merely built on the caste-building trends which were already apparent in the powerful seventeenth- and eighteenth-century realms discussed in Chapters 1 and 2. Some at least of these effects might well have followed from any process of economic expansion and modernisation affecting the subcontinent in the nineteenth and early twentieth centuries. What actually did occur was that, under unfavourable British military and land-settlement policies, large numbers of twice-born patricians experienced unprecedented insecurities. Such people therefore turned increasingly to the language and usages of purity and pollution in an attempt to subordinate so-called field servants and other labouring groups who had not hitherto been bracketed with unclean pollution-removers. In some though not all cases, these moves were reinforced by caste-specific colonial law and administrative practices, and also by the precepts of popular sectarian faiths which taught conformity to the sober norms of a 'civilised' dharmic moral order.

Of paramount importance, however, in creating the context for these transformations were the combined effects of deforestation, forced sedentarisation, population growth and the spread of commercial cash-cropping. It was in response to these profound changes in the subcontinent's physical and social environment that mobile pastoralists and 'tribals' – whose forebears had been either outside or on the fringes of this increasingly purity-conscious 'caste society' – found themselves drawn into a world in which they were defined, both by colonial officials and by other Indians, according to the reference points of jati and varna.

Other groups too in turbulent rural areas acquired a new and more militant sense of 'community' consciousness. For many non-polluting cultivators, this sense of identity was often fiercely anti-Brahmanical, as groups with the non-elite social patterns of the Jat, Kurmi or Goala/ Ahir confronted the thread-wearing patricians who tried to coerce them in much the same way that they sought to subordinate 'untouchables', that is, by treating the claims of varna theory as a code of ritualised servility. At the same time, there were many successful 'clean-caste' groups who embraced the norms of piety and social refinement which they observed in the lives of their localities' rich merchants and other purity-conscious grandees. Much like 'twice-born' patricians and traders, these superior 'peasants' made much of their superiority to the labourers, artisans and service providers whom they were able to stigmatise as being of unclean or ritually polluted birth.

The 'modern' colonial city of the nineteenth and early twentieth centuries was yet another environment in which stricter and more pollution-conscious manifestations of jati and varna came into being under British rule. This may seem paradoxical since recruitment into many of these new urban occupations was largely caste-free. Yet quite a number did recruit on a caste basis, as in the case of the burning-ground attendants and other ritualists who proliferated in the fast-growing funerary and pilgrimage towns. Another important case was the specialist pollution-removers who found themselves in demand to serve the households of the colonial towns' great armies of purity-conscious clerical and service people. And in addition, there were numerous forms of 'modern' labour which were either formally or informally caste-specific, hence the large numbers of very lowly urban migrants who were recruited as military and municipal 'sweepers', tanners and factory hands.

As was seen in Chapter 3, many of these changes were reinforced by the colonial state through its mammoth exercises in ethnographic investigation and data-collection. After mid-century, caste became one of the main categories of enumeration in an enormous array of official and quasi-official reportage, most notably in the decennial Census, as well as in the writings and operations of missionaries, medics, jurists, land settlement officers, military recruiters and 'orientalist' scholar-officials.

It is not the case, however, that India came to look or behave like a 'traditional' caste society because Europeans perceived and made it so. The British were far from being the first of the subcontinent's rulers to count or classify Indians by 'kind' or 'community', though there were certainly novelties in their techniques, most notably their attempts to label, count and rank all their female as well as male subjects by caste and 'community', and to do so on an all-India basis. In other respects, however, much that the British did in the way of collectively stereo-typing, classifying and 'essentialising' their Indian subjects was adapted directly from the statecraft of their Hindu and non-Hindu predecessors.

At the same time, British commentators of the colonial period emphatically did not all subscribe to the same simplistic view of India as a homogeneous caste society. Nor did they all hold that every Indian (or even every Hindu) was to be seen as radically inferior to the white European because the subcontinent was 'enslaved' by the morally enfeebling tyrannies of Brahman-centred jati and varna principles. On the contrary, Western writers differed profoundly from one another in their understanding of caste, and in the degree to which they considered it a manifestation of bio-racial, religious or material and political circumstances. Ironically, in some cases these colonial 'orientalists' saw caste status as a matter of individual will and strategy rather than immutable codes and customs shared in common by entire 'communities'. This is a view contrasting strongly with the modern form of 'orientalism' for which Dumont has been attacked, this being the claim that the element of individual human agency is given little or no importance in caste society, and hence that in India, the land of *homo hierarchicus*, there is no true concept of the individual as it exists in Western value systems.

Although its importance has not been widely recognised in modern accounts of so-called colonial discourse, the most powerful and persistent element in orientalist writing on India throughout the colonial period was not the theme of caste, but that of race. Much that was said in these writings on race, and indeed much that was quoted from them in this volume, will strike a contemporary ear as grotesque and offensive, and will be rightly abhorred by modern readers. But this should not lead us to ignore the remarkable and lasting worldwide enthusiasm for these theories of racial evolution, primordial race wars and collective racial essences, and the eagerness with which colonial commentators attempted to apply these ideas to their analysis of Indian society. Nor should we overlook the eagerness with which such ideas were taken up in India, China and many other extra-European societies, only becoming discredited (though not every-where abandoned) because of the contribution of Western race science to the genocidal beliefs and practices of Nazism.

The chief application of ethnological principles before Independence took the form of attempts to identify racial qualities of 'vigour', 'virility' and even nationhood among potential military recruits and other important clients of the colonial state. The idea of India as a domain of ethnologically superior 'Aryans' had a profound influence throughout the colonial period on those who considered themselves advanced and scientific in their application of contemporary race theory both to the practical problems of empire and to the wider concerns of contemporary science and global strategic thinking. Yet even more importantly, by the later nineteenth century these same theories were being actively embraced and transformed by an extre-mely wide range of educated south Asians. For these members of the subcontinent's vocal and politically active intelligentsias, race science was a source of deep and lasting inspiration in their formulation of secular as well as religious ideologies of nationhood and anti-colonial resistance.

As was seen in Chapter 7, the effects of this thinking can still be seen in the persistence of ethnological terms and categories in both official and scholarly writing on India's so-called tribal peoples, and in some cases – including the officially sponsored *People of India* project – in the discussion of supposed cultural and physical differentiations between individual 'clean' and 'untouchable' caste groups. Race theory is also very much alive in the polemics of the subcontinent's Hindu supremacist organisations. In the decades since Independence, it has remained a strong influence too on the many other political extremists who have claimed a right on 'scientific' racial grounds to advance the interests of particular religious, ethnic or linguistic 'communities'. These have included militant spokesmen for Sri Lanka's Sinhala Buddhist population, as well as many champions of India's so-called Dravidians and underclass Dalits, for whom the use of race theory has been reinforced since the early twentieth century by polemical references to caste and anti-Brahmanical ideals.

Notwithstanding this preoccupation with race and ethnological theory, in the late nineteenth and twentieth centuries the issue of caste became a major focus in debates between Indian intellectuals and social reformers about the alleged ills and moral failings of their homeland. How could India advance to true and independent nationhood, these thinkers asked, if it remained a 'caste society'? The answers to this question were extremely diverse, but there can be no doubt that the phenomenon of caste was of deep concern to most if not all of India's leading politicians and social commentators in the decades before Independence.

The 'uplift' of the so-called depressed or Harijan castes was a central theme in these debates. Opinion was deeply divided between those, including Gandhi and the Hindu sage-reformer Swami Vivekananda, who condemned the usages of untouchability while still identifying other aspects of caste as benign and valuable, and such polemicists as the 'untouchable' leader B. R. Ambedkar for whom caste was wholly pernicious. There were other important 'reformists' too who propounded vehemently anti-Brahmanical ideals, often embracing forms of so-called liberal or casteless faith through which they hoped to transform and purify the entire Indian social order.

As was seen in Chapter 6, even 'secular' nationalists like Nehru did not dismiss caste as an orientalist fiction or an irrelevance to the concerns of the modern nation. Indeed, the views of pre-Independence Hindu 'reformists' and of those who stood forth as defenders of pious caste norms often had much more in common than one might expect.

This was most evident in many of these commentators' paternalistic or openly hostile attitudes towards low-caste and other 'depressed' groups, including Muslims. The most striking area of this convergence was in the widely shared view of the 'pure' Hindu nation as a domain with little if any tolerance for such improprieties as cow-killing, and for the other so-called social impurities for which both 'untouchables' and Muslims had come to be so widely reviled. (It goes without saying that Nehru, together with many other important twentieth-century nationalists, did not evince this kind of hostility towards Muslims and the 'depressed'.)

In the second half of the book, there were again two complementary concerns, with the focus falling first on the workings of independent India's powerful and heavily bureaucratised modern state, and then on the moves made by ordinary citizens of the new 'secular' republic to challenge, embrace and reformulate the norms of caste in their everyday lives. In the early years of Independence, the leaders of the Indian National Congress committed the country to ideals of 'secularism' and casteless social justice. Yet, simultaneously, as was seen in Chapter 7, they also gave state agencies an obligation to accept the social reality of caste in fulfilling the 1950 Constitution's mandate to relieve the so-called backwardness of the country's 'untouchables', 'tribals' and other 'weaker sections'.

Since Independence, the state's attempts to pursue these goals through policies of so-called reservations (caste-based compensatory discrimination) have aroused persistent controversy as well as intermittent mass violence. Such schemes have certainly not expunged the social and economic disparities between Indians of 'clean' and 'unclean' caste origin. There are of course much-publicised individual exceptions. The career of Jagjivan Ram proved that a Harijan-'untouchable' politician could achieve senior ministerial office, and the leaders of virtually every Indian political party now routinely extol such champions of low-caste 'uplift' as Ambedkar and Phule. Even so, and in spite of the laws and constitutional provisions outlawing the formal usages of untouchability, most of India's poorest and least advantaged citizens are either Muslims or people of 'untouchable' or 'tribal' descent.

Thus, even though the state's moves to 'uplift' so-called Dalits have been anything but revolutionary in their effects, the debates which these official schemes have engendered have done much to keep awareness of caste alive in public consciousness since Independence. The language of contemporary politics has been suffused since the 1950s with forms of caste-related jargon which are familiar to virtually all those who vote, read newspapers or have reason to feel either threatened or inspired by the steps taken by state and central government to allocate college places and other benefits to so-called OBCs, Backwards, Dalits, Scheduled communities, non-'Manuvadis' and so on.

As Chapter 7 showed, the usages of modern electoral democracy have proved to be highly favourable to expressions of populism which have been framed around either direct or covert appeals to the moral and practical allegiances of caste. The political outcome in these cases has been just as complex and unpredictable as the workings of 'tribe' as a basis of electoral mobilisation in many African societies, or of religious and ethnic 'community' in the decision-making processes of many Western electorates, including those of Northern Ireland and the United States. Nevertheless, while regional caste groups have certainly not behaved according to the crude logic of the so-called vote bank, jati and varna themes had unmistakable power in the underpinning of the dramatically new forms of political allegiance which took shape in the years following Nehru's death.

These became visible first in the anti-Congress and 'banish poverty' electoral upheavals of the 1960s and early 1970s, which brought the so-called middle peasant to political prominence in the era of the Green Revolution. This period saw the dawning of militant Dalit agitation, and the new assertiveness of the 'son-of-the-soil' or clean-caste tiller, demanding massive reservations benefits for those of 'Other Backward' caste origin. Yet another wave of new electoral affinities came into being from the 1980s and well into the 1990s with the emergence of so-called Mandal–Mandir political confrontations. These had their origins in the rise of the Hindu supremacist *'sangh parivar'*, and its assault on so-called Ambedkarite social justice and reservations schemes in the name of unity, 'merit' and the advancement of Hindutva, or Hindu nationhood.

Caste was of course very far from being the only potent reference point for the advocates of these compelling new political causes, and indeed virtually all modern politicians proclaim their opposition to 'casteism' and 'casteist' electoral tactics. Even so, it would be absurd to claim that the idea of Jat, Kamma, Yadav or Dalit origin as a source of superior worth and entitlement has been anything other than a real and potent feature in the forging of these assertive post-Nehruvian mass political movements. The most notable examples of this in the 1990s have been the rise of Gangetic north India's highly successful 'peasant'/OBC Samajwadi Party (SP), and the Dalit-based Bahujan Samaj Party (BSP).

For all its power, the Indian state is still far from being the sole or even the paramount agent in the perpetuation of caste language and caste usages in the years since Independence. The conventions of jati and varna difference described in Chapter 8 have retained a notable degree of power in the lives of both urban and rural Indians, including many of those who see themselves as embodiments of modern goals and values. The observations of many social scientists have shown that in contemporary India there are still real economic and other practical advantages to be gained from the sustaining and affirming of caste ties.

This has been true of both of the forms of caste logic which were discussed in Chapter 8. These were, first, caste in its supposedly 'traditional' forms exalting gradations of *gotra*, or sub-caste, and the asymmetrical symbiosis of interacting high- and low-status jati groups; and secondly, the modern-minded or 'substantialised' idea of caste as an exclusive and often militant bond of allegiance with moral claims resembling those of other modern 'imagined communities', especially those of the nation and the ethno-religious community. It has been the capacity of these two contrasting conceptual systems to interact and reinforce one another in contentious circumstances which has made references to caste such an enduring feature both of politics and of everyday social interaction.

There are, of course, other claims, including those of class, ethno-religious 'community', and even the ideals of the modern 'casteless' nation, to which Indians regularly respond in everything from the making of marriages to the recruitment of office staff. Nevertheless, the active pursuit of caste-specific strategies, even by those who in some respects lead substantially 'casteless' lives both within and beyond the home, is still prevalent throughout the country. This can be seen not only in such arenas as the wording of marriage advertisements and the preservation of ritualised household purity norms, but also in the interactions of the ostensibly casteless industrial or bureaucratic workplace, as well as in many competitive commercial and 'peasant' environments.

Even with the curtailment of 'permit Raj', such usages have certainly not disappeared from the lives of successful business and trading people. They have been even more a source of significant advantages for many poor and vulnerable groups, especially those struggling to keep afloat in insecure agrarian environments. Yet even in rural India, where 'good' blood is still a desirable asset in a world of change and uncertainty, there is far more to 'caste society' than conformity to rigid norms of purity and hierarchy. Indeed one of the striking features of contemporary caste life is an apparent resurgence of the Kshatriya-like or power-centred ideals of moral endowment which were formerly so prominent in the emerging 'dharmic' kingdoms of the seventeenth and eighteenth centuries.

For a variety of reasons, including the partial discrediting of both 'secular' and Gandhian ideals of modern Indian nationhood, these Kshatriya-like models of the way of life of the 'good Hindu' have become decidedly more attractive to many Indians than the norms of caste-denying renunciatory asceticism or pacific Vaishya-style *ahimsa*. Of course this does suggest that now as much as in the lifetime of the self-made Kshatriya *chhatrapati* Shivaji Bhonsle, the leading of a caste life may be a matter of personal choice and calculated strategic options rather than an inheritance of age-old codes and scriptural norms.

Yet the one manifestation of so-called traditional caste values that still pervades everyday life is the compelling power of the pollution barrier. Certainly there are Dalit activists who fervently contest the claims and usages of ritual purity and pollution, and many descendants of so-called untouchables now subscribe to religious or 'secular' class-based ideologies which emphatically repudiate the logic of 'Manuvadi' teachings. Nevertheless, one need only look at the widespread phenomenon of so-called caste war, as described in Chapter 9, to see how powerful and persistent the usages of caste have been in situations where both embattled elites and more vulnerable populations have found advantage in appeals to those of like 'kind' and 'community', in some cases with official approval and support. These are certainly not expressions of primordial essences or allegiances. Furthermore, there are areas of India where so-called caste feuds do not regularly occur.

Yet where these outbreaks of so-called caste war have been widespread, those most vulnerable to coercion and violence have been those of Harijan/Dalit descent. In many areas, even the 'modern' city has become an arena for this kind of mass violence, and those caught up in such outbreaks are told by both the press and politicians that the divisions between them are, above all, those of caste rather than class, faith or ethnolinguistic identity.

It is true of course that the most sophisticated modern anthropological studies have strongly challenged the kinds of judgements that an old-style 'orientalist' would make both in the case of so-called caste feuds and in those of the more benign expressions of caste consciousness described in the final chapters. It has been widely observed that contemporary manifestations of jati and varna consciousness are very different from the purity-loving, 'holistic', *gotra*-conscious forms of caste identity that became widespread both before and during the colonial period. Dumont's concept of 'substantialisation', as developed and modified by Barnett, together with the further insights and theoretical innovations of such scholars as Veena Das, T. N. Madan and André Béteille, have all taken the modern understanding of caste very far from the idea of an innate and dehumanising south Asian cultural 'essence'.

Yet it is still important to recognise the power of caste norms in a world of both competing and intersecting affiliations and allegiances. These complexities can be observed in unexpected places, including the most solemn enactments of the modern Indian state. In July 1997, just three weeks before the fiftieth anniversary of Indian Independence, the Malayali diplomat Kocheril Raman Narayanan capped a brilliant career in public service by becoming the tenth President of the Indian Union, thus attaining India's highest national office. The Indian press, together with many foreign newspapers, gave intensive coverage to the new President's 'Dalit' origins, with much being said about the excitement his election had aroused among the country's low-caste or 'Dalit'/toiler populations, as well as the unprecedented nature of this achievement on the part of a descendant of 'untouchables'. Newspaper headlines hailed the President's inauguration as a decisive breaking of 'caste barriers'.

Following his swearing-in ceremony in the sumptuous setting of Edwin Lutyens's imperial capital of New Delhi, President Narayanan rode from the former viceroy's residence, now the presidential palace, in a horse-drawn carriage. This conveyance was another legacy of the Raj; it was used by India's British Viceroys in the colonial era's great ceremonies of state. The new President was attended by mounted cavalrymen, and by retainers who shielded his head with a fringed

12. Shielded by an umbrella signifying righteous rule, and guarded by horsemen in Rajput regimental uniform, Mr K. R. Narayanan rides in a Victorian-style coach after being sworn in as India's first 'Dalit'/Harijan head of state on 25 July 1997.

ceremonial umbrella like those used to signify the dharmic kingship of Hindu maharajas and the *mahant*s (chief preceptors) of ascetic renouncer orders. This honour-guard wore the resplendent full dress uniforms and turbans which the British had originally designed for their Rajput military regiments, using as their model the court dress of 'traditional' rulers from the so-called martial races. Thus both the press coverage of this event and the faithful replication of colonial and pre-British ceremonial usages comprised a remarkable amalgam of themes and reference points, with allusions to the particularities of ethnicity, race and class, as well as the unifying claims of the modern nation-state.

Caste themes were certainly not paramount here. Yet they were still a significant element in the way that both the staging of the event and its media representations took for granted the existence of caste as a potent reality of Indian life, at least in the past as well as the immediate present, if not necessarily for the future.

India then is not and never has been a monolithic 'caste society'. It may even be that one day the principles and usages of jati and varna will lose much or all of their meaning for Indians living both within and beyond the subcontinent. Nevertheless, if one is to do justice to India's complex history, and to its contemporary culture and politics, caste must be neither disregarded nor downplayed – its power has simply been too compelling and enduring.

GLOSSARY

Abbreviations

Ar	Arabic
Ben	Bengali
Hin	Hindi
Mar	Marathi
Skt	Sanskrit
Tam	Tamil
Tel	Telugu

ahimsa (Skt) Hindu principle of reverence for animate life

Ahir caste title of non-elite north Indian 'peasant'-pastoralists known also as Yadav (qv)

AIDMK 'All-India' DMK (qv)

Arya Samaj activist Hindu 'revival' association founded 1875

Aryan from Skt *arya* (a self-identification of ancient Sanskrit-speakers); used as a racial category differentiating speakers of Indo-European languages from so-called Dravidians (qv)

bania term used for members of castes associated with commerce, trade or money-lending

begar (Hin) unpaid labour services exacted from low-caste groups (see *rasad*)

bhadralok lit. 'good people' (Ben); educated high-caste Bengali Hindus

bhakti lit. 'devotion' (Skt); spiritual traditions emphasizing adoration of personified Hindu deities

Bhangi caste title of Gujarati 'untouchable' waste-removers

Bhil title of central Indian 'tribal' people

Bhumihar caste title of north Indian Brahmans with traditions of land-holding and soldiering

BJP Bharatiya Janata ('Indian People's') Party founded in 1980; Hindu supremacist political party devoted to the goal of Hindutva (qv)

Brahman member of Hindu 'priestly' caste; highest and purest order in the fourfold varna (qv) scheme

Chamar caste title of north India's major 'untouchable' population; alternative title Jatav now preferred

383

Chandala designation for low-status east Bengal cultivating caste; alternative title Namasudra (qv) now preferred

Chitpavan caste title of Maharashtra Brahmans with tradition of elite service under Maratha (qv) dynasts

Congress Party (or Indian National Congress, founded 1885) political organization spearheading anti-colonial 'freedom struggle'; independent India's ruling party 1947–77 and 1980–96

Dalit 'the oppressed' (Mar/Hin); term for low-caste/'untouchable' groups now used in preference to Gandhian appellation Harijan (qv)

deshmukh (Mar) head of an armed elite family vested by Maratha (qv) rulers with authority over a grouping of villages (*pargana*)

dharma lit. 'way', 'duty', 'law', etc. (Skt); code of morality, worship, conduct prescribed for a caste or 'community'; hence 'dharmic', referring to righteous norms or environments where *dharma* prevails

Dhed designation for 'untouchable' groups in Gujarat

DMK Dravida Munnetra Kazhagam. Tamil non-Brahman political party, founded 1949

dora lit. 'lord' (Tel); regional landlord in the Telengana region

Dravidian term for speakers of southern and 'tribal' Indian languages; regarded by race theorists as racially distinct from so-called Aryans (qv)

dwija 'twice-born' (Skt); members of caste groups entitled to wear the *suta* (qv) or sacred thread, i.e. Hindus who claim membership of the three superior varnas (qv)

Ezhava caste title of low-status Malabar cultivators and toddy (palm-wine) producers

gharibi hatao lit. 'poverty begone!' (Hin); slogan used in the 1970s in populist Congress Party (qv) campaigns of mass 'people's justice'

girasidar (also *girasia*, anglicised as Gracia, *girisi*, etc.) western Indian term for lord with ancestral raiding and revenue-taking rights

gotra Skt/Hin term usually translated as clan or sub-caste, i.e. non-intermarrying segment of a larger jati (qv) whose members claim common ancestry

Gujar title of north Indian 'peasants' with warrior-pastoralist origins

Harijan term coined by Mahatma Gandhi for 'unclean' or ex-'untouchable' castes, usually translated 'child of God'

Hindu Mahasabha 'Great Hindu Association'; all-India Hindu supremacist pressure group founded in 1915

Hindu revivalism term for activist movements to 'reform' or 'revive' the Hindu faith

Hindutva   lit. 'Hindu-ness' (Skt/Hin); term popularised since 1920s by campaigners exalting Hinduism as India's true national faith

Holeya   caste title of Kannada-speaking 'untouchables'

Jat   title of north India's major non-elite 'peasant' caste

jati   lit. 'birth', 'name', 'breed', 'order' etc. (Skt/Hin with variants in other vernaculars); caste in the sense of a specific named 'birth-group' (see varna)

Kabirpanthi   follower of the anti-Brahman sectarian tradition or *sampradaya* (qv) inspired by the Hindu weaver saint Kabir

Kallar   title of rural groups in Tamilnad with warrior-pastoralist ancestral traditions

Kamma   title of Telugu-speaking south Indian 'peasant' caste

Kanbi   see Patidar; western Indian 'peasant' caste title

Kayastha   title of predominantly north Indian caste with tradition of scribal livelihoods

Khatri   caste title of north Indians with military and scribal traditions

kisan   'peasant' (Hin); often used interchangeably with equivalent term *khedut*

Koli   title of western Indian warrior-pastoralist population

Kshatriya   (Skt) person of lordly/kingly virtues and livelihood; second highest 'order' in the fourfold varna (qv) scheme

Kurmi   caste title of non-elite 'peasants' in eastern Gangetic plain

Lingayat   caste title of Kannada-speaking 'peasant' population with distinctive Shaivite sectarian religious tradition

lokika   from Skt/Hin *lok* 'world'; used of Brahmans (qv) who follow non-priestly, i.e. 'secular' or worldly, callings

Mahar   title of a large 'unclean' labouring caste in Maharashtra

Manu   mythical Hindu author of classical Hindu text propounding the doctrine of varna (qv) hierarchy

Maratha   caste title of superior 'peasants' in Maharashtra with traditions of arms-bearing and privileged land rights

Marava   title of Tamilnad rural population with warrior-pastoralist ancestral traditions

math   Hindu monastic foundation

mirasidar   (from Ar *miras*, to inherit) superior south Indian landholder

Nadar   caste title of Tamil entrepreneurial groups, adopted by low-status tillers formerly known as Shanars

Namasudra   caste title of low-status rural Bengalis known formerly as Chandalas (qv)

Naxalite term first applied in late 1960s to Maoist rural insurgents in Naxalbari region (West Bengal), now used for other 'peasant' and 'tribal' militants

Nayaka south Indian term designating warrior chief, ruler

Nayar caste title of Malayalis with distinctive matrilineal descent system and traditions of martial lordship

NWP North-Western Provinces

Pallar title of a large 'unclean' south Indian labouring caste

pandit (Hin) Sanskrit-derived term for person with knowledge of classical Hindu scriptures and sciences

Paraiyar title of a large 'unclean' south Indian labouring caste; source of English term 'pariah'

Patidar caste title of superior 'peasant' tillers in Gujarat

patil (Mar) village headman

Peshwa title of hereditary Brahman chief ministers to pre-colonial Maratha (qv) ruling dynasts (see Chitpavan)

poligar (Tam *palaiyakarar*, domain-holder) ruler of petty south Indian chiefdom

purana (Skt) mythology of the Hindu gods

Rajput north Indian caste title with connotations of lordliness and royal refinement

Ram divine Hindu warrior-king, hero of the Hindu epic poem the *Ramayana*; inspiration for contemporary Hindu supremacist campaigns

rasad (Hin) dues in kind demanded from low-caste groups by those claiming authority over them (see *begar*)

Reddi caste title of Telugu-speaking south Indian 'peasant' cultivators

RSS Rashtriya Swayamsevak Sangh ('Association of National Volunteers') founded 1925; paramilitary Hindu supremacist organization

sampradaya (Skt) Hindu devotional order or sect

Sanskrit ancient language of the Vedas (qv) and other Hindu classical texts

sastric embodying the values of Hindu scriptures (Skt *sastras*) propounding the doctrine of varna (qv); sanctioned in scripture, hence proper or orthodox

sat-sudra 'clean-caste' (Skt/Hin); usually used of members of non-elite peasant caste groups (see Shudra)

sati (Skt) ritual self-immolation of Hindu widows

seva lit. 'service' (Skt/Hin); privileged devotional services, e.g. to gods and human spiritual preceptors

shakti   Skt-derived term for activated energy endowing deities, especially goddesses, with power to heal, protect, destroy

Shudra   (Skt) the lowest of the orders defined in the fourfold varna (qv) scheme

suta   (Skt/Hin) sacred thread worn by members of 'twice-born' (*dwija*) castes, signifying membership of one of the three superior Hindu varnas (qv)

swadeshi   literally 'own country'(Skt/Hin); home industry; early twentieth-century nationalist campaigns featuring boycotts of British goods

Thug   lit. 'trickster' (Hin); member of a purported secret religious cult of thieves and murderers

UP   United Provinces of Agra and Awadh/Uttar Pradesh

Vaishya   third in the rank order of the fourfold varna (qv) scheme; usually designating commercial livelihoods

varna   lit. 'colour', 'rank', 'class' (Skt); the idealised fourfold scheme of ranked human callings or orders as set out in ancient Hindu scriptures including the *Laws of Manu* (qv)

Vedas   India's most ancient classical religious scriptures, compiled *c.* 2000 BC

Vellala   High-status Tamil caste title denoting superior landed background

VHP   Vishva Hindu Parishad ('World Hindu Council'), founded 1964; organization devoted to worldwide 'revitalization' of Hindu faith

Vijayanagar   medieval south Indian ruling dynasty

Yadav   north Indian caste title signalling kinship with the deified Hindu pastoral hero Krishna; now used in preference to Ahir (qv)

zat   (Hin) see jati; innate and distinctive caste 'essence' or identity

BIBLIOGRAPHY

Abbreviations

CIS   *Contributions to Indian Sociology*
CSSH   *Comparative Studies in Society and History*
EJS   *European Journal of Sociology*
EPW   *Economic and Political Weekly*
IESHR   *Indian Economic and Social History Review*
ISR   *Indian Social Reformer*
JAS   *Journal of Asian Studies*
JESL   *Journal of the Ethnological Society of London*
JPS   *Journal of Peasant Studies*
JRAS   *Journal of the Royal Asiatic Society*
MAS   *Modern Asian Studies*
MASL   *Memoirs of the Anthropological Society of London*
TESL   *Transactions of the Ethnological Society of London*
THES   *Times Higher Educational Supplement*

Official surveys and gazetteers

Buchanan, Francis [Hamilton] 1925 *Journal of Francis Buchanan [Hamilton] Kept During the Survey of the Districts of Patna and Gaya in 1811–1812* (ed. V. H. Jackson) Patna
    1930 *Journal of Francis Buchanan [Hamilton] Kept During the Survey of the District of Bhagalpur 1810–1811* (ed. C. Oldham) Patna
Crooke, William 1896 *The tribes and castes of the North-Western Provinces and Oudh* Calcutta
Hodson, T. C. 1937 *India. Census ethnography, 1901–1931* Delhi
Iyer, L. K. Ananthakrishna 1909–12 *The Cochin tribes and castes* Madras
Logan, William 1887 *Malabar* 2 vols. Madras
Luard, C. E. 1908 *Central India State Gazetteer Series. II Indore* Calcutta
Nanjundayya, H. V. and L. K. Ananthakrishna Iyer 1930 *The Mysore tribes and castes* Mysore
Nesfield, J. C. 1885 *Brief view of the caste system of the North-Western Provinces and Oudh. Together with an examination of the names and figures shown in the Census Report, 1882* Allahabad
Oldham, Wilton 1870 *North-Western Provinces. Historical and statistical memoir of the Ghazeepoor District* Allahabad
    1876 *History of Ghazeepoor and the Benares Province from 1781 to 1795 A.D.* Allahabad

Russell, R. V. 1916 *The tribes and castes of the central provinces of India* 4 vols. London

Ternan, A. H. 1869 *North-Western Provinces. Report of the Jaloun District, historical, geographical, statistical* Allahabad

Thurston, Edgar 1909 *Castes and tribes of southern India* 9 vols. Madras

Censuses

Census of the North-Western Provinces 1872 Vol. 1 *General Report*, by W. C. Plowden (Allahabad, 1873)

Census of British India 1881 Vols. 1–3 *Report*, by W. C. Plowden (London, 1883)

Census of the North-Western Provinces and Oudh 1881 *Report*, by Edmund White (Allahabad, 1882)

Census of India 1891 Vol. 1 *General Report*, by J. A. Baines (London 1893)

Census of India 1901 Vol. 1, Pt 1 *Report*, by H. H. Risley and E. A. Gait (Calcutta, 1903)

Census of India 1911 Vol. 1, Pt 1 *Report*, by E. A. Gait (Calcutta, 1913)

Census of India 1921 Vol. 1, Pt 1 *Report*, by J. T. Marten (Calcutta, 1924)

Census of India 1931 Vol. 1, Pt 3 *Ethnographical* Section A *Racial Affinities of the Peoples of India* (by B. S. Guha); Section B *Ethnographic Notes* (ed. J. H. Hutton) (Simla, 1935)

Census of India 1931 Vol. 18 *United Provinces of Agra and Oudh* Pt 1 *Report*, by A. C. Turner (Allahabad, 1933)

Census of India 1961 Vol. 10 Pt 7B *Maharashtra. Fairs and Festivals in Maharashtra* (Bombay, 1969)

Census of India 1971 Series 19: *Tamil Nadu*, Part VB – Schedule C – *Ethnographic Notes* 2 vols. (Delhi, 1975)

Government publications

Proceedings of the Public Services Commission Scts. 1–3 Calcutta, 1887

Report of the Backward Classes Commission [K. Kalelkar, Chairman] 3 vols. (1st publ.) 1955: repr. Delhi 1983)

Report of the Backward Classes Commission [1978–80, B. P. Mandal, Chairman] 2 vols. Delhi 1981

Padmanabha, P. 1981 *The Indian Census and anthropological investigations* New Delhi

Singh, K. S. (ed.) 1992 *People of India: an introduction* (Anthropological Survey of India, Calcutta)

Singh, K. S. (ed.) 1995 *People of India* II: *The Scheduled Castes* Anthropological Survey of India (Delhi: Oxford University Press)

Singh, K. S., V. Balla and V. Kaul 1994 *People of India. National Series* vol. 10 *The biological variation in Indian populations* (Delhi: Oxford University Press)

Social Welfare, Department of 1969 *Report of the Committee on Untouch-*

ability, Economic and Educational Development of the Scheduled Castes
New Delhi

Newspapers and other serial publications

Congrès International des Sciences Anthropologiques et Ethnologiques
Economic and Political Weekly
Frontline (Madras)
The Hindu (Madras; and International Edition)
India Today (New Delhi)
Indian Social Reformer (Bombay)
Outlook (New Delhi)
Sunday (Calcutta)
The Times of India
The Week (Kochi [Cochin])

Secondary works

Abu'l Fazl, 1891 *The Ain-i-Akbari* (trans. H. S. Jarrett) 2 vols. Calcutta
Ahmad, Imtiaz (ed.) 1973 *Caste and social stratification among Indian Muslims* New Delhi
Ahmed, R. 1981 *The Bengal Muslims 1871–1906. A quest for identity* Delhi
Alam, Javeed 1989 'Political articulation of mass consciousness' in Z. Hasan *et al.* (eds.), *The state, political processes and identity. Reflections on modern India* Delhi: 237–55
— 1993 'The changing grounds of communal mobilization' in Gyanendra Pandey (ed.), *Hindus and others. The question of identity in India today* New Delhi: 146–76
Alam, Muzaffar 1986 *The crisis of empire in Mughal north India. Awadh and the Punjab, 1707–48* Delhi
Alavi, Seema 1995 *The sepoys and the company. Tradition and transition in northern India 1770–1830* Delhi
Ambedkar, B. R. 1936 *The annihilation of caste* (ed. Mulk Raj Anand, 1990) New Delhi
— 1946 *Who were the Shudras?* [repr. 1970] Bombay
— 1948 *The untouchables. Who were they and why they became untouchables* New Delhi
Amin, Shahid and Dipesh Chakrabarty (eds.) 1996 *Subaltern studies IX. Writings on south Asian history and society* Delhi
Anant, S. S. 1972 *The changing concept of caste in India* Delhi
Appadurai, Arjun 1974 'Right and left hand castes in south India' *IESHR* 11 (2–3): 216–59
— 1986 'Is homo hierarchicus?' *American Ethnologist* 13 (4): 745–61
— 1992 'Putting hierarchy in its place' in G. E. Marcus (ed.), *Rereading cultural anthropology* London: 34–47
Archer, Mildred and Toby Falk 1989 *India revealed. The art and adventures of James and William Fraser 1801–35* London

Arnold, David 1986 *Police power and colonial rule. Madras 1859–1947* New Delhi
1993 *Colonizing the body. State medicine and epidemic disease in nineteenth-century India* Berkeley and Los Angeles
Arunima, G. 1996 'Multiple meanings. Changing conceptions of matrilineal kinship in 19th & 20th century Malabar' *IESHR* 33 (3): 284–307
Babb, Lawrence A. 1972 'The Satnamis – political involvement of a religious movement' in Michael Mahar (ed.), *The untouchables of contemporary India* Tucson
1987 *Redemptive encounters. Three modern styles in the Hindu tradition* Delhi
Bailey, F. G. 1957 *Caste and the economic frontier. A village in highland Orissa* Manchester
1960 *Tribe, caste and nation. A study of political activity and political change in highland Orissa* Manchester
Baker, Christopher John 1976a *The politics of south India 1920–1937* Cambridge
1976b 'Tamilnad estates in the twentieth century' *IESHR* 13 (1): 1–44
Balfour, Arthur 1873 *Cyclopaedia of India* (2nd edn) 5 vols.
Banaji, Jairus 1994 'The farmers' movements' *JPS* Special Issue 21 (3–4): 228–45
Bandyopadhyay, Sekhar 1997 *Caste, protest and identity in colonial India. The Namasudras of Bengal 1872–1947* Richmond
Bandyopadhyay, Sekhar, Abhijit Dasgupta and W. van Schendel (eds.) 1994 *Bengal. Communities, development and states* New Delhi
Banton, Michael and J. Harwood 1975 *The race concept* Newton Abbott
Barkan, Elazar 1992 *The retreat of scientific racism. Changing concepts of race in Britain and the United States between the world wars* Cambridge
Barnett, Marguerite Ross 1976 *The politics of cultural nationalism* Princeton
Barnett, Steve 1977 'Identity choice and caste ideology in contemporary south India' in K. David (ed.), *The new wind* The Hague
Barrier, N. Gerald (ed.) 1981 *The Census in British India. New perspectives* New Delhi
Barstow, A. E. 1928 *The Sikhs. An ethnology* (repr. 1985) Delhi
Basu, Durga Das 1982 *Introduction to the Constitution of India* New Delhi
Bates, C. N. 1984 'Regional dependence and rural development in central India, 1820–1930' Ph.D. dissertation, University of Cambridge
1995 'Race, caste and tribe in Central India' in Peter Robb (ed.), *The concept of race in south Asia* Delhi 219–59
Baxi, Upendra 1990 'Reflections on the reservations crisis in Gujarat' in Veena Das (ed.), *Mirrors of violence. Communities, riots and survivors in south Asia* Delhi: 215–39
Bayly, C. A. 1975 *The local roots of Indian politics. Allahabad 1880–1920* Oxford
1983 *Rulers, townsmen and bazaars. North Indian society in the age of British expansion, 1770–1870* Cambridge

391

1988 *The New Cambridge History of India II. 1: Indian society and the making of the British Empire* Cambridge

1996 *Empire and information. Intelligence gathering and social communication in India, 1780–1870* Cambridge

Bayly, Susan 1989 *Saints, goddesses and kings. Muslims and Christians in south Indian society, 1700–1900* Cambridge

1995 'Caste and race in colonial ethnography' in Peter Robb (ed.), *The concept of race in south Asia* Delhi: 165–218

1999 'The evolution of colonial culture in Asia' in Andrew Porter (ed.), *The New Oxford History of the British Empire* III *The nineteenth century* Oxford

Beck, Brenda E. F. 1972 *Peasant society in Konku. A study of right and left subcastes in south India* Vancouver

1976 'The symbolic merger of body, space and cosmos' *CIS* ns 10 (2): 213–43

Bell, Morag, Robin Butlin and Michael Heffernan (eds.) 1995 *Geography and imperialism, 1820–1920* Manchester

Bennett, Lynn 1983 *Dangerous wives and sacred sisters. Social and symbolic roles of high-caste women in Nepal* New York

Bennett, Peter 1990 'In Nanda Baba's house. The devotional experience of Pushti Marg temples' in Owen Lynch (ed.) *Divine passions. The social construction of emotion in India* Delhi: 182–211

Bernier, François 1914 *Travels in the Mogul Empire, A.D. 1636–1668* (trans. A. Constable) (2nd edn), Oxford

Berreman, Gerald D. 1979 *Caste and other inequalities. Essays on inequality* Meerut

Béteille, André 1981 *The backward classes and the new social order* Delhi

1986 'Individualism and equality' *Current Anthropology* 27 (2): 121–34

1991a 'The reproduction of inequality: occupation, caste and family' *CIS* 25 (1): 3–28

1991b *Society and politics in India. Essays in a comparative perspective* London and Atlantic Highlands

1992a *The backward classes in contemporary India* Delhi

1992b 'Caste and family in representations of Indian society' *Anthropology Today* 8 (1): 13–18

1996 *Caste, class and power. Changing patterns of stratification in a Tanjore village* (2nd edn) Oxford

Bhambhri, C. P. 1989 'The Indian state: conflicts and contradictions' in Z. Hasan *et al.* (eds.), *The state, political processes and identity. Reflections on modern India* New Delhi: 73–87

Bhattacharya, Jogendra Nath 1896 *Hindu castes and sects* (repr. 1973) Calcutta

Bhattacharya, Neeladri 1992 'Agricultural labour and production' in Gyan Prakash (ed.), *The world of the rural labourer in colonial India* Delhi: 146–204

Biardeau, Madeleine 1992 *Hinduism. The anthropology of a civilization* New Delhi

Bloch, Maurice 1989 'Power and rank as a process' in M. Bloch (ed.), *Ritual, history and power. Selected papers in anthropology* London and Atlantic Highlands: 46–88

Blunt, E. A. H. 1969 *The caste system of northern India* (1st publ. 1931) Delhi

Borrodaile, H. 1884–7 *Gujarat caste rules. Published from the original answers of the castes with the sanction of Her Imperial Majesty's High Court of Judicature, Bombay* (ed. M. Nathoobhoy) 2 vols. Bombay

Bose, P. K. 1985a 'Mobility and conflict. Social roots of caste violence in Bihar' in I. P. Desai *et al.* (eds.), *Caste, caste conflict and reservations* Delhi: 180–200

1985b 'Social mobility and caste violence' in I. P. Desai *et al.* (eds.), *Caste, caste conflict and reservations* Delhi: 135–47

Bose, Subhas Chandra 1946 *The Indian struggle 1920–1942* London

Bose, Sugata 1986 *Agrarian Bengal. Economy, social structure and politics, 1919–1947* Cambridge

1997 'Nation as mother', in S. Bose and Ayesha Jalal (eds.), *Nationalism, Democracy and Development. State and Politics in India* Delhi: 50–75

Bose, Sugata and Ayesha Jalal 1998 *Modern south Asia. History, culture, political economy* London and New York

Bouglé, Celestin 1927 *Essais sur le régime des castes* Paris

Bourdieu, Pierre 1962 *Sociologie de l'Algérie* (1st publ. Paris 1958) Boston

Brass, Paul R. 1974 *Language, religion and politics in north India* Cambridge

1985 *Caste, faction and party in Indian politics* vol. 2 *Election Studies* Delhi

1990 *The New Cambridge History of India. IV. 1: The politics of India since Independence* Cambridge

1997 *Theft of an idol. Text and context in the representation of collective violence* Princeton

Brass, Paul R. and F. C. R. Robinson (eds.) 1987 *The Indian National Congress and Indian society 1885–1985* Delhi

Brass, T. (ed.) 1994 'New farmers' movements in India' *JPS – Special Issue* 21 (3–4)

Breckenridge, Carol A. and Peter van der Veer (eds.) 1993 *Orientalism and the postcolonial predicament. Perspectives on south Asia* Philadelphia

Breman, Jan 1974 *Patronage and exploitation. Changing agrarian relations in south Gujarat, India* Berkeley

1985 *Of peasants, migrants and paupers. Rural labour circulation and capitalist production in west India* Delhi

1992 'The Hali system in south Gujarat' in Gyan Prakash (ed.), *The world of rural labour in colonial India* Delhi: 248–81

Briggs, George W. 1920 *The Chamars* Calcutta

Brimnes, Niels 1996 'European authority and caste disputes in south India, 1650–1850 – British and Danish perspectives' Ph.D. dissertation, University of Cambridge

Brittlebank, Kate 1997 *Tipu Sultan's search for legitimacy. Islam and kingship in a Hindu domain* Delhi

Browne, James 1788 *India Tracts. Containing a description of the Jungle Terry districts* London

Burghart, Richard 1978a 'The founding of the Ramanandi sect' *Ethnohistory* 25: 121–39
    1978b 'Hierarchical models of the Hindu social system' *Man* ns 13: 519–36
    1983a 'Renunciation in the religious traditions of south Asia' *Man* ns 18: 635–53
    1983b 'For a sociology of Indias' *CIS* 17 (2): 275–99
Burghart, Richard and Audrey Cantlie (eds.) 1985 *Indian religion* London and New York
Burnes, Lt. Alexander 1834 'Notice of a remarkable hospital for animals at Surat' *JRAS* 1: 96–7
Campbell, George [n.d.] *The ethnology of India*
    1868–9 'On the races of India as traced in existing tribes and castes' *JESL* ns I: 128–40
Cannadine, David 1998 *The rise and fall of class in Britain* New Haven
Carman, J. B. and F. A. Marglin (eds.) 1985 *Purity and auspiciousness in Indian society* Leiden
Carroll, Lucy 1978 'Colonial perceptions of Indian society and the emergence of caste(s) associations' *JAS* 37(2): 233–50
Cashman, Richard I. 1975 *The myth of the Lokmanya. Tilak and mass politics in Maharashtra* Berkeley
Cassen, Robert and Vijay Joshi (eds.) 1995 *India. The future of economic reform* Delhi
Chakraborty, R. L. 1994 'A caste movement in Mymensingh' in S. Bandyopadhyay *et al.* (eds.), *Bengal. Communities, development and states* New Delhi: 120–34
Chanda, Ramaprasad 1916 *The Indo-Aryan races. A study of the origin of Indo-Aryan people and institutions* Rajshahi
Chandavarkar, Rajnarayan 1994 *The origins of industrial capitalism in India. Business strategies and the working classes in Bombay 1900–1940* Cambridge
Chatterjee, Partha 1986 *Nationalist thought and the colonial world. A derivative discourse?* London
    1989 'Caste and subaltern consciousness' in Ranajit Guha, (ed.), *Subaltern Studies VI. Writings on South Asian history and society* Delhi: 169–209
Chatterji, Joya 1994 *Bengal divided. Hindu communalism and partition 1932–1947* Cambridge
Chattopadhyaya, Sudhakar 1973 *Racial affinities of early north Indian tribes* New Delhi
Chaudhuri, B. B. 1979 'Agrarian movements in Bengal and Bihar' in A. R. Desai (ed.) *Peasant struggles in India* Bombay: 337–74
Chowdhury-Sengupta, Indira 1995 'The effeminate and the masculine: nationalism and the concept of race in colonial Bengal' in P. Robb (ed.), *The concept of race in south Asia* New Delhi: 282–303
Cohn, Bernard (ed.) 1987 *An anthropologist among the historians* New Delhi

Cole, J. R. I. 1988 *Roots of north Indian Shi'ism in Iran and India. Religion and the state in Awadh 1772–1859* Berkeley and Los Angeles

Commander, Simon 1983 'The *jajmani* system in north India' *MAS* 17: 283–311

Conlon, Frank F. 1977 *A caste in a changing world* Berkeley and Los Angeles
    1981 'The Census of India as a source of the historical study of caste and religion' in N. Gerald Barrier (ed.), *The Census in British India. New perspectives* New Delhi: 103–17

Courtright, Paul B. 1985 *Ganesa Lord of obstacles* Oxford

Cox, Edmund n.d. [*c.* 1911] *Police and crime in India* London

Crawfurd, John 1863 'On the antiquity of man' *TESL* ns 2: 170–81

Crooke, William 1890 *An ethnological hand-book for the N.-W. Provinces and Oudh* Allahabad 1890
    1907 *The native races of the British Empire: natives of northern India* London

Daniel, E. Valentine 1984 *Fluid signs. Being a person the Tamil way* Berkeley

Darling, Malcolm 1925 *The Punjab peasant in prosperity and debt* (repr. 1977) Delhi

Das, Veena 1976 'The uses of liminality. Society and cosmos in Hinduism' *CIS* ns 10 (2): 245–63
    1982 *Structure and cognition* Delhi
    1990 (ed.) *Mirrors of violence. Communities, riots and survivors in south Asia* Delhi

Dasgupta, B. N. 1982 *Rajah Rammohun Roy. The last phase* Delhi

Datta, Nonica 1997 'Arya Samaj and the making of Jat identity' *Studies in History* ns 13 (1): 97–119

David, Kenneth (ed.) 1977 *The new wind. Changing identities in south Asia* The Hague and Paris

Davis, M. 1976 'A philosophy of rank from rural west Bengal' *JAS* 36 (1): 5–24

Delïège, Robert 1985 *Bhils of Western India*
    1988 *Les Paraiyars du Tamil Nadu* Nettetal: Steyler Verlag
    1989 'Les mythes d'origine chez les Paraiyars' *L'Homme* 109: 107–16
    1992 'Replication and consensus' *Man* ns 27: 155–73
    1993 *Le système des castes* Paris

Desai, I. P. 1976 *Untouchability in Gujarat* Bombay

Desai, I. P., Ghanshyam Shah and Pradip Kumar Bose (eds.) 1985 *Caste, caste conflict and reservations* Delhi

Desai, Neera 1978 *Social change in Gujarat. A study of nineteenth-century Gujarati society* Bombay

Desai, S. V. 1980 *Social life in Maharashtra under the Peshwas* Bombay

Deshpande, Madhav M. and Peter Edwin Hook (eds.) 1979 *Aryan and non-Aryan in India* Ann Arbor

Dhanagare, D. N. 1986 *Peasant movements in India 1920–1950* (2nd edn) Delhi

Diamond, A. (ed.) 1991 *The Victorian achievement of Sir Henry Maine* Cambridge

Dikötter, Frank 1992 *The discourse of race in modern China* London

Dirks, Nicholas B. 1982 'The pasts of a *Palaiyakarar' JAS* 41 (4): 655–83

1987 *The hollow crown. Ethnohistory of an Indian kingdom* Cambridge

1989 'The invention of caste: civil society in colonial India' *Social Analysis* 25: 42–52

1992a 'From little king to landlord' in N. Dirks (ed.) *Colonialism and culture*., Ann Arbor: 175–208

1992b 'Castes of mind' *Representations* 37: 56–78

1992c (ed.) *Colonialism and culture* Ann Arbor

Divekar, V. D. 1982 'The emergence of an indigenous business class in Maharashtra in the eighteenth century' *MAS* 16: 427–43

Dumézil, Georges 1957 *Les dieux souverains des Indo-Européens* Paris

Dumont, Louis 1960 'For a sociology of India' *CIS* ns 4: 82–9

1966 'Marriage in India', *CIS* 9: 90–114

1970 *Homo hierarchicus. The caste system and its implications* London

1986 *A south Indian subcaste. Social organisation and religion of the Pramalai Kallar* (trans. M. Moffatt and A. Morton) Delhi

Dutt, Nripendra Kumar 1969 *Origin and growth of caste in India* II. *Castes in Bengal* (1st publ. 1931) Calcutta

Eaton, Richard Maxwell 1978 *Sufis of Bijapur 1300–1700. Social roles of Sufis in medieval India* Princeton

Elliot, Henry M. 1869 *Memoirs of the history, folklore and distribution of the races of the North Western Provinces of India* 2 vols. London

Elliot, Walter 1868–9 'On the characteristics of the population of central and southern India' *JESL* ns I: 94–128

Farquhar, J. N. 1967 *Modern religious movements in India* (1st publ. 1914) Delhi

Flood, Gavin 1996 *An introduction to Hinduism* Cambridge

Forbes, James 1813 *Oriental memoirs* 4 vols. London

Forbes, L. R. 1894 'The Cheros' *North Indian Notes and Queries* 2 (4): 25

Fox, R. G. 1971 *King, clan, raja and rule. State–hinterland relations in preindustrial India* Berkeley

1985 *Lions of the Punjab. Culture in the making* Berkeley

Frankel, Francine 1978 *India's political economy 1947–1977. The gradual revolution* Princeton

1989 'Caste, land and dominance in Bihar' in F. Frankel and M. S. A. Rao (eds.), *Dominance and state power in modern India. Decline of a social order*, I: 46–132

Frankel, Francine and M. S. A. Rao, 1989–90 *Dominance and state power in modern India. Decline of a social order* 2 vols. Delhi

Freeman, James 1986 'The consciousness of freedom among India's untouchables' in D. K. Basu and R. Sissons (eds.), *Social and economic development in India* Delhi: 153–170

Freitag, Sandria B. 1985 'Collective crime and authority in north India' in
A. Young (ed.), *Crime and criminality in British India* Tucson: 140–63
1989a *Collective action and community. Public arenas and the emergence of
communalism in north India* Berkeley
1989b (ed.) *Culture and power in Banaras. Community, performance and
environment 1800–1980* Berkeley
Fruzzetti, Lina 1982 *The gift of a virgin. Women, marriage and ritual in a
Bengali society* Delhi
Frykenberg, Robert Eric 1965 *Guntur district 1788–1848. A history of local
influence and central authority in southern India* Oxford
1982 'On roads and riots in Tinnevelly' *South Asia* 4 (2): 34–52
Fuller, C. J. 1975 'Kerala Christians and the caste system' *Man* ns 11: 53–70
1979 'Gods, priests and purity. On the relation between Hinduism and the
caste system' *Man* ns 14: 459–76
1984 *Servants of the goddess. The priests of a south Indian temple* Cambridge
1988 'The Hindu pantheon and the legitimation of hierarchy' *Man* ns 23, 1:
19–39
1989 'Misconceiving the grain heap' in J. Parry and M. Bloch (eds.), *Money
and the morality of exchange* Cambridge: 33–93
1992 *The camphor flame. Popular Hinduism and society in India* Princeton
1996 (ed.) *Caste today* Delhi
Gagnik, Achyut and Anil Bhatt 1984 'The anti-Dalit agitation in Gujarat'
South Asia Bulletin 4 (1): 45–60
Galanter, Marc 1984 *Competing equalities. Law and the backward classes in
India* Berkeley
Galey, Jean-Claude 1981 'Louis Dumont – an intellectual profile' *CIS* ns 15
(1&2): 3–29
1989 'Reconsidering kingship in India' *History and Anthropology* 4:
123–87
Geertz, Clifford 1974 *Agricultural involution. The process of ecological change
in Indonesia* Berkeley
Gellner, David 1986 'Language, caste, religion and territory. Newar identity
ancient and modern' *EJS* 27: 102–48
1991 'Hinduism, tribalism and the position of women. The problem of
Newar identity' *Man* ns 26 (1): 105–25
Gellner, David and Declan Quigley 1995 *Contested hierarchies. A collabora-
tive ethnography of caste among the Newars of the Kathmandu valley,
Nepal* Oxford
Ghugare, Shivaprabha 1983 *Renaissance in Western India. Karmaveer V. R.
Shinde (1873–1944)* Bombay
Ghurye, G. S. 1963 *The Mahadev Kolis* Bombay
Gill, S. S. 1994 'The farmers' movement and agrarian change' *JPS* Special
Issue 21 (3–4): 195–211
Godelier, Maurice 1978 'Infrastructures, societies and history' *New Left
Review* 112: 84–96

1986 *L'idéel et le materiel* (*The mental and the material. Thought, economy and society*: trans. M. Thom) London

Gokhale, Jayashree B. 1990 'Dalit consciousness in Maharashtra' in F. Frankel and M. S. A. Rao (eds.), *Dominance and state power in modern India. Decline of a social order* vol. II. Delhi: 222–65

Gold, Ann Grodzins 1988 *Fruitful journeys. The ways of Rajasthani pilgrims* Berkeley

Good, Anthony 1991 *The female bridegroom. A comparative study of life-crisis rituals in south India and Sri Lanka* Oxford

Gooptu, Nandini 1997 'The urban poor and militant Hinduism in early twentieth-century Uttar Pradesh' *MAS* 31 (4): 879–918

Gordon, Stewart 1993 *The New Cambridge History of India II. 4. The Marathas 1600–1818* Cambridge

Gore, M. S. 1989 *Non-Brahman movement in Maharashtra* New Delhi

Gough, Kathleen 1973 'Harijans in Thanjavur' in K. Gough and H. Sharma (eds.), *Imperialism and revolution in south Asia* New York: 222–45

1989 *Rural change in southeast India 1950s to 1980s* Delhi

Gould, Harold A. 1990 *The Hindu caste system. III. Politics and caste* Delhi

Grant Duff, James Cuninghame 1921 *A history of the Mahrattas* (1st pub. 1826) 2 vols. London

Grewal, J. S. 1990 *The New Cambridge History of India II. 3. The Sikhs of the Punjab* Cambridge

Guha, Ramachandra 1990 'An early environmental debate. The making of the 1878 Forest Act' *IESHR* 27 (1): 65–84

Guha, Ranajit (ed.) 1989 *Subaltern studies VI. Writings on south Asian history and society* Delhi

Guha, Sumit 1985 *The agrarian economy of the Bombay Deccan 1818–1941* Delhi

1995 'An Indian penal regime. Maharashtra in the eighteenth century' *Past and Present* 147: 101–26

1996 'Forest polities and agrarian empires. The Khandesh Bhils, c. 1700–1850' *IESHR* 33 (2): 133–53

Guha-Thakurta, Tapati 1992 *The making of a new 'Indian' art. Artists, aesthetics and nationalism in Bengal, c. 1850–1920* Cambridge

Gunthorpe, E. J. 1882 *Notes on criminal tribes residing in or frequenting the Bombay Presidency* Bombay

Gupta, S. K. 1985 *The scheduled castes in modern Indian politics. Their emergence as a political power* New Delhi

Hamilton, Walter 1828 *The East-India Gazetteer* 2 vols. (2nd edn) London

Hardgrave, Robert L. 1969 *The Nadars of Tamilnad. The political culture of a community in change* Berkeley and Los Angeles

Hardiman, David 1981 *Peasant nationalists in Gujarat. Kheda district 1917–1934* Delhi

1996 *Feeding the Baniya. Peasants and usurers in western India* Delhi

Harris, Marvin 1976 'A philosophy of Hindu rank from rural west Bengal' *JAS* 36 (1): 5–24

Hasan, Zoya 1994 'Shifting ground: Hindutva politics and the farmers' movement in U.P.' *JPS* Special Issue 21 (3–4): 165–94
Hasan, Zoya, S. N. Jha and R. Khan (eds.) 1989 *The state, political processes and identity. Reflections on modern India* New Delhi
Hauser, Walter 1991–2 'Swami Sahajanand and the politics of social reform' *Indian Historical Review* 18: 1–2
    1994 (ed.) *Sahajanand on agricultural labour and the rural poor* Delhi
Hawley, J. H. (ed.) 1994 *Sati the Blessing and the Curse* New York, Oxford
Hawthorn, Geoffrey 1984 'Some political causes of class and caste hostility in India' in C. Clarke, D. Ley and C. Peach (eds.) *Geography and ethnic pluralism* London: 141–56
Haynes, Douglas E. 1991 *Rhetoric and ritual in colonial India. The shaping of a public culture in Surat city 1852–1928* Berkeley and Oxford
Haynes, Douglas and Gyan Prakash (eds.) 1991 *Contesting power. Resistance and everyday social relations in south Asia* Berkeley and Los Angeles
Heesterman, J. C. 1985 *The inner conflict of tradition. Essays in Indian ritual, kingship, and society* Chicago and London
    1989 'King and warrior', *History and Anthropology* 4: 97–122
Heimsath, Charles M. 1964 *Indian nationalism and Hindu social reform* Princeton
Hocart, A. M. 1950 *Caste. A comparative study* London
Hodgson, J. S. 1857 *Opinions on the Indian Army* London
Humphrey, Caroline and James Laidlaw 1994 *The archetypal actions of ritual. A theory of ritual illustrated by the Jain rite of worship* Oxford
Hunt, James 1863 'On ethno-climatology' *TESL* ns 2: 50–83
    1863–4 'On the Negro's place in nature' *MASL* 1: 1–63
Hunter, W. W. 1897 *Annals of rural Bengal* (7th edn) London
Hutton, J. H. 1946 *Caste in India. Its nature, function and origins* Cambridge
Huxley, T. H. 1868–9 'President's address' *JESL* ns 1: 89–93
Ibbetson, Denzil 1916 *Panjab Castes* Lahore
Ilaih, K. 1996 'Productive labour, consciousness and history' in S. Amin and D. Chakrabarty (eds.), *Subaltern Studies IX* Delhi: 165–200
Inden, Ronald 1975 *Marriage and rank in Bengali culture* Berkeley
    1990 *Imagining India* Oxford
Irschick, Eugene F. 1969 *Politics and social conflict in South India. The non-Brahman movement and Tamil separatism, 1916–1929* Berkeley and Los Angeles
    1994 *Dialogue and history. Constructing south India 1795–1895* Berkeley
Isaacs, Harold R. 1965 *India's ex-untouchables* Bombay
Iyer, Raghavan (ed.) 1986–7 *The moral and political writings of Mahatma Gandhi* 3 vols. Oxford
Jacob, John 1857 *A few remarks on the Bengal army* (1st edn 1851) London
Jaffrelot, Christophe 1995 'The idea of the Hindu race' in Peter Robb (ed.), *The concept of race in south Asia* Delhi: 327–54
    1996 *The Hindu nationalist movement and Indian politics 1925 to the 1990s* London

Johnson, Gordon 1973 *Provincial politics and Indian nationalism. Bombay and the Indian National Congress 1880–1915* Cambridge
Jones, Kenneth W. 1976 *Arya Dharm. Hindu consciousness in 19th-century Punjab* Berkeley
1989 *The New Cambridge History of India. III. 1. Socio-religious reform movements in British India* Cambridge
1998 'Two *sanatan dharma* leaders', in William Radice (ed.), *Swami Vivekananda and the modernization of Hinduism* Oxford: 224–63
Jones, Sir William 1807a 'Sixth Discourse – On the Persians' *Asiatick Researches* II: 43–66
1807b 'Eighth Discourse' *Asiatick Researches* III: 1–16
Joshi, G. N. 1940 *The new Constitution of India* London
Joshi, Vijay and I. M. D. Little, 1996 *India's economic reforms 1991–2001* Oxford
Juergensmeyer, Mark 1982 *Religion as social vision. The movement against untouchability in twentieth-century Punjab* Berkeley
Kamble, N. D. 1981 *Atrocities on Scheduled Castes in post independent India* New Delhi
Karve, Irawati 1988 'On the road: a Maharashtrian pilgrimage' in E. Zelliot and M. Bertsen (eds.), *The experience of Hinduism. Essays on religion in Maharashtra* Albany: 142–73
Karve, Irawati and V. M. Dandekar, 1948 *Anthropometric measurements of Maharashtra* Poona
Kasturi, Malavika 1994 'Law and crime in India. British policy and the female infanticide act of 1870' *Indian Journal of Gender Studies* 1 (2): 169–93
Kaul, Rekha 1993 *Caste, class and education. Politics of the capitation fee phenomenon in Karnataka* New Delhi and London
Kaul, Shiv Kishan 1937 *Wake up Hindus (A plea for mass religion) Aryanism* Lahore
Keer, Dhananjay 1981 *Dr. Ambedkar. Life and mission* (3rd edn) Bombay
Kemper, Steven 1979 'Sinhalese astrology, south Asian caste systems and the notion of individuality' *JAS* 38 (3): 477–97
Ketkar, Shridhar V. 1909–1911 *History of caste in India* 2 vols. London
1911 *An essay on Hinduism. Its formation and future* vol. II London
Keyes, Charles F. and E. Valentine Daniel (eds.) 1983 *Karma. An anthropological inquiry* Berkeley
Khan, Ali Muhammad 1965 *Mirat-i-Ahmadi. A Persian history of Gujarat* [c. 1664] (trans M. Lokhandwala) Baroda
Khan, Mumtaz Ali 1980 *Scheduled castes and their status in India* New Delhi
Khare, R. S. 1976 *The Hindu hearth and home* New Delhi
1983 *Normative culture and kinship. Essays on Hindu categories, processes and perspectives* New Delhi
1984 *The untouchable as himself. Ideology, identity and pragmatism among the Lucknow Chamars* Cambridge and New York
1990 'Indian sociology and the cultural "other"' *CIS* ns 24 (2): 177–99
Khilnani, Sunil 1997 *The idea of India* London

Klass, Morton 1980 *Caste. The emergence of the south Asian social system* Philadelphia

Knox, Robert 1863 'Ethnological inquiries and observations' *The Anthropological Review* 1: 246–63

Kohli, Atul 1987 *The state and poverty in India. The politics of reform* Cambridge

Kolenda, Pauline 1964 'Religious anxiety and Hindu fate' in Edward B. Harper (ed.) *Religion in South Asia* Seattle: 71–81

1967 'Toward a model of the Hindu *jajmani* system' in G. Dalton (ed.), *Tribal and peasant economies* Garden City NY: 285–332

1976 'Seven types of hierarchy in *Homo Hierarchicus*' *JAS* 35 (4): 581–96

1978 *Caste in contemporary India. Beyond organic solidarity* Menlo Park and London

1980 'Hindu caste in a regal tradition: the native view' *Rice University Studies* 66 (1): 125–36

1983 *Caste, cult and hierarchy. Essays on the culture of India* New Delhi

1984 'Woman as tribute, woman as flower: images of "woman" in weddings in north and south India', *American Ethnologist* 11 (1): 98–117.

1986 'Caste in India since Independence' in D. K. Basu and R. Sissons (eds.), *Social and economic development in India* Delhi: 106–28

Kolff, Dirk 1990 *Naukar, Rajput and sepoy. The ethnohistory of the military labour market in Hindustan, 1450–1850* Cambridge

Kopf, David 1979 *The Brahmo Samaj and the shaping of the modern Indian mind* Princeton

Kothari, Rajni (ed.) 1970 *Caste in Indian politics* New Delhi

Kulke, Hermann 1995 *The state in India, 1000–1700* New Delhi

Kumar, Dharma 1965 *Land and caste in south India. Agricultural labour in the Madras Presidency during the nineteenth century* Cambridge

1992 'Caste and landlessness in south India' in Gyan Prakash (ed.), *The world of the rural labourer in colonial India* Delhi: 75–106

1994 'Indian secularism: a note' *MAS* 28 (1): 223–4

Kuper, Adam 1988 *The invention of primitive society. Transformation of an illusion* London and New York

1991 'The rise and fall of Maine's patriarchal society' in A. Diamond (ed.), *The Victorian achievement of Sir Henry Maine* Cambridge: 99–110

Laidlaw, James 1995 *Riches and renunciation. Religion, economy and society among the Jains* Oxford

Leach, Edmund (ed.) 1971 *Aspects of caste in South India, Ceylon and North West Pakistan* Cambridge

Leonard, Karen 1978 *The social history of an Indian caste. The Kayasths of Hyderabad* Berkeley and London

Leopold, J. 1974 'British applications of the Aryan theory of race to India' *English Historical Review* 89 (3): 578–603

Lodrick, D. O. 1981 *Sacred cows, sacred places. The origin and survival of animal homes in India* Berkeley

Lokhande, G. S. 1982 *B. R. Ambedkar. A study in social democracy* New Delhi
Lorenzen, David N. 1987 'Traditions of non-caste Hinduism: the Kabir Panth' *CIS* ns 21 (2): 263–83
Ludden, David 1985 *Peasant history in South India* Princeton
Lutgendorf, Philip 1989 'Ram's story in Shiva's city' in S. B Freitag (ed.), *Culture and power in Benares* Berkeley: 34–61
Lynch, Owen M. 1969 *The politics of untouchability. Social mobility and social change in a city of India* New York and London
Macfarlane, A. D. J. 1991 'Some contributions of Maine to history and anthropology' in A. Diamond (ed.), *The Victorian achievement of Sir Henry Maine* Cambridge: 111–42
Madan, T. N. 1982 'Anthropology as a mutual interpretation of cultures' in Hussein Fahim (ed.), *Indigenous anthropology in non-Western countries* Durham, North Carolina: 4–18
1991 'Auspiciousness and purity: some reconsiderations' *CIS* 25 (2): 287–94
1992 'The ideology of the householder among the Kashmiri Pandits' in Ákos Östör, Lina Fruzzetti and Steve Barnett (eds.), *Concepts of person. Kinship, caste and marriage in India* Delhi: 99–117
1993 'The structural implications of marriage alliance in north India' in P. Uberoi (ed.), *Family, kinship and marriage in India* Delhi: 287–306
Madan, T. N. *et al.* 1971 'On the nature of caste in India. A review symposium on Louis Dumont's *Homo hierarchicus*' *CIS* ns 5: 1–81
Maddock, Peter 1993 'Idolatry in western Saurashtra' *South Asia* 15: 101–26
Mahar, J. Michael (ed.) 1972 *The untouchables in contemporary India* Tucson
Malamoud, Charles 1981 'On the rhetoric and semantics of purusartha' *CIS* ns 15 (1&2): 33–54
Malcolm, Sir John 1832 *A memoir of central India including Malwa and adjoining provinces* 2 vols. (repr. Shannon, 3rd edn 1972)
Manor, James 1989 'Caste, class, dominance' in F. Frankel and M. S. A. Rao (eds.), *Dominance and state power in modern India. Decline of a social order*, I, Delhi: 326–43
Marriott, McKim 1968 'Caste ranking and food transactions' in Milton Singer and Bernard S. Cohn (eds.), *Structure and change in Indian society* Chicago: 133–71
1969 (ed.) [1955] *Village India* Chicago
1976 'Hindu transactions: diversity without dualism' in Bruce Kapferer (ed.), *Transaction and meaning: Directions in the anthropology of exchange and symbolic behaviour* Philadelphia: 109–142
1989 'Constructing an Indian sociology' *CIS* Special Issue 23 (1): 1–40
Marriott, McKim and Ronald Inden 1977 'Toward an ethnosociology of south Asian caste systems' in Kenneth David (ed.), *The new wind: changing identities in south Asia* The Hague and Paris: 227–38
Marshall, Peter 1987 *The New Cambridge History of India. II. 2. Bengal the British Bridgehead: Eastern India, 1740–1828* Cambridge
1996 'Reappraisals: the rise of British power in eighteenth-century India' *South Asia* 19 (1):

Masselos, James C. 1974 *Towards nationalism. Group affiliations and the politics of public associations in nineteenth-century western India* Bombay

Massey, James 1995 *Dalits in India* Delhi

Mateer, Samuel 1871: '*The land of charity'. A descriptive account of Travancore* London

Mathur, K. and C. Agarwal (eds.) 1974 *Tribe, caste and peasantry* Lucknow

Mayer, Adrian C. 1985 'The king's two thrones' *Man* ns 20: 205–21

McGilvray, D. B. (ed.) 1982 *Caste ideology and interaction* Cambridge

McLane, John R. 1977 *Indian nationalism and the early Congress* Princeton

Mcmunn, Sir G. 1932 *The martial races of India* London

Meillassoux, Claude 1973 'Are there castes in India?' *Economy and Society* 2, 1: 89–111

Mencher, Joan P. 1974 'The caste system upside down' *Current Anthropology* 15: 469–93

　1978 *Agriculture and social structure in Tamil Nadu. Past origins, present transformations* Durham, North Carolina

Mendelsohn, Oliver and Marika Vicziany 1998 *The untouchables. Subordination, poverty and the state in modern India* Cambridge

Menon, Dilip M. 1994 *Caste, nationalism and Communism in south India. Malabar 1900–1948* Cambridge

Metcalf, Thomas R. 1979 *Land, landlords and the British Raj. Northern India in the nineteenth century* Berkeley

　1995 *Ideologies of the Raj* Cambridge

Mines, Mattison 1984 *The warrior merchants. Textiles, trade and territory in south India* Cambridge

　1992 'Individuality and achievement in south Indian social history' *MAS* 26 (1): 129–56

Mishra, R. C., D. Sinha, and J. W. Berry 1996 *Ecology, acculturation and psychological adaptation. A study of Adivasis in Bihar* New Delhi

Mitra, Babu Rajendralala 1867–9 'On the Gypsies of Bengal' *MASL* 3: 120–33

Mitra, Subrata K. 1982 'Caste, class and conflict. Organisation and ideological change in an Orissa village' *Purusartha* 6: 97–133

　1990 (ed.) *Politics of positive discrimination. A cross national perspective* Bombay

　1992 *Power, protest and participation. Local elites and the politics of development in India* London and New York

　1994 'Caste, democracy and the politics of community formation in India' in M. Searle-Chatterjee and U. Sharma (eds.), *Contextualizing caste. Post-Dumontian approaches* Oxford: 49–71

Moffatt, Michael 1979 *An untouchable community in south India. Structure and consensus* Princeton, NJ

　1990 'Deconstructing McKim Marriott's ethnosociology: an outcaste's critique' *CIS* 24 (2): 215–36

Moon, Vasant 1982 *Dr Babasaheb Ambedkar. Writings and speeches* Pune

Morris, Charles 1881 *The Aryan race. Its origins and its achievements* London

Morrison, Charles 1984 'Three styles of imperial ethnography. British officials as anthropologists in India' *Knowledge and Society* 141–69

Fani, Moshan 1973 *Oriental literature, or The Dabistan* (trans. D. Shea and A. Troyer) Lahore

Mukherjee, S. N. 1970 'Class, caste and politics in Calcutta, 1815–1838' in Edmund Leach and S. N. Mukherjee (eds.), *Elites in South Asia* Cambridge: 33–78

Mukherjee, S. N. and Edmund Leach (eds.) 1970 *Elites in south Asia* Cambridge

Nag, Kalidas and Debajyoti Burman (eds.) 1945 *The English works of Raja Rammohun Roy* Calcutta

Naik, Murahari 1989 *Agrarian unrest in Karnataka* New Delhi

Nandy, Ashis 1983 *The intimate enemy. Loss and recovery of self under colonialism* Delhi

Natarajan, S. 1959 *A century of social reform in India* London

Nelson, J. H. 1881 *A prospectus of the scientific study of the Hindu law* London

Nigam, Sanjay 1990 'Disciplining and policing the "criminals by birth"', Pts 1 & 2 *IESHR* 27 (2): 131–64; 27 (3): 257–87

O'Flaherty, Wendy Doniger (ed.) 1981 *The Rg Veda. An Anthology* Harmondsworth

1988 (ed) *Textual sources for the study of Hinduism* Manchester

1991 (ed.) *The Laws of Manu* London

O'Hanlon, Rosalind 1985 *Caste, conflict and ideology. Mahatma Jotirao Phule and low caste protest in nineteenth-century Western India* Cambridge

1993 'Historical approaches to communalism' in Peter Robb (ed.), *Society and ideology. Essays in south Asian history* Delhi: 247–66.

1994 *A comparison between women and men. Tarabai Shinde and the critique of gender relations in colonial India* Madras

forthcoming: a 'Imperial masculinities. Gender and the construction of imperial service under Akbar' *IESHR*

forthcoming: b 'Warriors, gentlemen and eunuchs. Some meanings of manliness in late Mughal India' *Journal of the Economic and Social History of the Orient*

O'Hanlon, Rosalind and D. A. Washbrook 1992 'After Orientalism: culture, criticism and politics in the Third World' *CSSH* 34 (1): 141–67

Oman, J. Campbell 1907 *The Brahmans, Theists and Muslims of India* London

Omissi, David 1994 *The sepoy and the Raj. The Indian army, 1860–1940* Basingstoke and London

Omvedt, Gail 1976 *Cultural revolt in a colonial society. The non-Brahman movement in western India 1873–1930* Bombay

1978 'Class struggles or caste war' *Frontier* 30 Sept. 1978

1980 'Adivasis, culture and modes of production in India' *Bulletin of Concerned Asian Scholars* 12 (1): 15–22

1982 (ed.) *Land, caste and politics in Indian states* Delhi
1994 *Dalits and the democratic revolution. Dr. Ambedkar and the Dalit movement in colonial India* New Delhi
1995 *Dalit visions. The anti-caste movement and the construction of an Indian identity* London
Ovington, J. 1929 [1696] *A voyage to Surat in the year 1689* London
Pande, B. N. 1985 *A centenary history of the Indian National Congress (1885–1985)* vol. II New Delhi
Panikkar, K. N. 1995 *Culture, ideology, hegemony. Intellectuals and social consciousness in colonial India* New Delhi
Panini, M. N. 1996 'The political economy of caste' in M. N. Srinivas (ed.), *Caste. Its twentieth century avatar* New Delhi: 26–68
Pant, R. 1987 'The cognitive status of caste in colonial ethnography' *IESHR* 24 (2): 145–62
Parekh, Bhikkhu and Subrata Kumar Mitra 1990 'The logic of anti-reservation discourse', in Subrata Kumar Mitra (ed.), *Politics of positive discrimination. A cross-national perspective* Bombay: 91–109
Parkin, Robert 1990 'Ladders and circles. Affinal alliance and the problem of hierarchy' *Man* ns 25 (3): 472–88
Parry, Jonathan 1970 'The Koli dilemma' *CIS* ns 4: 84–104
1974 'Egalitarian values in a hierarchical society' *South Asian Review* 7 (2): 95–121
1979 *Caste and kinship in Kangra* London
1980 'Ghosts, greed and sin' *Man* ns 15: 88–111
1981 'Death and cosmogony in Kashi' *CIS* ns 15: 337–65
1985 'Death and digestion: the symbolism of food and eating in north Indian mortuary rites' *Man* ns 20: 612–30
1991 'The Hindu lexicographer? A note on auspiciousness and purity' *CIS* ns 25 (2): 267–85
1994 *Death in Banaras* Cambridge
Patnaik, Utsa and Manjari Dingwaney (eds.) 1985 *Chains of servitude. Bondage and slavery in India* London
Peabody, Norbert 1991 'In whose turban does the Lord reside?: The objectification of charisma and the fetishism of objects in the Hindu kingdom of Kota' *CSSH* 33 (4): 726–54
1996 'Tod's *Rajast'han* and the boundaries of colonial rule in nineteenth-century India' *MAS* 30 (1): 185–220
Pearson, M. N. 1975 *Merchants and rulers in Gujarat. The response to the Portuguese in the sixteenth century* Berkeley, London
Peers, D. M. 1991 ' "The habitual nobility of being": British officers and the social construction of the Bengal army' *MAS* 25 (3): 545–69
Perlin, Frank 1978 'Of white whale and countrymen in the eighteenth-century Maratha Deccan' *JPS* 5 (2): 172–237
1985 'State formation reconsidered' *MAS* 19 (3): 415–80
Pick, Daniel 1989 *Faces of degeneration: a European disorder c. 1848–1918* Cambridge

Pike, L. Owen 1865–6 'On the psychical characteristics of the English people' *MASL* 2: 153–88

Pinch, William, R. 1996 *Peasants and monks in British India* Berkeley

Pinney, Christopher 1988 'Representations of India: normalisation and the "other"' *Pacific Viewpoint* 29 (2): 144–62

1990a 'Classification and fantasy in the photographic construction of caste and tribe' *Visual Anthropology* 3 (2–3): 259–88

1990b 'Colonial anthropology in the "laboratory of mankind"' in C. A. Bayly (ed.), *The Raj. India and the British 1600–1946* London: 252–63

Pitt-Rivers, Julian 1971 'On the word "caste"' in T. O. Beidelman (ed.), *The translation of culture. Essays to E. E. Evans-Pritchard* London: 231–56

Pocock, David 1972 *Kanbi and Patidar. A study of the Patidar community of Gujarat* Oxford

1973 *Mind, body and wealth. A study of belief and practice in an Indian village* Oxford

Poliakov, Leon 1974 *The Aryan myth* New York

Potter, Sulamith Heins and Jack Potter 1990 *China's peasants* Cambridge

Pradhan, M. C. 1966 *The political system of the Jats of northern India* London

Prakash, Gyan 1990a *Bonded histories. Genealogies of labour servitude in colonial India* Cambridge

1990b 'Writing post-Orientalist histories of the Third World' *CSSH* 32 (2): 383–408

1991 'Becoming a Bhuinya' in D. Haynes and G. Prakash (eds.), *Contesting power. Resistance and everyday social relations in south Asia* Berkeley: 145–74

Preston, Lawrence W. 1989 *The Devs of Cincvad. A lineage and the state in Maharashtra* Cambridge

Price, Pamela 1996 *Kingship and political practice in colonial India* Cambridge

Prior, Katherine Helen 1990 'The British administration of Hinduism in north India, 1780–1900' Ph.D. dissertation, University of Cambridge

Punalcker, S. P. 1985 'Caste ideology and class interests' in I. P. Desai *et al.* (eds.), *Caste, caste conflict and reservations* Delhi: 148–79

Puntambekar, S. V. 1929 'The Ajnapatra or royal edict' *Journal of Indian History* 8 (1–3): 81–105, 207–33

Puri, B. N. 1988 *The Khatris. A socio-historical study* New Delhi

Quigley, Declan 1993 *The interpretation of caste* Oxford

Rabitoy, Neil 1974 'Administrative modernisation and the Bhats of British Gujarat 1800–1820' *IESHR* 11 (1): 46–73

Radhakrishnan, Meena 1992 'Surveillance and settlements under the Criminal Tribes Act in Madras' *IESHR* 29 (2): 171–95

Radhakrishnan, Sarvepalli and Charles A. Moore (eds.) 1957 *A sourcebook in Indian philosophy* Princeton

Raheja, Gloria Goodwin 1988a *The poison in the gift. Ritual, prestation and the dominant caste in a north Indian village* Chicago and London

1988b 'India: caste, kingship and dominance reconsidered' *Annual Review of Anthropology* 17: 497–522

1989 'Centrality, mutuality and hierarchy' *CIS* 23 (1): 79–101

Ram, Jagjivan 1980 *Caste challenges in India* Delhi

Ramaswamy, Uma 1978 'The belief system of the non-Brahmin movement in India: the Andhra case' *Asian Survey* 18 (3): 290–300

Ranade, M. G. 1900 *Rise of the Maratha power* Bombay

Randeria, Shalini 1989 'Carrion and corpses: conflict in categorizing untouchability in Gujarat' *EJS* 30: 171–91

Rao, Raghunatha 1908 *The Aryan marriage* Madras

Rao, N. J. Usha 1981 *Deprived castes in India. (A profile of Karnataka)* Allahabad

Rao, V. N., D. Shulman and S. Subrahmanyam (eds.) 1992 *Symbols of substance. Court and state in Nayaka period Tamilnadu* Delhi

Raval, R. L. 1987 *Socio-religious reform movements in Gujarat during the nineteenth century* New Delhi

Ray, Rajat K. 1984 *Social conflict and political unrest in Bengal 1875–1927* Delhi

Raychaudhuri, Tapan 1988 *Europe reconsidered. Perceptions of the West in nineteenth century Bengal* Delhi

Raz, Ram 1836 'On the introduction of trial by jury' *JRAS* 3: 244–57

Reynolds, Lt. 1836 'Notes on the T'hags' *JRAS* 4: 200–13

Richards, J. F. (ed.) 1978 *Kingship and authority in south Asia* Madison, Wisconsin

1993 *The new Cambridge history of India I. 5. The Mughal empire* Cambridge

Richardson, David 1801 'An account of the Bazeegurs' *Asiatick Researches* 7: 457–85

Risley, H. H. 1886 'Primitive marriage in Bengal' *Asiatic Quarterly Review* 2: 71–96

1894 'The progress of anthropology in India', *Imperial & Asiatic Quarterly* ns 7 (13&14): 432–7

1908 *The people of India* London

Robb, Peter (ed.) 1993 *Society and ideology. Essays in south Asian history* Delhi

Ronaldshay, Lord 1925 *The Heart of Aryavarta. A study in the psychology of Indian unrest* London

Rosen, Stephen Peter 1996 *Societies and military power. India and its armies* Ithaca and London

Rudner, David 1994 *Caste and capitalism in colonial India. The Nattukottai Chettiars* Cambridge

Rudolph, Lloyd I. and Susanne Hoeber Rudolph 1987 *In pursuit of Lakshmi. The political economy of the Indian state* Chicago

Sangari, Kumkum and Sudesh Vaid (eds.) 1989 *Recasting women. Essays in colonial history* New Delhi

Saradamoni, K. 1973 'Agrestic slavery in Kerala during the nineteenth century' *IESHR* 10 (4): 371–85

Sarasvati, A. Rangasvami 1926 'Political maxims of the emperor-poet Krishnadeva Raya' *Journal of Indian History* 4 (1–3): 61–88

Saraswathi, S. 1974 *Minorities in Madras state. Group interests in modern politics* Delhi

Saraswati, Swami Dayananda 1975 *Light of Truth, or an English translation of the Satyarth Prakash* (trans. C. Bharadwaja) New Delhi

Sarkar, T. 1985 'Bondage in the colonial context' in U. Patnaik and M. Bingwaney (eds.), *Chains of servitude. Bondage and slavery in India* London: 97–126

Sato, Masanori 1997 'The Chamars of south-eastern Rajasthan' in H. Kotani (ed.), *Caste system, untouchability and the depressed* New Delhi: 31–53

Saumarez Smith, Richard 1985 'Rule-by-records and rule-by-reports. Complementary aspects of the British imperial rule of law' *CIS* ns 19 (1): 153–76

Scholberg, H. *The District Gazetteers of British India* Zug

Schwartzberg, J. 1981 'Sources and types of census error' in N. G. Barrier (ed.), *The Census in British India. New perspectives* New Delhi: 41–60

Seal, Anil 1968 *The emergence of Indian nationalism* Cambridge

Searle-Chatterjee, Mary 1981 *Reversible sex-roles. The special case of Benares sweepers* Oxford

— 1994 'Urban "untouchables" and Hindu nationalism' *Immigrants and Minorities* 13 (1): 12–25

Searle-Chatterjee, Mary and Ursula Sharma (eds.) 1994 *Contextualizing caste. Post-Dumontian approaches* Oxford

Seesodia, Thakur Shri Jessrajsinghji 1915 *The Rajputs. A fighting race* London

Sen, Amiya P. 1993 *Hindu revivalism in Bengal 1872–1905. Some essays in interpretation* Delhi

Sen, S. P. (ed.) 1979 *Social and religious reform movements in the nineteenth and twentieth centuries* Calcutta

Senart, Emile 1894 *Les castes dans l'Inde. Les faits et le système* Paris

Sengupta, K. S. 1979 'Agrarian disturbances in 19th century Bengal' in A. R. Desai (ed.), *Peasant struggles in India* Bombay: 189–205

Seth, Motilal 1904 *History of the Khattris* Agra

Shah, A. M. and I. P. Desai 1988 *Division and hierarchy. An overview of caste in Gujarat* Delhi

Shah, Ghanshyam 1985a 'Caste in contemporary India' in I. P. Desai, G. Shah and Pradip Kumar Bose (eds.), *Caste, caste conflict and reservations* Delhi: 1–43

— 1985b 'Anti-untouchable movements' in I. P. Desai et al. (eds.), *Caste, caste conflict and reservations* Delhi: 102–23

— 1990 *Social movements in India. A review of the literature* New Delhi, London

Shakespear, John 1820 'Observations regarding Badheks and T'hegs' *Asiatic Researches* 13: 282–92

Shankaradass, R. D. 1982 *The first Congress raj* Delhi

Sharma, K. L. (ed.) 1994 *Caste and class in India* Jaipur and New Delhi

Sharma, K. N. 1975 'For a sociology of India. On the word *"varna"*' *CIS* ns 9 (2): 293–7

Sherring, M. A. 1872 *Hindu tribes and castes as represented in Benares* London

Sherwood, Richard 1820 'Of the murderers called Phansigars' *Asiatic Researches* 13: 250–82

Sheth, D. L. 1979 'Caste and politics: a survey of literature', in Gopal Krishna (ed.), *Contributions to Asian Studies, 1* Delhi: 161–97

Shukla, K. S. and B. M. Verma 1993 *Development of Scheduled Castes and administration* New Delhi

Singh, Chetan 1988 'Conformity and conflict. Tribes and the "agrarian system" of Mughal India' *IESHR* 23 (3): 319–40

Singh, Parmand 1982 *Equality, reservation and discrimination in India. A constitutional study of Scheduled Castes, Scheduled Tribes and Other Backward Classes* New Delhi

Singh, Sita Ram 1968 *Nationalism and social reform in India* Delhi

Singha, Radhika 1998 *A despotism of law. Crime and justice in early colonial India* Delhi

Sivaramayya, B. 1996 'The Mandal judgement' in M. N. Srinivas (ed.) *Caste. Its twentieth-century avatar* New Delhi: 221–43

Skaria, Ajay 1992 'A forest polity in western India. The Dangs, 1800s–1920s' Ph.D. dissertation, University of Cambridge

Smith, V. A. 1894 'Thuggee' *North Indian Notes and Queries* 3 (4): 41–2

Srinivas, M. N. 1965 [1952] *Religion and society among the Coorgs of south India* Bombay

  1969 [1955] 'The social system of a Mysore village' in McKim Marriott (ed.), *Village India* Chicago

  1989 *The cohesive role of Sanskritization and other essays* Delhi

  1996 (ed.) *Caste. Its twentieth-century avatar* New Delhi

Steele, Arthur 1868 *The law and custom of the Hindoo castes within the Dekhun Provinces subject to the Presidency of Bombay* (1st publ. 1826) London

Stein, Burton 1980 *Peasant state and society in medieval south India* New Delhi

  1989 *The New Cambridge History of India I. 2. Vijayanagara* Cambridge

Stepan, Nancy 1982 *The idea of race in science. Great Britain 1800–1960* London

Stern, Henri 1977 'Power in traditional India: territory, caste and kinship in Rajasthan' in R. G. Fox (ed.), *Realm and region in traditional India* Delhi: 52–77

Stocking, G. W. 1968 *Race, culture and evolution. Essays in the history of anthropology* New York

Stokes, E. T. 1978 *The peasant and the Raj. Studies in agrarian society and peasant rebellion in colonial India* Cambridge

  1986 *The peasant armed. The Indian rebellion of 1857* Oxford

Subrahmanyam, Sanjay 1990a *The political economy of commerce. Southern India, 1500–1650* Cambridge

409

1990b (ed.) *Merchants, markets and the state in early modern India* Delhi

Tagore, G. M. 1863 'On the formation and institution of the caste system – the Aryan polity' *TESL* ns 2: 369–86

Tambiah, S. J. 1973 'From varna to caste through mixed unions' in Jack Goody (ed.), *The character of kinship* Cambridge: 191–229; (reprinted 1985 in S. J. Tambiah (ed.), *Culture, thought and social action* Cambridge and London: 212–51)

1996 *Levelling crowds. Ethnonationalist conflicts and collective violence in south Asia* Berkeley and London

Taylor, Miles (ed.) 1994 *The European diaries of Richard Cobden 1846–1849* Aldershot

Thapar, Romila 1984 *From lineage to state. Social formations in the mid-first millennium B.C. in the Ganga valley* Bombay

1989 'Imagined religious communities? Ancient history and the modern search for a Hindu identity' *MAS* 23 (2): 209–31

1992 *Interpreting early India* Delhi

Tharu, S. and Niranjana, T. 1996 'Problems for a contemporary theory of gender' in S. Amin and D. Chakrabarty (eds.), *Subaltern studies IX* Delhi: 232–60

Thorne, Christopher 1985 *The issue of war. States, societies and the Far Eastern conflict of 1941–1945* London

Timberg, Thomas A. 1978 *The Marwaris. From traders to industrialists* New Delhi

Tod, James 1920 *Annals and antiquities of Rajasthan* 3 vols., ed. W. Crooke (1st publ. 1829–32, new edn 1971) Delhi

Tomlinson, B. R. 1993 *The new Cambridge history of India III. 3: The economy of modern India 1860–1970* Cambridge

Tone, W. H. 1799 'Illustrations of some institutions of the Mahratta people' *Asiatic Annual Register 1798–99*: 124–50

Trautmann, Thomas R. 1997 *Aryans and British India* Berkeley, Los Angeles and London

Uberoi, Patricia (ed.) 1993 *Family, kinship and marriage in India* Delhi

Unnithan, Maya 1994 'Girasias and the politics of difference in Rajastan' in M. Searle-Chatterjee and U. Sharma (eds.), *Contextualising caste. Post-Dumontian approaches* Oxford: 92–121

Upadhyaya, Prakash Chandra 1992 'The politics of Indian secularism' *MAS* 26 (4): 815–53

Vambery, Arminius 1865–6 'On the dervishes and hadjis of the East' *MASL* 2: 14–24.

van der Veer, Peter 1987 'Taming the ascetic: devotionalism in a Hindu monastic order' *Man* ns 22: 680–95

1988 *Gods on earth. The management of religious experience and identity in a north Indian pilgrimage centre* London and Atlantic Highlands

1994 *Religious nationalism. Hindus and Muslims in India* Berkeley

Viswanatha, S. V. 1928 *Racial synthesis in Hindu culture* London

Vivekenanda, Swami 1989–92 *Complete works* (Mayavati Memorial edn) 8 vols. Calcutta

Wake, C. S. 1870 'The aim and scope of anthropology' *The Journal of Anthropology* 1: 1–18

Ward, Helen 1997 'Worth its weight: gold, women and value in North West India', Ph.D. dissertation, University of Cambridge

Ward, Revd. William 1817–20 *A view of the history, literature and religion of the Hindoos* (3rd edn) 4 vols. London

Washbrook, D. A. 1975 'The development of caste organisation in south India' in C. J. Baker and D. A. Washbrook (eds.), *South India. Political institutions and political change 1880–1940* Delhi: 150–203

1990 'Caste, class and dominance in Tamilnadu' in Francine Frankel and M. S. A. Rao (eds.) *Dominance and state power in modern India. Decline of a social order*, II Delhi: 204–63

1993 'Economic depression and the making of "traditional" society in colonial India' *Transactions of the Royal Historical Society* 6 (3): 237–63

Weber, Max 1958 *The religion of India. The sociology of Hinduism and Buddhism* (trans. H. H. Gerth and D. Martindale) Glencoe, Illinois

Westphal-Hellbusch, S. 1974 'Changes in meaning of ethnic names' in L. S. Leshnik and G. D. Sontheimer (eds.), *Pastoralists and nomads in south Asia* Wiesbaden: 117–138

Wilson, John 1843 'Account of the Waralis and Katodis' *JRAS* 7: 14–31

Wink, André 1986 *Land and sovereignty in India. Agrarian society and politics under the eighteenth-century Maratha Swarajya* Cambridge

Wise, James 1883 *Notes on the races, castes and trades of eastern Bengal* London

Wolpert, Stanley 1989 *Tilak and Gokhale. Revolution and reform in the making of modern India* Delhi

Yadav, K. C. 1994 *India's unequal citizens. A study of OBCs* Delhi

Yang, Anand (ed.) 1985 *Crime and criminality in British India* Tucson

1989 *The limited Raj. Agrarian relations in colonial India: Saran district 1793–1920* Berkeley

Young, Richard Fox 1981 *Resistant Hinduism. Sanskrit sources on anti-Christian apologetics in early nineteenth-century India* Vienna

Zelliot, Eleanor 1970 'Learning the use of political means' in Rajni Kothari (ed.), *Caste in Indian politics* New Delhi: 26–69

1988 'Congress and the untouchables, 1917–1950' in Richard Sisson and Stanley Wolpert (eds.), *Congress and Indian nationalism. The pre-Independence phase* Berkeley and Los Angeles: 182–97

1992 *From untouchable to Dalit. Essays on the Ambedkar movement* (2nd edn 1996) New Delhi

Zelliot, Eleanor and Maxine Berntsen (eds.) 1988 *The experience of Hinduism. Essays on religion in Maharashtra* Albany

Ziegler, Norman P. 1973 'Action, community, power and service in Rajasthani culture: a social history of the Rajputs of middle period

Rajasthan', Ph.D. dissertation, Department of History, University of Chicago

Zimmermann, Francis 1987 *The jungle and the aroma of meats. An ecological theme in Hindu medicine* Berkeley, Los Angeles and London

INDEX

Adi-Dharm movement, 245n., 246
Adivasi, 248, 279; *see also* tribal populations
Advani, L. K., 303
affirmative action, 270; *see also* 'reservations
Agarwals, 210, 212–13, 320
Agra, 111
Ahirs, 40, 50, 62, 84, 104, 200, 204–5, 209, 325, 347
Ahmedabad, 40, 219, 221, 223, 321, 356
Ain-i-akbari, 45–6, 104, 108
Ajnapatra, 76n.
Akali Dal, 283
Al-Biruni, 103–4
Ali, Haidar, 89
All-India Backward Classes Federation, 288
Allahabad, 72, 216–17
Ambedkar, B. R., 2, 231, 239, 254, 256–62, 264–5, 270, 280–1, 354–5, 375–6; on caste, 257, 260, 375; on Hinduism, 259–60, 262, 300
Amritsar massacre, 127n.
Anavils, 197–9
Andaman Islands, 123n.
Anthropological Review, 126
Anthropological Survey of India, 275–6
anthropometry, 120, 132n., 143n.; post-Independence survivals of, 276
Arcot, 62; *see also* Carnatic
Aroras, 212–13
arthashastra, 76
Arya Samaj, 60, 90, 129, 149–50, 161, 166, 168–70, 173, 176, 183, 208, 221–2, 229, 239, 261, 264, 288n.
Aryan Brotherhood, 175
Aryans, 114–15, 127–9, 132, 134–8, 140, 141n., 153, 156, 158, 164, 167, 173–5, 179, 181–2, 209, 237, 240, 242, 246, 293, 374–5; *see also* race, theories of
'Aryavarta', 127
ascetic, *see* renouncers and renunciation
astrology, 146, 315–16, 362
Aurangabad, 353, 355
Aurangzeb, 35
Aurobindo, Sri, 153–4
auspiciousness and inauspiciousness, 15, 55

Awadh Rent Act (1868), 206
Awadh, 74, 200, 206–7; *see also* United Provinces/UP
Ayodhya, 302n., 319

Backward Castes (or Classes), 234, 241n., 256–7, 280, 284, 288, 292, 330; *see also* OBC
Backward Classes Commission (1953–5), 288–92
Backward Classes Commission (1978–80: 'Mandal Commission'), 272n., 290–2; 294–6, 301
Bahujan Samaj Party (BSP), 298, 302–3, 345, 358, 378
bahujan samaj, 240–2
Bailey, F. G., 12
Banaras, 59, 68–9, 71, 86–7, 89, 145, 217–19, 319–21, 355, 359
Bandit Queen, 362–3
Bangalore, 318
*bania*s, 96, 106, 184, 200, 210, 212–13, 214–222, 358; *see also* traders
Bapu, Subaji, 146–7
Bardoli civil protests (*satyagraha*s), 243
Baroda, 111
Bediyas, 133
begar, 204, 206–7, 210, 326–7
Bengal, 47–8, 74, 80–1, 112, 115, 121–2, 133–6, 140, 193n., 199, 204, 205n., 207, 212, 216–17, 230–1, 245–6
Bengal Army, 202–3
Besant, Annie, 183
Béteille, André, 13, 313
bhadralok, 199, 234n., 237
Bhagavad Gita, 13–14
bhaiachara, 37, 350
bhakti (devotional worship), 27, 46–8, 68–9, 170, 240, 249, 263, 323, 339, 370
Bhangis, 194, 226–7, 250–1
Bharatiya Janata Party (BJP), 281, 297–303
Bharatiya Kisan Union (BKU), 350
Bharatiya Kranti Dal (BKD), 282–3
Bharatiya Lok Dal (BLD), 282–3, 294
Bharatpur, kingdom of, 43, 89; raja of, 241
Bhats, 45, 67, 87
Bhattacharya, Jogendra Nath, 163–5

413

THE NEW CAMBRIDGE HISTORY OF INDIA

I The Mughals and their Contemporaries

II Indian States and the Transition to Colonialism

III The Indian Empire and the Beginnings of Modern Society

IV The Evolution of Contemporary South Asia

* Already published   + Available in paperback